A Doctor's Life

A DOCTOR'S LIFE

Dr R.P. Cookson

BG

The Book Guild Ltd.
Sussex, England

This book is sold subject to the condition that it shall not, by way
of trade or otherwise, be lent, re-sold, hired out, photocopied or held
in any retrieval system, or otherwise circulated without the publisher's
prior consent in any form of binding or cover other than that in which
this is published and without a similar condition including this condition
being imposed on the subsequent purchaser.

The Book Guild Ltd.
25 High Street,
Lewes, Sussex.

First published 1991
© Dr R.P. Cookson 1991
Set in Baskerville
Typesetting by Ashford Setting & Design,
Ashford, Middlesex.
Printed in Great Britain by
Antony Rowe Ltd.,
Chippenham, Wiltshire.

British Library Cataloguing in Publication Data
Cookson, R.P. (Robert Power) 1918-
    A Doctor's Life
    1. Yorkshire (England). General practice
    I. Title
    362.172092

ISBN 0 86332 656 0

CONTENTS

LIST OF ILLUSTRATIONS

FOREWORD

This book is dedicated to colleagues and friends past and present, to former patients, and to all those whose lives helped to make mine such a happy one. To my wife there are special acknowledgements. Without her patience, encouragement, and coercion, this story would never have been penned. To Christine, of Yours Faithfully, Scarborough, I record my most grateful thanks for her skill, courtesy, and willingness to decipher my hand-writing.

1

Early Days

I was born six weeks before the armistice was signed on 11 November 1918, terminating World War One. The event took place at Tivoli Place in Cheltenham, and I was delivered by a lady doctor, which was unusual in those days.

My father was a solicitor serving with the Queens Royal West Surrey Regiment. My paternal grandfather was a surgeon/major, and had spent many years serving in the Indian Army Medical Service. He operated on the Raj. He trained in Edinburgh. Shortly before his fiftieth birthday he married. His bride was almost half his age, bore him two sons, my father, and his elder brother, who qualified in medicine in Edinburgh, and became a consultant pathologist in Sunderland until 1948 when he emigrated to Canada; he died in Toronto in early 1949 after a short illness.

She died while still a young woman, but he survived in good health and died aged eighty-four years in 1921.

My maternal grandfather was an estate agent in Cheltenham. He had a flourishing business, but as a result of an unwise investment after the war, he lost everything, and lived in a flat in London in a subdued style. However, his health was good and he died aged ninety-three years. He had three children, my mother, a younger sister, and a younger brother.

I had a sister two years older than myself. Unfortunately she must have suffered brain damage at birth, and although able to read and write and attend to herself, her behaviour was unpredictable and beyond the capability of my parents. My father's experience during the war in the trenches, his near death in the 1918 influenza pandemic, and the sadness of having a daughter with a mental disorder, rendered him incapable of coping with many situations. This resulted in my sister being admitted to a private institution in Teddington when she was ten years old, quite customary treatment at that time. She died there in 1946 from bronchopneumonia at the early age of thirty years.

My mother was quiet, guided by my father, and never overcame the disappointment of her father's misfortune and her daughter's mental handicap. She was an excellent pianist, and a skilled gardener.

This sad situation must have had some impact on my early upbringing, though I was to a large extent sheltered from it by my parents.

After hostilities ceased in 1918 my father was employed by a firm of solicitors in Ramsgate in Kent. The senior partner was Mr Daniels. My father did not enjoy working in an office, nor did he like Ramsgate. Although he was only in his early thirties, he was unwell, and was advised to undertake lighter work. As a result my parents moved to Swanage on the Dorset coast where he had been stationed in the early days of the war, and he liked the place. They moved house in the year of the General Strike in 1926.

I have few memories of Ramsgate. I can remember a square shaped garden surrounded by a high wall with a surrounding path. I had a tricycle and loved to cycle round and round the path. I have recollections, too, of a small school there. We stood in a row, and mathematical tables and basic arithmetical sums were questioned. If you knew the answer, you moved up one, and down one if you did not know the answer. It was not nice being at the bottom of the row, but it was possible to climb to the top during a session. I can also remember Sandwich with a large sandy beach, wet, as the tide receded, and the appearance of sand worms.

After the move to Swanage, my father was employed by the same firm at Ramsgate, but received his work through the post. He worked in that manner for over twenty years. Obviously it was not lucrative, but he managed to pay for my education, see me through the medical training, and provide for my sister up to her death. I know it was difficult for them.

Perhaps it was not surprising that I was interested in medicine from an early age. I had bilious attacks frequently; the cause was usually excitement, over-indulgence with food, or a long tiring day, especially if a train journey was involved. Recovery was overnight. As I became older, these attacks were replaced by severe headaches which throbbed, were incapacitating, but were always relieved by a night's sleep.

From eight to thirteen years of age I went to a co-educational preparatory school as a day boy in Swanage. It was a boarding school for boys and girls, but there was a large day pupil component. The school had excellent grounds, and we played cricket in summer and football in winter. The girls played tennis and hockey. In the summer time we walked to the beach ten minutes away and bathed from the school hut. Bathing started without fail on 1 June and the summer term ended at the end of July. We learned to swim using water wings; there was a raft anchored some ten yards out of our depth where we learned to dive.

It seemed to be a good school with a full academic curriculum, including Latin. The headmaster and his family were Quakers, but we went to a Church of England Service on Sunday mornings, walking in a crocodile. The Common Entrance Examination for entry to public schools for boys and girls was the educational aim, and most successful the pupils were too.

I was entered for Weymouth College, a small independent public school affiliated with Trent College. Shortly before I was fourteen it was decided I should sit their entrance scholarship examination. I did so and to everyone's surprise I was awarded a modest scholarship for the length of time I was at the school. This, of course, exempted me from the Common Entrance exam.

Weymouth College turned out to be quite a tough school. There was a fagging system, cold baths every morning winter or summer at six forty-five am, 'prep' for half an hour before breakfast, and very strict discipline. It soon became very clear that it was a disgrace to be poorly, and that to get on in life, physical fitness, toughness, and the ability to endure hardship, featured prominently in the everyday life of the school. It was, however, a happy and good school, with a dedicated staff. The results of examinations and sports were excellent.

Most of the boys parents were in the services, the professions, or the ministry, and this may explain why there was a twenty minute church service in the school chapel every morning and evening. On Sundays there was a morning and evening service lasting an hour. If you had been confirmed there was an eight am service as well. To miss this service one ran the gauntlet of getting on the wrong side of the school 'priest', an unsatisfactory position to be in. Paradoxically it was not considered an unduly religious school!

At the preparatory school in Swanage we used to have hot baths after football in the afternoons. Three small boys would fill a standard bath. On one occasion I was sitting at the taps end of the bath when a boy turned on the hot tap. Almost boiling water poured over my buttocks, and I sustained a painful burn with large blisters.

The school doctor was sent for, and I remember the embarrassment of daily dressings to this part of the anatomy and the subsequent journey home kneeling on the passenger seat of a car. On another occasion I caught a finger on the door latch. There was a deep cut and copious bleeding, and I was taken to the school doctor. The wound was not stitched and it took a long time to heal.

One day a boy fell out of a dormitory window from the first floor on to concrete. He was unconscious and we thought he was dead. He disappeared, and spent the rest of the term in the school pavilion shaded with a parasol, and away from all noise. He had concussion, was in bed seven weeks but he made a full recovery; his name was Petrie-Hay, and the accident subdued the school.

There was an epidemic of measles. This was a severe illness in those days. Quite apart from the high temperature, up to 105° Fahrenheit plus sometimes, and the burning rash, there were nasty complications involving the chest, ears, and eyes. A mastoid operation was often a sequel to measles. There were no antibiotics to deal with infection, and a small pill of calomel was administered at the first sign of earache, the rationale being that catharsis would reduce the inflammation.

When I was nine years old I developed an enlargement of the cervical glands on one side. After a week there was no sign of improvement and the doctor was called. I felt perfectly well, but to my surprise I was wrapped up in a blanket and taken to the local children's hospital. I was put to bed in a room by myself. It was late when a nurse came into the room; her starched head cap terrified me. She ordered me out of bed and said we would walk to the theatre. I was delighted, thinking I was going to see a Charlie-Chaplin film. I remember climbing a stairway with nurse to a door with 'Theatre' written across it. The door was opened and I was in the operating theatre, confused and frightened at what I saw. I was lifted on to a high table, a mask was placed over my face and I was told to breathe. I was too terrified to speak or cry. I recall a nasty sickly smell and a dreadful feeling of suffocation, and then I was asleep.

When I awoke my head was between sandbags. I was sick and a very old nurse sat by my bed for the rest of the night. I spent a fortnight in this hospital, unhappy and puzzled why I was there. My father said the glands had been removed. After a few days I was transferred to the children's ward which I enjoyed. It was several weeks before I held my head straight. I was back at school the next term with a red scar down the side of my neck, and plenty of boys came and had a look.

One unpleasant boy squeezed my neck and I thought I would die from the pain he caused me. When I was sixteen years old my father told me one day that I was very lucky to be alive as I had Hodgkins disease. This was considered to be a fatal illness. There was no follow-up. Presumably I had an acute lymphadenitis which nowadays would have responded quickly to a course of antibiotics. There was no recurrence.

One day in the school summer holidays when I was ten years old there was a girl of my own age having a donkey ride on the beach; there was an attendant controlling the donkey with reins. As she passed by, the donkey threw her off and she fell on the sands. She was not unconscious but obviously in pain, very white and shocked and I thought she would die on the beach. An ambulance arrived on the road above, and a stretcher was assembled to take her to hospital. Although it was a glorious hot summer day, the accident caused such an upset to the others on the beach that they left and went home.

I was most alarmed about this; as the days passed nobody knew or would say what had happened to the girl and I thought she must have died. After a fortnight I walked to the children's hospital, unknown to my parents, and rang the pull-bell. I was taken to an office and Matron appeared. I explained the situation, and asked if she knew what had happened to the girl. She was very kind and told me that when the donkey threw her she ruptured her spleen and was taken straight away to a large

13

hospital. Her spleen had been removed, and she had been so ill she nearly died. She said she was nearly better now. I remember thinking how wonderful it was to be able to save a life.

At Weymouth there was a maths-master whose name was Mr Major. He was a very large and obese man, and for this reason he was nicknamed 'Gobi'. He had been at the school for many years. One day he died rather suddenly, and the headmaster called an assembly and informed us he had died. He finished by saying that no boy must leave the dormitories between nine pm and midnight on any account. News soon spread that his body would be moved that night. The boys were very quiet, and there was conjecture as to how he would be moved on account of his extreme weight. We never saw or heard anything. His death was another reason why I thought I would like to be a doctor; I was always interested in illness and treatment.

While I was at school I noticed that several boys seated at desks in front of me had curved surgical scars behind their ears, evidence of a mastoid operation. Some showed quite deep cavities lined with skin. These boys did not appear to be deaf, nor did they have discharging ears. It was a situation I did not like to see and it alarmed me. The word 'mastoid' was a frightening one, associated with nasty surgical procedures and sometimes death. Happily I never had earache, but I am very sympathetic with those who have experienced a mastoid operation.

Once a term at my public school there was a medical inspection of all borders. It usually took place near half-term. At that time removal of the tonsils and adenoids was almost a routine procedure at the age of five years. It was thought that if the tonsils were chronically infected, sore throats, nasal blockage, nephritis, and possibly endocarditis, could follow. Streptococcal throat infections were not uncommon, they lowered resistance and caused debility. There were virulent germs in those days. I had heard alarming stories of tonsils and adenoids being removed on the kitchen table at home. My father's dislike of doctors saved me from this assault.

However, the school doctor was determined about the need for the removal of unhealthy tonsils. At the termly inspection, always in the late evening, we trooped down to the sick quarters by dormitories and lined up in a queue, wearing pyjamas and dressing gowns. The examination involved a listen to the heart

14

and chest using a Bell stethoscope. Then the mouth was opened and the tongue held down with a spoon. I dreaded the termly medical inspections. If you had enlarged tonsils, the doctor's eyes rolled upwards towards the matron, and with a look of horror he would pick up a red ink pen and make an entry. No words were spoken, and we were quickly ushered back to the dormitory wondering whether we should land up on the kitchen table for the operation next holidays. The doctor was an austere, erect figure in striped grey trousers and a black morning coat. He wore a white winged collar and we regarded him with awe. Over five years and fifteen inspections never once did he alter his routine, nor was I ever invited to speak. However I kept my tonsils whilst at school! Subsequently I learned that the doctor was a general practitioner surgeon with the FRCS and was highly respected.

We were a healthy crowd at this school. Out of 130 boys and over five years I cannot recall any boy with epilepsy, or a boy unfit to play games or steeple-chase. I cannot recall any boy having appendicitis or having a fracture. There was one boy who had osteomyelitis and had numerous incisions on his body presumably to drain pyaemic abscesses. Nocturnal enuresis was very unusual, and the offenders unpopular. Left handed boys were rare, but popular as bowlers on the cricket field. I cannot recall anyone with asthma. One boy had an operation for undescended testicles and this caused quite a stir!

There were two epidemics of influenza in spring-terms when three quarters of the school were ill at the same time. Dormitories became sick wards. Treatment was aspirin, and inhalations of Friars balsam under the bed clothes. I coughed, and upset some boiling balsam over my chest and received a painful burn. Matron was not pleased with me. During one epidemic of influenza some boys experienced severe tracheitis, and they coughed up strands of elastic tissue which must have been shed from the trachea. I have never encountered this condition again during my medical life.

School terms were thirteen weeks in summer and autumn, and ten or eleven weeks in the spring. There were two half-day exeats per term from one pm to six pm with your parents, provided there was no influenza or other epidemics in the town. There were no half term holidays.

Parent-teacher contact was not encouraged. However, with

the other boys I was happy in this spartan regime and we seemed to thrive. I enjoyed my school-days at Weymouth. Although I did not realize it at the time, in retrospect, I am very sure that this school, at which we were taught to work and play hard always, prepared me for the busy years which lay ahead. Our lives were governed by a large school bell with a clapper, and swung by a porter using a rope. It started to ring at six forty-five am, and continued at intervals of three quarters of an hour for a change of lesson, and again for meals, chapel and assembly.

The school-chaplain (always called 'Priest') was also a house-master. He taught divinity, and most of us sat this subject for the School Certificate exam. He was a bachelor, a jovial and kindly man, who was well-versed in the beauty and the geology of the Dorset coast. He was very popular with the boys whatever their age group. One day he was taken ill and we learned he had undergone an emergency operation for acute appendicitis. He was said to be very ill, and was in a nursing home close to the school. No visitors were allowed for some days. When he was well enough to be visited, small groups of three or four boys from various forms were selected to see him. I was one of those chosen, and looked forward to seeing inside a nursing home. It was a formal occasion and a nurse told us not to stay longer than five minutes.

We trooped into the room and stood around the bed: he wore pince-nez spectacles, and I thought he looked quite well. I was interested in the height of the bed; it must have been an orthopaedic bed and of such height that we had to look up to the Priest. He lay very still and was propped up with a pillow under his knees. This was the classic 'Fowler's Position', well known now to cause deep vein thrombosis and pulmonary embolism. He was only fifty-two years old, and it was many weeks before he was able to resume his school and chapel work. Nowadays he would have been up the following day after operation, and home a day or two after that.

From the first morning at school until a boy became a school prefect or a VIth form boy, a cold bath at six forty-five am was compulsory. We lined up, winter or summer, and plunged into a bath, brim-full with cold water. The cold taps remained on and the overflow poured on to a white tiled floor and then to gutters around the room to the drains. Prefects from each dormitory surveyed the scene and there was no dodging.

We washed in the dormitories from enamel basins set in long wooden frames the length of the room. The basins were filled with cold water from jugs, and carried by fags from the cold taps in the bathrooms. In winter there could be ice on the basins on waking. Plumbed wash basins were not a luxury for schools. There was hot water only for school prefects, again carried by fags. However, we had one hot bath per week (during prep), but in the games changing rooms there were troughs with hot and cold water for use after football. We had a haircut every three weeks in the changing rooms during 'prep'.

At bed making we turned the mattress every morning, applied the bottom sheet, and rolled back the upper sheet and blankets to the foot of the bed. The blankets were scarlet. Completion of bed-making was by domestic staff later in the morning when the beds were 'aired'. Then we had morning 'prep' from seven fifteen am to seven forty-five am and so to breakfast. We all kept in good health and no one came to harm from this vigorous discipline. Shoe cleaning was after breakfast, using black boot polish and a polishing brush in the toilets, which had no doors!

Breakfasts were good. There was porridge (often lumpy) every day, followed by a cooked meal which could be fried bread, or bacon, and herring, and on Sundays we had boiled eggs (hard boiled!). There was toast, a twist of butter, and we were allowed to take a two pound tin or jar of jam every term in a 'tuck box' as a spreader. Fifty years on, breakfast is a small meal, except in hotels and guest houses. There are many cereals to select. The boarding schools, however, still provide a cooked breakfast, but not necessarily every day. It is day pupils who so often attend school on a bag of crisps and little else. Teachers say that a low calorie breakfast causes poor concentration and has a deleterious effect on school work. They may well be correct.

We were weighed and measured for height each term, and this was recorded on the end of term school report.

In my day at public school we sat the Oxford and Cambridge School Certificate at sixteen years of age in English, maths, Latin, French, Religious Knowledge, history, geography and German. It was mandatory to pass in English, maths and a language and two other subjects at one and the same time. There was certainly a core curriculum in the 1930s, and long before that. My mother sat the London Matriculation in 1907 in five subjects!

My father was very anxious that I should study Latin. He wanted me to become a lawyer. Latin was necessary for the law and medicine then. I never liked the subject, but I managed a 'credit' pass as it was called then if you achieved good marks. The next two years until I was eighteen years old were spent working for the Higher School Certificate, for which I studied French and history as the main subjects, and German as the subsidiary.

One did not specialize or drop subjects so easily in those days, and science subjects often were not taught in some schools until the School Certificate was obtained. I did not study science at school because my father wanted me to study law, and this required a classical education.

During the holidays before my final term at school, my father suggested we should go to a lawyer's office and see a friend of his there. I noted the shelves of books, the tables piled high with legal documents, conveyances, and all the rest. I noted the stressed appearance of the lawyers and the heap of work waiting attention. Outside the dingy office the sun was shining and the birds singing. My mind was made up there and then! This was not the life for me. I did not want to be a caged bird. I could not go through with the law. I wanted to be a doctor.

On the way home I dropped the bombshell. My father was displeased, but he did not stand in my way. He did not like doctors. I think he was afraid of them. He regarded medicine as a hard life of toil and sacrifice with long hours and little leisure. The financial reward was meagre and he talked of bad debts which were difficult to recover. Despite his views I was certain I wanted to be a doctor, and gradually he accepted the idea, and paid for my training. He encouraged me but I have always thought it was a disappointment to him that I did not follow his footsteps.

I wrote letters to Edinburgh, and Oxford and Cambridge Universities enquiring about admission to their medical faculties. I provided details of my School Certificate result and explained I had not studied physics, chemistry and biology at school. I was accepted by all three universities.

Oxford and Cambridge were never seriously considered, the cost in excess of what my father could afford. My medical relatives all went to Edinburgh.

At Edinburgh University, there was a pre-registration exam

in physics and chemistry which had to be sat, and passed, before you could commence the medical course and matriculate.

No special course existed for these subjects, the assumption being that the candidate would have probably reached the standard required to pass the exam, whilst at school. It appeared I might require a year's work in the two subjects to reach the knowledge required. However, in Edinburgh, there was also a School of Medicine of the Royal Colleges, situated at Surgeons Hall in Nicholson Street. This school also had a pre-registration exam but it provided a revisionary course in physics and chemistry over one term followed by the exam in December. If you were successful it was possible to continue with the Higher Standard physics and chemistry for the following two terms sitting the exam at the end of the summer term in early July. Botany and zoology were also studied during the spring and summer terms of the first year and the examination taken in July as well. I could complete the pre-registration exam and the first year exams in the three subjects all in one year.

Normally, it would not have been too difficult a decision as I could probably have studied physics and chemistry at a technical college in Exeter, and then sat the pre-registration exam for Edinburgh University at the end of the year. I thought it wiser to be in Edinburgh where the revision course was held; also war seemed inevitable and it seemed sensible to get as far as possible in the training and probably be allowed to continue the course to its completion. There was no time to waste.

It was, therefore, for these reasons that I elected to go to the School of Medicine of the Royal Colleges, Edinburgh. If I was successful in passing the pre-registration exam, and the first year physics, chemistry, botany and zoology as well, no time would be lost. I realized it would be very hard work for me but I was keen and an optimist. I left school at the end of July 1937.

As events unfolded and World War Two commenced in September 1939, the assumption about deferment was proved correct and I was able to complete my medical education. I was lucky and I appreciated it.

How different is the situation now! Science subjects are started at an early age and basic subjects are quickly dropped. I think I was fortunate to have the benefits of a classical and scientific education, though it did involve a serious commitment to work hard. Now that the tax-payer pays for medical education, the available places are grossly over-subscribed leading to the necessity for high grades in the A level examination for admission to the course.

Financial grants also assist the modern student; in my time the cost had to be carried by parents, relatives, or whoever could help. There are many complaints about the grants, but the present day students seem well-off compared with their fore-runners of whom many were hard pushed indeed, but it would have been illogical to have complained.

In Edinburgh, many students were local, and lived at home, others lived in lodgings in and about Edinburgh; and a few lived in halls of residence, which were in short supply. Sometimes a group of three or four students would rent a flat. A small handful of students possessed a car, and a very old one at that; very few students married until they had completed their course and were established in work.

The usual procedure for a student requiring accommodation was to contact the students' union. On application the union would send a list of landladies, with names and addresses and their charges, who were willing to provide board and lodgings. There were large lists of landladies classified according to streets in Edinburgh.

Accommodation consisted of a room in a block tenement of four storeys. Breakfast, board, and evening meal averaged thirty shillings a week, and this included lunch on Saturday and Sunday. Twenty-seven and sixpence was not an uncommon weekly rate provided full board was not required at weekends.

I was duly sent this list of landladies. I had never been to Edinburgh so streets and districts meant little to me. I decided to arrive in Edinburgh a week before the autumn session commenced in order to learn the geography of the city, find lodgings and attend the correct place to register. I would have to find the various lecture rooms, timetables for my subjects, and, very important, find out the date of the pre-registration exam in December!

My parents had left Swanage and moved to a house near Ottery-St-Mary in Devonshire during 1936. It was very rural, and rather remote.

Towards the end of September 1937 I travelled from Exeter to Waterloo on my way to Edinburgh using the Southern Railway with the familiar dark green coaches. I had a small school trunk of clothes and personal effects in the luggage van, my ticket to Edinburgh, £5 in my pocket, and the list of landladies. My father warned me not to talk to strangers!

He came to Exeter to see me off. The whistle blew, a green flag fluttered, and I was off, full of excitement, and hope, and expectation. I was not to be disappointed.

On the continent Herr Hitler was in full swagger, and on the radio, there was the sound of marching feet. The clouds of war were gathering fast. From her yacht at Cannes Lady Docker was calling: 'Wake up Britain'. This was the background as the train gathered speed.

As the train sped through the luscious scenery of Devon in late September, I reflected that I had never travelled further north than Swindon, and I wondered whether it would be different. It was unusual to travel big distances in those days. Foreign travel was only for a few. School holidays were spent at home, and there could be few nicer areas than Dorset and Devon to spend them. The countryside was lovely, hilly and very green; there were also numerous small coastal resorts for the beach and bathing.

The trains were very efficient. Steam trains with clean coaches, and so comfortable. The network was intricate and few places were inaccessible. There was no shortage of porters to help with the heavier luggage, and at the main line stations there were more than sufficient to deal with most passengers as they alighted from the coaches. A porter would willingly find you. Tipping was expected, a tanner (6d.) was a standard sum, unless a special service was requested. Fares were very reasonable; it cost £5 return London-Edinburgh. The coaches were first or third class. In a coach, a side corridor ran its full length and sliding doors opened into compartments for six persons, three each side in confrontation. There was space for light luggage each side on racks above head-level. Every compartment had a railway map of the network, a mirror, and pictures of places of interest the railway served. There was a chain, the communication cord, to be pulled in an emergency to stop the train; £5 was the fine for improper use. The main line trains had first or third class restaurant coaches, and excellent breakfasts, lunches, and dinners were served at several sessions. The prices were most reasonable. These restaurant coaches were very popular with the travelling public.

It was nearly dark when the Exeter Waterloo Express pulled into the terminus. There was no difficulty, no confusion; a porter quickly found my trunk in the luggage van and led me to the taxi line-up. He found a taxi for me, placed the luggage aboard and away I went to Euston Station. Similar efficiency awaited at Euston and my luggage was placed in the left luggage office as there was a wait of two hours before the night train departed. I now had time to find the departure platform, check the time-table and enjoy a cup of tea and some sandwiches. The waiting room of Euston Station was spacious and luxurious with wooden panelling on the walls. The hubbub of a busy London terminus did not seem to penetrate this room. Time passed quickly and soon I made my way to the left luggage office to collect my trunk. A group of porters was on duty here and a porter willingly came forward with a trolley and wheeled the trunk to the luggage van of the night train to Edinburgh. I remember the train had a large number of coaches and there were several sleeping coaches for first and third class. There was plenty of seating accommodation and I found a corner seat facing the engine. It was the year 1937, the railways had not been nationalized and the four companies — Southern, Great Western, London Midland and Scottish and London North Eastern Railways provided the rail network for Britain. Each company had individual characteristics and provided a reliable service. The GWR was renowned for its gleaming engines, but I liked the LMS with the red engines.

The train travelled slowly on through the night. When it stopped at a station it was difficult to know your whereabouts because stations were poorly lit. Sometimes a porter could be heard shouting the name of the station as the train pulled in. Stops were lengthy as luggage, mail and newspapers were loaded and unloaded; there was time to leave the compartment and buy a cup of tea and a small packet of plain biscuits from tea-trollies on the platform. The night seemed long. As dawn came the train was making its way slowly through the Lowlands, north of Carlisle. The scenery was different from Dartmoor and Dorset; the hills, and the solitude at that early hour impressed me and over the years I have treasured memories of the Lowlands and the drive to Scotland's beautiful capital city. The train stopped for a few minutes at Carstairs Junction; at seven thirty am it arrived at the Caledonian Station, Edinburgh, which

22

was at the west end of Princes Street.

The journey was over! Again my trunk was deposited at the left luggage office and after a cup of tea at the station buffet, I left the station, crossed the road, and I was in Princes Street.

My first impression of Princes Street was the width of the road, and the clean maroon coloured electric trams in plenty traversing the middle of the road. There were numerous islands for intending passengers. Every tram had a driver and a ticket collector. Every tram had a swivelling arm projecting from the roof which was connected to an overhead cable to provide the power for its mobility.

I noted the fine shops, the Princes Street Gardens, the Scots Memorial, the Mound and Edinburgh Castle, high up, guarding the city. It was a most impressive sight.

The student's union had sent me a street map of Edinburgh. I had spent a considerable time studying it and I had come to the conclusion that the Marchmont District would be satisfactory for access to the university, the Edinburgh Royal Infirmary and Surgeons Hall in Nicholson Street. All were within easy walking distance.

It seemed to be a popular area, and there was a big choice of landladies.

It was a perfect autumn morning as I set out on foot anxious to stretch my legs and find lodgings. It did not take me long to walk up the Mound, and along George IV Bridge to the Royal Infirmary. I crossed the tree lined, traffic-free avenue to the 'Meadows', and reached the area at the end where whale's jaw bones had been fashioned into an archway over the path. Here was Marchmont Road and Warrender Park Terrace.

Autumn leaves formed a carpet as I walked. The air was crisp and clean, and I thought I had come to a lovely place.

My student days were about to commence, but that is a different story and another chapter.

2

Student Days

It did not take long to find suitable accommodation. At the third attempt I found digs in Warrender Park Terrace, which overlooked the 'Meadows', and I boarded here for my first year. My requirements were basic and simple. A table, a chair, a bed, a light, some form of heat, and above all, peace and quiet. I had been used to a spartan life at school, not a luxurious one at home either, and I was in no position to alter my life-style. Therefore to find a linoleum floor, and an iron-bedstead in Edinburgh came as no surprise and was what I had expected. The landlord was tall and pale, and in his late thirties. He had a club-foot. His wife was dumpy and there was a daughter of two years. Both he and his wife were kind, caring, and attentive to me throughout my stay. I was barely nineteen years, and they thought I was young to be on my own. There was no radio, and of course, no television in 1937, and I relied on the *Edinburgh Evening News* to keep abreast with topical events. A coal fire was alight when I reached the digs in the late afternoons after the lectures; at weekends the fire was alight all day. We wore more clothes in those days. Thick woollen underwear was usual, thick woollen socks, overcoat and gloves, and even a trilby hat if the weather was harsh.

Those who live on the Continent in more sheltered areas express astonishment at the inadequate outdoor clothing of the British in winter. Paradoxically, public buildings, shops and even hospitals are only too often grossly overheated. These digs were ideally suitable. Three minutes walk took me to a tram stop in Marchmont Road; from there it was direct to Princes Street, and anywhere else required. It was a superb tram system, and

2d. was the fare for a lengthy distance.

Shops were around the corner, a post office, chemist and newsagent. From my room on the fourth floor there was a fine view across the 'Meadows'. Ten minutes away over the 'Meadows' were the lecture rooms, the entrance to the Royal Infirmary, the medical book shops, Surgeons Hall, and the bank.

The weekly charge was thirty shillings for breakfast, high tea and accommodation. At weekends there was full board, and I was happy about this as there were few shops open on a Sunday pre-war. I agreed to these terms, paid thirty shillings in advance and arranged to arrive in the late afternoon with my luggage. I was the only lodger. There was no accommodation for another. The block tenements in Edinburgh were not spacious. I remember eight flats to a block, sharing a front door, and a stone stairway and iron rail going in a spiral from the ground floor to the top floor. Outside the main door a row of brass bell-pulls gleaned with the names of flat tenants on a brass plate below. These bells worked well, and the desired flat owners appeared at whatever floor levels and invited you upstairs. From the top floor my landlord had to shout to make himself heard. Coal was the usual source of heat, gas for cooking, and occasionally for light too. Electric fires, and central heating were not widely available. Coal was delivered by horse and cart, and stored in bunkers in the back yard of the tenement. Every tenant had his own bunker; small quantities were delivered at a time, and I think coal cost 1s.9d. per cwt. The tenant carried the coal to their flats in buckets, quite a haul from ground-floor to fourth floor.

By now I was beginning to feel hungry and I made my way to Princes Street: I had a splendid lunch in the restaurant of a large store. Well fortified I browsed away the rest of the afternoon. I saw the formidable Edinburgh Castle, the Walter Scott Monument, the Art Gallery and Princes Street Gardens. There was also an unusual building on Carlton Hill on the eastern side of the city. This building was incomplete, a monument to Scots killed in the Napoleonic Wars; to its pillars and Greek architecture Edinburgh owes its title of Athens of the North.

It was soon time to return to the Caledonian Station to collect my luggage. I took a taxi to Warrender Park Terrace again, and the driver helped me with the trunk up to the top floor.

I wonder whether a taxi driver would offer such a service today!

I unpacked, and concealed the trunk under the bedstead. Then I wrote a letter home describing the events of the past twenty-four hours. Letter postage was 1½ d., a postcard 1d., and an unsealed envelope enclosing an advert was only ½ d. A letter posted before six pm would arrive second post in rural Devonshire.

Cigarette smoking was the norm (for men!). You were not a proper man unless you smoked! Fifty years have changed that ideology. I bought a packet of five Players cigarettes for 3d. and returned to the flat. High tea was ready and I tucked it away. I was pleased with the day's events, and read the newspaper in a drowsy state. The next day had to be planned, and there would be plenty of walking.

I was used to being on my own, and it did not trouble me. I was never lonely. Soon sleep overcame me; I was tired. Out went the light, and I went out like a light. Next day dawned bright and sunny, giving promise of a lovely autumn. The landlady tapped on the bedroom door at eight am and announced she had placed a jug of hot water for shaving in the bathroom. Electric razors were unknown in 1937; cut-throat razors, or safety razors with replaceable blades, bought in packets of five, were used by most men.

It was painful, and inefficient, to shave with cold water and I welcomed the landlady's care.

In those days the tenements had the standard, stoved, type of kitchen range with the fire set high up. Coal was the fuel. A large black iron kettle sat close to the fire and could be moved to hang over the flames on a hook. Although the kitchen range was able to heat water in a back boiler, the storage tank for the hot water was always small. The result was that the bath which was larger and deeper than those of today was filled to a level of only seven-eight inches of hot water! Provided the water was near boiling, necessitating several inches of cold water to produce a comfortable temperature, one could have a good bath. If the water was not very hot, one had a small and chilly bath. The landlord liked to know when a bath was required so that the fire could have special stoking. He made out a rota, and a cold bath was avoided.

I cannot recall any discomforture during my stay there. There was gas-lighting; gas-mantles broke easily and were brittle. For breakfast there was porridge every morning and sometimes it was lumpy, no doubt due to inadequate stirring during the cooking process. As I was a Sassenach eyebrows were not raised when I applied sugar to the porridge! There was always a cooked breakfast of fried bread, a rasher of bacon, a fried egg, or a kipper, followed by toast and marmalade. Importance was attached to breakfast in order to have a good foundation for the start of the day. There were no heated cars to drive to lectures, and the lecture rooms were not heated at 70°F + as is the custom now. I walked to lectures in all weathers and a good breakfast was essential.

My plans for the day centred on finding the medical school, and learning about the various courses. The opening day of the autumn session was several days away. As I strolled across the Meadows towards the University buildings it soon became clear that there were many people in a similar situation to myself, finding their bearings and looking all around. I did not think it would be long before I made acquaintances.

Students have changed in many ways. We were reasonably well dressed, but we had few clothes. It was unfashionable to have long hair, and we were clean shaven. Everybody wore a tie. We had a good dark suit worn for examinations and orals; for day to day use most students wore flannel trousers with one and a half inch turn ups, and a sports jacket with pullover. I remember one student had plus-fours, and he was the envy of us all. If you appeared untidy, the lecturer was likely to hold you up to ridicule before the class. On the whole, by today's standards, behaviour was exemplary, possibly a little uncouth at weekends if the beer flowed too freely, but we respected the law.

Politically ignorant, we never saw the ghastly scenes that take place today where jeering, yelling, mobs of students, and others, disrupt meetings and even cause physical injury to the police and politicians invited to speak to them. We had the goodwill of the citizens of Edinburgh, and we were grateful for this.

It did not take long to discover when and where the various courses for the lectures and practicals in physics and chemistry for the first year medical course were to be held, and I drew up a timetable. I learned as well that the pre-registration examination was in mid-December, only ten weeks away. I was up against it!

In Teviot Place, opposite the University, and adjacent to the Royal Infirmary were several excellent bookshops selling text books for all faculties, new and second hand. I remember Baxendale's Book Shop and Forsyth's Book Shop. There was an awesome range of books, and knowledgeable and proficient counter staff who were very helpful. I estimated I would require to spend about £10 to fit myself out with text books. I left home with £5 and had already spent thirty shillings on the digs, and small sums for taxis, newspapers and sundries. My father had decided that as I was under-age (a minor under twenty-one years) I could not open a bank account. He would send me a registered envelope monthly to cover my expenses, and ten shillings weekly pocket money. Tuition fees were reasonably cheap, and he also sent money for these and the necessary books. I was left in no doubt that further requests before a month was up would fall on deaf ears!

I had been accustomed to 3s.6d. per week when I was eighteen years old, so ten shillings was a big increase, and what a long way it went. A daily newspaper, five cigarettes daily, a two-course lunch five days a week, and a film show on a Saturday night!

On such a tight budget there was little opportunity to do other than work hard. I was certainly not 'one off'; my contemporaries fared no better, and some worse. However, we were happy, contented, and had a sense of purpose. There was good friendship, nearly fifty years duration in many instances. Today's students would think we were deprived, but we never thought so.

In the remaining few days before the session commenced I explored as much of Edinburgh as I could. The Castle, Arthur's Seat, with the fine view from the summit, and the Forth Rail Bridge were all visited; Holyrood Castle, the Royal Mile and St Giles' Cathedral stand out in my memories. I was delighted at the thought of five years in Edinburgh.

I did not realize World War Two was quite so near, and naively thought Hitler would never provoke the catastrophe that was to change, and in many cases destroy, the lives of millions of innocent people. As students we did not talk about the likelihood of war, preferring to address ourselves to our work.

It was now early October, and I bought a paper. It was a big day for the *Daily Telegraph*, having announced the union with another well known newspaper, the *Morning Post*. For many years afterwards it was the *Daily Telegraph*, and in smaller print below, the *Morning Post*. This was dropped many years later, and the newspaper became the *Daily Telegraph* again.

The lectures on the first day embraced physics and chemistry as expected, and this was the daily pattern, with practical work in addition most days. It was with some trepidation that I crossed the 'Meadows' that morning armed with notebooks, and mingled with the other students in the lecture rooms.

Chemistry came first. The blocks of desks were in tiers, and a blackboard ran the full width of the room wall behind the lecturer's desk. There was a modest stamping of feet on the wooden floor as the lecturer entered. He seemed pleased to see us and bade us good morning. He was elderly and dignified in manner. The lecture commenced with his query 'How many have never studied chemistry before?' There was an uneasy silence. I glimpsed around and saw no elevated hands, so I decided to keep quiet. I thought it probable that I would be odd man out, and I had no desire to be embarrassed on my first day, and start off on the wrong footing!

The lecturer continued. He was a clear speaker and was very helpful with his advice on text books and practical guides he regarded essential for the course. Much of the work he said would be revision, and he would highlight the most important areas, but we would have to read up plenty of material ourselves. This was not an understatement! As the hour and a half drew to a close I discovered I had enjoyed scribbling down his words as fast as I could write, and that this was a great improvement on the history of the Renaissance, or trying to untangle passages from Goethe with the aid of the crib. As we met after the lecture it was evident that most of the students had experienced a term or two of physics and chemistry at school, but had not achieved the standard of the pre-registration exam. A handful had previously sat the examination and failed in one or both subjects.

We then moved to the physics laboratory, and I was relieved to see many of the same faces there. The lecturer wore a white jacket. The room was crammed with equipment, even on top of the cupboards. Dynamos, electric motors, and pendulums were articles I could recognize. There were power points all round the lecturer's dais, and on a table close by were pieces of equipment set up for experiment and demonstration.

The lecturer started. He was excellent. He spoke earnestly, with clarity, and it was evident he was master of his subject and liked teaching. He started off with specific gravity, and demonstrations followed. There was floor stamping at the end of every successful demonstration. I noted that the stamping was louder and prolonged if an experiment went wrong, but this happened rarely. The lecturer enjoyed these demonstrations. How different from school days! Behaviour like that would have seen the ring leaders on their way to the headmaster's study.

By the end of the first lecture I thought I was going to enjoy physics, though I was well aware I would meet problems galore. Once again the lecturer produced some textbooks and named the authors.

Lunch hour was near. Close to Surgeons Hall in Nicholson Street were numerous restaurants. All had waitress service and they looked inviting. A two-course lunch for 1s.3d. was advertised on a sandwich board outside.

After the trials of my first morning I needed food and decided on the lunch. The restaurant was very clean, with individual tables, and white table cloths. It was busy as well. I found a seat, when a student I recognized at the lectures invited me to another table. I rose, and joined three other students all doing the same course, and all were to sit the pre-registration exam in December. Thus began friendships which lasted for many years, and I remember all their names today. Their company was a tremendous help, especially during that first term; three heads were better than one in unravelling workaday problems! Just as there was a syllabus for school subjects, so there must be a syllabus for the pre-registration exam. After I had purchased the recommended text books it was difficult to appreciate what knowledge was required. Happily the university faculty booklet was a mine of information. 'The Candidate for this examination is expected to know so and so, to show a reasonable knowledge of . . . so and so; the candidate will need to understand certain practical procedures of chemical analysis.' It did not take me long to realize that knowledge of the text books from cover to cover was necessary, and all in ten weeks too!

It was a daunting prospect. Fleeting glimpses of the lawyer's office haunted me that evening. Had I made a mistake? We had an English master at school who said there was no such word as can't in the English language. My father had similar ideology.

I felt it would be very feeble to even think of giving up the course at the end of Day One. What a disgrace! By bedtime I had pulled myself together. I should have to work and work and work. There was no option. I would have to become a swot, attend lectures, write up notes, plough through books, disappear from view after the lectures, not a pleasing manner in which to spend your first term. Next day I received valuable help from the colleagues I had encountered the previous day. They loaned me specimens of questions asked by the Scottish Examination Board for schools, and also a few past specimens of the pre-registration exam. This really helped me. I now had the books, the lectures, test papers and everything that was required. It was up to me. The days passed rapidly, and out of the dark the stars began to shine as I started to understand what I was doing and what I was being taught. I found the balancing of chemical equations very difficult until one day I suddenly understood and made rapid progress thereafter. I was lucky to have a good memory and good recall. I really began to think I could reach the requisite standard by mid-December.

The physics lecturer spurred us on; he seemed to know the areas in which we would experience difficulty. I shall never forget his lecture on the Doppler Sound Effect. It must have been a good lecture!

As the date of the pre-registration examination drew near so the busy days became even busier, and my light burned far into the night. I was learning, memorizing, attempting to pick possible questions, and modelling suitable answers. Although ten weeks ago it had seemed an insuperable task, on the eve of the examination I thought I felt ready for whatever lay ahead, and I doubted whether I could ever be better prepared. It had been a mammoth slog.

Luck was with me on the examination day, and by late afternoon the written papers in physics and chemistry were over. I was geared up and estimated sufficient marks to satisfy the examiners. Practical chemistry the next day was straight forward, but it was the oral physics that I found a trial.

Two examiners sat at a small table and I was offered the vacant chair. On the table was a gold-leaf electroscope. One question led to another and a wide area was covered but there was no indication from either examiner whether I was right or wrong. This unnerved me and I began to lose my confidence. When the gold-leaf electroscope was touched with an imaginary charged rod I was asked the reaction to be expected from the instrument. I was unsure of myself and I think I confused divergence and convergence, and may have given the wrong answer!

The oral finished rapidly and I was told to go. There was a sleepless night for me but next day the pass list was on the board, and I had passed in both subjects! My friends also passed. We were all delighted and elated at our success, and looked forward to meeting again next term.

Christmas was ten days away, and I felt light hearted as I joined the crowd of shoppers in the brightly lit Princes Street. Fifty years ago Christmas was not an event for which celebrations started many weeks ahead, and continued for at least ten days after Christmas Day. Although shops were gaily decorated, and lighted trees were sited at strategic positions, there was little commercialization. Never did the church have to remind us to put Christ back into Christmas. The holiday was Christmas Day and Boxing Day, and work as usual on 27 December.

New Year's Day was always a holiday in Scotland, but a normal working day in England. Money was tight and although modest presents were exchanged, and families brought together at Christmas, there was little opportunity for prolonged indulgence in food and drink. It was a religious festival and a happy time for children and their parents.

I sent a telegram home with the good news of my examination success. My parents always expected me to pass exams first time and I was pleased not to have disappointed them! I made arrangements to travel home to Devonshire the following night, and spend the holidays there. I had a school friend who lived in Salisbury and worked in London. He was able to get the day off and we arranged to meet at Euston at seven thirty am, the expected arrival time of the night train from Edinburgh. I travelled light, leaving books and heavy luggage in the 'digs'. The train departed from the Caledonian Station at the west end of Princes Street at ten pm. It was made up of first and third class coaches, and a long sleeper compartment. A sleeper cost £1 but I was unused to the facility and preferred a compartment.

It may surprise the present generation to learn that to arrive in London unshaven and untidy after a night journey was not the right way to behave. To go into a Lyon's Corner House for breakfast with facial growth would have incurred disapproving glances. To overcome this difficulty main-line stations in London had barbers shops on the platform where cafes now abound. It was normal to see a dozen men in chairs, faces well lathered from shaving soap, a brush and hot water being shaved by barbers using a cut throat. They were quick and smart in their white jackets. They did a good job and the charge was reasonable. Many times on my journeys between Edinburgh and Devon I had a shave on the platform.

My friend was a most helpful guide and introduced me to the sights of London over the years. We used the underground, or tubes, as the system was frequently called, and sometimes the buses to reach our destination. The underground seems to have changed very little in fifty years, apart from the cost and the congestion. For two pence you could travel a good distance. The rolling stock seems identical. The noise, the uncomfortable ride, the white tiled corridors and the waves of air intermittently rushing along these corridors to improve ventilation, have not altered. Cigarette smoking was widespread in the underground, the dangers were not appreciated, but I cannot recall a greater incidence of fires, nor do I think there were more staff than now.

It was always a most exhausting day in London with my friend. Quite apart from a disturbed night in the train I walked big distances all over, and we usually finished up in a small cinema adjacent to Waterloo Station to fill in time before the Exeter train departed at four thirty pm. If it was on Friday my friend travelled with me to Salisbury; any other day he returned to his lodgings. By the time the train had reached a small junction some eighteen miles from Exeter, and I had changed to a branch line for another twelve miles travel, it was nearly eight pm before I reached my destination. The station was rural, no taxi, the last bus had left and a two and a half mile walk awaited me to my parents home. Self-help was the order of the day. This was normal procedure and I thought nothing of the effort required, even with a suitcase. Traffic was light. It was dark but I knew the road.

Unwinding after ten weeks intensive study, and enjoying the euphoria of the successful examination result I had time to review my position, and peer into the future. I was indeed elated at my success; after ten weeks I was not a beginner and I was on an equal footing with those on the first year course. There seemed no reason why I should experience difficulty with the higher level of physics, chemistry, or botany and zoology as well, provided I worked hard.

The first year obviously was going to be my most difficult year, and if I could complete it successfully, I would not be disadvantaged, and my colleagues and I would start the second year course with similar levels of knowledge. I wanted, however, to enjoy my student days and work in a more relaxed way. I was not keen to take up sports; I had plenty of compulsory sport at school over many years: golf was too expensive and took up too much time. There was really very little time for leisure during the week, and even on Saturday mornings there was practical work. The medical course seemed intensive compared with other faculties.

After a fortnight's holiday I was back in Edinburgh again, and soon absorbed in the studies. There was always the companionship of other students, always the laughter at incidents during the lectures and above all, never any boredom.

After lectures finished in the afternoons, four of us would occasionally play snooker. Nobody knew the rules properly and amazing shots were made. To pot a ball into a central pocket we would hit the ball so hard it went back and forth across the table and eventually might land in the pocket! We improved with time.

None of us had female friends, and this was the norm — in the 1930s boys and girls tended to be segregated. There were schools for boys, and schools for girls, and it was not unusual to reach the age of nineteen years with very little knowledge of the opposite sex, especially if there were no sisters in the family.

In mixed schools run by local authorities the staff were strict, and there was little chance of irresponsible behaviour. Teenage marriages were rare. Students were invariably single; it was unusual to marry until the male partner was able to support a wife: this involved a job, and the provision of a home. Fewer married women had jobs: most were at home bringing up their children. Student behaviour was morally good. It was a serious matter to put a girl in the family way, for the girl and the student. Contraception was limited to barrier methods, and it was not common knowledge to seven year old children, teenagers, and often students. Sex before marriage was frowned upon, promiscuity or sleeping around associated with prostitution. We did not feel sex-starved; what you do not have you do not miss, and we were content to wait until the right person appeared, and we were in a position to do something about it.

It was at this time there was a major accident in the London Underground. From the newspaper one of the dead was a boy who had been at Weymouth College with me. He was studying dentistry in London. He had a twin brother, also at Weymouth, who survived the sinking of the *Royal Oak* in Scapa Flow. I was very upset and sad about this tragedy.

Back in Edinburgh, the spring term passed rapidly, and there were no exams. The pressure was less, and I was able to cope with chemistry and physics at a higher level. I was enjoying zoology too, dissecting and labelling vital structures of the frog, skate, and earthworm: with daily lectures we covered a great amount of material. There were so many lectures that there was little time for other activities.

The summer term was most pleasant; longer light evenings compared with the South Coast, and fine, sunny, bracing days. The Aurora Boreolis was active that summer. I had not seen the phenomenon before. There were entertainments in the 'Meadows', bands in Princes Street Gardens, and open air political and religious meetings in the Mound and outside the Art Gallery. Mr Neville Chamberlain had flown to see Adolf Hitler at Berchtesgaden, and he returned waving a slip of paper bearing 'Peace in our time'. Peace lasted a year longer and gave a disarmed and unprepared country a chance to organize for a war which seemed inevitable.

The first year examinations in physics, chemistry, botany and zoology took place at the end of June, and I was fortunate in passing all the subjects. I was awarded the Silver Medal in physics. It was an immense relief and I had succeeded in what I had hoped to achieve. Looking back the first year caused me more work and anxiety than any of the later years. I felt now that I would be able to fulfil my ambition to become a doctor. It was with a light heart that I returned to Devonshire after another day in London. Three months' holiday lay ahead.

Foreign travel was for a favoured few; package holidays, and cheap flights non-existent. Air travel was in its infancy, ensuring holidays were spent in the UK. I was particularly fortunate because there could be few counties for a better holiday than Devonshire. We had superb sunny days in July, August and September, and a large garden at home. Ten miles to the coast were small resorts, Seaton, Sidmouth, Ladram Bay, Exmouth and Beer. All had a shingle beach and crystal clear sea for bathing; each had its special characteristics. I had always enjoyed cycling. The roads were not too congested with cars and they travelled slower; it was safe to be out, and alone. I used to enjoy setting out on my cycle with sandwiches and a bottle of lemonade for a day on the beach. I travelled to a different resort every day. It was superb. Seaton made a special ice-cream cornet, yellow and egg-flavoured. I have never tasted better elsewhere at home or abroad. Cycling inland there were dairy farms to see: also we lived close to the orchards, their trees laden with small apples used in the manufacture of cider. Whimple was the name of the area. Always there was peace and quiet, a stark contrast to the hysterical screeching of Hitler and the goose-step march on the German stadia. I wondered how it would end. It seemed incredible there could be another world war only twenty years after the end of World War One. I could not visualize this country being over-run and forced to capitulate. This was the cloud hovering over that beautiful summer of 1938.

Holidays pass quickly and in early October I was back in Edinburgh for my second year. I changed 'digs', but stayed in the same area. The change was for the better, the cost the same. The room was larger, the level of comfort higher, and it was the first floor instead of the fourth. So much time was spent in 'digs' swotting that an annual change was desirable.

Once again the matriculation fee, and the course tuition fees for the year were paid, and work started. This year anatomy, physiology and organic chemistry were the subjects for study.

We assembled in the anatomy laboratory. In the middle of the room were four tables, each table bearing a cadaver. I understood these bodies were obtained from deaths in the workhouse! Every cadaver was very aged, but complete anatomically. There was a strong smell of formalin in the room. Around the room were 'pots': these were preserved specimens of part of the body with the salient features labelled. A glass cover protected the 'pots' and sealed them from the air.

We were split up into groups of half a dozen, and allocated to an arm or leg; the abdomen, thorax and skull were for later.

Dissecting manuals were available; we were told to equip ourselves with dissection tools, a knife, scissors and forceps. We had already dissected in zoology, and there was nothing so very different about human tissues. One or two students were adept with the knife and took over, receiving advice and encouragement from the remainder of the group. It was impractical for everyone to be cutting, mistakes would occur, and there was risk of being cut yourself. Good progress was made, and surveying the scene at the end of the day it was very clear that work had been done! Nobody fainted or changed colour, but conversation was subdued and we were glad for a smoke in the lobby. Anatomy lectures took place daily as did dissection. I did not appreciate that every muscle, every blood vessel, every nerve, or every groove, projection, or cavity in a bone had a name, and a Latin name too, and in my student days it was the Latin name to be learned. Latin at school was a great help. No matter how good your brain, or how sharp your memory and recall, anatomy was a factual subject and it had to be learned in detail. Either you knew it or you did not. Guessing was hazardous, and in an oral could quickly leave you on the wrong side of the door and advice to come back in three months. It was therefore no surprise to learn that the second year examination claimed many victims, and this was aggravated by the fact that both subjects, anatomy and physiology, had to be passed at one and the same time.

Physiology, the function of the human body was another large subject with a great deal of detail. The professor held up Samson-Wright's big fat textbook and said: 'Gentlemen, this is your Bible.' We shuddered, knowing too well there was another larger Bible in the 'digs' called Gray's Anatomy. There were physiology practicals too, and experiments with muscle tissue, electrically stimulated, producing a contraction, which was recorded on a revolving smoked drum. Frogs were used for the experiments, and there was no shortage. Histology, embryology and biochemistry were auxiliary subjects.

Clearly it was going to be a busy year and the sooner we addressed the task and kept up to date with the lectures, the better.

I enjoyed anatomy and physiology. Knowledge could be gained from sitting in a chair and reading, supplementing the information given by the lecturers. Professor Jamieson was the anatomy chief in Edinburgh University, and he published what were known as 'Jimmy's Plates'. These were detailed and beautifully illustrated anatomical pictures of all parts of the body. They could be acquired second-hand, and were invaluable, far superior to staring at a dismantled cadaver whose arteries and veins were the same dismal colour and hard to identify. There were also cram books which fitted into your pocket, useful for the beach and elsewhere.

There were certain structures, for example, those that were situated over the inner side of the ankle joint, whose initial letters formed a word. This was called a nemonic; a nemonic could be very useful if there was a memory lapse. Anatomy made heavy demands on memory, and there was an enormous amount to read and learn.

Physiology was always interesting, but there was a great amount of detail as well. The structures and function of the blood, the kidneys, the gall bladder, liver, and enzymes made fascinating reading. A difficult subject to teach. The professor pointed the direction, we did the reading. Over and above there was the organic chemistry course. The lecturer was brilliant, and we all enjoyed the course. It was a great help, and it made the biochemistry reading much easier to understand.

I required all my time and energy to deal with the second year's work. The examination in the two subjects took place as usual at the end of June. Once again I had the good fortune to pass them all. I remember the anatomy oral clearly. I was examined on the gluteal region, the sciatic nerve, and a 'pot' with a urinary bladder, prostate gland, ureters and urethra under the glass cover.

To complete your second year successfully was a landmark for a medical student and you really felt you were on the way. Several students went to a pub that night and drank draught cider. The atmosphere was very jovial indeed. I was there.

On the 3 September 1939 while I was on holiday in Devonshire, Hitler invaded Poland, and Mr Neville Chamberlain, the prime minister, declared Britain was at war with Germany. Mr Chamberlain spoke gravely on the radio, and barely had he finished speaking before there was the wail of an air raid siren. There was initial confusion and radio broadcasts stopped that day. A news bulletin was broadcast in the late evening but there was little information. After a day or two there was an evacuation of many school children from London to the country. Many arrived in Devonshire and were billeted. Many returned to London after a few weeks to be reunited with their families. In retrospect it seemed a pointless exercise, but nobody knew the immediate turn of events. London could have been bombed early on in the war.

I was not quite twenty-one years old, and for a week or so, I did not know whether I would be called up. Shortly afterwards it was announced that medical students after their second year were to continue their studies. I remember completing a form delaying call up until qualified. There was a proviso that examination failure would negate the deferment.

The pattern of life changed rapidly. Those on holiday in Cornwall and Devon returned home by road and rail. The roads were very busy. Black-out curtains replaced existing curtains. Wardens patrolled the streets, and a chink of light from a window or door way invited a knock and a demand that the fault be corrected forthwith. Out went all the street lights, and the headlamps of motor cars were fitted with a cover similar to a top hat with three slots on the front to allow a trace of light to emerge. It was better not to be on the roads at night, so poor was the vision. Petrol rationing and petrol coupons soon followed, and private cars began to disappear from the roads.

Gas masks arrived at the village hall. I remember checking them and packing them in a cardboard box for issue to the public. Everyone had a gas mask tucked away, but very few carried them. The mood was sombre, the nation subdued.

I was relieved to return to Edinburgh in October 1939 to another and final change of 'digs'. Edinburgh seemed more remote from the war; it was the south coast which was so vulnerable. My father had a theory that Germany would invade Britain and the South could be cut off from the North, and indeed such an event might have taken place had it not been for the heroic air battles over the South-East coast in September 1940 by the Battle of Britain pilots in their fighter aircraft. Their actions destroyed the Luftwaffe, and invasion became unlikely without air support. As a result of my father's theory he managed to give me six months finance for 'digs', course, and pocket money. I opened a bank account opposite the Royal Infirmary in Forest Road. I was cautioned to budget carefully.

I was soon at studies again. This third year was taken up with pathology, pharmacology and materia medica, and medical jurisprudence.

Pathology, the study of diseased tissue was another subject to keep the mind active. There was plenty to read. Every illness produces pathological changes. Microscopic examination of diseased tissue on slides and blood films, took up the time allocated for practical work. In the practical examination there were half a dozen or so microscopes with a slide focussed. A question paper required knowledge of the organ, cells and disease. Slides could be difficult, and practice was valuable. An entire organ such as the liver might be presented, and an examiner there to ask questions about the specimen.

Pharmacology and materia medica brought us nearer to the real world of treatment. A detailed knowledge of drugs and preparations, their dosage, and side effects was required. I was taught to write prescriptions in Latin, and continued to do so for many years after I was qualified. We were asked to make up a bottle of medicine, an expectorant, for example. Care had to be taken that the various ingredients were compatible, and that the cork was not blown out of the bottle! As time went by there were a large number of proprietary preparations manufactured by drug companies, and these were prescribed by a proprietary name. Prescribing in Latin became unnecessary. The standard of prescribing in fact deteriorated rapidly, and it was only too easy to write up a proprietary medicament without knowing its ingredients. The pendulum is swinging back and generic prescribing is becoming better practice, and often cheaper.

We all enjoyed medical jurisprudence and the work police surgeons have to tackle. Drowning, asphyxia, sexual crimes, and correct procedure in the witness box were discussed. Rigor mortis was a popular examination question, and the determination how long ago death had occurred was a stimulating exercise.

In the spring term of 1940, as I was struggling with these new subjects, the anatomy lecturer notified us that we should sit for the Hill-Pattison-Struthers Bursary in anatomy and physiology. This bursary was open to students who had passed the professional examination in those subjects during the year. The examination consisted of written papers only in those two subjects. The prize for the winner was a certificate and the sum

40

of £50. The response was not enthusiastic; it was a major interruption of the work in hand. Having put the detailed knowledge behind us for the time being, many students were loth to rake out the anatomy and physiology textbooks again; some thought it might jeopardize their chances for the examination in July on the current subjects. Clearly an examination of that calibre would not be easy and a high standard would be expected for the prize to be awarded. I entered for the exam. I had a good memory, good morale, and an optimistic attitude about most things.

There was nothing to lose, no disgrace in failing, and £50 was a dangling carrot. As hoped, my memory did not let me down, and on the examination day I was in confident mood. There were only six candidates, and the questions were no more difficult than those of the professional examination.

After a few days I was notified in writing that I had won the award, and there would be a formal presentation at the next meeting of the Royal College of Physicians on a certain date. When the day arrived I had to present myself at the Royal College at three pm. I donned my best suit, white collar and a non-flashy tie. My black shoes gleamed. A uniformed porter conducted me along a corridor and up a flight of wide stairs. It was an imposing building. Portraits of past presidents of the Royal College lined the walls, and chandeliers hung from sculptured ceilings. At the top of the stairs I was handed over to two uniformed attendants guarding a wide large door. I was instructed to watch the door, and when it opened, make my way to the table at the end of the room, receive the award, shake hands, and retrace my steps.

The door opened and I walked in. The room was large. Fellows of the College sat in rows on each side of the passage as I walked to the large highly polished table at the end of the room. There was the president of the College with other Fellows seated on either side of him. He rose as I approached. He had magnificent robes and was a very dignified figure. He congratulated me, handed me my certificate rolled into a cylinder, and an envelope bearing a cheque for £50. He shook hands and I retraced my steps to the door midst applause from the assembled gathering. I was soon in the street again and on my way to the 'digs' to find a safe place for my newly won possessions. It had been my day although it lasted less than five minutes! I have always treasured the certificate, and it is hard to believe that fifty years have elapsed since that great day. £50 was a large sum and it was soon safely in the bank. I decided to spend the bulk on books for my future courses and I derived great pleasure and benefit from an excellent text book on diseases of the eye, and an illustrated book on radiology as well as many others. £10 was allotted for the purchase of a second-hand radio. I used to listen to Lord Haw-Haw speaking from Germany after midnight, as well as concerts. Before the nine pm news on a Sunday evening the national anthems were played of all the countries involved in the fight against Hitler. The list grew longer every year. I enjoyed the radio, and the set proved to be reliable. The war was not going well. The Germans had reached the Siegfried Line, and our forces in France had their backs to the wall. They retreated to the Dunkirk beaches and were evacuated in their thousands to Britain by naval vessels and by fleets of boats of all sizes and types, including small fishing boats, paddle steamers and rowing boats. This evacuation of the British Expeditionary Force from France was an outstanding achievement. All the time this armada was mercilessly under air attack from the Luftwaffe. Many naval vessels were sunk or damaged, as were the smaller civilian vessels; there was loss of life, but the bulk of the British Expeditionary Force was evacuated.

Belgium, Holland, and now France, were under German domination and Britain stood alone that summer of 1940. An invasion of the south coast was possible and if Hitler had struck then there could have been a very different end to the war. However, he paused. Barbed wire, concrete bollards and pill boxes sprang up along the south and east coasts and feverishly the country worked on munitions and fighter aircraft manufacture to combat the assault when it came.

Life had to continue for those not involved with the forces. The trains still ran, bus services continued, but shops became short of certain commodities. Bananas and eggs disappeared. Egg powder appeared. Cigarettes were scarce and sold in small quantities at a time; if you were unknown to a shop, your chances of obtaining cigarettes were slim. Rationing of food commenced, controlled by ration books. Most foods were rationed, some items appeared on the black market. If you relied on the rations there seemed little to eat. It is claimed that the nation's health was at its best during the war years, but I would be unsure whether that claim applied to civilians ineligible for canteen meals which were provided over and above the rations.

I was still able to travel between Edinburgh and Devonshire, but the journeys became increasingly uncomfortable. The night trains from the north were full of service personnel travelling south, on leave or other postings, from Naval vessels at Scapa Flow and Invergordon. Men slept where they could, across a table, along a corridor, heads on packs, or standing propped up between others. I shared their discomfort. The lights were dim, little was said, and many were fatigued. Positions of ships were never discussed nor questions asked. There were quislings about and one did not know who they were. Information must never reach the enemy.

My London friend was still a civilian. He was shortly called up, and survived the war. He married and lived in Salisbury but sadly died from cancer many years ago. Summer 1940 was the last long vacation I had as a student. I had passed the exams in pathology and materia medica, and medical jurisprudence in July, and travelled home. (I was awarded the class medal in materia medica.)

I shall never forget summer 1940. The sun blazed out of a cloudless sky day after day as the Luftwaffe under the command of Herr Goering crossed the English Channel. They were confronted by a tiny force of Spitfire and Hurricane fighters. Our pilots were grossly outnumbered. Despite this, hundreds of German fighters were shot down, or limped back across the Channel, and gradually the Battle of Britain was won, and the Luftwaffe left seriously weakened and undermined. Many brave pilots lost their lives; many had just left school; many of my contemporaries joined the RAF, experienced a few weeks training, before they were in the air and fighting the Luftwaffe. The course of the war was changed, and Britain was no longer under serious threat of invasion. Hitler miscalculated and paid the penalty. It was a dreadful time, but the success was outstanding. The country had been saved.

October 1940 saw me back in Edinburgh. I was now in my fourth year when clinical work commenced, and I came into contact with hospitals and patients.

Surgery, medicine, midwifery and gynaecology were the main subjects for study over the next two years before the final

Edinburgh Royal Infirmary, facing the meadows. Courtesy of The Scotsman Publication.

examination. Then there were the special subjects such as ear nose and throat, eyes, skins, VD, fevers and diseases of children, and mental illnesses. These specialities were fitted into the curriculum over the next two years and there was a class examination held in each speciality before a certificate was issued, stating you had completed the course and satisfied the clinical tutors. You could not sit the final examination unless you had completed certificates of attendance for the various specialities.

The lectures in surgery, medicine and midwifery and gynaecology, were held in Surgeons Hall, but there was a clinic held in the Royal Infirmary several times a week where we met patients, examined them, and had tutorial instruction from chiefs, registrars and clinical tutors.

We were advised to buy a stethoscope. It had to be a basic 'Bell type Stethoscope', and an unostentatious model. Some students had ideas of their own and produced magnification models. They were invariably picked out by the professor to examine a patient in front of the class to find out what they heard through that type of stethoscope! The first time a stethoscope is used is a disappointment. Little can he heard apart from a rush of air. The bell piece of the stethoscope must be flush on the patient's skin and there must be no handshake. There was sarcasm from our instructors if the hand shook! A bony chest can make it difficult to place the stethoscope flush on the skin. Gradually and with experience one learns to exclude extraneous sounds, so that one can concentrate on the heart sounds or the breath sounds. The clinical tutors were very skilled at picking up abnormal sounds and heart murmurs. I found a mid-diastolic murmur difficult, but no doubt today, with amplification loud and clear, this is no longer a problem for students.

We were taught in the wards to be systematic in the examination of a patient. Physical signs had to be found and interpreted. A student would be asked to take a patient's pulse. To say it was normal was a disaster. The rate, the rhythm, the regularity in time and force, and the state of the arterial wall had to be announced. Inspection, palpation, percussion and auscultation were vital in the examination of a patient's chest and to make a diagnosis without a proper examination was a serious omission.

A considerable amount of time was spent in the laboratory

— side rooms off the main wards. Here there was a sink, hot and cold water, a Bunsen burner, and a microscope with low, high, and oil-immersion lenses. Boxes of microscope slide covers were in abundance. There was an endless supply of cylindrical glass urine beakers about ten inches high, all well filled with the urine from the In-Patients. Bottles of urine testing reagents fitted into racks, and there were small booklets of pink and blue litmus paper to test the reaction of the urine. There was a hydrometer to measure the specific gravity.

Urine had to be heated in a glass test tube to test for albumen. As soon as the urine was warmed over the Bunsen burner a cloud of whiteness would appear. A drop of glacial acetic acid would clear the whiteness produced by phosphates, but would not alter albumen. There was Benedicts solution for sugar testing, and a range of colours in the test tube indicated roughly the quantity of sugar present in the sample.

There were more complex tests for bile, blood and acetone. An Esbach tube was always to be found to estimate the quantity of albumen as a percentage. Every test was made, recorded, and the result recorded on the patients case sheet. There was a centrifuge as well, powered by electricity or hand for -spinning' a small sample of urine in order to collect the sediment at the bottom of the test tube. The deposit was drawn up into pipette, a drop placed on a microscope slide, a cover glass applied, and a search made for crystals, cells and pus. It was very important to be proficient at testing urine. Time and time again this knowledge was required at the bed-side during a ward round, and if there was a lack of knowledge, the patient, other students and the ward sister looked on in obvious discomfort. Today there is a dipstick to dip into urine and it will read off eight-ten tests within seconds. This saves a great deal of time and energy. I do not know whether students today are taught the former tests. I suspect samples make their way to the pathological department and a printed 'read out' follows to the ward!

I was always surprised at the length of the ward in a big hospital. The beds seem to stretch as far as the eye could see along both sides and across the far end as well. Portable, curtained screens on wheels which could fold up, were used for privacy. They were clumsy obstacles, easy to trip over. Gliding curtain rails had not been invented.

The advantages of early ambulation were not appreciated.

An operation involved confinement to bed until the stitches had been removed for a couple of days. A hernia repair took fourteen days flat on your back and then seven days with a pillow before ambulation. A gynaecological repair, and a Caesarean section involved twenty-one days in bed. If you were in hospital you were in bed! How necessary it was in those days to have a bedpan per patient, and a sluice-room to empty, wash and sterilize these pans. How difficult it was for the patient to use them lying on their backs, or sitting on them in bed, arms behind them supporting their position. If the pans were cold it was an uncomfortable experience. Bedpans were heavy work for the nurses, and the situation was worse in a female ward.

Another component of the training in the medical wards was writing up a 'case'. A student was allocated three patients in a term. A full history had to be taken, age, marital status, family, past medical history and any relevant information. Symptoms, past and present were queried and finally a physical examination had to be carried out.

Subsequently the student was required to make a diagnosis, a differential diagnosis, and the completed work handed in to the clinical tutor for evaluation. It took time but it was a valuable exercise. There was always a problem. The case history necessitated 'out of hours' work, and permission had to be granted by the ward sister to enter the ward. In those days, ward sisters could be dominant and were often curt with students. Sometimes permission was refused. There was nothing to be gained from an argument. Of course students were a nuisance: screens had to be placed round the bed, a nurse sent to chaperone, and often they were otherwise occupied. Again, many patients were very ill and resented questioning and examining all over again. However, we had our work to do as well, and everything was settled in the end.

While the medical work was in progress, surgery also was studied. Again, apart from the main lectures in the medical school, there were clinics in the surgical wards. Again, the importance attached to a correct and detailed examination was paramount. Great emphasis was placed on the diagnosis of the 'acute abdomen'. A diagnosis of an acute abdomen involved emergency surgery to save life. It was therefore imperative to appreciate the physical signs which were produced by an acute abdomen. To miss an acute abdomen was, naturally, quite shocking. It could be tricky, and safer to err on the side of caution.

There were well known surgical chiefs. I remember Sir John Fraser, Mr Pirie-Watson, Professor Learmonth and Mr Jardine during my clinical years.

A chief's surgical ward had a night on call in rotation. This meant that every surgical admission arrived at that chief's male or female surgical wards. It could be a very busy night indeed. I cannot recall the chief being on the scene at night, but the registrar, tutors and house surgeons were. They operated all through the night. Some already held the FRCSE or were close to it.

Most of the surgery was heavy. There were perforations, so common in those days, appendicitis, small and large bowel obstructions, and the relief of acute urinary retention if an attempt to pass a catheter failed. Suprapubic cystostomy was not a pleasant procedure. It was always followed by a bladder infection necessitating daily bladder irrigation. Prostatectomy followed later and it had a high mortality. Urogenital surgery was not a speciality and formed part of the load of a general surgeon's work.

Students were attached to a chief and his surgical wards. On the on-call nights we were expected to be there sizing up the situation, getting adjusted to the hustle and bustle, and making ourselves useful. We did a great deal of work in the anaesthetic room lifting patients on and off trolleys, holding the anaesthetic mask on the patient's face whilst the anaesthetist attended to more pressing problems. Anybody wearing a white coat was utilized. There was a great opportunity to see emergency admissions. Physical signs and diagnoses were pointed out to us if the pressure of work was not excessive. We soon became accustomed to blood and abdominal content. I disliked amputations and nearly passed out one day during the amputation of a forearm.

The operating theatre of a teaching hospital has a gallery with tiers of seating overlooking the operating table. A good view was possible. One was not allowed to enter the gallery without a green cap, gown, face mask, and foot covers extending as far as the knee. There was an adjacent dressing room leading to the gallery. We had experienced the operating conditions from above before we ventured on to the floor. Anaesthesia was gas, oxygen and ether via the Boyles machine, or open ether; chloroform was reserved for midwifery.

I had completed my fourth year and it was July 1941. For some time I had been troubled with sore throats; looking at my tonsils in the mirror I thought they were large and unhealthy and showed debris in the crypts. I was concerned. So many serious illnesses started with a sore throat. I consulted one of the ENT surgeons. He was adamant that my tonsils were bad and should be removed, and soon. A date was fixed for the following week and I was instructed to report to the students ward early in the evening prior to the operation next day. The school doctor had been correct!

The procedure was severe. No supper and no breakfast next morning. I was surprised to have to submit to an enema as I thought it irrelevant for a throat operation, though I appreciated the stomach must be empty, and I accepted the starvation. I was given two soneryl tablets around ten pm and I sank into deep sleep. Life started around six am when the curtains were pulled back. A bowl of hot water was brought to the bed table and I washed and shaved using a safety razor. There were only two in the ward, but plenty of nursing staff. The bed was made with me in it. I felt fit and could have run a mile. The care was remarkable and touching; a pleasant young nurse brushed and parted my hair! Sister appeared and I was instructed to lie still and not derange the bed clothes. She said my throat would be painful after the operation for a few days. Then I was given a pre-medication presumably Morph gr 1/4 and Atropine gr 1/100 which was widely used at that time. (Morph gr 1/6 if your gender was female.)

I was light-headed after this. I was being pushed at fair speed along corridors but indifferent to my fate. I had a hazy recollection of being in the theatre. There were voices and I was lifted off the trolley and placed in a high backed chair. I saw the ENT Surgeon capped, masked, and gowned confronting me. He said he was operating under local anaesthesia as it was safer. Had it not been for the pre-medication which had confused me I am sure I would have panicked and rushed out of the hospital and across the Meadows to my 'digs' as I was. The back of my throat was sprayed, and after a short time the operation started. It was most unpleasant. I had to open my mouth as wide as the temporomandibular joints would allow and it was held in that position with a metal cage, inserted into the mouth; my tongue was pulled forward as far as it could go. It was a horrible and uncomfortable position and I concentrated on breathing. My eyes were bandaged. There was no pain, I heard the clink of instruments and the ratchets of artery forceps. It seemed a long time when suddenly the bandage slipped and I saw instruments sticking out of my mouth. I fought to breathe and flaked out. I came round with my head near the floor between my knees. The operation proceeded. I was told to keep breathing. A voice said: 'He's going to do it again,' and I did!

I came round in a recovery room. The instruments had gone, a nurse was feeling my pulse and I was lying on a trolley. I felt groggy. An hour later I perked up and was wheeled back to the ward and to bed.

Although I understood tonsils were frequently removed under local anaesthetic I have never met anyone during my practice life who had experienced it. I cannot recommend it.

As the effects of the anaesthetic spray and local infiltration wore off the discomfort by mid-afternoon was acute. I was encourage to swallow but it was torture. Next day I felt better and was able to sip cold water. For tea some thin strips of bread and butter with a brown spread arrived. It was torture, the brown spread was Marmite!

I begged the nurse not to give it to me again. Two or three days later there was improvement and I could swallow soft food and liquids with some discomfort.

It was now that I began to appreciate Louise Petrie. Louise was an attractive and most pleasant nurse. She had recently become an SRN. She was chatty and a comforting person to have around when unwell. She came from the Manse, and lived some miles south of the city at Loanhead. There was little chance to see as much of her as I would have liked but discipline was strict and she had her work to do. I was discharged on the eight day; the ENT specialist said the sloughs were separating and that everything was normal. The end result was most satisfactory, but it had been an unpleasant experience. I had lost some weight and felt frail as I crossed the Meadows to my 'digs'. I decided to have a week to pick up my strength, and then spend a month in the casualty department of the infirmary. After that I would return home for a week or two until the start of the autumn session.

After a few days I was much better. The fresh air at the summit of Arthur's Seat was a tonic. I reported to the casualty department and donned a white coat. It was a busy place, with numerous rooms and side rooms and rows of patients awaiting treatment. It did not take long to understand the working of the system. There were numerous house doctors and nursing staff. I learned how to apply bandages correctly, even the capeline bandage for the head. There were numerous wounds or leg ulcers for dressings. Eusol (Edinburgh University Solution of Lime) was widely used and cleaned up a septic wound. Pink lint, oiled silk, hot fomentations and kaolin poultices were frequently used. Magnesium sulphate paste was a popular dressing spread on gauze. Students were there to observe and digest, but if you wore a white coat, and you were expected to, you were asked to lend a hand. It was a valuable experience and I have never regretted it. It was not a compulsory part of the course.

At the end of the day there was time to revise, read and check up on the notes of the courses attended during the year. During that month I saw Louise in the corridor and I asked her out. She agreed to come. Nurses worked long hours eight am to eight pm, and handed over to the night staff before going off duty. Also they had to be back in the nurses home before midnight: there could be some nasty trouble if they were late. The evening therefore was very short indeed. Shops were shut, the war news depressing, and there was little to do apart from strolling about. I thought how attractive she was in mufti. It was most enjoyable and we agreed to meet again before long. She was always agreeable and a pleasant companion to have on your arm.

The next meeting was soon after, when I was invited to the Manse at Loanhead for tea. It was Sunday. I had not seen the inside of a church since leaving school, and I knew I would require my best behaviour. I arrived by bus in the main street and Louise was there to meet me. We strolled about the area and into a wooded park before returning to her home. Her parents were formal, very courteous and we sat down to the table. Conversation was not easy, and I had not expected it to be so. Sunday afternoon was a quiet time in the Manse. I left before the evening service as buses were few at that stage of the war. We agreed to write to each other.

I went to Devonshire for a couple of weeks after another

unpleasant journey by night. Hitler, frustrated at his failure, vented his anger on London, Coventry, Liverpool, Plymouth, Hull, Sheffield and Exeter by dropping bombs as soon as there was cover of darkness. Loss of life was heavy and the destruction severe and devastating. The underground was used as air raid shelters at night in London. It was a different city each night for the raids.

In Africa the Eighth Army was sweeping Rommel's German and Italian forces out of North Africa but there was rarely good news.

The end of September 1941 came and it was time to return to Edinburgh for the last lap. The finals had been brought forward by six months, and I was to sit them in early January 1943. Vacation courses enabled the shortening of the normal length of training.

When I arrived at London, having left home early in the morning, there had been a raid the previous night. There were few people in the station and the underground was shut. There were no taxis and there had been damage near the station. It was necessary to reach Euston, and clearly I would require to walk it. I started off and had Westminster Bridge almost to myself. Half way across a taxi pulled up behind me and I was driven to Euston and very pleased to see it. There was no sense staying in London as further air-raids seemed imminent so I caught a train due to arrive in Edinburgh at ten pm. It was a slow journey with stops out in the country. It was after two am when Edinburgh was reached. Again, the black-out and no taxis.

I walked to the 'digs' to find the good landlady had stayed up, and had some food available. People were very helpful to each other during the war.

A letter came from Louise. She was now in a London Hospital having left Edinburgh, and said she would like to join the QAIMNS. I was depressed about this and decided there was little sense in having a girl-friend four hundred miles away and I tried to forget her. There was much work to do and I must pass my finals.

Midwifery lectures commenced. After the course there was attendance at a dozen deliveries on the district. Work on the specialities continued as well; there was plenty to do. Everybody enjoyed the lectures on midwifery given by two lecturers from the Simpson Memorial Maternity Block. Pelvic measurements were very important. The foetal stethoscope picked up the foetal heart sounds; it took time to become proficient in its use.

Scanning was years away and sounded like a dream. Foetal distress was diagnosed by the quality and rate of the foetal heart using the foetal stethoscope. The induction of labour was OBE (oil, bath or enema) and rupture of the membranes in suitable cases. A Caesarean section was a major event using the classical route, and there was a mortality rate. Puerperal fever was a nightmare until antibiotics arrived. White leg and a deep vein thrombosis were all too common. There conditions were caused by immobility.

We used to attend an anti-natal clinic in a poor area of Edinburgh. Urine was tested routinely for albumen, the haemoglobin tested on the spot using Haldane's Haemoglobinometer. In the corner there was a couch and about thirty women in their later weeks took turns to be examined. The obstetrician was our lecturer. Presentation, position, the site of maximum foetal heart sounds, and whether the presenting part was engaged in the pelvis finished the examination. We found this difficult at first, and the foetal heart sounds very difficult to hear, but time and experience made all the difference.

We went to the Simpson Maternity Block several times. We scrubbed up our hands, donned sterile gowns, caps, gloves and masks in preparation for delivery. The labour room was full of staff. We were kept in the background until the head was 'crowned'. If lucky we assisted in the extraction of the trunk. All primigravida had an episiotomy. The place was like a factory and I was not particularly impressed. It seemed far removed from our teaching.

Then I went to Leith to attend the twelve district cases. There was a house in Leith which accommodated half a dozen students at a time. We never left the building until the bell rang and we were given the address of a woman in labour. With a midwife I cycled to the address with a midder bag strapped to the rear of the cycle. In the black-out it was difficult to know where you were, but the police always helped us. They were 'on the beat' in those days. Leith was a poor area. The block tenements were overcrowded and the area extensive. As we entered the doorway into the passage by the stairway, we would brush past a drunk leaning against the wall. Methylated spirit was often drunk with wretched consequences for the liver. Despite the darkness and the eerie quietness of the streets we were never molested and we felt perfectly safe.

Midwife and I went up the stairs and into the flat. Neither knew what to expect as we reached the labouring woman. There was a black kitchen range and usually a big coal fire. The lighting was by gas and the gas mantles were often damaged, giving a very poor light. There was a large iron bedstead with little bedding. Often small children ran about the room while the husband sat by the fire. A dog was taken outside. On one occasion the baby was born before we arrived, but all was well.

Newspapers were placed under the mother on the bed, and the husband produced very hot water as required. He looked after the other children as well. Usually the patient was in the second stage of labour when we arrived, and there was time to assess the position and check the state of cervical dilation. This was carried out rectally using a finger-stall. Vaginal examinations were not allowed because of the dangers of infection, and we would be in serious trouble with examiners if it was suggested. We listened for the foetal heart, and had a large plate available to hold the placenta.

The midwife conducted the delivery, and the aim was to deliver the head without a perineal tear, even if primigravida. This was usually achieved. All our cases had received some ante-natal care and were considered normal. We had no problems with haemorrhage or retained placenta. It was a crime to pull on the cord. The baby was placed at the foot of the bed until the placenta was delivered. This was wrapped in newspapers and placed on the fire. Intramuscular ergometrine was always given.

Nurse washed the baby, wrapped it up and the mother took charge. The baby was always weighed using the old-fashioned spring and hook. Gratitude and thanks were profuse. If the baby was a girl it was named after the midwife, if a boy after me!

If there had been a problem we could not handle it was reported to the HQ in Leith and the patient was transferred to hospital.

A confinement used to be considered a physiological event. Nowadays it seems pathological! Very few mothers fall into a normal pattern as the criteria for normality multiply. When we returned to the HQ we had to write the case up in detail and hand it in for assessment.

Despite the unhygienic situations mothers and babies used to thrive, though the infant mortality rate was high throughout the country. Grand multiparity was common and families of nine or ten children were reared in these tenements.

I remember the skin disease clinics clearly. The chief was abrasive to patients and students alike. He was precise and expected precise answers but rarely achieved this satisfaction. He disliked any proprietary preparation, especially Germoline, used on the skin. The word 'eczema' upset him as well. He would be very irate if the cause of dermatitis was suggested to be occupational, though frequently this was the case.

Scabies was common, especially during the war years, and was usually transmitted by blankets, especially army blankets. It was treated with sulphur ointment. Clothes and blankets were disinfected. Acne vulgaris, rosacea, ringworm of the scalp and body, psoriasis and dermatitis were seen in the clinic. We learned how to examine and inspect the skin, indeed we learned much from him. It was a tense hour and we were relieved to be outside with our reputation untarnished.

The ENT Clinic was another difficult speciality for a student. An electric auriscope was not allowed. We had head-mirrors and visualization of the eardrum was achieved by reflecting a source of light adjacent to the patients chair down the external auditory canal. The pinna was drawn back and an aural speculum inserted using the thumb and index finger. Of course we saw nothing to start with, the reflected light would show up on the ceiling and we needed our imagination. It is certainly desirable to be able to use a speculum and head-mirror as it enables a free hand to be used for mopping out the canal. The electric auriscope had great attractions because apart from illuminating the canal, it provided magnification of the drum.

Acute otitis media was very common, especially so during a measles epidemic. It started with earache, usually in a child, which worsened and throbbed until the ear drum perforated with a gush of blood and pus giving instant relief. To prevent a perforation, a J shaped incision, a myringotomy, was performed under anaesthesia, the rationale being that a surgical wound healed quicker and better than a burst wound with ragged edges. Many burst drums healed without a hearing loss, but many never healed and the patient was left with a chronic discharging ear and poor hearing. Even if the discharge dried up the perforation was still there, but an upper respiratory infection would flare up the condition and cause the discharge to recur.

There were always young patients whose otitis media did not settle when the drum perforated. The infection spread to the air cells of the mastoid process producing an acute mastoiditis. When this took place, the temperature became raised, and the mastoid process tender to touch and it felt and looked puffy. If left untreated a brain abscess or thrombosis of the lateral sinus supervened, followed by death. The treatment was to incise over the infected mastoid, and drain the air cells. A chisel and hammer were required. The entire situation was unpleasant for patient and operator: drainage tubes were inserted and daily dressings followed. Often the cosmetic result left much to be desired.

Sulphonamide therapy stopped all the discomfort and pain, and usually prevented perforation; mastoiditis is rarely seen now. If the drum perforated because treatment started too late, it seemed to heal. I remember ENT specialists were slow to use sulphonamides, because it was thought their use could mask a mastoiditis. Penicillin is used now and is even better for the prevention and treatment of acute otitis media.

Otitis externa could be a problem too. Large wicks soaked in eight per cent aluminium acetate were in vogue, and boric powder was sometimes insoufflated. An otitis externa could be caused by the discharge from a chronic perforation and we looked for a pulsating discharge to help solve the problem. We were taught never to use ear drops in the presence of a perforation. This condition otitis externa used to cause a great deal of work over long periods of time because daily dressings were necessary.

Proof puncture of an antrum followed by antral lavage was a daily event in the clinic to relieve chronic sinus infection. The Caldwell-Luc operation was performed for chronic infection of an antrum. Nasal polpyi were very common and were snared again and again. The role of the ENT specialists has changed over recent years; intricate and delicate operations can now be carried out on the middle and inner ear, and radical surgery for cancer of the larynx.

We moved on to the Childrens Hospital in Sciennes Road. The atmosphere was more relaxed here. There was no casualty department, and children were not pouring into the hospital day and night. Our work concentrated on small babies and their feeding problems, and the correct way to inspect and examine an infant. The illnesses peculiar to infants such as intussussception received special teaching. It was dreadful to misdiagnose intussussception, which responded to surgery, but fatal if misdiagnosed. It had to be foremost in your mind when examining an infant. Congenital pyloric stenosis could be deceptive and difficult to diagnose. Leukaemia, all the varieties, received special mention, and we had to become efficient at differentiating the various types from blood films. The chief was Dr Patterson-Brown, a splendid teacher, and a quiet, dedicated professor; he had an excellent nursing staff. It was a fine hospital with conscientious, patient, and dedicated nurses and doctors. Many cases were heart-breaking and tragic at that time; medical advance could not come quickly enough.

I was awarded the Class Medal for 'Disease of Children'. We left the hospital with the message ringing in our ears, that to refuse a call to an infant or small child whatever the time of day or night was criminal.

Epilepsy in children was a difficult problem; a fit was controlled using paraldehyde rectally, the dose per kilo body weight. Intravenous phenobarbitone, a thick oily preparation used in older children and adults was quite effective. There is a wonderful array of preparations available now for the control of epilepsy. There used to be stigma for epileptics, and it was difficult for them to find employment. One rarely sees a person having an epileptic fit in the street now; it was very common once; help came as the handles of spoons were wrapped in gauze and lint, and carefully placed in the mouth between spasms to prevent damage to the teeth.

At this stage of the war Hitler was dropping incendiary bombs. These fell on roofs of houses and offices and could set fire to a building quickly. To lessen the task of the official fire watchers, and to free them for more important duties, it was the responsibility of the owners of shops, offices and other tall buildings to provide their own fire-watchers at night. Usually it was the male members of the staff who took over the responsibility, sometimes the boss. It was not a popular occupation and would be dangerous if there was a fire. Students were a source of man power for the job and many undertook it.

I decided to take it on and fire-watched two nights weekly for two months. I arrived at the building in George Street at nine pm. I had been given a key and could let myself in. A climb of about four or five flights up to the top of the building followed, passing offices on the way with their doors unlocked, in case entry was necessary. The fire watcher's room was up here: a basic bed, chair and electric fire were provided. Outside the door was a stirrup pump and a bucket of water. I knew where to find a telephone in an emergency. The lighting was dim and the windows blacked out; it could be very chilly at night. There was a gas ring in the passage outside the door and it was possible to make a hot drink. Now and again the air raid sirens wailed and I prepared for the worst. It was eerie up there at night on your own.

Happily I never had occasion to see or fight a fire. On the credit side I had the time and opportunity to revise, read, and check my lecture notes. It was the spring of 1941.

Shortly after Easter a notice was placed on the board in the university precinct stating that the University Army Training Corps was to patrol a stretch of coast over a weekend. Student volunteers were required. I had been in the Weymouth College Cadet Force for several years, knew drill, the compass, and I had attended large school camps at Tidworth. I had also carried a rifle. I signed up, and in no time I was issued with a kilt, glengarry, jacket and gaiters. I provided my own boots. I had been told that the Scots did not wear underpants when the kilt was worn, so I thought I had better conform though I did not relish the idea.

It turned out to be one of the most uncomfortable weekends of my life. Apart from having a heavy cold, the weather was extremely cold and I felt rotten. Security was tight and we set off in buses for a journey lasting about an hour. It was clear we were on the estuary of the Firth of Forth at Gullane. Accommodation was wooden huts and we had a paliasse of straw which was placed on the floor for sleeping. There was no heating and the food was unpalatable and scanty. We did a four hour stint on the cliff tops by day and another four hours during the night. There was plenty of beer and everybody drank far too much, but it kept us warm. Crude singsongs took place at night for those who were not on the cliff top. On the Saturday afternoon there was a football match versus a regular army team some miles inland. I was chosen and played right half. I felt too unwell to enjoy the match and the opposing team won easily. When the Monday afternoon came I was not sorry to leave. There was a hitch with the transport and we were dropped off near Musselburgh. We marched the rest of the way back to the university through streets and shoppers with our kilts swinging. It was several miles. In retrospect it seemed a pointless exercise, and it took me several days to restore my health and settle down to work again.

By now the venereal disease course was behind us. Mr Batchelor was head of the department. Gonorrhoea was prevalent in men and women, especially in the ports. Before antibiotics it was difficult to eradicate, men suffered from a chronic urethral discharge, prostatitis and stricture; women suffered from salpingitis, abdominal pains, adhesions and sterility. We were shown the primary chancre of syphilis and patients were presented with the long term effects of syphilis. The stamping gait of tabes dorsalis was particularly distressing, as were the children born with congenital syphilis. Gummata and bone syphilis were shown to us as well. Treatment of syphilis at that time was by intravenous injection of arsenic, and intramuscular injections of bismuth, given in courses of several weeks, followed by a pause, followed by repeat courses. It was a dreadful condition, the treatment toxic, and damaging to the liver.

The Wasserman and Kahn Tests on a sample of venous blood were diagnostic for syphilis. Permission was not asked for these tests; it was routine. I am puzzled that the same procedure does not apply routinely for investigation of HIV infection.

In practitioners of my age group the discovery of penicillin, and its ability to cure gonorrhoea and syphilis, was a wonder to behold.

During the winter of 1942 I decided to join the university union, a pleasant building close to the McEwen Hall. Lunch at modest prices was available on weekdays. Chiefs and tutors from the university shared the facility. A bar was available. In this room there was a piano, and small groups of students were engrossed in playing bridge. Ashtrays were piled high with cigarette stumps. It was a meeting place for your friends.

On Saturday nights the place really came to life. There was a band upstairs for the dance floor. Laughter, revelry, and the singing of a lusty song called the Ball of Kirriemuir added to the noise. About eight thirty pm the female company arrived; these girls were mainly from Atholl Crescent School of Domestic Science. They were very well behaved and great sports. Their behaviour on the dance floor was quite admirable. Often the lights would go out (by arrangement) during the dancing, and might stay out for five minutes if you were lucky. Small alcoves led off the main dancing area. We all had the whale of a time and the janitors who always appeared so severe took it all in good part. The girls left about eleven thirty pm. It was absolutely safe for them to go back to Atholl Crescent in the black out, on their own by tram, or even on foot. It was at least a two mile walk. Nobody would have thought of molesting them. Rape was very rare in Edinburgh; many did not even know the meaning of the word.

Throughout our work and pleasures the bombing of London and other cities continued. Our merchant fleet convoys suffered appalling losses in the Atlantic Ocean and Mediterranean Sea; the Eighth Army was out of North Africa and fighting in the difficult terrain of Sicily and Italy. One thing was clear. Hitler was certain to lose the war now.

As 1942 progressed, the main bulk of the medical course was drawing to a close. The finals in January 1943 loomed ahead. It was the time for revision, revision lectures, and special tutorials in everything we had been taught. Any specialities not studied, were completed at this time. Rows of instruments were put out for us to see and name; catheters, bougies, catgut, silk-worm-sutures and atraumatic needles filled the tables. Oxygen tents, pneumothorax equipment and a steam kettle found a stance.

In the midwifery department there was a dummy pelvis and dummy baby to freshen up our knowledge from the text books and district work. I began to see the five and a half years work fitting together to produce a final picture.

For those who felt sufficiently motivated final year students were more acceptable in the wards; it was helpful to watch a resident house surgeon pass a catheter and relieve urinary retention; bladder decompression over several hours was the rule; to empty a distended bladder in a single drainage was to invite loss of bladder muscle tone, a serious situation. In the medical wards an electrocardiograph would be demonstrated, and we learned to interpret an electrocardiogram. This work was very much in its infancy then, and the machines temperamental in function.

The long summer vacation of 1942 arrived. There was work to do, a course here and there to complete but a three week holiday was possible. I did not want to take the trying journey to Devonshire at this particular time, and previous experiences in London had proved the journey hazardous and difficult.

This was my last summer in Edinburgh and I was very anxious to see more of Scotland. There had been little chance to do this so far. A fellow student, Bruce Martin who lived in Ayr, agreed to accompany me. We decided to hire cycles and while we were discussing the terms we spotted a tandem in a shop for £7. It looked good value and we bought it.

Stirling was considered the gateway to the Highlands so we travelled there by train, and started cycling. We each had a small haversack, a cycle pump, puncture outfit and £50 between us. It was fine summer weather and we set off in high spirits, intending to spend the nights in Youth Hostels.

I was at the front handlebars and my friend pedalled tirelessly behind me. Half an hour after leaving Stirling the rear tyre softened and in a few minutes we were on the rim. I knew what to do as I had been cycling for years; the tandem was soon upside down, the inner tube eased out, the puncture identified, and sealed with a John Bull patch and rubber solution. We were quickly on the way again and the machine caused no further trouble.

During the war most sign posts at road junctions had been removed to confuse the enemy. It confused us, we took a wrong turn and had to retrace our way. It was starting to get dark, there was a steep hill and we had to push the tandem; we eventually reached Killin in complete darkness. Lights were illegal; happily traffic was virtually nil. It was far too late to find accommodation so we spent the night in a cattle truck in the railway yard. We fell asleep at once. We were up early with the sun and found a hotel for a wash, shave, and breakfast. We had overdone the miles on Day One, and decided to do less in future. That day we continued alongside Loch Tay midst beautiful scenery. We had the road to ourselves. Early evening we reached a YHA in a small village at Struan. The hostel was formerly a church. We opened a tin and had a meal and cups of tea and looked forward to a good sleep in a bed. There were others staying there making it a base for a walking holiday. Day followed day with perfect summer conditions. We entered the Pass of Killiecrankie, and had a pint now and again in isolated hotels in the country. The cycling was invigorating. The machine did not have a three speed gear so we walked up the hills, but, having reached the summit it was exhilarating to swoop down the other side at high speed. We reached a YHA every night and stayed at Blair Atholl, Kingussie, Aviemore, and at last we arrived in Inverness.

We decided to spend a day and two nights here to see the shops and have a rest from the saddle. The finances were barely touched and we had no difficulty in finding lodgings and increasing our diet. I remember the old bridge over the River Ness linking the main town to the road to Beauly, and the Castle on the River side.

I returned ten years later to find a new, wide and modern bridge had replaced the original. I liked Inverness.

On the return journey we decided to travel alongside Loch Ness, through Drumnadrochit to Fort Augustus, to Fort William. It was a splendid run through scenery second to none. We did not see the Loch Ness Monster! Ben Nevis looms over Fort William. There was a large YHA, well filled with climbers and it was a good place to stay. We crossed the water at Ballachulish in a small ferry and had a hilly but pretty journey to Crianlarich. Resting a while we cycled on to Ardlui at the head of the beautiful Loch Lomond. The scenery was wonderful, the tranquillity idyllic. Half way down the Lochside Road we stopped and admired a large building peeping out from the trees on the opposite side of the loch, which looked like a hotel. A motor launch slowly crossed the Loch and tied up at a landing stage; the owner said he was from the Inversnaid Hotel opposite and did we want to stay. We did. The tandem was lifted on to the launch and we chugged over to the hotel.

It was very isolated, there was no traffic, and we were the only guests. Food appeared such as we had not seen since before the war. There was every comfort. We sat in chairs, sipping beer and basking in the sun. There was total peace apart from the gentle lapping of the water and the chirping of birds. There were quiet walks along the side of the Loch along paths bordered by massive bushes of rhododendrons, enriched with the aroma from pine needles. It was utopia. I was there again in 1985.

Little had changed, and why should it? We stayed two days, and it was not expensive.

We did not cross the Loch the way we came. Instead we cycled eastwards through tree-lined narrow roads to Aberfoyle. The weather was beginning to break. We had been on the road for sixteen days and had travelled nearly 400 miles, so we rode back to Stirling to the train and reached Edinburgh once again. Next day we cleaned up the tandem and rode it back to the shop from which we had made the purchase. The owner was pleased to buy it back for the £7 we paid for the purchase!

That was the end of the holiday. It had been an outstanding success with perfect weather and unforgettable scenery. Our health had been improved. For my part I had memories of peaceful scenes and a beautiful country. I am always delighted to return. There were four months left before the finals. Occasionally I was depressed because it was impossible to know it all. Rumours of possible questions did not help. There was a rumour that the red nucleus in the brain was a likely question! It never was. I wondered who initiated such rumours. I felt that if you knew the important conditions well, there would be little to fear.

The autumn passed, the syllabus completed, leaving about three weeks for the last minute crash work before the final exam commenced. I did not get home for Christmas; it was the first I had missed but the situation rendered it impractical. I worked on in the solitude of the 'digs'.

A few days before the finals I was aware of a discomfort at the nape of the neck. It grew steadily worse, my joints ached and I had a raised temperature. I could not sleep or find comfort. It was evident I was building up a very large boil or even a carbuncle. The morning of the finals I did not feel able to get up and the walk to the Examination Centre seemed out of the question. I would have to obtain a medical certificate and explain the situation. Half to three quarters of an hour before the exam, a fellow student, Seymour Halkett, came to the 'digs' on his way to the Examination Centre. He was emphatic that I made the effort and he would see me into the exam room. With difficulty I dressed up in my best suit, collected pens and pencil, and we set off. I only just made it, and I must have looked awful. I was thankful to sit down. At that moment the large boil burst and its contents ran down the back of my collar and neck with immediate relief. I could only put a handkerchief there and turn up my jacket collar. What a rotten start to an important examination!

When we were told we could turn the question paper over and start, I did a quick appraisal and thought it was all very reasonable. The first question was on the investigation of a case of glycosuria. I had realized before that a raised temperature enhanced the sharpness of the brain, and it seemed to have that effect on mine. All the time I was beginning to feel more comfortable, mentally and physically.

It seemed customary for fellow students to point their thumbs up and down to indicate their feelings about the questions. Surveying the scene, some were raised, some were down, some were horizontal (whatever that meant!). Mine went up. The three hours passed quickly. There were five questions and I thought I had given a reasonable account in my answers. All questions had to be answered.

I felt very different by the end of the morning and was able to buy some dressings at a chemist and cover the boil. I have always been grateful to Seymour Halkett for goading me out of bed that morning.

That same afternoon we sat the examination in surgery. I think I was well prepared and managed to answer all the five questions without undue trouble. It was remarkable how quickly I improved in health after the boil burst. As I relaxed that evening in the 'digs' I felt confident that I had managed a satisfactory performance.

Next morning it was the turn for the examination in midwifery and gynaecology, and that completed the written part of the examinations. Orals and practicals were to follow.

Good marks in a written paper did not compensate for poor marks in an oral. It is easy to botch an oral and you have to be on guard all the time. A stupid or dangerous remark could finish your chances.

On the eve of the oral and practical examinations, conducted in the wards and side rooms, certain patients were moved from their customary bed positions, to near the ward entrance, and their bed charts removed. It was correctly assumed that these were the patients who would be presented at the examination. Students' anxious faces pressed against the glass in the doors to the wards which had been locked. There was no point asking

64

Sister or a staff nurse what was on show. Sometimes a junior nurse would mouth at you from the other side of the door until checked by her seniors. It was foolish to jump to conclusions about cases, and dreadful to blurt out a diagnosis after two minutes examination, a diagnosis, which had taken a learned professor a couple of weeks and a battery of tests to make!

I remember my oral and practical in the medical ward. I was tidily turned out in a dark suit. A stethoscope peeped from my jacket pocket. It was unwise to strut about with a stethoscope round your neck; that was the prerogative of professors, registrars, doctors and possibly house surgeons. We pulled them out as required, and unobtrusively returned them after auscultation was completed.

When my turn arrived I was conducted to a bed carrying a male patient and asked to examine the chest. Everything was wrong. He was breathless, had a cough, his pulse was fast and he could have been feverish. I did everything I had been taught viz inspection, percussion, vocal fremitus, and auscultation.

I thought he had a resolving lobar pneumonia on the left side. The patient was a young man and not a flicker of help did I get. Presumably he had been instructed to keep quiet.

The examiner reappeared with the temperature charts, and he asked me what I thought, and I told him. He said that the temperature had dropped to normal on the fourth day, and surely that was not the behaviour of lobar pneumonia. It was not, and after further questioning it became clear this patient had been taking sulphapyridine (M & B 693), the new antibiotic therapy, and this, of course, had altered the course of the illness. He went on about the possibility of the infection spreading to the other lung, and I thought that was unlikely. Then I moved to another bed to listen to a heart very carefully. I could find nothing wrong but I stuck to my guns, and when the examiner reappeared, I said it was a normal heart. He told me to move on to the side room.

We were taught that it was far worse to diagnose a heart as abnormal, when it was in fact normal, than to tell a patient his heart was normal when it was in fact abnormal. That was the way to cause a cardiac neurosis! As I moved towards the door I saw a fellow student listening to a chest with his stethoscope unplugged in his ears! A nurse saw the situation and tapped his shoulder. Sheepishly he corrected the situation. It was very good of her.

In the side room was a row of microscopes each with a focussed slide. Paper alongside was for your opinion on what you were looking at, 'spots' they were called. Then an examiner asked me questions on an X-ray plate, an intravenous pyleogram. The plate showed hydronephrosis and this led to much questioning. There was a plate of a carcinoma of the lower end of the oesophagus, and a bronchial carcinoma. I moved to a table strewn with the appliances peculiar to a medical ward. There was a rack with three tubes for measuring the sedimentation rate of the blood; this invited some questioning. I was then told I could go. That was it.

Anxious faces gathered in a coffee house after the examination was over and compared activities and post mortems. The surgery oral was next day. The procedure was very similar to that of the preceding day except we were in surgical wards. I was shown a young lad with a Brodie's abcess in his tibia. This was a manifestation of osteomyelitis, another condition curable with antibiotics subsequently. I doubt students are even taught about this now. The exam went quite well. There were questions on some pots, a little anatomy, and a few surgical instruments. (Cheatels forceps!) I was released and again we assembled in the coffee house afterwards.

Midwifery and gynaecology orals were next day. There was questioning on posterior positions. Pre-eclampsia cropped up, and there was the inevitable manoeuvres with the dummy infant and maternal pelvis. I was reasonably happy.

Thus the final exam terminated. We had done our best.

There was so much to learn and know, and the examinations were over in a flash, the culmination of five and a quarter years of hard work. The results were out in two days. I had passed along with twenty-five other fellow students. It was quite an anti-climax, but an immense relief. Nobody went over the top. It was relief, sheer relief. Five and a quarter years was a long time to be studying, and now it was over.

The graduation ceremony quickly followed. We agreed to abide by the Hippocratic Oath, were exhorted to uphold the good name of the medical profession, and to work diligently and not behave dishonourably. The certificates were individually presented concealed in a long cardboard cylinder. We registered with the General Medical Council soon after, and paid the fee.

We were now registered medical practitioners. It was 12 January 1943.

I wrote to a large maternity hospital, applying for a six months residency, in Liverpool. Six months hospital work after qualification was mandatory. I had visions of taking up midwifery and gynaecology as a speciality. I had been awarded the Class Medal. After a few days I was accepted for the post starting on 1 February, 1943.

On the strength of this I packed up, took my leave of Edinburgh, and made my way to Devonshire. My parents were pleased I had completed the course and had qualified in medicine.

I was very pleased indeed. I was just twenty-four years old and looked forward to the future. I had been delighted with Edinburgh as a medical centre, and thought there could be no better teaching centre elsewhere.

However I had not appreciated that there was a body called the Central Medical War Committee. This committee, formed during the war, was responsible for the allocation of house-appointments to newly qualified doctors, and I suspect, notified the War Office when their call-up date for the forces was due. Barely had I reached home before I received a letter from the Committee; they noted I was now qualified and directed me to commence work in Arbroath Infirmary on 1 February 1943! I did not really wish to go to Arbroath, and was even unsure of its location until I looked it up on the map. I was set on Liverpool.

Any problems with students at Edinburgh were dealt with by a charming man called Colonel Fitz-Gerald. He was the bursar of the Infirmary. I thought I had better see him. Back to Edinburgh I went and explained the position that I already had a post at Liverpool to fulfil. He was very pleasant. He had no jurisdiction with the CMWC and said I would have to go to Arbroath. As I trained in Scotland, was it not my duty to do the house appointment in Scotland?

He was right of course, and I had to accept the situation.

I wrote to Liverpool and explained that I was unable to accept the post. The hospital understood the directive from the CMW Committee.

I retraced my steps to Devon for a few days holiday before going to Arbroath. I required a rest.

This directive by the Central Medical War Committee was to reshape the entire course of my life.

However, this is another story, and another chapter.

3

Hospital Days

The days at home passed rapidly and I resigned myself to the six months appointment to Arbroath Infirmary as house surgeon.

Although my father had accepted the fact that I was now a doctor, he never exhibited much enthusiasm. I felt this because I had put so much work into the training. He never forgot my discourse on protoplasm in my zoology days, and seemed to think he must be protoplasm! He did not like it; he had little faith in doctors. This attitude was to his disadvantage as I could at least have advised him on many aspects of his failing health. He seemed to be suspicious of doctors and their motives, and would not hear or accept any advice about his own health. I blamed his legal outlook for this unfortunate position.

I had time to write to Louise again; she was still working in a London hospital. I asked if she would meet me in London on my way to Arbroath. It would probably be the last chance for a meeting for a long time. She agreed and we arranged to meet in the underground. It was unsafe in the London streets at night as air-raids were frequent as soon as darkness fell. When I reached London and the underground I found she was her usual pleasant self, seemed pleased to see me, and we passed a couple of hours chatting on many topics. I always had the impression she was a career girl, and I knew that my affection for her was greater than hers for myself. We parted sadly. I doubted whether I would ever see her again. Times were difficult and people lived from day to day during the war. However, after many months, and by a remarkable turn of the wheel of fortune we did meet again, unintentionally, and in a very different environment.

The journey to Arbroath continued, and after another cold and uncomfortable night we arrived in Edinburgh just as the shops were opening. I disembarked and had some breakfast. The absence of tea-trolleys at the main stations on route was a miserable feature of night travel during the war. The journeys were slow, and cold was an enemy. I had to walk about to warm up. The train did not leave the Waverley Station until two thirty pm, and I expected to arrive in Arbroath about four thirty pm.

There had been no mention of remuneration during my communications with Arbroath Infirmary, I had heard students mention £100 for the six months and all found. I hardly dared hope that I would be paid £100 as this was beyond the dreams of avarice. Unlike today, your salary was your own affair, and it was impertinent to seek knowledge about the salary of other people. The rate for the job was notified, and refused if unsatisfactory, but to accept the post and complain later was bad manners and unacceptable behaviour.

The train slowly crossed the long Tay Bridge and stopped at Dundee. In 1879 the previous rail bridge collapsed with heavy loss of life.

It was a short journey from Dundee to Arbroath, and dark as the train pulled into the station; a porter removed my luggage from the van and showed me to a taxi. After a short drive in pitch darkness I arrived at the main entrance to the Infirmary. I rang the bell and as I waited I could hear the sound of the sea.

The door opened; no light was allowed to escape and I was quickly in the lobby. A stocky man with a healthy complexion eyed me as I explained who I was. He said he would take me to the superintendent and would take care of the luggage. The office was nearby. He gave me a wink, rolled his eyes towards the door, and I sensed a message that the superintendent was a formidable figure. Later I found out his name was Mr Foster and a good friend to medical, nursing, and domestic staff. He tapped the door delicately, opened it, and I walked in.

The superintendent was a formidable figure. She was a lady, and matron as well. She was indeed the infirmary, and knew all the details of the daily life in the hospital; this knowledge applied to doctors, nursing staff, patients, porters, cooks and maids. It would be difficult to enter or leave the infirmary without her knowledge. She welcomed me to Arbroath, and motioned me to a chair. After some introductory courtesies she said the establishment catered for two house-surgeons and up until now had managed to find two, but due to the demands of the war I would be single-handed and would be required to undertake the work of two men. She said the present houseman was Dr Inch, but he had been called-up and was leaving in a week; his colleague had already left. There was no prospect of a second houseman during my appointment. She outlined the infirmary which like all hospitals at that time had its board of governors. There were over a hundred beds and the local practitioners attended their patients. Consultants in surgery, medicine, ENT and gynaecology came over from Dundee Royal Infirmary every week. They held clinics and the surgeons had operating lists weekly. There was a good X-ray Department and a busy casualty and out-patient Department.

Close to the infirmary was a small building, a VD clinic and part of my duties was to run this clinic on a Monday evening.

She was a short lady in a grey cloak and starched cap. She moved swiftly and was 'getting on' in years. Badges of her awards were pinned over the left chest. Her expressions varied from the severe to the forced smile.

A secretary was called in and I was asked if I belonged to a defence organization. I reassured them. The salary was £100 for the six months and included full board. I signed acceptance. She hoped I would enjoy my six months and to consult her if I had any worries. She said Dr Inch would initiate me and she sent for him; she concluded by remarking she expected exemplary behaviour from the house doctors, and that tact, as well as skill, was required for the post. I understood what she meant and promised not to disappoint her.

Dr Inch appeared. He looked tired and pale; obviously he had been busy. We walked along a corridor and up a flight of stairs to the residency. This consisted of a small sitting/dining room, two bedrooms, and a bathroom. A telephone was positioned to the walls of the bedrooms and sitting room; very comfortable, basic but all that was required. Two white coats hung from hooks on the door and mine was pointed out to me.

Dr Inch said he lived in Taymouth; he was very pleasant and discreet. He asked me if I was a good anaesthetist. I remember laughing merrily. How could I be, only qualified for three weeks! He remarked that I should be very skilled at the end of six months. After next Saturday I would be giving every anaesthetic required. There was no specialist anaesthetist attached. I expressed concern, and he told me not to worry. He would show me. He said he would have to leave now as he was busy. He would see me for breakfast and then we would get down to work. If I pressed the bell I might get some tea.

It was nearly six pm. I had a slight headache, and no wonder. Perhaps a cup of tea would help, so I pressed the bell. A young maid in black dress and spotless apron and cap appeared. I asked if I could have some tea. She was soon back bearing a tray with teapot, water jug, a cup, and small cake. I thanked her. She bridled and left the room.

Despite the cup of tea the headache worsened and I cursed myself as I realized I had one of those dreadful migraine headaches. I had been free from headaches for several years and I had no tablets. It seemed unthinkable to go to a ward and ask for two tablets of Codeine Co., and a poor start to a new job. There was no option but to sleep it off. Supper came but I could not face it, so I settled in the chair, hoping to overcome the throbbing temples.

There was a tap on the door. The assistant matron introduced herself and invited me along to meet the infirmary sisters. To decline would have been offensive, and I was very anxious to get off to a good start. We walked along the first floor corridor to a small room which initially seemed full of sisters with different uniforms and white caps. Some were in chairs, several on a sofa; SRN and SCM badges glistened on their chests; some had watches on chains, and pens peeped from their aprons. I was introduced individually, and invited to sit down. The heat of the room was intense; I was unused to central heating. Everyone was jovial and there was plenty of laughter. Accents confused me and there were expressions and words new to me which I would have to learn to understand. Various events of the day were discussed and it did not take me long to realize that Matron expected a high standard of nursing from them.

After about an hour my headache was so bad that I had to excuse myself. I felt sick. However, despite the headache I had noticed a sister in a pink uniform sitting on the top of the back of the sofa, black-stockinged legs stretched before her. She was very smart and most attractive, and seemed the life and soul of the gathering.

I went to bed and awoke next morning cleared of the migraine. Dr Inch and I breakfasted together as arranged. He named the doctors who came in to see their patients; they were all single-handed, mainly due to the war, their partners serving in the forces. There were, however, more single-handed practices than partnerships prior to the introduction of the NHS in June 1948.

Dr 'A' always arrived first; he was short and dapper. He wore spats, a dark suit and a black homburg hat. He walked briskly and his speech was curt. He would be sixty years at least. He was well known in the town and to his patients; he did not suffer mistakes, vagueness or inaccuracy. Clearly he had a high opinion of himself, and a poor one of his colleagues; even Matron could be flustered in his presence.

He was, undoubtedly, a very good practitioner; I watched him remove an acutely inflamed appendix in an emergency. He was regarded as the leading practitioner in town, and I am sure the claim was justifiable.

Dr 'B' was twenty years younger and commenced his hospital round after completion of his morning surgery. Always smart his dress was unostentatious, and occasionally he arrived wearing a sports jacket. Like Dr 'A' he moved very quickly and we were hard pressed to keep up with him in the corridors. Courteous always, he would chat to us as we raced along. I thought he was a skilled and experienced practitioner: his patients felt safe in his hands. At one time he had been a partner of Dr A, but left and set up on his own attracting many patients from his former practice! It had been a seven day wonder, but the situation had settled; there was of course no love lost between them and they never met in the infirmary.

Then there was Dr 'C'; at least sixty-fives years, he called a spade a spade and no nonsense. He seemed to be from a different generation, his treatment reminiscent of that used in World War One: he employed Iodoform dressings. He did not have as many patients in the hospital as Drs 'A' and 'B'. He walked slowly, arrived about noon, and went out of his way to upset Matron by word or deed. He would speak irreverently in my presence about her and shake with laughter; he could be extremely funny. Despite these quirks he was a kindly man and had many admiring supporters.

Dr 'D' arrived shortly before lunch. His hair was grey for his fifty odd years, and severely cut in Peterhead style. He was a pleasant, humorous character and spoke loudly in the ward for all to hear. He was well up on medical matters, and took care to be up-dated: he could manage most medical problems efficiently. Not a great friend of Matron, he upset her by teasing rather than by dislike; he would not be fussed. He was kind to me and took me out in his small Austin car some Sunday afternoons for a breather.

Dr 'E' was the youngest, and the untidiest. Paradoxically he would halt at mirrors and straighten his tie. I thought he was the most updated and this was to be expected because of his age. In many respects he was odd man out, though he had wise counsel for his colleagues who occasionally would ask for his opinion. He, too, removed an appendix in an emergency quickly and efficiently.

Dr 'F' lived at Carnoustie. His maternity patients came to Arbroath and I met him more at night than by day. He was a large jocular man and good at midwifery. He always came, whatever the hour, and usually wore a flower in his button-hole. He was very popular.

Dr 'I' was a rural practitioner from Friockheim. He was a friend of Dr 'C'. He did not use Arbroath so much and I think many of his patients were treated at Forfar Hospital.

These were the general practitioners I worked for; I was happy and proud to have worked with and for them; they were undoubtedly dedicated and sincere people. We would attend to their requests re blood and urine tests, and carry out minor surgical procedures. We wrote up case notes for every patient. If one of their maternity cases was approaching delivery we would contact them; they usually came and showed displeasure if they were too late.

Then there were the visiting consultants, a surgeon, gynaecologist, ENT specialist and a physician. All were chiefs in Dundee Royal Infirmary. They paid a weekly visit, except the ENT surgeon who came every fortnight.

There was Miss Kong, an efficient radiographer who never seemed to be off duty, and two physiotherapists. Ministers from the Scottish presbyteries, some, governors of the infirmary, often came to see Matron and their parishioners. They were dignified men and highly respected. There were porters, the cook, and one or two maids, and domestic staff.

The infirmary plan was uncomplicated. From the entrance

a corridor ran the length of the building: to the right a short corridor led to the casualty and OP department. At the end of this short corridor was the entrance to the female surgical ward. To the left of the main corridor was a small corridor where Matron had her office. To the right of this corridor was a small pharmacy. The female medical ward was at the end of the corridor. Continuing along the main corridor were the lift, and telephone room on the right; on the left, a small sun-room and clinical room. Further along on the left the entrance to the children's medical ward. Opposite this was the kitchen and back door. At the end of this main corridor were corridors to right and left with numerous small rooms for private patients. The area was called Drumsheugh. Above Drumsheugh were the nursing staffs' quarters: a house called Rosebrae in the grounds was for the use of the night staff, away from the noise of the main building.

Arbroath Infirmary, Scotland, about 1956.

Upstairs the male surgical ward was above the female surgical, male medical above the female medical, and children's surgical over the children's medical. Above the kitchen were the operating theatre, anaesthetic rooms and X-ray department. Above the clinical laboratory was a small room called the sun-room; it looked over the sea. There were one or two private rooms above Matron's office and the pharmacy, and another pleasant sitting room overlooking the sea where Matron entertained the consultants to afternoon tea during breaks from the theatre. The residency was to the left of the upstairs corridor and could be reached from downstairs as well.

Arbroath Infirmary, 1989.

As I trailed Dr Inch that day there was much to absorb and so many names to remember, staff and patients alike.

The Infirmary was always full. New admissions, except those on waiting lists, were arranged by Matron who spoke directly to the general practitioners. Nobody was ever turned away. The words 'We haven't any beds', were never heard. If the wards were full extra beds were assembled and made up. The operating lists were not cancelled, curtailed or postponed because the hospital was full. The wards were filled with post-operative, and major medical illnesses, especially respiratory infections.

Before Dr Inch left at the end of the week there were two operating sessions, a surgical and a gynaecological, and I had these two sessions in which to become proficient in anaesthesia. Already, I was familiar with the wire cage mask surrounded by a towel and pinned, with a gauze layer inside. After his six months Dr Inch was deft, competent, and confident with anaesthesia. He sprayed the inside of the mask with ethyl chloride until it was wet and then held it just above the patients face and not resting on it. The patient was asked to breathe deeply, and soon became unconscious; after a couple more sprays of ethyl chloride the mask was placed on the patient's face. Now real skill was required, the administration of ether to deepen, and then to maintain the anaesthesia; ether was an irritant and caused coughing if the patient was too light.

If you exercised the right skill, the patient moved swiftly from anaesthesia induced by ethyl chloride, to anaesthesia from ether, without coughing, and was maintained in the third stage with centrally fixed eyes, and semi-dilated pupils. When this stage was reached the patient was ready to be wheeled into the theatre and onto the operating table, ready for the knife. If you were unskilled or unlucky, the patient started to cough. Coughing, bronchial spasm, laryngeal spasm, the patient trying to 'come out' of the anaesthesia, moving, and having to be held, gave rise to scenes that made one think it had been a mistake to study medicine, but today, modern anaesthesia has eliminated these problems.

However, you stuck to your guns and improved the airway with a tube (if tolerated); and eventually the patient reached a satisfactory level of anaesthesia. The large, strong, and heavy patient influenced the induction; if the patient was a cigarette smoker or a bronchitic, the situation was aggravated.

We reckoned it needed twenty minutes to have a patient ready for the surgeon. During the induction the door would open a chink and you could see the anxious blue eyes of the theatre sister above her mask enquiring how much longer we would be.

Some surgeons understood the anaesthetist's problems and were calm and patient, others were touchy and irritable, demanding the patient in the theatre, ready or not. It was an unhelpful attitude, and of course the surgeon had to wait until the patient was ready.

Whether the patient was young or old, bronchitic or cardiac, the procedure was the same. Apart from nitrous oxide and oxygen, used for minor surgery, there was no alternative; the new intravenous anaesthetics for induction were not yet widely available. The problems, however, were not over, when the patient was anaesthetized, because there were no muscle relaxants. We watched the operation as much as possible. It was really necessary to achieve deep anaesthesia during the suturing of the peritoneum or the abdominal contents, small bowel usually, attempted to extrude from the abdomen.

Understanding and tolerant surgeons pressed on, holding the abdominal contents in place with a large metal spatula and suturing over it. Intolerant surgeons would snap at you to put the patient deeper! Often the patient was so deep that to go further would endanger life. A remark of that nature had to be ignored.

As soon as the peritoneum was closed we took the mask off, removed the airway, mopped out the back of the throat, and replaced the airway. A little oxygen was administered if deemed necessary. There was no recovery room; we did not allow the patients to lighten too quickly, preferring them to come round in the ward under the experienced eye of the ward sister. The final touch was to instil a drop of oil into each eye. I doubt whether modern anaesthetists would have enjoyed the experience.

Despite some inevitable and anxious moments I administered 260 general anaesthetics during my six months in Arbroath. There were happily no deaths, and so far as I knew, no one suffered any ill-effects; often I was surprised to see male patients smoking their pipes next morning after a lengthy operation!

Dr Inch left for the army. I met him in Bridlington fourteen years later when he came over for the day from Leeds with his wife and children. He was in general practice then.

I was now alone. The work was endless and demanding. The mornings were taken up with going round with the GPs and writing up case notes. Interruptions were the rule. To the Casualty for suturing, a fit, foreign bodies in the eye, and the hundred and one incidents making up a day's work in a casualty department awaited me. Back to the clinical laboratory to test urines, estimate haemoglobin with gowers instrument, the microscope for red and white blood cell counts, and differentials on certain patients, spin urine and look for pus cells, crystals and casts.

On operating days intravenous drips were set up. Then sister would ring to say a maternity patient was ready and would I come. Usually their own GP arrived for their deliveries; sometimes they were too late and it was up to me. Usually a midwife took control but I was always expected to deliver the head.

Fifty years ago to allow a perineal tear was bad practice, almost inexcusable: hostile eyes shamed you if you were unlucky. To prevent this disgrace, insofar as was humanly possible, the mother lay on her left side with flexed hips and knees. As soon as a pushing pain arrived a nurse would elevate the right lower limb, and the accoucheur was able to maintain flexion of the presenting head with his left hand, and control the perineum with his right. It was amazing the degree of control available, and amazing, too, the extent of stretch of the perineum. Gradually, fraction by fraction, the head was delivered. This process could take fifteen minutes, and time and time again primigravada were delivered intact. Episiotomy was a last resort. The trunk followed with the next pain. The infants cried straight away and the uterus contracted firmly and quickly. Light chloroform inhalations numbed the pains but anaesthesia was not sought. We were taught never to pull on the umbilical cord. We waited until the placenta separated, one hand resting on the fundus of the uterus. With a separated placenta, a firm uterus, a gentle push from mother, and from the accoucheur on the fundus, the placenta was delivered. Ergometrine was given intramuscularly or intravenously as soon as the placenta was delivered. Perhaps I was lucky; I never saw a post-partum haemorrhage or a retained placenta in Arbroath. Indications for Caesarean section were few, mainly performed to save a maternal or infant death, and never for convenience. The operation was hazardous and had a mortality rate. Pulmonary embolism and deep vein thrombosis were complications, and most unwelcome.

Few young women smoked cigarettes fifty years ago and this spared us from many of the troubles of today, which are now known to be related to cigarette-smoking.

Intravenous therapy was quite a performance and could be time-consuming. Solutions commonly used were five per cent glucose-Saline, Ringers solution, plasma and blood. These solutions were made up in glass bottles containing one pint; the bottles were sealed with a screw cap, which, when unscrewed, showed a firm rubber bung in the neck of the bottle; two partly manufactured perforations existed in the bung. Made up sterile giving sets were unknown. Inserted into one of these perforations was a wide-bored needle protruding about a quarter of an inch into the solution (with bottle inverted). This was connected by a short piece of rubber tubing to a drip chamber which was connected by a long piece of rubber tubing to a metal connector designed to fit an intravenous needle or a cannula. Inserted into the remaining perforation in the rubber bung was a long needle which extended to within half an inch from the bottom of the bottle (when inverted) to allow air into the bottle. All these separate items were sterilized in the ward and set out on a 'giving tray'. Frequently boiled rubber did not always ensure a good fit at connections, and slight leaks were usual.

Intravenous needles were about an inch long and wide bored, necessitating a large vein for their insertion. Provided only one or two pints were used, blood being the usual fluid, this needle could be inserted into a good vein in the cubital fossa, strapped down, and the elbow joint immobilized by fastening it to a back-splint. It was unwise to do this if the patient was likely to be moved from bed to trolley and vice-versa; the needle could move, puncture the vein and as the drips continued a haematoma was produced. In obese women it is well known how difficult it can be to locate a big vein in the bend of the elbow.

If the intravenous therapy was intended to last twenty-four to twenty-eight hours, it was necessary to 'cut down' over a vein in the cubital fossa, or over the saphenous vein at the inner aspect of the ankle, and insert a cannula which possessed a blunt end: there were several sizes for various bores of veins. This 'cut down' could be finicky: local anaesthesia was infiltrated into the skin over a vein and an incision made transversely over the vein without nicking it. Then the vein was mobilized, catgut passed beneath it using an aneurysm needle, the vein partially opened and the cannula inserted and tied in with the catgut over the vein. The skin wound was then closed.

If this technique was skilfully performed the drips would commence in the counting chamber, continue to drip, and were less likely to stop when the patient was moved.

On a surgical operating day a 'cut down' was carried out on three or more patients before the surgeon arrived. All the drips were set up before or during the lunch hour. It gave me considerable satisfaction to find the patients in the anaesthetic room with their drips functioning satisfactorily, and continuing to do so during the operation. Drips, however, blocked easily due to the equipment available, and frequently I had to set up the apparatus again during the night after the operation, using a different vein. Certainly the drips caused a great deal of work, but the advantage to the patient outweighed the problems of administration. The fluid input and output were carefully charted.

The operating session for the surgical list was a busy day; apart from attending to the GPs requirements during the morning, the four or five surgical patients, admitted the previous evening, were carefully checked over, and notes brought up to date. The chest and heart were auscultated and blood pressure recorded. Care was taken to see that the correct site for surgery was recorded and it corresponded with the patients statement. General questions were asked about previous operations. I then entered the pre-medication on the chart. Scopolamine gr 1/150 and atropine gr 1/100 were standard. The administration time was left to the ward sister who contacted the theatre for advice about the operation time. Urine had been tested on admission for albumen and sugar. Those cases requiring intravenous therapy were prepared. By two pm the stage was set: I had checked out the theatre and the staff were ready, sterile instruments concealed with sterile towels. At five past two pm I was at the entrance, white coated, and awaiting the surgeon.

The surgeon was about fifty years, and a chief in Dundee Royal Infirmary; he arrived in his own car, driving himself. He was a tall, well built man, moved slowly and held himself erect. He was a serious man and he rarely smiled; there was little conversation. He knew what to expect on the operating list because it was customary to ring his home after the BBC news on a Sunday evening to select the cases from the Waiting List Book. He usually chose two major cases, and three or four smaller cases. If a patient cancelled his operation, I chose another identical case, but I had to be careful about this, because for reasons only known to himself he often objected to my choice!

When he arrived we went straight away to the out patient clinic where perhaps a dozen patients would be waiting by appointment: this clinic could last three quarters of an hour. I wrote while he examined, and I learned a great deal from watching him. He was always the strong, silent, man. The conditions seen were similar to those of today. Herniae, varicose veins, a grumbling appendix, cholecystitis, gall stones and prostate trouble, were soon added to the waiting list. Lumps in breast were placed high on the list, and other suspected malignancies as well.

When the clinic was over it was near three pm. Matron was always about ensuring everything was in order as we made our way to the operating theatre to start the first case.

As the surgeon went to the changing room to don his white operating suit and scrub up, I knew he would be occupied for the next twenty minutes: I had those twenty minutes to change myself, and have the patient fully anaesthetized ready to be wheeled in. If the drip was functioning well it was good for morale. More often than not, I was ready when he was; occasionally I had trouble if the patient was large, heavy, and a bronchitic, and this delayed me.

The theatre atmosphere was tense; we all had work to do. Little was said. I tried some light-hearted conversation on one occasion, but I noted theatre sister's facial expression showed displeasure, so I kept quiet on future occasions.

All the time the ether slowly dropped from the bottle on to the mask maintaining a pleasing state of anaesthesia.

When Case One was completed, I had to work fast to have Case Two ready in time. On this occasion the surgeon had only to change his gown, and scrub up; this required less time. I managed quite well, and with experience I found I was able to have the patient wheeled into theatre as soon as the airway was tolerated. By the time he was on the table, draped, and the skin sterilized with mercuric perchloride the patient was at the correct stage of anaesthesia. It made my day if I was able to announce that the patient was ready rather than the reverse!

When Case Two was finished there was an afternoon tea-break; tea was always ready and we never had to wait. Matron, surgeon, and myself moved to the pleasant room overlooking the sea and enjoyed comfortable seats. Conversation was light, the war never mentioned, and there were gaps when no one spoke. After his tea the surgeon selected a cigarette, but he never offered me one. Cigarettes were scarce and I understood. I had my own meagre supply but my lungs were so full of ether vapour I feared my breath could catch fire. In those days cigarettes were considered good for you, and you were not a proper man unless you smoked!

We were soon back in the theatre. Cases Three and Four might be hernia repairs, inguinal, or femoral in a woman, or varicose veins: these were usually tied off in the groin, and the saphenous vein cut and tied at various levels.

Gastroenterostomy was a popular operation for a peptic ulcer and radical mastectomy the usual operation for a malignant mass in the breast: I set up a blood transfusion for a radical mastectomy. The results were good. Prostatectomy was a serious operation; shock, haemorrhage and infection were sequelae. It seemed to take a long time to establish a flow per urethram, though there were good results too. The operation was always a traumatic experience for the patient and house-surgeon post-operatively, because drainage tubes blocked easily from blood clot, and bladder irrigation was required frequently, a messy business for the doctor and nurses.

When the list was completed about six thirty pm the surgeon left for Dundee and I had plenty of work to keep me occupied for some time; post-operative medication had to be ordered, there were intravenous drips to check, and queries from the ward sisters to answer. A note was made of the new gynaecological admissions for operation the following day. New patients admitted during the afternoon, while I was in the theatre were examined and the case-notes written up; treatment had usually been initiated by the GP over the telephone.

I was glad to sit down for supper.

There was little respite next day because this was the visiting consultant gynaecologist's afternoon. The list usually comprised an abdominal hysterectomy, a colporrhaphy and three or four D & Cs and cautery to the cervix, most weeks. The professor was a middle-aged lady, and she, too, travelled from Dundee in her own car, chauffeur-driven. The professor and Matron were well-suited to each other's company.

She was a slick operator and we usually finished in good time; light anaesthesia was adequate for the D & Cs and quicker for me.

On one occasion I was invited to perform a D & C. All went well until she announced I had perforated the body of the uterus with the curette, and she took over again! I did not really believe her; she told me it was a common occurrence and quite unimportant. I thought she was very skilled and generally very pleasant in the tea-room.

The ENT specialist came every fortnight. Sometimes he was difficult in the theatre and upset the staff by impatient requests, and irritable behaviour.

His list could be an adult tonsillectomy, and eight or nine T & As on children aged about five years. Everybody was strained. During my first theatre session with him there was an adult patient for tonsillectomy. Theatre sister had advised me that he liked nitrous oxide, oxygen, and ether supplied via a tube from the Boyles machine to the connection on the mouth gag, so that when the mouth was wide open the gases flowed into the respiratory tree. However when the adult patient arrived in the theatre, suitably anaesthetized initially with open ether, I was instructed to make my way to a far corner of the room taking the Boyles machine with me. Several yards of rubber tubing were tossed at me to catch. I connected my end to the Boyles machine, and he connected his end to the nipple on the mouth-gag. The operation started and the patient went slightly blue but this was corrected with additional oxygen. I stood at least twelve paces from the patient and would have required opera-glasses to check visually that all was well.

It was not very easy for me moving back and forth from patient to machine making adjustments. However, this was the procedure he liked, and in those days the surgeon was in charge. I disliked T & As on children. I think the pre-medication was seconal gr 3/4 only: they were all asleep when they arrived in the anaesthetic room. The procedure was to make sure the surgeon was ready: the patient was anaesthetized using ethyl chloride and quickly wheeled into the theatre and on to the table.

I used to increase the depth of anaesthesia for a short time knowing that as soon as the mask was removed the patient would quickly lighten. Deftly the surgeon removed both tonsils with the guillotine, and quickly curetted the adenoidal pad. The patient was rotated to lie on the abdomen with the head hanging over the end of the table facing a basin. With a cold sponge the mouth, nose, and entire face indeed, were sponged. If your anaesthesia was right the patient started to cough, or cry, or both, and the danger was over. Seven more cases followed with identical procedure. The theatre staff and I were physically drained after this session; the only relief was the knowledge that it would be a fortnight before he came again. It was a messy procedure, and a bloody one too.

I must pay tribute to the theatre sister and her staff. She was superb. Young, motivated to a high degree, skilled and knowledgeable, she ran her department in a most efficient

Matron Brander,
1943

manner. She could be shrill when annoyed, blushed easily, usually when angry, and had a range of northern expressions and words unknown to me. The theatre was also the labour room, and I soon learnt never to send a maternity patient there, on an operating day, for obvious reasons. I had differences of opinion with her on some matters but we never quarrelled, and we enjoyed a good relationship based on mutual respect.

The nursing staff, too, were very efficient. They worked long hours, and every one seemed dedicated to the work. Matron expected high standards, and she obtained them. The infirmary was a nurses' training school: ex nurses, years later praised their training, regarding it as second to none, and it had stood them in good stead in their nursing careers.

One and all admired Matron. Demanding, yes, but a wonderful example of care, compassion, and goodness. After a few weeks in the infirmary I was able to develop some sort of routine. Despite being permanently on call I was enjoying the work and responsibility; confidence increased and morale stayed high. I had also received my first pay packet after four weeks work. The envelope contained £13.2s.6d. I was delighted. I had no living expenses, and with zero-inflation it went a long way.

Despite the busy days I was increasingly aware of the presence of the dark-haired sister in the pink uniform I had met on my first day. She was in charge of Drumsheugh, the private patients area. She was always there when I visited the patients with their GPs. I thought she was very attractive, efficient, and she exhibited a mischievous attitude which appealed to me. It was difficult to concentrate in her presence. One morning she was missing; a week passed and she was still away. I missed her very much. Reticent by nature I did not wish to ask others where she was.

I had fears she might have changed her work and left the Infirmary. After a day or two more she appeared out of the blue in the clinical laboratory, and was I pleased. It turned out that we had missed each other. She had been to her home in Huntly, Aberdeenshire on holiday. Human chemistry is a remarkable science and will no doubt remain mystical and inexplicable.

This was the start of a secret romance. The clinical laboratory was a useful room to meet in and there was always an excuse for her to be there. Our work had to continue and we did not

At Arbroath Infirmary 1943.
Dr Inch is in uniform on the left, the author is on the right and
Barbara is on the author's right.

wish to invite hospital rumours. I was so busy I thought I could not possibly have further reserves to tap. I was wrong. There was still one left.

Three special incidents occurred in the theatre. On one occasion Dr 'C', the elderly GP, had a surgical emergency. He contacted a surgeon himself, a friend of his. This surgeon at one time had been a house-surgeon in Arbroath Infirmary; he was in his late thirties, a good-looking man and he was also a slick and competent surgeon. On the first occasion he was removing a huge ovarian cyst, the size of a football. I was in my usual place with the ether bottle. After clamping the pedicle, mobilizing the cyst, he eased the cyst slowly out of the abdomen and held it up with two artery forceps. Sister, taken aback at its sheer size was not ready quickly enough with a suitably sized vessel to receive it. Deliberately he dropped it on the floor where it burst, shedding a couple of pints of straw-coloured liquid over a wide area. My feet were drenched, and the floor around the table became a slippery mess.

On another occasion the elderly GP and the same surgeon were performing a laparotomy. The GP's spectacles slipped off his nose into the abdominal cavity! The surgeon retrieved them and a nurse took them away for cleaning. She replaced them on his nose and the patient was none the worse for the experience.

Finally, the ENT surgeon had a scare. He had removed a large cyst from the posterior pharyngeal wall with some difficulty, but after the operation the cyst was missing. Sister thought she had it on gauze ready for transfer to a formalin bottle, but it could not be found. Thinking the cyst might have slipped into the trachea he was irate and upset. However, I found the cyst floating in the bucket for swabs by the operating table, whilst he was having tea. He was pleased and subsequently taught me how to remove tonsils with the guillotine. I found it tricky removing the left tonsil using the guillotine in the left hand. It was very important that the guillotine blade was blunt so that the tonsil was gripped and twisted off, allowing the blood vessels to contract and stopping the haemorrhage. If the tonsil was sliced off with a sharp guillotine blade, clotting was delayed and there could be serious haemorrhage, but that situation was not seen in Arbroath during my time there.

The professor of medicine from Dundee Royal Infirmary came monthly to Arbroath. He was a quiet man, his patients took time in the wards, and he was happy to go and see them on his own. The GPs would contact him personally if they wished for his opinion. He wrote up his findings and suggestions on the case sheets himself. Diabetes mellitus was a large and important part of his work and I learned a great deal from him.

Pleural effusions which were often seen before the arrival of antibiotic therapy, were not uncommon. Sometimes I had to carry out a paracentesis or chest drainage. I had heard of 'pleural shock' as the needle was inserted into the chest wall and I was always a little uneasy. The procedure was to infiltrate a suitable part of the chest wall with a local anaesthetic (two per cent Novocaine was popular). There was a thirty cc glass syringe available, with a two-way tap. A long wide-bored chest needle was attached to the syringe and pushed into the anaesthetized area and through the pleura. Aspiration often produced a straw-coloured liquid. When the syringe was full, the tap was turned through a right angle and the fluid conducted to a suitable vessel via a rubber tube.

A couple of pints were drawn off and the process repeated after a week. It made a striking difference to the patient's welfare. The fluid was sent to the lab, and occasionally there was a report that malignant cells were present: this signalled lung cancer and a death sentence.

Fluid collected, as well, in the abdominal cavity producing ascites. Sometimes this was malignant, sometimes not; I remember a patient with myxoedema showing ascites and the condition resolved using thyroid tablets. Fluid was removed in large quantities by a paracentesis. A cannula with introducer was pushed into a selected area of the abdominal wall. Fluid escaped via a tube into a bucket over several hours, controlled by a tap. Eight to twelve pints were sometimes removed; as the girth decreased, a multi-tailed bandage was tightened up. Patients were relieved and comfortable; it was not pleasant for patients and myself when we could see and feel malignant nodules after a paracentesis.

Thyrotoxicosis in youngish women was controlled using Lugol's iodine for some ten days prior to surgery. This operation was also carried out in the infirmary by the general surgeon. Again, open ether was used and I was very near the site of operation. The result was good. Looking back it was quite remarkable what was achieved in the Infirmary during those difficult war years, and at that era.

About a mile outside Arbroath on the main road to Friockheim was HMS Condor, a Fleet Air Arm Naval Base. During the war years it was an important training centre for naval pilots and contained a large establishment of officers and men. Occasionally a rating would arrive at the casualty department, in the care of a medical officer, complaining of acute toothache. Between us we decided the tooth was so decayed that there was no hope of saving it. It was not always possible to contact a dentist, especially at a weekend.

In the theatre instrument cupboard were half a dozen dental forceps. When theatre sister arrived these forceps were boiled and sterilized and laid out ready for use.

The medical officer opted to give the anaesthetic and I was the dentist. I had never extracted a tooth before. He used pure gas (nitrous oxide) until the patient was unconscious, removed the mask and I had about ten to fifteen seconds to extract the tooth. By gripping the tooth firmly with the forceps, loosening it with a rotary movement, the tooth could be levered out with little exertion, and quickly transferred to a crucible for examination later. As the patient recovered consciousness, the laughing gas had its effect and soon everybody was laughing. Although Matron looked stern afterwards I think she enjoyed these incidents. She liked the infirmary to work at its full potential.

There were fractures to deal with, dislocations as well. I remember one man fell off a ladder and dislocated a hip joint. He was very shocked. I gave a full anaesthetic with the patient lying on the floor of the theatre, and his GP reduced the dislocation successfully.

I suspect that fractures of the femoral neck were not as common then as now. The patients were usually women and very aged. Before the days of the Smith Peterson Pin which fixed the fragments, treatment was immobilization with the lower limb between long heavy sandbags. Often it was a terminal event, the patient dying from hypostatic congestion, or despondency. Some recovered after many months but I suspect the fracture may have been impacted in those cases.

Plaster of Paris bandages were as good then as they are now.

Open reduction was in its infancy. The materials were not adequate, screws and plates caused tissue reactions and sepsis. Suitable antibiotics were not generally available for bone infection.

Fractures, therefore, were reduced using traction and manipulation. Colles fractures caused little trouble in their management. Patients were seen in the streets walking about with what were called 'aeroplane splints'. The fracture involved the upper end of the humerus, and the splint immobilized the joint in abduction. It must have been a most uncomfortable situation for the patient. In severe and serious fractures outside the skill of the Infirmary there was an EMS hospital called Stracathro. It was near Brechin in rural and beautiful surroundings, and a few Arbroath patients were treated there as occasion arose.

Our X-ray facility was good. The radiographer, Miss Kong, spent her working life in the Arbroath Infirmary, and died a short time ago. She worked from nine am to six pm, and could always be contacted outside usual hours and at weekends. She always arrived whatever the hour, and was a willing worker.

Epithelioma of the lower lip in men was common. The treatment was excision, but cosmetically the results often left much to be desired; clay-pipe smoking was considered to be the cause of the condition. Radiotherapy was available at Dundee Royal Infirmary for suitable patients.

I did not see many patients with coronary thrombosis in the medical wards: those who were there had their attack as an in-patient for some other condition. It was considered very bad practice to transfer patients to hospital after a coronary thrombosis; the ambulance journey, and the six weeks bed rest required in hospital were not conducive to a tranquil outlook, so necessary for the treatment. Those who were not killed outright were treated in the calm of their homes. Apart from bed-rest and good nursing care there was little to be done. Ventricular fibrillation did not respond to treatment. Sometimes I thought I must have seen the worst possible attacks; a patient's blood pressure was barely recordable, 80/50 and often lower; shock, cold, clammy sweat and prostration were evident, and hearts sounds barely audible. Around the third day after the attack the temperature would rise to 100°F due to toxicity and absorption of the infarct. It was not until the temperature returned to normal and the blood pressure climbed to 100/75 that the outlook was reasonably good. After six weeks mobilization slowly started; up for five minutes the first day, and gradually increasing until the patient was up all day. There were many first class recoveries. Those patients who had milder attacks never came my way; perhaps they carried on working.

The ward sisters, by the end of the seventh day without a bowel movement from a patient who had a coronary thrombosis became concerned and I had to decide whether a small enema should be given. It was thought to be dangerous to lift a patient on to a bedpan, and with a blood pressure of 80/50 anything could happen if the patient attempted to strain! However, an enema was usually given with benefit to the patient. I still think I saw the extreme cases, and it was gratifying when they recovered.

The infirmary had a small convalescent home two miles from the centre of Arbroath. It was a pleasant house in the country, and was staffed by a sister and a handful of nurses. The patients were either post-operative, or convalescent from respiratory illness: they were all up and about and many assisted with the domestic management. I used to go in the early evening now and again, or when asked.

I mentioned that the infirmary had a VD clinic. It was a separate building away from the main block. The clinic was held on a Monday evening at seven pm and was men only. With a sister accustomed to this sort of work, and a nurse, we would arrive to find twenty or more men, mostly members of the forces, waiting for us. Each had a record card. Their treatment was initiated by specialists who organized the courses of injections.

Syphilis was the main concern. The treatment usually involved ten intravenous injections of arsenic and an intramuscular injection of bismuth into the upper outer quadrant of the buttock. Great care was taken that the arsenic did not escape into the tissues as it caused a nasty reaction. Urine was tested for albumen before the injections and we were looking for rashes and other signs of toxicity.

These injections were repeated at weekly intervals until the course of treatment was complete. The patients then were followed up by the specialist, and further courses organized. The atmosphere was jovial and there was much laughter, surprising considering the horror of the illness. Happily the patients I used to see would have been cured by penicillin a few years later but I was unaware of such a development then.

The infirmary had its own ambulance. It was a high-sided solid Austin. Mr Foster, the porter, used to drive it. Occasionally he drove to Dundee Royal Infirmary for certain stores.

If the work was under control I would travel with him and he allowed me to drive (I had passed my test in 1937 for motor cars). The steering was heavy but it was frisky and had a nice touch of speed. The engine sounded as though it would run for ever. There was never time for a tour of Dundee Royal Infirmary; I was on duty and had to return quickly.

Traffic was very light. The private motorist, who lived in a rural area away from shops, was allowed petrol coupons for two hundred miles per month. Key workers, doctors included, were allowed considerably more.

The romance flourished; never a day passed without seeing Barbara Ann Mair. Clearly we were so attracted that Cupid's arrows did not miss their mark.

Sisters were allowed two hours off duty, afternoon or evening; on an operating day some sisters elected to go off-duty at six pm.

As the days lengthened, and the pressure from respiratory illness lessened, and as I became familiar with the hospital regime, so it became possible to leave the hospital for an hour or two after eight pm, provided everything was under control. Night sister was experienced and competent, and in a dire emergency the patient's GP would come to the Infirmary.

Summer 1943 was good, and the long light evenings were inviting for a stroll in the balmy air. I had barely set foot outside the entrance door for two months and I looked forward to seeing what Arbroath had to offer. Barbara knew the area well, having trained in Arbroath and qualified as an SRN. She also trained in Aberdeen Infirmary and gained the SCM. Subsequently she worked in a general hospital at Torphins before returning to Arbroath as a sister. It was arranged we would meet round the corner a quarter of a mile from the infirmary and go for a stroll. Barbara resided in the nurses' home and we did not want to be seen leaving the area together.

This meeting was the start of many romantic walks. It was an idyllic time for both of us. We returned to the Infirmary independently, and no one knew about these clandestine outings for over a month. Eventually, and predictably, we were discovered and it was soon common knowledge that we were walking out, a situation happily and unexpectedly acceptable to Matron.

The days and weeks passed in a whirl of work; the evenings, whenever possible were reserved for walks in the gloaming. There was a lovely walk along the Queen's Promenade to the cliffs, and then on to the Deil's Heid and Auchmithie. With only two weeks left before the termination of my appointment our attention was inevitably drawn to the future. What was the future? For me, service in the RAMC lay ahead, and an overseas posting seemed a certainty. I had been so busy I was rather out of touch with the war. How long would it last? Hitler was now fighting on two fronts; Mussolini facing defeat as the First and Eighth Armies slowly succeeded in the difficult terrain of Italy. An invasion of France by our forces was expected, and impatiently awaited by Russia. A secret weapon promised by Hitler arrived; it was called the doodle-bomb, and it caused further damage and loss of life for Londoners. The end of the hostilities was not yet in sight, though victory for the forces of freedom was a certainty.

Barbara had decided to continue nursing at Arbroath, come what may; this was a relief to me and I knew she would be safe there. I would have to wait discharge from the forces after the war and build up my life from there. We were in love, and would wait for as long as it would take. These happy days could not last for ever; storm clouds were for ever overhead and we could not forecast what lay ahead.

Another newly-qualified doctor was appointed and arrived a week before I departed. He was already a chemist, and he was a mature character. It was a relief to have another pair of hands even for a week, a week in which I introduced him to the workings of the infirmary just as Dr Inch had done for me.

A few days before I was due to leave the Infirmary Dr 'C', the elderly GP whose spectacles dropped into the abdominal cavity asked me if I would act as locum in his practice while he went away for two weeks holiday. I was delighted to have the opportunity to spend another two weeks in Arbroath and agreed readily with his suggestion. Next morning Dr 'B' asked me the same question and of course I was only too pleased to accept his invitation as well. Another month in Arbroath was forthcoming.

A locum's salary was around £10 a week; an assistant was paid £700-£800 annually.

During the next few days I received intimation from the Central Medical War Committee that I was to serve in HM Forces; I was required to state my preference for army, navy or air-force. I preferred my feet on the ground and elected the army. In no time I was notified to report to the RAMC Base Depot at Crookham, Hants, on 16 October: a uniform allowance followed and a warrant for my journey from my home in Devon to Crookham. It was all highly efficient.

The immediate future was now clear, namely a month in general practice. I was very sorry to leave the Arbroath Infirmary; six months had passed quickly and I felt I had gained great experience in many areas of medicine. It had been a delight working with such a splendid staff; the end-result was so very different, and so much better than what I anticipated. Over and above I had met Barbara, the girl of my dreams. Love at first sight? Yes. No wonder I have never had regrets about my posting to Arbroath Infirmary.

Matron was complimentary about my work, and the consultant staff wrote most generous testimonials which I hoped would help me on my return to civilian life.

I commenced work as a locum. The doctor's house had surgery and waiting room facilities; it was a nice old house. I received a brief explanation of the various NHI medical certificates, the prescription pad, and an array of 'Winchester Bottles'. These contained concentrated solutions of everyday medicaments to be diluted 1-3 with water. The water was called aqua tappae for obvious reasons. Mist Expect, Mist Ipecac and Morph, Mist Kaolin and Morph, Mist Magnesium Trisilicate Co., and Gee's Linctus (lint scill c opio) had prominent positions on the shelves. Mist Pot Brom was popular as a mild sedative and it was also used in the first stage of labour: if a patient showed a depressive state and nerves were at screaming point, a dose of Valeria was added to the mixture: the taste was revolting, the results excellent. There was also a Winchester of what was known as 'cat's medicine' (Mist Pot Cit & Hyoscyamus). The taste warranted the name, but patients swore by it for cystitis. There was also a strange mixture called Mist Pot Brom & Nuc Vom. It was a maroon colour, used as a pick-me-up, and again, very popular with the patients.

Tablets were coming into vogue and he had a modest array of tabs phenobarbitone gr 1/2, tabs ephedrine gr 1/2 and tabs thyroid gr 1/2 on the shelves. Tabs amphetamine mgm V and the proprietary dexedrine were known, and occasionally a student took one before an exam. I tried one myself as an experiment and I must say I felt very bright. No dispensary was properly equipped without castor oil; bowels were moved with the help of senna pods or cascara sagrada, and occasionally liquid paraffin and phenolphthalein for long-term therapy. There was a locked cupboard containing morphia, atropine, scopolamine, and carbachol. Carbachol stimulated the parasympathetic nervous system and if you were lucky relieved acute urinary retention, when caused by an alcoholic indiscretion, superimposed on an early prostatic enlargement. It was dispensed as a small white table in a thin glass vial. The tablet was placed in a teaspoon, water (aq tappae) added, and the spoon was gently heated over a gas ring or a meth spirit burner carried in the medical bag. When it had dissolved the liquid content was drawn into a one cc glass record syringe already boiled, and injected subcutaneously. If the patient was then able to relax in a generous hot bath micturition might be re-established. If you were successful news travelled quickly on the grape-vine, and you could expect the practice to increase and prosper. Glass ampoules were rare; I think Coramine was one of the first preparations to appear in an ampoule: we all carried small metal 'saws' in our pockets to cut across the glass necks of these ampoules. Sterile water was dispensed in ten cc rubber capped bottles, and presumably was not sterile for long; not that untoward reactions from its use by injection were ever seen by us.

After the doctor had mentioned the names of various patients requiring follow-up, and his hospital patients, which I knew, he and his wife departed on holiday. He left his daughter, who was a medical student at the University of St Andrews, to drive me about to patient's houses. She was very helpful in other ways, knowing where certain items were kept, and also having knowledge of the patients as well.

There was a morning and evening surgery, nine to ten am and six thirty to seven thirty pm (including Saturdays). The work was light compared with my infirmary days. Patients had tremendous faith in a 'bottle', and few left the room without some medication. Mixtures were dispensed on the spot for those in the consultation room: after the bottle had been filled with the correct concentration it was corked, and labelled. Instructions were always a tablespoonful three times daily, except for a linctus which was only a teaspoonful. The bottle was then wrapped in white paper and sealed with red sealing wax; for those who had signet rings now was time to use them. There was a right and a wrong way to pack a bottle; it had to look clean and be professionally wrapped and not to look as though it had come from a fish and chip shop. To hand a patient an unwrapped bottle was embarrassing for dispenser and recipient. (Remember that Mist Pot Cit & Hyoscyamus looked very like a bottle of urine!)

I must remind my readers that the National Health Insurance Scheme was introduced by Lloyd George's Liberal Government in 1911, and it was only for the male working members of the household. Wives and children, grandparents and others were private patients. It was not until 6 June 1948 that the NHI was replaced by the NHS and everyone was entitled to its benefits. The charge, for a consultation was in 1943 2s.6. (half a crown) and 3s.6d. for a visit. Medicine and tablets were extra and were cheap.

Records were simple, and showed the patients name, address and age. Every consultation or visit involved the selection of a record card from a drawer or cabinet, and the treatment, diagnosis, and fee were entered. Consultations were usually paid on the spot, those visited were sent a bill every quarter. Many never paid, and were unable to pay, and the practice acquired Bad Debts. It has to be remembered that the NHI got off to a poor start; World War One devitalized the nation; the general strike of 1926 inflicted further financial damage, then came the problems of the 1930s, the Jarrow March, unemployment, the disaster of prime minister Ramsay-MacDonald, and disarmament culminating in World War Two. There was very little money about, and the doctor's bills were the last to be settled.

NHI patients had an envelope similar in size and construction to the present day NHS envelopes. Even today these old envelopes can still be seen, folded inside the present day envelopes of some of the older patients in the practice. They have worn well.

When I started GP work in Arbroath patients were wary of me; after all, I was only twenty-four years old. Initially the work was follow-on: sickness certificates and repeat medication kept me occupied; new illnesses tended to keep away from me unless it was urgent, preferring to wait until their own doctor returned.

After a few days however visiting became heavy and necessary; children especially, with measles, whooping cough, chickenpox and rubella always on the list. All these conditions were severe compared with today. Measles could involve three or four visits, possibly many more if complications occurred. Whooping cough was a dread in babies and young children, the paroxysms of coughing at their peak frightening for mother, infant and doctor. Often I felt I had to stay on in the house to lend support. There was a preparation called eumydrin, an antispasmodic, given in drops directly into the mouth. It was invaluable and undoubtedly saved life at the peak of the illness. It is rarely used now, because whooping cough has become a mild illness and is modified by immunization. No longer is it a threat to life.

Occasionally chickenpox could be so severe, the patient so ill and toxic, that smallpox had to be considered. I remember having rubella myself as a student with a high temperature and a fierce erythematous rash for forty-eight hours.

The exanthemata of children took up a great deal of time, and families were large then. Nowadays a punctate erythema associated with a sore throat is dismissed as a toxic rash, the condition cured by five days of penicillin. Previously, the sore throat was a real haemolytic streptococcal infection, with a strawberry tongue, and a severe rash all over the body. It was called scarlet fever. Treatment was six weeks in an isolation hospital, until desquamation was complete, and the danger of nephritis reduced. It was a serious illness and often produced serious complications, nephritis, and endocarditis.

Other illnesses on the visiting list were acute cystitis, and pyelitis; (this could be confused with acute appendicitis if the pyelitis was acute) and on the right side. Gastroenteritis, peptic ulcer, respiratory illness, and terminal malignancy kept me going.

An average-sized practice could attract forty-fifty home confinements annually; most had some ante-natal care especially in the later weeks. District midwives were extremely efficient and I thought they were the salt of the earth. They had an uncanny accuracy in determining when a patient was ready for delivery, and this, in the daytime, was a great help in the management of the work. Forceps were used at home if necessary and some doctors were extremely skilled in their use, using chloroform as the anaesthetic. Post-natal visits were daily for ten days. I never saw puerperal fever.

Although many people reached an advanced age, fewer of course did so, and those that survived were not as fit as those of the same age today. Osteoarthritis maimed many; others succumbed to congestive cardiac failure prematurely caused by mitral stenosis, incompetence, and aortic stenosis. Granny was in the rocking chair in black clothes by the fireside at sixty years old, her life's work done. Today great-grandmother sets out for Benidorm for the winter months expecting to dance the time away at the disco, and to dabble her feet in the swimming pool.

The fortnight passed without serious incidents, and the elderly doctor returned refreshed from his holiday. I had enjoyed the experience, and I enjoyed being paid. He seemed pleased. The same day I moved on to Dr 'B's' practice. He had a larger, more modern house, again with surgery and waiting room accommodation. The practice was active, larger, and it took some time to hand over the essential knowledge. His wife and he then departed to their cottage in the Glen.

I had the house to myself, apart from a domestic who lived out; she came and stayed all day, prepared meals, and dealt with the telephone when I was out. He also left for my use a very nice, bright red, open-seated car with folding hood. It was a sporty model and the exhaust emitted a pleasant cackle.

This practice had a large rural component, and it was very busy all the time I was there. The aim was to complete the morning surgery, deal with the Infirmary and try to get most of the new calls completed before lunch. After lunch the red car moved out to the rural areas and small villages.

Although I had a map, signposts were removed during the war, and I often had difficulty in finding my destination. There was little sense in asking; country folk were reticent during the war, and they were frequently advised to be cautious. Perhaps they thought I was a quisling! On my return it was time for the evening surgery at six thirty pm.

When Barbara was off-duty in the afternoons she came with me in the red car and I really felt I had climbed up the ladder!

One busy morning there was a string of new calls and one was written down as having a 'bit of a tummy ache'. By the time I had dealt with many calls, in the town and rurally, it was five pm before I reached the 'bit of tummy ache'. I was surprised and alarmed to find a young lad with a perforated appendix. He went straight to the Infirmary and a surgeon came over from Dundee. It was indeed a perforated appendix. It was removed and two thick rubber drains were inserted, one into the peritoneal cavity, the other between the muscle layers. He recovered, but there was anxiety for several days because paralytic ileus was not uncommon, and a most dangerous threat to life.

The fortnight passed rapidly. I had enjoyed this experience too, and I began to think I would like to undertake general practice. Every patient had to be followed through; it was impossible to send for the ambulance and transfer a patient except in the most extenuating circumstances. The doctor was pleased with my efforts and would have liked me to become a partner. The work required more than one man. I would have liked it as well, but it was impossible to commit myself when war service lay ahead. Once again I enjoyed being paid for my labours.

It was at this stage that Barbara had some leave and I was invited to her home near Huntly in Aberdeenshire, to meet her mother, brothers and sister; her father had died in the influenza pandemic of 1918. It was a quiet and peaceful farm set amid rolling countryside only one and a half miles from the small market town of Huntly and thirty-six miles north-west of Aberdeen. At that time harvesting was about to commence and the countryside was at its best. I received great kindness and courtesy. I have clear memories of a horse gently neighing in its stall at daybreak, and stamping a foot with impatience.

It was here in this pleasant place that I proposed to Barbara, was accepted, and we became engaged. It is said that love is blind, and no doubt it often must be so, but in our case the blindness has lasted forty-seven years and it has not been detrimental to us. A great deal of discussion and thought went into the decision due to the instability of the times.

We decided on marriage if I was posted abroad, and marriage in 1943 was a commitment for life. Little did I envisage standing at the altar steps in just over two months' time, but that is exactly what happened.

We went to Aberdeen for a day's sight-seeing, and to buy an engagement ring. We decided to go to Henderson, an imposing jewellers shop in Union Street. There was a great selection and we were not disappointed with the final choice.

Aberdeen was a fine city, and still is. It had an efficient tram system similar to Edinburgh but the trains were painted an apple-green instead of the maroon of Edinburgh. Union Street was wide and straight with high grade shops on either side. Plenty of warm restaurants invited you in for high tea or coffee and biscuits; always busy, the shopping centre teamed with smart well-dressed people. A day out in Aberdeen was an exciting and interesting occasion.

Sadly these happy days came to a close only too quickly; it was time for Barbara to return to Arbroath to continue her work, and it was time for me to find my way to Devonshire to see my parents and to sort out my affairs before joining the army.

It was sad to say farewell, and difficult to know when we would meet again; it would probably be on my first leave. We had, however, found each other and this kept us alive during the difficult and wearisome days that were ahead.

The situation at home was quiet and depressing. My parents seemed overcome with the events and horrors of the war; it was the second time round for them, having married in 1915. The trench warfare and the horrifying loss of life in World War One had upset my father to such an extent that he never recovered from the shock and horror of his experiences. To add to the trouble Exeter had been severely bombed and damaged on many occasions with great loss of life and the noise and thudding of the attacks had driven them to seek shelter under the stairs at night. Also rationing for two people without access to supplementary calories was meagre; without their garden and their ability to grow vegetables they would have fared badly.

My parents were not enthusiastic that I was engaged so soon after qualification, still less that marriage was contemplated at the present stage of hostilities. There was little that I could do to help them: they were more concerned with the past and the present, but it was the future that attracted me. Their reaction was predictable.

16 October, 1943 dawned bright and sunny as I slowly rejected my civilian clothes, dressed up in my new uniform and posed for a photograph in the garden. My orders were to proceed to a certain platform at Waterloo Station and board a certain train for Fleet. From there the army would take over.

My luggage was a valise containing a World War One sleeping bag belonging to my father, and a small suitcase. As the taxi sped along the country road to the small station I knew that life would never be quite the same again. I was full of excitement, hope, and expectation. I was not to be disappointed.

Another chapter lay ahead.

4

Army Days

Officers travelled first class whenever possible. I felt slightly embarrassed as I entered the carriage and sank into cushioned comfort: such luxury was alien, but it made the journey to Waterloo much more comfortable than on previous occasions.

When I reached the appointed platform it was evident that I was not alone; other young men with RAMC badges and new uniforms strutted uncertainly here and there. All wore the double pips of a lieutenant like myself, and we were all heading for the RAMC Base Depot at Crookham, Hants. When the coaches were shunted to the platform and we took our seats, I noticed that one RAMC officer had his Sam Browne Belt on back to front! The buckle was fastened at the back! I cannot imagine how he managed to do this. He was surprised and a little irritated when his error was pointed out and unwilling to correct the fault. We persisted and eventually dressed him properly in the train. I am sure there would have been much laughter in the officers mess if he had reported incorrectly dressed. When we reached Fleet one and a half hours away we were met by covered army trucks and conveyed to the Base Depot at Crookham. It was not a comfortable ride.

The mess and sleeping accommodation were better than I had anticipated: it was a brick building, with good facilities, a bar, and it was modestly cosy. We were raw recruits and perhaps the military was trying to impress! There were notices all over the place, daily orders, regulations, and standing orders. There were about fifty of us, and it soon transpired that we were on a fortnight's course to break us in. The greater part of the day was to be spent square-bashing, interspersed with lectures on map-reading, the field hygiene manual, handling sick-parades, and learning how to avoid and prevent gonorrhoea.

We were soon issued with battle dress and a beret for everyday use, and black army boots.

I am sure we all enjoyed our first evening in the mess. It was like a social gathering without the ladies. Beer flowed freely. Doctors love to talk shop. Not so enjoyable was the parade on the square next morning for several hours of drill.

Backwards and forwards we marched, halting, marking time, right and left wheeling, and shuffling into line. It was not new to me as I had been in the Officers Training Corps at school; the severity and toughness of the sergeant-major and his insistence on perfection were unnerving.

It is a remarkable fact that when any group of new recruits starts to march there is always one who has incorrect co-ordination; he puts the left foot forward and at the same time he extends the left upper limb. This produces an extraordinary gait and completely ruins an orderly display. We had one in our group and it reduced our sergeant-major to a state of exasperation. We did not know whether to laugh or cry. With intense concentration the unfortunate medical officer achieved the correct swing, but quickly reverted to the former situation if, even for a moment, he allowed his mind to wander. In all other respects he was Grade A. Many times on parade most of us were called out to march the group hither and thither. We learned to shout out orders without coughing, turning dizzy or getting into a tizzy. Things went quite well and you felt in control until an order such as 'at the halt, on the right, form platoon', was demanded. This was too much for doctor's intelligence and we would land up in odd places, sometimes with the platoon fragmented. It was embarrassing and we were scared to laugh at our discomfiture.

As the mornings passed in this invigorating manner, slowly the colour drained back to our cheeks, and eyes looked brightly alert. Quickly our appetites improved. Army food at Crookham, stodgy though it was, was plentiful, and after civilian stringency, we made the most of it.

On one occasion we were instructed to open a bank account with Glynn Mills Bank. This was the bank the army used for payment of their personnel. There was a branch at Aldershot.

I remember completing many forms, opening an account and

hoping everything would be satisfactory. I authorized this bank to transmit the greater part of my pay to Barbara, and she paid it into a bank at Arbroath. Over the years it accumulated to a healthy sum, and another chapter will describe the use we made of it.

Many of my readers will, no doubt, be familiar with the shiny black-toe-capped regulation army boots. The leather was tough, the soles strong and the weight considerable; they were designed to stand up to the rigours of the battle-field, whether sandy deserts or concrete fortifications. The posterior part of the heel was extra thick and protective, and it coincided with the insertion of the Achilles tendon into the calcaneum. On purpose the boots were slightly on the large size when issued to allow room for some gravitational oedema after a day on the march. It was no surprise that the continual slipping of the boot on the heel, produced, after a few days, a painful tenosynovitis at the insertion of the Achilles tendon. The rustling of the inflamed tendon sheath was easily felt, and heard. Unfortunately the treatment was not an injection of hydrocortisone acetate locally, and rest for the affected part on a couch; the treatment was more marching using the same boots! The condition had to be fought, to be marched off, and twenty-four hours sick leave for officers or men was just not on. It really was very painful easing the boot over the inflamed heel, and sheer torture to walk. Happily the symptoms subsided over a few days, the boots were broken in, and there was no recurrence.

During the evenings in the mess I met Dr J.D. Little, a lieutenant like myself. He was an Oxford graduate, married, and met his wife, who came from Liverpool, at Oxford, where she was a student. Quite apart from being medically qualified he could play the cello and frequently played in an orchestra. He was well versed in the fine arts and his knowledge of music and musicians was remarkable. There was wit in his conversation, an appeal about his manner, a similarity of ideology, and we soon struck a friendship which is now in its forty-seventh year. There were doctors from all over the country, including one from Tarbet, and another from the coast bordering the Pentland Firth.

The two weeks passed rapidly and we became adjusted to our uniform and to the salutes of other ranks, which were always reciprocated at the base depot. It was impractical in the streets.

Then came a major announcement. We were to proceed to Edinburgh for a twenty-one day course in tropical medicine at the university. It appeared that we would be on the high seas sooner than expected. We travelled to Edinburgh by train and we were billeted at the prestigious 'Old Waverley Hotel' in Princes Street. The army was doing us proud! It was a fine hotel, the dining room tables were spotless with white table-cloths, and the cutlery engraved: the food was good too. Lounges had most comfortable armchairs, and there were quiet rooms, tables and note-paper. It was a delight to be back to the familiar sights of Edinburgh, and the university class-rooms too.

The tropical course was intensive and lasted the entire day, every day except Sunday. There was a manual on the subject, a thick paper-back from the War Office, and this kept us quiet in the evenings.

I was delighted at the thought of seeing Barbara sooner than I dared hope. If you left Edinburgh, you had to be back in the hotel on Sunday night. There would be just time for a quick day-trip.

It was impossible to leave Edinburgh before ten am. I travelled from the Waverley Station, through Princes Street gardens, and arrived in Arbroath before lunch. Barbara met me at the station and we had a lovely lunch in Keptie Street, the home of Mrs Crockatt. Mrs Crockatt was a most generous and kind-hearted person; her husband had died suddenly early in the year and Barbara knew her from her early nursing days; she was most kind and motherly to her. Mrs Crockatt was a valued pillar of strength to both of us right up to her death in 1982; we miss her very much. The day passed very rapidly indeed, and I had to break the news that after the tropical medicine course was over I was to take embarkation leave for fourteen days.

We had decided previously to marry if this situation arose: there was great excitement and Barbara was left to fix a date, and plan the programme. I would be able to return to Arbroath the following Sunday, and find out what had been arranged.

It was after ten pm before I reached Edinburgh on a packed train. The course continued and by the following Sunday when I reached Arbroath, the wedding day was fixed up for 30 November (St Andrew's Day). The church service was to be held in a country church at Drumblade, three miles from Barbara's home, and the reception at a hotel in Huntly. We decided to spend eight days in Edinburgh on honeymoon and then return to Arbroath for the last few days and stay with Mrs Crockatt.

It was difficult to arrange a wedding during the war years. Clothes were rationed, and coupons quickly disappeared: catering was difficult, vital constituents of cake were rationed or unobtainable. It was difficult for me too. I bought a wedding ring in Edinburgh not knowing the size, hoping it would not be too small!

I had a disappointment as well. My best man (from the south) had to cancel at the last minute, and my parents were not well enough to undertake a journey of that magnitude.

On the eve of the wedding I arrived at Aberdeen from Edinburgh, and spent my last night of bachelorhood on my own in a hotel near Union Street. I caught the last post informing Barbara I had arrived in Aberdeen and would be there!

I was there, and a lovely church wedding we had. The sun shone, the air was crisp, and the surrounding mountains were already snow-capped. Barbara was radiant in her wedding dress, and I was in service dress. Photos were taken and we had a splendid reception in the Huntly Hotel in the square. The display of good food was quite extraordinary, baked by relations and good friends of the family.

We left the hotel around four thirty pm by taxi. It was dark. Strong, exuberant men lifted the taxi a few feet off the ground, rear wheels spinning; it dropped and we shot off to the station. Another lively scene took place on the platform until eventually we found seats in the train. We reached Edinburgh, and stayed at the Learmonth Hotel. It had been a great day and we were so happy.

The honeymoon passed quickly; we attended a service in St Giles Cathedral on the Sunday, a memorable event. We visited many places of interest and historical significance. The red Forth Railway bridge, always an attraction for visitors, received a visit from us too. We lived for the present, the future was unpredictable, and every day was a treasure.

We moved to Arbroath. I said farewell to the matron of the infirmary; she had helped us so much and we shall never forget her many kindnesses.

It was now time for us to part, Barbara to the infirmary to continue her work and I had received a posting to a unit in

The author and bride, 30th November 1943.

Newmarket. These partings were a dread; we had no idea when we would meet again.

I reached Newmarket eventually; it was quicker to travel to London, change trains for Newmarket, rather than attempt a cross country journey via Peterborough. After I had reported to the CO of the establishment it was obvious the posting was a temporary one, and that I was filling in time. My duties involved sick-parades at several different areas, at present being carried out by general practitioners in Newmarket. It was bitterly cold and I never seemed to find any warmth. The atmosphere in the mess was quiet and reserved, the inmates discontented. The *esprit de corps* I had been accustomed to recently was sadly absent. The work was light and I was able to roam about the town.

After a week I was posted to Cambridge. There were several units in the area and I carried out sick-parades in various places daily. I was billeted at a private house close by.

I had never been to Cambridge. It was an impressive place with splendid university buildings; King's College stands out in my memories, and so does the cold.

One day I was duty officer and I was required to carry out an inspection of the barracks including the cook house. An orderly accompanied me to the kitchen where the lunchtime meal was in preparation. As the room was brought to attention I sensed hostility: a cook lodged a complaint about some grain. The situation required defusing, so I asked for the grain. From a sack I picked up a handful of grain and let it run through my fingers: it looked and smelled satisfactory. I asked why there was a complaint, and was told it was infested with the weevil. Obviously there was a gap in my education: I knew nothing about the life style of the weevil, its size, or whether it was even visible to the naked eye. I did not want to show my ignorance, still less did I want an outbreak of gastroenteritis in the unit. I still think I was taken for a ride and condemned a good sack of grain. Some years later I was talking to a colleague and he had experienced a similar situation in the army with the weevil. He condemned his sack too!

I spent Christmas Day with the unit. It is an army custom that on Christmas Day the officers serve the other ranks with their fare. There was a full turkey dinner enjoyed by one and all. We toasted the King.

I shall never forget the house where I was billeted. It was about a mile from the HQ, owned and occupied by a refined lady who had numerous dogs. These dogs received far better treatment than was bestowed on me, and I envied them their position, stretched out before the fire. I had the use of a bedroom; she provided breakfast, and I sat in the sitting room with her in the evenings. The living room was full of greenhouse plants; a large castor oil plant prevented me from getting close to the fire. In the bedroom there was a double bed against a wall; as I climbed into it the central springs sagged to the floor and the piece of mattress over this area dipped to the floor and I went with it. There was no sense in trying to climb out of this undignified and uncomfortable position and seek the sides of the bed, because I slipped back into the pit. If it had not been so cold I would have preferred the floor. I mentioned the situation to the lady next morning; she was surprised I felt it necessary to complain, and I had a hot water bottle for comfort subsequently! No change was made to the bed.

A couple of days after Christmas I was notified to proceed to the RAMC Base Depot at Crookham again, prior to embarkation; 5 January 1944 was the reporting date; meantime I could take seven days leave. Travel warrants were issued for my journeys.

The CO told me that very morning he had been notified I was entitled to the married officer's allowance and it had been approved. He wished me good luck on my travels and shook my hand. I bridled and thanked him. I had not enjoyed the Fens.

This was it. I knew now that I was leaving the country, destination unknown, duration unknown. I must travel to Devon to say farewell to my parents and then spend the last few days with Barbara in Scotland. I spent two days at home, and made a very early start to catch the train to London, and on to Scotland.

The country road was dark and dismal as the taxi threaded its way to the station; I wondered whether I would ever see my parents again, and I think they thought the same about me.

I reached Aberdeen at eight am on a Sunday morning. Matron had allowed Barbara a few days leave and she travelled ahead of me on the Saturday. There were no trains out of Aberdeen on a Sunday: I was advised to travel to Huntly by bus and I received instructions where to find the bus station.

Lieut. R.P. Cookson, 1943

It was appropriate it left from near a surgical instrument shop called Whitelaw. Previously I had always travelled to Huntly by train so it made a pleasant change to travel the country road. Luckily the roads were free of snow.

The bus stopped in the Huntly Square, and I was relieved to see Alick, one of Barbara's brothers there with a Morris 10; he had anticipated my movements, and drove me over to the house.

What a relief it was to see Barbara again, and to enjoy the peace, and comfort of their home for the final three days. It was mid-winter and the weather uninviting, but we went out for walks as much as possible.

The day we had dreaded dawned. I had to catch the evening train from Aberdeen to King's Cross; Barbara came with me and disembarked at Arbroath to return to work. Mrs Crockatt was at the station to meet us; the train only stopped a minute or two as we parted. Steam hissed from the connecting pipe between the two carriages, and Barbara was lost in the steam. Little did we realize it would be nearly three years before we met again. I returned to the compartment, saw her empty seat, and I cursed Hitler, the war, and everything else.

The train moved steadily on through the night; there was another medical officer in the same compartment with a newly married wife en route for Crookham; both were taking the situation badly. The medical officer told me he had developed haematuria and did not intend to go to Crookham! I met many of the medical officers whom I had met previously, at Crookham, but never saw the medical officer with haematuria again.

We were in a hutted area, and the conditions were uncomfortable. Next morning we were issued with tropical kit and we assumed India or the Middle East would be the most likely destinations; the issuing sergeant-major said that Iceland was, of course, a possibility! What miserable humour! Later on that day there was briefing about the journey to the port of embarkation: we were given an embarkation code number; mine was RC 000, easy to remember because the letters made my initials.

We were split up into small groups of four or five medical officers, and the group leader handed a sealed envelope with orders within, and not to be opened until we were in the train. About eight pm that same evening a small truck carried us to

Fleet station in time to catch the next train travelling westwards. Our compartment was empty and we opened the envelope. We were instructed to disembark at the next stop, destroy the instructions by burning them, and catch the next train eastwards for three stops. We were then to disembark, and catch another train eastwards for two more stops. We were to remain there until the main troop train arrived, and join it.

Security was tight and we hoped we had followed the instructions correctly as we disembarked at the final station. It was like a paper chase!

The station might have been Woking. We did not know. It was unmarked, and railway staff were reticent.

After a wait of an hour and more a long troop train pulled into the station. It was very full, but with only a small suitcase each we managed to push aboard. We left about midnight. It was an appalling journey; officers and men were crammed into whatever space was available. It was cold, and dark; we had no food, and the train never stopped on its journey. No one spoke.

At six thirty am somebody came to life and announced we had passed through Chester Station. He was correct; in half an hour the long train pulled into the dockland area of Merseyside (probably Birkenhead) and stiffly we disembarked and formed into our groups. After a lengthy wait we walked the gang-plank into the ship.

The ship was the *Stirling Castle*, one of the luxurious liners which used to sail the route Southampton to the Cape. We were allotted cabins; I was given the top bunk of a twin-bedded cabin. We were going to be very comfortable by all accounts on board this liner. After a shave, a wash and tidy-up we made our way to the main dining saloon for breakfast; we required it. The dining saloon was luxurious. As I sat down at the table I looked across the room, and there, resplendent in her QAIMNS uniform was Louise!

Oh dear! It is indeed a small world. I crossed over to her table and we expressed our surprise and pleasure at meeting in such circumstances. It was a year since we met in the Underground. She was in the company of other QAs, but I told her I had been married just over a month. Always pleasant was Louise, no more so than on this occasion, as she congratulated me graciously. I thought I discerned a trace of surprise, a transient elevation

112

of eyebrows, and I understood; after all it had been quite a shotgun marriage. I left and thought there might be another chance of a chat during the voyage.

Apart from creaking and groaning, she was a splendid ship. It would have been more enjoyable if we had known where we were going. There was a temporary letter-box on one of the decks which would be taken ashore just before the ship sailed. All mail was censored now, and information about the ship, the port, and possible destination was not allowed in case it could help the enemy. I wrote a note to Barbara and my parents; it would be a long time before they received another letter. Barbara had my RC 000 Code, and that was all.

We sailed in the late afternoon as dusk was falling; I had never travelled on a large liner before and it was interesting as tugs manoeuvred the vessel. Soon we were heading slowly down the Mersey towards the open sea. It was 9 January 1944. Next morning it was a guess where we were but probably off the mouth of the Clyde. During the day other ships joined us and by nightfall it was clear that a convoy was forming. By the following morning we were one of a large convoy of ten or twelve large liners flanked by naval vessels. The liners had the well known names of those we knew in peace-time; all had lost their distinctive colours and were painted a dull grey. During the day the convoy was widely dispersed, but at night it closed up, and the ships were so close you could easily discern people on the decks. Every fifteen minutes the convoy zig-zagged to confuse us, and the enemy.

We were treated as though we were fare-paying passengers with a full menu, immaculate waiters and every attention.

Unfortunately this did not apply to other ranks who were deep down in the bowels of the ship wherever there was space. Men slept in hammocks; there was gross congestion. As duty officer one day I made my way down below and I thought the conditions were pretty grim. Morale, however, was good, and it was unusual to hear a grumble, however justifiable.

It was compulsory to carry your life jacket at all times and a serious offence to be without it. At night it was vital to know exactly where it was.

Most nights there were entertainments given by ENSA (Entertainments National Service Association). There were comedians, musical artistes and singers, occasionally a high-powered concert. ENSA was an association of professional entertainers, who travelled to entertain British troops overseas often in way out places, often in unpleasant conditions. It was very popular. There was a library on board and I think the ship was dry.

Clusters of people played bridge all day. There were several medical officers of high rank, top brass, and presumably specialists in various fields of medicine on board; they were keen on their deck walks daily and would pace backwards and forwards relentlessly for hours, talking ernestly amongst themselves.

After a week to ten days there seemed little change climatically. The weather was cold and wet, the seas moderate, and it seemed likely we were in the Atlantic. An officer with a sextant took some measurements. People clustered round him and he said we were near the Azores! Right or wrong, the weather changed quickly and the air became bland and mild. Those of us on deck that evening saw the lights of Tangier and we knew we were in the Mediterranean. The naval men donned white clothes, and we assumed lighter clothing ourselves.

The Mediterranean had not long been opened for convoys, which previously had to travel round the Cape to reach Suez. There was still anxiety from enemy aircraft from Crete, and everyone was extra alert in case of trouble. Three days into the Mediterranean a gale blew up very quickly with a rough sea. People turned green as they spoke, and many disappeared below deck and sought refuge in bunks and hammocks.

I was untroubled and found a sheltered spot on the leeward side of the ship and swayed against the pitching. I was amazed to see the propellers of the liners out of the water as the ships pitched; I never realized the sea could be quite so rough in the Mediterranean. However, the conditions subsided very quickly. At night, if the sea was calm, the bow waves from the liners were phosphorescent. It was very beautiful.

Three weeks after leaving the Mersey we arrived at Port Said, probably a journey of a week or less in normal times. The sky was blue, the sun pleasantly hot, and we wondered whether we would disembark or continue through the canal to India.

On the last night before reaching Port Said, a medical officer in our group announced his engagement to a Wren; a courtship of three weeks, and both unknown to each other previously. He beat me!

I spoke to Louise several times on board, and we agreed that the world was so small we might meet again. We did, unintentionally, and in a very different environment, two and a half years later.

We disembarked at Port Said, and formed up in a gigantic square near the railway sidings. Troublesome natives laden with low grade oranges and tangerines, tried to tempt us, and steal. Baksheesh! Baksheesh! was the cry around us.

While we stood in lines waiting, there was subdued laughter around me. An officer shouted across! 'Have you brought it all the way from Blighty?' The laughter was on account of my small suitcase which had RPC engraved. These initials could stand for 'Retained Products of Conception'! In my esteemed medical school it was considered sloppy to use abbreviations, and the initials meant little to me! As I forced some laughter myself we were moved on to an Egyptian train. The coaches had wooden seats and the ride was uncomfortable and noisy. On and on it travelled parallel with the Suez Canal. Now and again a large ship slowly passed along the canal, giving the impression of moving along the desert. Sand was soft and windswept in this area. Camels were numerous, legging it through the sand, and ridden by men in white galabiyas. Platforms along the route were crowded with men, women, and children. Many lay down attempting to sleep with flies crowding over their closed lids. Eye disease was rife, blindness and trachoma, common to all.

By late evening after an exhausting ride we arrived at Cairo, and rode in a 15cwt truck to the RAMC Base Depot at Helmiah. As I walked into the mess for some food, there, sitting at a table was Lieutenant J.D. Little. He had been in the same convoy in another liner, the *Durban Castle* sailing from Clydeside. The Base Depot was moderately comfortable and we slept in wooden huts surrounded by soft, loose sand: it was seven or eight miles from the centre of Cairo.

Egyptian cigarettes were available in the mess and the aroma was pungent and nasty; suggestions were made as to the composition of these cigarettes! The base depot was the transit camp and posting centre for medical officers in the MEF, and we were to remain there waiting for our posting to units or hospitals. We were allowed into the centre of Cairo provided

115

we went in parties of three or four at a time and stayed together. British troops were not too popular with the indigenous population, who hoped the Germans would win the war. There was a tram from Helmiah to the centre of Cairo; it was called the 'little brown tram'. It was thronged with Egyptians, some even sitting on the roof, or buffers. We had been warned to guard our service identity cards; not that there were many safe pockets to hide them. Small Egyptian boys were skilled pickpockets and usually found what they wanted. On our first trip into Cairo we were pestered by small boys darting out on the pavement and pouring a black sticky substance over our shoes, followed by a demand to clean them for baksheesh. After several incidents of this harassment, one medical officer, who was carrying a cudgel type of walking stick, went over the top, and hit out.

In seconds we were surrounded by a yelling mob of youths; the situation was ugly and we made a quick decision to break up. It was every man for himself. I finished up behind a counter of a jeweller's shop to the astonishment of the Egyptian owner. He was, however, understanding, and I stayed there until the fracas subsided.

Eventually we met up again and reached the base depot without further ado. I lost my fountain pen in the incident.

On another day a small party of medical officers braved the Cairo streets again and we made our way along the Mena Road to the Pyramids of Giza. The air was heavy with the smell of vaporizing petrol and sheer dirt. It was, however, an interesting day. The Sphinx gazed at us with its inscrutable smile; we climbed to the top of the Great Pyramid, step by step, and we entered the Blue Mosque of Mohammed Ali. It was an amazing experience.

Finally we mounted camels and were photographed with the Sphinx and Great Pyramid in the background.

After a couple of days I developed a severe headache, a high temperature, and pain at the back of the neck. My eyeballs were acutely tender to touch, and an attempt to rotate the eyeballs produced acute discomfort. Happily I was in the base depot and was able to lie about for a couple of days. This was sandfly fever, a virus infection, and one attack produced immunity for life. Apart from analgesics there was no treatment. I recovered quickly and was soon back to my norm.

On another occasion in the base depot I had placed my tropical

The author can be seen on the second camel from the right. Dr J.D. Little is on the left of the standing front row.

jacket over a chair while I was in the wash room. When I returned there was an unusual black object on the sleeve of the jacket which looked ominous. I showed it to another officer who snatched the jacket from my grasp and shook the offending object to the ground, grinding it to death with his boot. This was the black scorpion. There are two main types of scorpion, the black, and the sand-coloured. Both have long tails which flick over, penetrating the skin of its victim and injecting a toxin. There is intense pain, and shock.

The toxin of the black scorpion is potent and it can kill. The Sudanese seemed to be particularly vulnerable to the black scorpion, and if they died it was the will of Allah. They did not respond to treatment. British troops suffered the intense pain but they responded to local injections of novocaine two per cent, and they did not die. The sand-coloured scorpion is less virulent and produces pain without systemic upset. Scorpions like to hide inside shoes and boots, inside sleeves of jackets, and pockets. We treated them with respect and shook our clothes with care as we dressed. I was beginning to wonder if I was going to get away from the base depot alive, so many were the hazards!

Every day one or two medical officers disappeared having received their posting, and I never saw them again. Some went to Paiforce, (Persian and Iraq Force) and learned about Baghdad! Dr Little went to Khartoum River Hospital for the Sudanese. One medical officer kicked up a fuss and wanted to fight the enemy literally. I do not know what the ADMS decided to do with him! My turn came and I was posted to a Sudanese Infantry unit at present stationed in Tripoli, Libya. I was to leave that night and travel from Cairo to Castel Benito Airport outside Tripoli. Just before I left I received a very welcome batch of letters from Barbara; they had taken more than a month to arrive. It was over two months before she heard from me.

My valise had now arrived at the base depot and just in time. Shortly before midnight an army truck left the base depot with a driver and myself. We travelled a long way through the centre of Cairo, and then struck out into the desert until we reached a small airport, possibly only used by the RAF. A mug of tea at a canteen was welcome. Soon ten people assembled, several RAF personnel, one or two naval officers, a Wren, and myself. I had never flown before. We moved towards a Dakota aircraft and climbed aboard. Luggage followed. There was a metal seat

118

the length of the fuselage on each side, unpadded. The centre of the plane was empty except for the Wren who slept on the floor. Propellers on each wing started to rotate and we taxied slowly down the runway, and turned ready for take-off. At that time each engine was individually screamed up to maximum revs before take-off, and the plane vibrated uncomfortably. When the pilot was satisfied we sped down the runway. Suddenly smoke and fumes filled the inside of the aircraft. Somebody shouted an obscenity. Power was cut and we stopped. We left the plane and made our way back to the canteen for another mug of tea. After an hour we boarded the plane, went through the procedure again, and this time we were airborne. The lighting was dim, the seat uncomfortable, but I was able to doze fitfully.

Daylight was early and we came in to land on a desert strip; I think the place was Marble Arch! Although miles from anywhere it was quite an establishment with tents and hutted areas.

There was breakfast in a tent and I was delighted to be eating eggs and bacon, toast and marmalade and drinking mugs of tea.

We boarded the plane and took off again. After an hour, the main door to the outside burst open and hit the fuselage with a tremendous clang. I was opposite the door; the roar of wind was alarming and I held on tight. The co-pilot arrived and with metal grab hooks and ropes, we formed a human chain and pulled the heavy door shut. Dakota aircraft were unpressurized, did not fly high or fast, and I suppose there was no real danger; it was however unpleasant until the door was closed. As we flew on our way I noticed some oil slowly trickling along one of the wings, and I was unhappy about this.

At last we landed at Castel Benito Airport, and I reported to the RTO (Regional Transport Officer). He notified the various surrounding units of arrivals and requested transport to their units.

After a very long wait, a staff car driven by a Sudanese corporal arrived. He wore a turban and I remember his large sandals. He could not speak English and at that time I could not communicate in Arabic. We drove about eight miles across a bleak piece of desert and entered a compound consisting of a large tent and many smaller tents. This was the HQ for medical officers attached to the Sudan Defence Force; it was commanded by Lieutenant Colonel Corkhill, or Corkhillbey given his Sudanese title. He had lived and worked in the Sudan for many years. His room was unusual and looked at though it might have been a concrete pill-box at one time; it overlooked the sea. Oil lamps swayed from the roof. Conversation was not so easy because he had not been to England for a long time, and felt out of touch: the Sudan was his home. We had some supper and I was given a glass of neat whisky; it was very welcome. He told me that I was posted to No 3 Infantry Battalion SDF as their medical officer; the unit was stationed in Tripoli and I was to join next morning. All the officers of this unit were British and he hoped I would enjoy my experiences.

There was a bed for me in the big tent. When I woke up next morning there was another medical officer in the tent. I had been posted to relieve him as he had been posted elsewhere. He apologized for leaving me on my own with the boss but he had spent the evening with another unit to say farewell after some months there.

Shortly after breakfast a truck arrived and I was driven to the HQ of my new unit No 3 Infantry Battalion SDF. (Sudanese Defence Force).

The building was two storeys, and situated on the eastern side of the main promenade; it overlooked Tripoli harbour; it might even have been a school before the war. I was introduced to the CO, and the other British officers. It was quickly evident that we did not have much in common; certainly they were amusing, were very addicted to the alcohol available, and could tell jokes which made your hair stand on end! Most had been overseas three years or more and had travelled with this SDF unit from the Sudan in the wake of the Eighth Army. Women were the main topic discussed, and this was boring after a few days. I was not going to be able to change them, though I did try over the five months I was with the unit, and they were unlikely to change me. I thought it was going to be very difficult for them to rehabilitate after the war. The transport officer however, was a sensible man and there was little he did not know about army trucks, small and large: he told me he had ring trouble. I did not know what he meant, and he never elaborated. Perhaps he was referring to piston-rings. One officer sang *Silent Night*, repeatedly; it seemed to be the only carol he knew. However we had to live together, and as I have mentioned before, there was friendship in the army, and we all coped as best we could. After their three years in the area I was very surprised that I was never questioned about Blighty, having been there five weeks previously.

Leading off the mess was a balcony and it was rather pleasant out there in the evenings with a glass of beer. The sun set every night in a red ball of fire, and as the last rim dipped beneath the horizon a green flash lit up the sea. I shall never forget the beauty of the Mediterranean Sea.

There was no shortage of accommodation in the HQ and we had a room to ourselves; the floors were marble and ice-cold to the feet in late February. Electric light bulbs were in short supply; they were the screw-thread type and we moved them from room to room as required. The electric wiring was very dangerous, and it was easy to sustain an electric shock.

The war had swept through Tripoli and the damage and destruction was not too severe. The harbour suffered badly and was full of sunken or scuttled ships. A large Red Cross liner was submerged across the harbour entrance. There was a British military general hospital, 48th General, a large white rectangular building, and an attractive dome-shaped white building, subsequently to become a small transit hotel. The main town was typically Italian: one area was out of bounds on account of a brothel within. Palm trees adorned the promenade, and the climate seemed pleasant. The place had potential. I would be pleased to return were it not for Colonel Gedaffi, and survey the place with nostalgia.

I held sick-parades every morning, and I was, of course, always available at other times. It is not easy handling sick people when there is a lack of communication. Fortunately I had a very good medical orderly, a Sudanese corporal, who knew all the members of the unit and was helpful. There was a wooden box containing basic needs, its contents controlled from HQ and replenished by the British military hospital. The young Sudanese generally were strong and tough, but unfortunately they did not thrive in North Africa on the coast, a thousand miles north of their homeland. Those who came from Juba, nearest to the equatorial line suffered most. They lost resistance and developed pulmonary tuberculosis. Modern therapy was unknown: the condition was fulminating and many went home to die. I learned very soon that if a Sudanese reported sick with a fistula-in-ano,

121

the probability was that he had pulmonary TB, only too frequently confirmed radiologically. Discipline for the Sudanese ordinary ranks was very severe; no matter how trivial the offence, the punishment was lashes (jelda). Twelve lashes was a standard punishment. This was administered by a Sudanese sergeant (shawysk) using a leather thronged whip. The unfortunate recipient lay on the ground, buttocks bared; a wet cloth was placed over the buttocks. The punishment did not seem to cause great distress as their hides were thick. One soldier received forty lashes for theft, two sergeants at a time brandishing the whips. I asked him later how he felt. He said ('schadid') very strong, and laughed.

I travelled with the unit wherever it went and learned other skills in administration, totally unconnected with medicine. One day we went a hundred miles due south of Tripoli to a desert township: there was a fort there manned by Sudanese. It was late at night when we arrived back to HQ. It was eerie in the desert at night; small tents and bivouacs, faintly lit were alongside parts of the track. It did not feel too safe. By day, miles from anywhere, young men with perfect physique galloped across the desert on magnificent steeds with real skill. Who they were, and how they lived remains a mystery.

The Germans and Italians were now out of Tunisia and out of North Africa; nor were they succeeding in Italy.

It was time for the Sudanese defence forces to return to their homeland, and arrangements were in hand. The journey involved returning to Alexandria in army transport, on to Cairo, to Aswan, thence to Wadi Halfa by Nile paddle steamer and home across the Nubian Desert to Khartoum. The journey was interesting, but slow, and I doubt whether we covered a hundred miles a day due to the state of the road and the heat of the sun. For miles the terrain was stark desert, hard, stony, sandy ground with parched scrub. At strategic intervals there were water points at an oasis; the water was poured into skin receptacles which were slung alongside the vehicles; air movement kept the water cool. We ate where and when we could. There were tins of M & V (meat and vegetables), nourishing no doubt, but unpalatable when cold. Biscuits, not unlike dog biscuits, were in plentiful supply.

In the daytime it was very hot, and the absence of protection from the sun was exhausting; it burned relentlessly from a cloudless sky. We all looked forward to sunset. When it came a cold chill quickly enveloped the desert and we were only too ready to put on our thick khaki jerseys. At night I crawled into my sleeping bag, wrapped myself in blankets, and eventually warmed up. I slept under the truck hoping there would be no oil leaks from the transmission.

Here and there were quite delightful small clusters of trees, and settlements, made by Italian immigrants. The small, mass produced dwellings had a small garden and were fenced off from their neighbours. They were derelict, but undamaged by the war: there must have been thousands of immigrants in Tripolitania pre-war. Derna was a pleasant coastal settlement, and town. The ports of Tobruk, Benghazi, and Tripoli provided access to their homeland. How did these immigrants live? What did they do and what is the situation now? I would like to return and see for myself. The journey continued, and we reached Tobruk. Ten Sudanese developed measles en route; the rash was difficult to diagnose on their dark skins. The journey was uncomfortable for them lying together on the floor of a covered truck, with their high temperatures and coryzal symptoms, but the unit had to press on. They all recovered.

Tobruk had a fine harbour, full of sunken ships. The sea was deep blue and the water warm. The unit stayed several days here, and we bathed, swimming from wreck to wreck. As I swam on one occasion my watch was still on my wrist and it soon stopped. It was very easy to be burned by the sun, even in the water; sunburn was a self-inflicted wound and there could be serious trouble for offenders. There were still quite a number of British troops in Tobruk, and an army pay-master; I remember cashing a cheque there. Tents were our accommodation just outside Tobruk; one night a sandstorm blew up; it was uncomfortable and fine sand stung the face and hurt the eyes; sand found a place everywhere. The wind was so strong we feared the tent could have blown away.

After four weeks, passing through El Alamein, and Sidi Barrani the unit arrived outside Alexandria, and we stayed here several days and I caught up with Barbara's letters again. What a difference it made knowing there was still another way of life back home; I lived for her letters. Alexandria was a pleasant place with fine beaches and promenades. The town was large with good shops and I took my watch for repair.

Horse-drawn vehicles conveyed people here and there; the place was clean, fashionable and had a surfeit of wealthy Egyptians.

A party of us went into a garden where drinks were available; to my surprise a school pal from Weymouth came into the garden. His name was Kennedy, and he was an officer in the RASC, I think. We had a great reunion and celebration after four weeks in the shag. We finished by having a carriage drive; the Egyptian driver was determined to drive us to the red light area and I remember an undignified scene as horse and carriage at our insistence, tried to turn in a narrow street, and move to a more respectable area.

The unit then travelled to Cairo by train and we spent a few days in a basic camp near the Pyramids, and the Mena Hotel, where Winston Churchill and President Roosevelt conducted one of their World War conferences. The cooks had specialized in making curries and they were as hot as any I had ever tasted.

We moved south by train again and after a hot and dusty journey arrived at Aswan. The temperature was alleged to be 130° plus F, quite intolerable, and there had been no rain within living memory. One night here was long enough and then we were on our way. There was time to see the Aswan Dam, but unfortunately we were unable to see Luxor. We embarked on a Nile steamer for the journey to Wadi Halfa. The Nile steamers had a large paddle wheel at the stern, and very reasonable accommodation. Iced drinks were a luxury, taken slowly to avoid stomach cramp. On the way we stopped at Abu Simbal to see the remarkable sculptures three thousand years old; since then they have been moved with great difficulty to another position to avoid damage from the high rise of the Nile water due to the building of the High Dam completed in 1972. The slow journey continued, the scenery mainly wide river and desert. We met Egyptian boats (fellukas); they had a characteristic shape and a peculiar sail, but were a good form of transport on this river.

On this paddle-steamer there was a medical officer who was travelling independently to Khartoum. He showed the white knees and the inexperience of recent arrivals from the UK. Eccentric indeed he was; his views on medicine were unorthodox and bizarre, his behaviour out of keeping with his position, and totally unpredictable.

As the steamer slowly churned its way along a narrow part of the river a small herd of cattle came into view on the opposite side. Most animals in the east are desperately thin and look dejected; dogs, donkeys and cows shared the emaciation, and the bare ground had little to offer. This herd was no exception but there were three cows rather worse than the rest. This medical officer was angry at what he saw and demanded a service rifle and three bullets from a Sudanese infantry-man: they were forthcoming, and in fact the infantry man had little option and would never refuse an order from a British officer. Startled and speechless we watched the scene. Three shots rang out, and three beasts sank to their knees, and rolled over, presumably mortally wounded. 'Now they are at peace,' he said. The steamer moved away from the scene; those beasts would have been the livelihood of some poor Egyptian farmer. What would happen? Would there be trouble at Wadi Halfa?

We arrived at Wadi Halfa and there was no trouble, and no apparent knowledge of the event, no doubt due to the isolation and paucity of communications.

We were now in the Nubian Desert, the most northerly area of the Sudan. We boarded a Sudanese train to convey the unit to Khartoum. As far as the eye could see, the terrain was flat, hard desert, and an occasional hillock. The Sudan, at this period of history, was a condominium, ruled by Britain and Egypt; the railway was a narrow track, and the entire system was British built. It was clean, comfortable, and efficient. The coaches were reminiscent of the sleeping compartments of trains in Britain. Meals were served by servants in white robes wearing a red kummelbund (cloth strap) around the waist. Electric fans moved the sultry air.

After some hours in the Nubian Desert the train reached greener and more pleasant terrain. There were trees, and acres of cultivated land producing cotton, wheat, dura and gum-arabic. Small communities were scattered here widely. There were hundreds of small circular dwellings built of mud, sticks, and straw for the roof. Older men wore a white galabiya and white turban, younger people, shorts and a khaki shirt. Their feet were bare, or encased in thick leather sandals. The clothes were exceptionally clean, shorts pressed with a major crease. A charcoal iron was essential. Women were heavily veiled if married, and wore black robes; younger women wore white.

Several wives were permitted by Islam. When the train stopped at a village, it remained for half an hour or so and it seemed the entire community turned out to see it. They were a laughing, happy, people, ruled by a district commissioner who was British at that time, but gradually, control was being handed over to Sudanese officials. Every village had its chief and local customs. Their faces had scars on both cheeks, and sometimes the forehead. Certain tribes had a particular designation of scar, so everybody knew at a glance, their tribe, and probably their village. I was never able to elucidate how the scars were made but my impression is that a two inch scratch was made, grease applied, and that epithelialization occurred over the grease. The scars never gave the impression of ever having been septic, nor can I believe they were deep cuts made in infancy. The scars seemed keloidal. The Sudanese were reticent about their customs, and one required a good command of Arabic to discuss such subjects and also one did not wish to intrude upon their privacies.

We reached Khartoum, but did not stay. Most of the Sudanese in the No 3 SDF Infantry Battalion came from El Obeid, in the heart of the Sudan, and were eager to return to their villages and wives. Trains were changed again and we travelled south-west to the heart of the Sudan. The distance would have been about 400 miles, but the journey required two nights and three days through rather similar scenery to the previous journey. At last we reached El Obeid in the province of Kordofan, and here the railway line ended; to reach El Fasher, another town at least 200 miles further west, it required a sturdy vehicle or a camel. Many soldiers in the unit lived in El Fasher and were happy to be nearly home.

El Obeid had sandy streets, a small hospital, a mosque, and a sug (market). The population was mainly Moslem. There was no evidence of a pending disbandment of the unit and duties continued. Sick parades were similar, the conditions seen mostly minor and I had little trouble in dealing with their illnesses, thanks to the trusty medical orderly. My Arabic was improving too and this was a major help, not only for the sick-parade, but also for the administrative duties that I was asked to undertake.

After a few days I suffered an acute gastroenteritis; the symptoms were so acute I feared dehydration. There was no improvement after two days so I went to the hospital and was admitted. I had a parasitic infection with giardia lamblia and a short course of mepacrine quickly relieved the symptoms. A Sudanese medical orderly attended me, and I was well cared for. A large ceiling fan, slowly rotating, helped the hot humid conditions.

Three days treatment cured me and I returned to the unit. Several events took place in El Obeid which the passage of time has not dimmed. The Sudanese killed their hens by decapitation. I was amazed to see these unfortunate creatures running in circles for a full minute before they collapsed dead. It was horrible to witness, but that was the mode.

On another occasion a British officer, older than most of us, and with a wife at home, went through a matrimonial ceremony with a Sudanese girl. We heard all the details about the dowry, the cost and the wedding-feast, and how finally he was conducted to a hut for the consummation of the marriage. When he emerged he was carried triumphantly through the streets. It was incredible. To add to the astonishment were the stories about female circumcision. This was commonly practised at that time, but I understand it is a dying custom now, and a good thing too.

About half a mile from the camp a large ostrich strutted importantly here and there, picking up scraps of vegetation from the barren ground. It looked old, feathers were missing and it did not look healthy. Another British officer succeeded in mounting its back, his arms encircling the long tubular neck. The bird suddenly took fright, and set off. Old it looked, but it was capable of running at forty miles per hour with the terrified officer hanging on, too frightened to let go at such a speed. Eventually he was thrown off unharmed.

The unit practised field exercises now and again. One day the unit received orders to march to Jebel El Obeid. A Jebel is a sandy miniature mountain in the scrub. Jebel El Obeid must have been six miles from the camp, probably more. Conditions were hot and humid, and the sun beat down on us. I had notified the CO that I thought it a risky procedure to march that distance in the mid-day heat. He pooh-poohed the suggestion and we set off. I had a rather unhygienic water bottle strapped to my khaki belt, and I made sure it was filled to the brim. My fears about the heat were justifiable, and we must have lost pints of sweat and salt. Every hour we stopped for fifteen minutes and lay on the ground; only small quantities of fluid were allowed

127

hourly in case of gastric colic; we did not have salt tablets. However, we did reach the Jebel and sought shelter from the burning sun by hiding beneath parched, skeletal twigs for two hours. By then the worst of the heat was over and we marched back to El Obeid.

The Sudanese were in their element. They possess long legs, have protective skins, take big strides, and are of course used to such conditions. As they marched back they sang a marching song, Ay jy, Ay, jy jy, Ay jy, Ay, jy, jy. It went on for hours, loud and raucous. I began to chant as well, and after all my training, I wondered what on earth I was doing! Perhaps it was a touch of sun-stroke! I comforted myself in the knowledge that I was a mere fragment in a massive military machine; remove a piece, and the entire machine might grind to a halt!

It was always a major occasion when mail reached the unit; sometimes two months would elapse without word, but when it came there could be as many as twenty-five letters from Barbara, all numbered externally, so that I knew the correct order to open them. I wrote several times a week, as and when I could, and eventually my letters reached Barbara. Letters, in general, had a good effect on the morale of the troops, but there were always some who received the bad news that their marriages were disintegrating, that girl friends had broken off engagements, or perhaps a new baby had arrived on the scene, the husband having been in the desert for the past two and a half years. There was a large psychiatric hospital not so far from Cairo; I think it was the 49th General. It was always well filled, the inmates suffering from depression, and other conditions as well. A posting back to the UK, or even compassionate leave was unusual, and, under active service, extremely rare. There was an organization called SSAFA (Soldiers, Sailors and Airmen's Family Association) in the UK, which performed sterling work during the war assisting members of the Forces in obtaining a compassionate posting to the UK in cases of bereavement, a broken home, or a wife's illness; such situations could produce a psychiatric disturbance in the serving member. Many deserving cases received help, but many applications, too, fell on stony ground. There was a war on, of course, and under active service conditions with transport problems, such requests could be unrealistic, and had to be rejected. Times were hard. Often we felt a little isolated so far away in the centre of the

Sudan, and there was little knowledge of the progress of the war. We knew the long expected invasion of France had taken place, but little else. The unit did not possess a short wave radio; such a possession would not have lasted long; transistors were not invented and radio valves often went wrong, and required replacing.

I was offered fourteen days leave and I decided to spend it in Khartoum. I returned on my own and stayed at the army transit camp and enjoyed looking around the area in the company of other officers in different corps who were also on leave. While I was there I met Lieutenant J.D. Little again who had spent time at the SDF Base Hospital in Khartoum. He introduced me to the Sudan Club where there was a good swimming pool. Despite the intense heat I found Khartoum a pleasant place and I enjoyed my leave there.

Barely had I returned to El Obeid to rejoin my unit when I was reposted to Khartoum and ordered to report to the ADMS there. I returned, and met Nobby Clark, the ADMS. He was a jovial and pleasant character in the Sudan Medical Service. He said I was to travel to Asmara, the capital of Eritrea, and further instructions awaited me there on arrival. I was pleased to be leaving the unit and moving elsewhere. I travelled with another British officer who spoke Italian fluently. My rank was elevated to captain. This time the journey was east of Khartoum and we travelled by train again as far as Kassala where the railway terminated. The journey lasted two days. Kassala had been the scene of heavy fighting in the early days of the war: many British troops lost their lives in Abbysinia. It must have been very hot, the terrain rough and mountainous, and military operations hard going. The crests of British regiments were carved on the mountains, and visible a long way off. We were now near the Sudan/Eritrea border; a large, aged, Italian bus conveyed us for three hours along a rough pot-holed tarred road through desert and scrub to Agordat. From there we boarded a rack railway which took us up, up and up through the mountains to Asmara.

Asmara was very high up; it was cold and we donned battle dress. We were slightly breathless from the altitude as we walked about; it was a sudden change, and not unwelcome.

The Sudanese defence force had been serving in Eritrea as well. I was based at the transit camp in Asmara. I travelled daily along cleverly engineered roads with numerous hairpin bends built by the Italians. I was provided with an ambulance with a large Red Cross on its sides, and a Sudanese driver.

I conducted sick-parades and sometimes conveyed sick Sudanese to the military hospital at Mai Habar, nestling in the mountains.

One day I was requested to take a medical package to a small naval establishment at Massawa on the Red Sea coast. The heat was unbelievable and the flies profuse. The naval establishment had air-conditioning. As I left I felt as though I might be walking into an oven and it was a relief to reach higher ground again.

While I was in Asmara I had a short leave. Asmara had a cinema, typical Italian buildings, tarred streets, churches and a little traffic. The transit camp was so good, and the air cool that I thought a few days there would be beneficial. Other officers arrived on leave to enjoy the pleasant conditions, and we went visiting. I remember a pleasant day at Addi Ugri, when Griffin, Parsons and Atkinson, made up the party. We had a drink under a large parasol. Another day we climbed to the summit of Mount Briezen where there was a monastery. We were well received by the monks who looked strong and fit. It was a long climb and took most of the day.

In Eritrea there was an Italian brewery, and Melotti beer was the main product. It looked good, the colour was right, and it had a frothy head. It was however, potent, and when iced it could produce symptoms of acute cystitis. We were wary of it, and drank a litre now and again.

Back on duty after the leave I was sent miles out into the scrub where the Eighth Infantry Battalion SDF was serving. They had no medical officer and I was temporarily attached. Help was needed because of an outbreak of measles. It was as bleak a piece of desert that could be found, but there was a white shack which I took over as a sick-bay, well away from the main camp. I had a tent alongside, and the medical orderly's tent was near mine. The commanding officer told me to watch myself as gazelle were in the area. A gazelle is a powerfully built animal not quite the size of a full grown pig; it has a thick neck and can move quickly. I had seen a dead one and estimated it could easily knock a man down and kill. They roamed at night. I was not too happy under my mosquito net in a small tent alone and away from the main camp.

It was so hot that the tent-flap must be left open in order to breathe. One night I woke suddenly; I was sure I heard movement and could hear breathing. I lay as though dead, terrified to move. Was it a gazelle? Was it imagination? I don't think so. Next morning I told the CO and he suggested I kept a small oil lamp outside the tent at night. I thought a light might attract them but there was no further incident.

The measles situation was contained and I returned to Asmara, to be informed I had been posted to No 1 SDF Base Hospital, Khartoum. It was early September 1945.

I retraced my steps and reached the transit camp in Khartoum. It was really a basic camp; there was a toilet block and ablution room. Excreta went into buckets, and these were collected daily and placed on a cart drawn by a camel. A camel is an intelligent animal; this one knew exactly what it had to do, and it walked nimbly with its unpleasant load. I liked camels. They had humorous faces, but if displeased they could turn nasty and spit and snarl.

Next day I reported to the base hospital to find John Little was still there. He suggested I moved to the officers quarters called the 'Pink Palace'. This was a compound consisting of numerous wooden huts, each with a verandah. Nearby was a pink building containing a dining room, a bar, and a place to sit down. The huts had large ceiling fans, a bed, table, chair and electric light. It was luxurious compared with my present quarters. There was a Sudanese servant who washed and ironed the tropical clothes. He was called the dhobi. The mess bills were modest and I decided to move. We ate well here. I remember the curries; it seemed strange to consume such hot food in such a sweltering climate.

No 1 SDF Base Hospital was a rectangular-shaped building and one storey high. It overlooked the Nile. A long tarred road extended from the Pink Palace, passed in front of the hospital, continued through the Governor General's palace to the Grand Hotel on the southern end of the water-front. Khartoum Bridge across the Nile was very close. The hospital establishment comprised a commanding officer (a lieutenant colonel), three more British doctors, a Palestinian doctor, and a Sudanese doctor called Dr Zein. There was a secretary called Shooshah, a Palestinian, a dispenser, and numerous nursing orderlies.

Dr Zein was trained at Khartoum medical school; he was

131

efficient, spoke English well, and was very familiar with the illnesses and psychological behaviour of the Sudanese.

Apart from pulmonary tuberculosis, measles, and gonorrhoea, I had not seen many medical conditions so far, and it was high time I was back in hospital. Because the hospital was the base hospital we received patients from far and wide.

Malaria was common, invariably a recurrence, and responded well to quinine and mepacrine. Malignant malaria patients were very ill; they responded well to intravenous quinine. Bilharzia was seen occasionally.

Khartoum was hot all the year round and unbearable at certain times of the year. 115°F was not uncommon, but 98°F and high humidity was more uncomfortable. British troops suffered from prickly heat rash, a sweat rash. Chest, shoulders, neck creases were involved, and the chaffing from coarse khaki was unpleasant. Calamine lotion helped. A change of weather produced a dramatic improvement.

My working day in Khartoum started at six am when a Red Cross Ambulance arrived outside the Pink Palace. A Sudanese driver would convey me considerable distances to three or four units well out in the desert. Sick parades were conducted here. Most of the patients were M & D (medicine and duty) on the written form for the commanding officer; a few were excused duties for twenty-four hours, and occasionally there was a hospital patient. The CO, or another British officer was available, and we often had a chat.

It was the best part of the day, the sun barely risen, and though hot, it was pleasant compared with the grilling heat later on in the morning. I returned to the Pink Palace for breakfast, and then cycled to the Military Hospital. The hospital work was similar to the work in a hospital at home. Everything we did took time largely due to the language difficulty, but also to the extreme heat. Perspiration dripped from us and there was no air-conditioning in the hospital.

X-ray facilities existed at the British Military Hospital, the patients travelling to and fro by ambulance. Surgical emergencies were very rare. I remember a patient with appendicitis having the operation in Khartoum General Hospital. There was difficulty because the appendix was intra-mural, and not grossly pathological.

There were notes to write up, and a fair amount of paper

work in triplicate, always a feature of army life. We had visits from a Major Wardell. He was a British medical officer but was attached to the ADMS office in an administrative capacity. He was a jovial character, had a tidy mind, and was well briefed in army regulations. Every situation, large or small, was a problem and his favourite expression when the problem was solved was: 'that's the answer to that one'. Unfortunately for him he developed acute appendicitis and underwent surgery in the British Military Hospital, and 'that was the answer to that one'.

The heat did not help his immediate post-operative state, but he made a complete recovery.

Three hours in the hospital each morning soon passed, and I cycled back to the Pink Palace for lunch. This was the only time of day I wore a pith hat and I was grateful for the protection it provided for the nape of the neck. These hats were unpopular; they were clumsy, and had a chin-strap. We felt uncomfortable and self-conscious wearing them. After lunch, everybody disappeared to their huts, switched on the fans, and tried to sleep until the worst of the heat was over. It was absolutely vital to wrap a towel round the front of the abdomen whilst you slept; failure to do this resulted in abdominal colic and diarrhoea; sometimes I fought the heat, attempting to read a book, or writing a letter, stuck to the wooden chair with perspiration.

About three thirty pm the heat eased a little as the sun moved lower. John Little, myself, and sometimes one or two others would cycle to the Sudan Club. This club was the property of the British officials and their families employed by the Sudanese Government. The club was surrounded by trees which masked the sun, a lawn was kept green with repeated soakings, but above everything it had a fine swimming-pool. It was white-tiled, possessed a high diving platform, and the water was changed weekly. We were admitted free of charge as honorary members due to the generosity and kind thoughts of the British officials.

We all derived much pleasure from the pool, the peace, and the protection from the sun. Scattered on the lawn were comfortable chairs, and tables; if you took a seat a beaming Sudanese waiter, immaculate in white galabiya and turban, and wearing a crimson waist band came with a tea-tray and some cakes. We paid for that service, of course. Sometimes we met some of the British expatriates. I remember a Mr and Mrs Nye who were most kind to invite us to their house. Having been out of England for so long, and now accustomed to efficient service from their servants, they were real pukka-sahibs, and I thought they would find it difficult to adjust to the shortages, and political changes which were certain to follow the end of the war. The majority had no intention of going back to the UK after the war to settle, provided their three months' annual leave was resumed. Every adult member of a household was allocated six bottles of Johnny Walker whisky per month! I think it was necessary!

On our return journey to the Pink Palace John Little and I would return to the hospital, see the orderlies, examine all new patients admitted during the afternoon, and deal with any queries.

Anchored close to the bridge crossing the Nile and twenty yards out, were a dozen or so small sailing dinghies. Instead of going to the Sudan Club Dr Little and I would hire one of these boats and go for a sail. Usually we headed north and with a fair breeze we went a considerable distance down river out of sight from Khartoum. Sometimes we thought we saw small crocodiles at the water's edge, but they turned out to be pieces of wood. It was deceptive. In the early evening the wind dropped and it was a slow journey back to Khartoum bridge. Once we sailed south to the junction of the Blue and White Niles and met waters so turbulent we feared for our safety, but John Little was a skilful navigator.

It was dark by seven forty-five pm all the year round. After a light supper we used to go to a small open-air picture house near the hospital. The film changed twice a week. We enjoyed the newsreels, rather out of date, but we obtained a better insight of the progress of the war. Frank Sinatra was a young man in 1945 and his crooning carried us away.

Khartoum was a pleasant place; there were good buildings, a cathedral, churches, a museum, and statues of General Gordon in the sandy streets. There were some good shops. I was able to purchase a good Swiss watch at a reasonable price to replace the one I damaged in the sea at Tobruk; despite the repair in Alexandria it was never the same again. There was a good bookshop and one by one I purchased novels by Jane Austen, Trollope and Charlotte Brontë. I had time to read them. Once we went to Omdurman. There was a large and well-known sug with clever work performed on elephants' tusks. The tools were very basic and ivory was cut with saws controlled with the feet! I bought an ivory dressing-table set in Omdurman and managed to get it home: it is still used daily and has never discoloured in the way that ivory so often does.

During my sojourn in Khartoum, the Governor General, Sir Hubert Huddlestone and his wife were very kind to British troops; one evening we had a trip down river in his launch and we all enjoyed it.

This posting to Khartoum was a pleasant experience. The conditions, apart from the heat, were excellent. Happily it continued for several months. It was almost Christmas 1945, the war in Europe was over, and Japan had just signed the peace treaty too.

Out of the blue one morning I was instructed by the ADMS to proceed to Gebeit, north east of Khartoum, close to Port Sudan, and relieve a medical officer, stationed at a prison camp full of Palestinians; they were political refugees. It did not sound a pleasant posting but it was only to last for a fortnight.

After another long journey by train at last I reached Gebeit. It was very hot, fairly close to the Red Sea, and a dusty barren area. I was soon inside the heavily wired prison cage, and once inside it was difficult to get outside! There were about a dozen British officers and other ranks handling the situation. The inmates were Jewish and there were racial customs which caused problems with the food.

I did not find them easy to deal with. Many had haematuria caused by renal stones; some had X-rays with them to confirm the diagnosis. A handful demanded surgery for removal of their stones. I could only satisfy myself that no lives were in danger, and I had the impression these refugees were resentful, trying to be difficult, and trying, naturally, to get away from the prison cage.

Half-way through my fortnight in the camp, one of the British private soldiers developed a sore throat. His temperature was 105°F; he had delirium and was acutely ill. Examination of his throat showed huge red tonsils meeting in the mid-line. The cervical glands were swollen and tender; I had a supply of sulphapyridine and a course was started. This man seemed ill out of all proportion to the cause, presumably a haemolytic streptococcal infection. I could not detect other troubles. I stuck it out for two days, but there was no improvement, in fact he was dehydrated due to the heat and inability to sip adequate fluids. I thought about diphtheria but by now it was difficult for him to open his mouth due to trismus. Clearly he had to be moved, and quickly.

It took some time to contact the ADMS. He listened to the story and when he realized the patient was in no state to travel to Khartoum by rail (there were only two trains per week I think) he said he would contact the RAF.

After about two hours a small RAF plane circled the Camp, and made a landing on rough desert ground; it was not an airstrip and I thought the pilot had done well. The soldier was strapped to a stretcher and placed in the care of an RAF medical orderly and lifted on to the small plane.

Anxiously we watched as the plane gathered speed on the bumpy ground; it became airborne and soon was a speck in the distance. When I returned to Khartoum I found my diagnosis was correct, and he recovered in the British Military Hospital.

I was relieved when I left Gebeit for Khartoum, and did not give it a backward glance. Back in the SDF Base Hospital, and relaxing in the pleasant Sudan Club garden, I appreciated the comforts of Khartoum.

Fellow-officers, and expatriates too, had warned us that after a year or two there the country possessed a magnetic attraction, a mystique, drawing people to like the charm of its happy inhabitants, and to cherish a desire to live and work there. I was falling under the spell. At night, the croaking of thousands of frogs along the Nile's banks, the distant off-beat native drum music wafting across the still sultry air were having their effect on me: even the call of the muezzin to prayer in a mosque had an appeal! I made some enquiries about joining the Sudan Medical Service, and it would not have been difficult to sign along the dotted line. However I fought this urge and rejected the idea from my mind. How could I possibly ask Barbara to leave the Scottish hills for a native village, hundreds of miles from anywhere? A challenge, yes, a chance to improve the medical welfare of a community, yes: if I was single I might have fallen victim. In retrospect, and knowing the problems the country has suffered since the war, I am sure I made the correct decision.

Now that the war was over, Python, a demobilization scheme

was introduced and troops returned to the UK for demobilization. It was rightly first in, first out. There was also leave in the UK, called Liap, (leave in addition to Python) but I was not offered this facility.

New medical officers arrived to replace those taking leave or returning for their release from the Forces. They were easy to spot with their white knees below their khaki shorts. We had acquired sallow complexions, aggravated no doubt by the daily tablet of Mepacrine. One newly arrived medical officer caused consternation in the mess one night. He asked us what we knew about the rhesus factor (an additional factor in a blood group, very recently discovered, and of major importance in midwifery); of course we could not know. There was a silence until a medical officer with glass in hand shouted:- 'Rhesus Jesus! what do you know, boys!' It certainly was witty and funny. Everybody enjoyed the laughter. We all had to learn about the rhesus blood grouping at a later date and it has always reminded me of Khartoum.

I had by now been promoted to the rank of major, but there was a surprise in store. I received a posting to return to Tripoli (Libya), another tedious journey; the purpose was to wind up a small SDF remnant left there and hand over. It would take about three weeks, and then I was instructed to return to Khartoum.

I flew from Khartoum to Cairo. It was a much better aircraft and had proper seating accommodation the length of the fuselage. It held about thirty passengers, service personnel, civilians, women and some children. In the hot air the plane suddenly dropped several hundred feet and then rose to its former altitude. 'Air pockets' they were called. I found it uncomfortable and felt a little sick. As we approached a runway at Shellal, the plane dropped, and we hit the ground with a massive thud. I have never enjoyed flying after these experiences. I reached Cairo and was conveyed to the base depot by army truck. After twenty-four hours I flew to Tripoli.

It was two years since I first arrived in Tripoli and I was agreeably surprised. All the sunken ships in the harbour had been removed, and it was in active use. The main street and sug had been opened up, the gardens were tidy, the natives walking the streets and promenade, and the area was reverting to its pre-war mode.

The Sudanese compound, awaiting disbandment was at the rear of Tripoli, and approached by traversing a long, straight, tree-lined avenue, into a side road and thence to the camp entrance. There was little comfort, the facilities were poor because the bulk of the unit had already left. Gradually I examined the remaining soldiers and completed forms in triplicate necessitating the application of a grade to any soldier showing illness or injury attributable to military service. Whilst here I met Dr Little again; he had been on an assignment to Misurata, some miles east of Tripoli, and also had in-patient experience in the British Military Hospital at Tripoli; he was about to return to Khartoum with an SDF unit, travelling by sea from Tripoli to Egypt with another medical officer.

After a few days the remaining Sudanese departed in army transport and commenced their long journey home. With the compound almost empty, a British corporal and myself sorted out the remaining equipment and stores, checked it against the establishment, and laid it out for inspection. The equipment was mainly army blankets and great coats. It was not easy for us to guard against theft, and small Arab boys would wriggle under the wire enclosing the camp and make off with some items, not that there was much of value remaining. Happily we seemed to be over-establishment, and one afternoon we were able to hand everything over to top brass.

The work was complete, not quite my line, but interesting to see Tripoli again. It was time to return to Khartoum.

I flew back to Cairo, and the journey was uneventful; the RAMC base depot was changing now that the war was over and was being used by other corps, part of the unwinding mechanism. Although travelling on my own, and sleeping in a large hut with twenty other officers and all strangers, it was remarkable what good friendship there was in the services. I was never made to feel ill at ease, everyone was helpful, and many had an unusual tale to tell.

While I was waiting arrangements for the journey to Khartoum I went into Cairo to meet an officer I had met before, at the officers club: by now I was bolder with so much travel, and with a knowledge of the language I was able to curse at strangers in their own tongue if they attempted to molest me, and walk the streets alone in fair safety.

I found the club, met the officer, and we walked to a table

for some food. As I sat down I looked round the room, and there, still resplendent in her QAIMNS uniform was Louise! She looked well and was escorted by two officers: it was over two years since I last saw her aboard the *Stirling Castle*. I went over to her table, and in her usual light-hearted way she gave a précis of her activities. I could not linger, nor did I wish to intrude, but it was the last time I saw Louise. I have often wondered about her destiny. It is not, however, in the best interests of your marriage to wonder about your first flame, and I left it at that.

I returned to Khartoum by train, steamer, and train again; I was soon back in the Pink Palace and returned to the Base Hospital. The commanding officer was on his way home, and I was appointed to his place with the rank of Lieutenant-Colonel. It was a surprise. The work pattern was changing; as the Sudanese were demobilized, so the number of sick lessened. Instead, the work involved a medical examination of every Sudanese soldier for demobilization. Some thought they had an illness or injury attributable to military service. They arrived at the hospital in large numbers and we had to work very hard indeed. We required our knowledge of Arabic.

One evening I arranged to meet a fellow-officer at the Grand Hotel overlooking the river. He was going on leave to the UK and I went to bid him farewell. We had a meal and a chat. I left on foot about eleven thirty pm for the two mile walk to the Pink Palace. I had barely walked a hundred yards when an RAF staff car pulled up alongside and an RAF officer asked me if I would like a lift to the end of the road. I accepted willingly. He set off at once, and it did not take seconds to realize he was 'well over the limit'. Faster and faster we went, fifty miles per hour, maybe more. I remonstrated, advising him that the Governor-General's palace was ahead and the two gates would be closed at that time of the night. He must slow down and take a right turn. He took no notice, and went faster. I told him again he was crazy not to slow down. I was petrified, but it was too late: the closed gates loomed in the glare of the headlights. He jammed on the brakes, swerved, lost control, and we crashed at high speed into the rear of a stationary car parked at the side of the road, killing a young woman sitting on the rear seat. Neither the RAF officer nor myself were hurt; I have no recollection of getting out of the staff car. There was pandemonium and a very nasty situation. Sudanese police arrived, followed by RAF police and the RAF driver was taken from the scene. I was surrounded by an angry mob but after interrogation I was allowed to return to the Pink Palace, shaken, lucky to be alive, and distressed at such an extraordinary and tragic turn of events.

For a fortnight I had a sharp pain between my shoulder blades. I was notified the RAF driver was facing a court-martial; I was his only witness, would be required to give evidence, and on no account was I to make any attempt to contact him. I did not even know his name.

On the day of the court-martial I had to put on service dress, Sam Browne Belt and carry my baton. The heat was intense for such clothing. The first day was a wasted day and I was never called. Next day I was. It was left, right, left, right, up the room to the witness-box saluting as I went. It was a serious occasion. High-ranking officers flanked one side of a table; the charge was manslaughter. These situations are always difficult and I had, of course, no knowledge of the amount of alcohol involved, or the accused officer's story. Looking at him in the box he was expressionless, and I did not recognize him. The prosecution could not understand why we had failed to see the parked car. The answer was that the car must have been parked just off the road. I was concentrating on those closed wrought-iron gates; to have crashed those would have killed both of us outright. Eventually I was dismissed; more saluting and I was on my way back to the Pink Palace to cool off. In the Khartoum evening paper I read that the officer had been reduced to the ranks and was awaiting transfer to the UK. He was not a regular, and I assumed he would be demobbed. It was a shocking experience, and I think he was lucky to escape a prison sentence.

1946 was not a good year for Khartoum. The rainy season at the origins of the Blue and White Niles had been unusually heavy and the Nile overflowed its banks. It was humid and unhealthy. The water slowly seeped into the Pink Palace compound, and my hut, well down towards the river was surrounded by murky water. The river itself was a fast-flowing torrent, and only a narrow gap separated the water level from the arches of the bridge. The flood of 1988 was far worse, but that of 1946 came second.

We attended a wedding in Khartoum Cathedral. One of the

medical officers attached to the SDF Base Hospital married a QA from the British Military Hospital. It was a great occasion.

Victory Day was celebrated in Khartoum on 8 June, 1946. At the SDF Hospital we organized a garden party. There were flags, a Sudanese band, and a demonstration by Sudanese ambulance men. Tea, cakes, and beer followed. The occasion raised the question: 'When was I going to be released?' It could not be far off.

Our work in the hospital continued, and slowly but steadily the volume of medical examinations lessened; we were coming to the end of grading the eligible soldiers. I was becoming stale; I had been in areas where 'leave' was inappropriate, and I felt in need of a change or a rest. It was time to return to the UK. The summer of 1946 had been unpleasant, the river was still in spate, and this limited activities; it also caused a high humidity which was almost intolerable.

I have not mentioned the Moslem festival of Ramadan; this played an important part in the life of Sudanese troops. Ramadan occurred during the ninth month of the Moslem calender, and was comparable to Lent. During Ramadan there was fasting during daylight hours, and alcohol and sexual activity forbidden. Prayer played an important part of the festival, Moslems prayed in mosques, in groups, and as individuals. Most Sudanese were practising Moslems though I did come across one or two who said they were Catholic. My ambulance driver was a devout Moslem, and often I waited patiently while he knelt and prayed before getting behind the wheel. To interrupt was unthinkable; we respected their religion, and never criticized. It can easily be understood that to exist in a hot climate between sunrise and sunset without food or drink made heavy demands on health, morale, and well-being. Some troops had to drop out from exhaustion, some became depressed, and British officers understood this and adapted to the situation. There was general relief when Ramadan was over, and it took a little time before a normal pattern was resumed.

My great day eventually arrived and at the end of August 1946 I was instructed to return to the UK for demobilization. I could hardly believe it was true. I wrote to Barbara at once, and addressed the air mail letter in red ink as arranged beforehand so that she would know at a glance I was on my way home. Although it was possible to travel some of the way home by air, it was standard to travel by land and sea. I had not enjoyed my flights and I elected to travel overland with the prospect of a Mediterranean cruise as well!

On the morning of departure the entire staff of the Base Hospital came to Khartoum Railway Station to see me off, and a large number of Sudanese as well. The platform was thronged with people. I was presented with a beautifully made jewel box with a typical Sudanese design externally. Although elated to be returning home to Barbara and the continuation of my medical career I was sorry to be leaving friends, and the mystique of the Sudan. I had found the Sudanese to be excellent soldiers, loyal and trustworthy, and I liked and admired them. It has always been my wish to return but so far I have not been able to do so and it is rather late in my life for a holiday there now.

There is a legend that once you have seen the Blue Nile, you always go back. Perhaps I shall manage it. I enjoyed the journey back to the base depot in Cairo, and felt a sense of peace and freedom such as I had not known for many a day. With the Nile in spate, the river journey was quicker and I was in Aswan sooner than I expected.

I had one spare day in Cairo, so I went into the city to see Shepperds Hotel, and I also spent a pleasant afternoon at Gezira where there was a sports club. Cairo was an impressive place with wide streets and numerous mosques with fascinating architecture. Desperate poverty and unseemly wealth, co-existed. These were the days of King Farouk of Egypt who loved life and self-indulgency. I saw him once in an open car in the centre of Cairo.

I left Cairo for Alexandria by train next day, a journey of several hours. It was a miserable trip. All the stations were crowded with impoverished Egyptians. Ismalia was particularly unpleasant. Dirt, sand and flies prevailed, and there were extraordinary stenches. Many adult eyes were severely damaged, and showed corneal scarring, scleritis, and trachoma. Many people were blind or nearly so. I was left with a poor impression of Egypt. I wonder whether, nearly fifty years later, the ocular situation in Egypt has improved with modern chemotherapy. There was a mammoth task ahead for Egyptian doctors.

When I arrived in Alexandria I was driven to a large, tented, demobilization transit camp. To my surprise I met John Little there.

I thought he would have arrived home because he started his journey before me. However he developed jaundice and was admitted to hospital with infective hepatitis, (as the illness was known then). Happily the attack was mild but it set him back by three weeks. He accompanied me to the UK. There was a jovial and relaxed atmosphere about this camp, and no wonder!

In the morning we were wakened by Wakey! Wakey! The bad news, though, was that we were not travelling home on luxury liners, but on a liberty ship, as far as Toulon; from there across France to Calais, and so back to the UK. Liberty ships were built in sections in the USA, ferried across, and bolted together. This was part of the lend-lease package arranged by President Roosevelt: these ships were very much smaller than a cross-Channel ferry.

We embarked after twenty-four hours in the Transit Camp; the vessel, as feared, was basic, with a lack of comfort that bode ill for the journey, especially if the sea was rough. Everything was bare metal, and the metal floor had recently been painted with a red oxide paint. It stained our boots, our clothes and our hands. Meals were at trestle tables. I doubt whether there were more than a hundred people aboard.

Despite the rough accommodation we were in good spirits as we slowly sailed into the sunset. Egypt was receding into the distance; there was the smell of the sea, and the excitement of new horizons ahead.

Even though the sea was calm there was a peculiar motion about the ship which was uncomfortable; no one was sick, but I suffered a dull frontal headache. Leaning over the ship's rail, only a few yards from the water-line, and peering into the blue sea, fish of all kinds could be seen. Some were several feet long with fins, like small sharks. After three days we were informed that the ventilation system in the engine room had broken down and there was mutiny down below. A medical officer went down to assess the situation. He reappeared, red-faced and gasping for air and said the temperature was 140°F. However the crew were prepared to take the vessel to Malta (out of our way) for repairs. We steamed slowly into Valetta Harbour, berthed, and hoped for the best. It was a wonderful harbour with very attractive fishing boats, not unlike the gondolas of Venice. We were not allowed ashore. Malta had suffered the ravages of air-attack over a long period of time, and severe damage could be seen from the boat. The island was presented with the George Cross by King George VI for its heroism during the war.

We were nearly twelve hours in Malta; whether repairs were carried out I know not, but we put to sea. We were never provided with any information, and the attitude suggested indifference. As soon as we were out of the harbour a large sail-chute was constructed to conduct air down the ventilator to the engine-room, and it appeared to satisfy the engine-room staff. We steamed on and after a journey of seven days we reached Toulon, a French naval port, and another splendid harbour.

Army trucks conveyed us to a large transit camp at least ten miles inland. Regulations were minimal and we had forty-eight hours to fill in before crossing France. It had taken fourteen days to travel from Alexandria to Toulon. Three of us decided to stretch our legs. We did not know where we were then, but subsequently I learned we were near Hyeres. After walking a short distance along a narrow country road, an aged bus overtook us and stopped. Did we want to go to Le Lavandou? Yes, but we had no French money so the driver gave us return tickets 'on the house'. He said Le Lavandou was 'très bon'; after a ride of half an hour or so we arrived. It was a lovely sea-side resort, quite a deep bay, with sand and shingle beaches. The water was inviting; it was 12 October 1946, but we bathed and it was one of the best bathes I ever experienced. The sea was still warm and we had the beach to ourselves. To the east of the bay was a small port, and the town was in that area as well. The place was shabby and had been occupied by the German military. I thought I would like to come back again.

I returned to Le Lavandou in 1975 and again in 1981. There was a surprise waiting for me. Certainly the shape of the bay was unchanged, and the small port recognizable, but to the west of the bay a large marina complex had been built. There were boats, yachts, and vessels of all sizes and expense. Chandlers, yachts, boats, bars and souvenir shops were plentiful. Tall modern buildings surrounded the bay alongside a promenade. The beach was packed; sail boards darted hither and thither, and the town centre had been rebuilt.

Topless women lay brazenly on the sand. It was indeed La Belle France. I immersed my ageing bones in the warm sea and thought how good it was to be alive.

Next day, the 13 October 1946 we were on our way across

France, a journey of seven hundred miles, and it took the best part of two and a half days. The rolling stock was old, worn down by the war and neglect, the seats wooden and comfortless. We had been issued individually with a food pack for the journey; occasionally we stopped to relieve ourselves on the track; there were long delays, and it became colder as we slowly travelled north. At last we reached Calais, but like other French Channel ports it had suffered the ravage of war, with most of the town centre destroyed. The French are excellent at manufacturing and erecting exact replicas of buildings that were destroyed, and this certainly applied to Calais. It is now an imposing, clean, and attractive port.

We were back in battle dress and berets and it felt strange; the transit camp supplied tea and food and we were soon on our way across the Channel in small ferries. There was general excitement; we were nearly home and the white cliffs of Dover welcomed us. It was late afternoon, early autumn in Britain; as we were nearing Dover a large merchant ship moving at a good speed seemed to be bearing down upon us; I do not know the rules of the sea, but it was clear no one intended to give way. Sirens and hooters were ignored, and we gripped the rails ready for the disaster which seemed certain. At the last minute our skipper took avoiding action and the two vessels missed each other by a few feet. It was a nasty moment, and the incident inexcusable.

From Dover we travelled by train to a demobilization centre where we spent the night. The place was geared up for its task and in no time we were handing in certain documents, and were issued with travel warrants and application forms for food and clothing coupons. I was not familiar with the south-east of England but I think this demobilization centre was near Guildford. Next morning we were to visit a clothing centre and select a demob suit. It was dark when I found a telephone kiosk and phoned my home in Devonshire. My father answered.

He was pleased I was safely back. I remarked how impressed I was to see the green fields of Kent, the trees and the orderly way of life, all so different from the desert. He warned me that the country had changed, and I must not expect too much. It would take many years to recover from the war and there were political changes to aggravate the recovery. I said I would come to Devon with Barbara as soon as I could. I was faintly

145

depressed. He was always the pessimist, but I was an optimist.

Next morning we went to a large warehouse packed with suits and sports jackets. There was little time, everybody was in a hurry to get away, and no clothes were tried out to see if they fitted. I chose a grey suit with a white pin-stripe, and it lasted many years.

A truck conveyed us to a station and soon we reached Waterloo. Everybody, troops and civilians, dispersed quickly in all directions. I was a little bewildered as I looked about the station; I was alive, I was demobbed, a free man, and once again, on my own. I had been away two years and nine months and it had seemed a life time, but the war was over. A loud-speaker voice above a platform brought me to my senses.

I knew where I was going. My wife would be waiting for me at Arbroath. A new life and a new chapter lay ahead. It was 16 October 1946.

5

Post-Demobilization Days

When Barbara received my air-mail letter addressed in red ink, a red letter day, informing her I was on my way home she resigned from her post at Arbroath Infirmary, and went home. The two years nine months had been a long weary wait for her. Initially many weeks passed without news from me; it was two months before my first letter arrived informing her I was in the Middle East and I knew only too well the frustration I felt myself as it was six weeks before I received her first letter. Every move to another unit added to the delay before her mail reached its destination.

As it had not been possible to receive mail during my journey home, I was unsure of Barbara's whereabouts, though I assumed she would be in Huntly. I decided to send a telegram notifying the arrival time at Arbroath the next morning.

It was strange travelling on the Underground again; however I reached King's Cross Station, and discovered the night train still left at seven thirty pm, reaching Arbroath about seven thirty am the next morning. I left the station and found a post office close by from where I sent a telegram on its way to Huntly.

Telegrams have fallen from fashion now that so many houses have telephones; every post office had a container for telegram forms which cost 1s. for twelve words, and the words were carefully counted by the counter-staff. A telegram used to take one or two hours to reach the addressee, and it was delivered by a telegram boy wearing a special cap to distinguish him from the postman. He waited whilst it was opened and always asked if there was a reply.

The night train did not leave King's Cross for over six hours;

147

I was weary as it had been a long and tiring journey back to the UK of over four weeks. I did not relish walking the streets so I went to a picture-house where it was warm; by the time I had seen the film through, and enjoyed a restaurant meal, it was time to retrace my steps to King's Cross.

The night journey passed very quickly. I was asleep in a first-class compartment before the train left the station, and I woke in Waverley Station, Edinburgh! As the train passed through the familiar scenery, and across the Forth Rail Bridge there was mounting excitement. I could not believe our separation was nearly over. Soon the train crossed the Tay Bridge and came to a stop in Dundee Station; half an hour later Elliot came into view, and soon I could see Arbroath Infirmary standing out overlooking the sea. At last the train arrived at the station. The platforms were quiet at such an early hour, but there waiting for me was my beloved wife, just as I pictured. We swore we would never be apart again, and with the exception of a few days now and again we have never been separated since that home-coming.

There was so much to talk about, and plans to formulate. Next day we travelled to Aberdeenshire, back to the peaceful hills. Here there was plenty of activity. Barbara's sister, who had been a QA, had recently returned from India, where she met her husband. Her first baby, a boy, was just a few weeks old.

After a few days we moved south again, by train, en route for Devonshire. Barbara had never travelled south of the border and it was a new experience for her. How different the journey was; the black-out was over, and stations, roads and bridges were ablaze with lights. We travelled by night, and spent most of next day in London seeing some of the sights, and in the late evening reached my parents home. This was the first opportunity there had been to introduce Barbara, and no doubt an unnerving experience for her. She need not have worried, for they were very pleased to see her.

A leisurely time followed. We spent a day in Torquay and walked for miles. My father owned a 1935 Morris 8 Saloon, and I drove it to Sidmouth, Seaton and Budleigh Salterton. Although this car was twelve years old and had covered over 60,000 miles, the exhaust system was the original, a testimony to the solid construction of vehicles then. It cost £145 brand new, and £10 less if the model had a fixed roof.

It was such a pleasant late autumn that my parents decided to accompany us to Swanage, and we spent a week in the Grovenor Hotel, a landmark, overlooking the beautiful deep bay. There are many things to see and do at Swanage. The Great Globe and Tilly Whim Caves at Durlston are unusual and interesting. There is a fine walk from Swanage to Studland over Ballard Down, and further west another memorable walk from Lulworth Cove to Durdle Door. A trip to Bournemouth via Sandbanks Ferry was another splendid outing.

When we returned to Devon, Barbara and I decided to spend a long weekend in London ourselves: we stayed at the Kenilworth Hotel, climbed the Monument, and saw the numerous attractions for tourists. Madame Tussaud's gallery was fascinating; some wax models were dressed as attendants, and it was amusing to see visitors talking to them and asking questions!

Christmas was approaching; it was the second Christmas since the cessation of hostilities, and buildings in Oxford Street were decorated with coloured lights; Christmas trees were set up at railway stations and outside the larger stores. My parents suggested we spend Christmas with them. As soon as the New Year was in, it would be time to decide and plan the future.

Service personnel received full pay for ninety days after their official demobilization date; holding the rank of Lieutenant-Colonel I had built up a pleasing sum of savings in a bank in Arbroath. I had little opportunity to spend money overseas, in fact I never carried any money on my person; there was a free issue of fifty cigarettes weekly, and my expenses for mess bills with the SDF unit, and Pink Palace had been low. Also Barbara had been self-supportive, and had never had occasion to draw a penny from the account; thus, by the end of the ninety days when the army pay ceased, there were just over £2,000 in the bank. In 1947 with near zero inflation, that was a useful sum and would have to go far.

There are times when decisions have to be taken which influence and change your future. When recently qualified I was interested in taking up obstetrics and gynaecology, but this idea was thwarted by the Central Medical War Committee. As time passed, my experiences at Arbroath Infirmary, and latterly in the Forces, led me to consider a broader medical life, and that general practice was probably my goal. The future of medicine was in the melting pot, and it was a near certainty that the NHS would be implemented despite the massive opposition from the medical profession and their leaders. Hospitals would be nationalized, and inevitably bureaucracy would interfere with patient care. I had experienced bureaucracy in the forces and the thought of a similar situation occurring in hospitals did not appeal to me. I was rather used to working on my own and making my own decisions, and I thought I could give my best to patients untrammelled and unmolested by others. Moreover, Barbara was now pregnant and a baby expected at the end of August. I had just turned twenty-eight years. It was time to find a practice and a home.

I have no idea how many medical officers ex Forces felt the need for some refresher work before embarking on their careers. There were those, of course, who felt they would have to return to general practice forthwith to lighten the load of their senior, and frequently elderly partners, who had held the reins for five war years, often solo. Many elderly partners demanded that their former partners return at once, enabling them to retire. There would be many budding ex-forces enthusiasts wishing to specialize in various branches of medicine, and it would, of course, have been mandatory for them to have taken an appropriate hospital post, and slowly ascend the ladder to consultancy.

Now that I had taken the decision to enter general practice, I realized that I needed a refresher experience first; there are, after all, other conditions than malaria, Gonorrhoea, fistula-in-ano, leprosy, measles and helminth infection which had occupied me for the past two and three quarter years. I had experienced a most valuable house appointment in 1943, ideal for a future GP, and I doubted whether I could do better than repeat the experience in Arbroath Infirmary. I knew that the appointment would be from 1 February to 31 July so I put in an application forthwith.

Matron was still there, but an administrator had been appointed to lighten her load, and conduct future management. He wrote back stating that there had been many applicants, but mine had been added to the list. I was to phone him on a certain date to learn the result. Mrs Crockatt, with her usual generosity asked Barbara to live with her for the six months appointment if I was accepted.

Whether Matron had any say in the matter I shall never know, but when the hospital governors had held their deliberations I phoned to find that I had been appointed.

Barbara and I considered we had been most fortunate to be accepted for the post, and to be in the same town among good friends so that we could see each other in my off-duty. Two medical officers had been appointed to the Infirmary, so there would be less pressure than previously.

We were back to Aberdeenshire by now, and the last two weeks before work commenced on 1 February, passed very quickly. I had at last shed my army uniform and bought civilian clothes, and the demobilization suit turned out to be a successful choice. The ninety days were up and I really was a civilian again. I missed my army beret most, it kept my head warm; it was now unfashionable for men to wear hats, and in any event, I did not wish to use up valuable clothes coupons for a hat.

On 1 February Barbara and I arrived in Arbroath again. Mrs Crockatt met us at the station and we went to her house. I left Barbara there and made my way to the Infirmary.

It felt strange to be back after four years to the day since arriving on that dark winter night in 1943. Many of the nursing staff were still there and it was pleasant to see them again.

Matron was the same as ever, bustling here and there. After the spacious desert and scrub-land, the infirmary appeared small and compact. The second house-surgeon had already arrived; he was recently qualified and I remember he was engaged to be married. I made my way to the residency and to my old bedroom.

There had been staff changes. Dr 'A', the leading practitioner had retired and his place taken by a young practitioner. He was keen on motor cars, and sadly both he and his wife lost their lives in a car accident a few years ago. Dr 'B' had taken on two partners, one was the doctor/chemist who took my place when I completed my first spell there in 1943.

The Doctor 'C', whose spectacles dropped into the abdominal cavity during an operation, had been joined by his son and daughter; the elderly doctor had retired.

The consultants were the same, but in addition there was now a lady anaesthetist who came from Dundee for the consultants operating sessions. Pentothal sodium had replaced Evipan sodium as an intravenous anaesthetic. She used this for induction and then went straight over to the Boyles Machine using gas, oxygen and ether. Trilene had arrived but was mainly used in obstetrics.

I became involved very quickly and knew the ropes. I found the assistance of the other medical officer most valuable, and he was able to fill in some gaps for me; the rhesus factor was one! It was surprising how quickly drugs, doses, and diagnoses came back to memory; also what I found so valuable was the time available to browse in the clinical laboratory room with microscope, blood smears and urine beakers. Instead of giving the anaesthetics I was now assisting the surgeons and gynaecologist at operations and I enjoyed this. When off-duty I was able to walk down the road, collect Barbara, and we would go into the town for a cup of tea. Mrs Crockatt provided superb fish teas; the local fishing fleet sailed daily and fish was absolutely fresh. I have never tasted better.

Winter 1947 was one of the hardest for many many years; it did not start until early February, and when it came it lasted for two months. Deep snow with heavy drifting blocked many roads for weeks on end. Snow was piled up at the sides of the roads, and I remember an afternoon trip to Friockheim when the snow was many feet above the height of the car; it was like driving through a tunnel. I was lucky to be in the warm centrally-heated infirmary for my first winter home after the tropics. Mrs Crockatt kept good fires and Barbara kept warm as well.

The months passed swiftly. Barbara's pregnancy proceeded normally and her health was excellent.

Treatment had changed just a little whilst I was away. Sulphadimidine had been added to the antibiotic scene. Diuretics included tabs salygran, and mersalyl by injection; they were mercurials and better than nothing. Radical mastectomy was still performed. The infirmary remained full, and the routine lists of hernia repairs, Varicose veins, colporrhaphies continued. Anticoagulants, penicillin and steroid therapy had not arrived for general use.

There was an improvement in the 'giving sets' for intravenous fluid therapy, and I assumed these were used in the Normandy Landings in 1944; they had not reached Khartoum.

The six months drew to a close. Again I was very grateful to Arbroath Infirmary for the assistance and encouragement I had received. I felt able to enter general practice and reasonably confident that I would be able to cope and not make mistakes. It is experience and care that make a safe doctor and this is just as true today as it was nearly fifty years ago. Yes, I was sorry to leave, but time was marching on; Barbara was due within a month, and I knew it was not going to be easy to find a niche in general practice. I did not possess medical relatives in the country; my uncle had emigrated to Canada and died abruptly at Toronto shortly after arrival. His son, my cousin, who also qualified in Edinburgh, had left the UK for Canada too. We said farewell to Arbroath and Mrs Crockatt, and I left Barbara at her home in Aberdeenshire. The baby was to be born in the Huntly Hospital; she was having ante natal care, and was among many good people who would drive her to the hospital when she started labour.

I was now free to travel about and try to get started off in a practice.

The British Medical Journal was the weekly magazine used by doctors who were advertising for assistants, assistants with a view to partnership, or for the sale of their practices. Prior to the NHS, practices were bought and sold, and a prospective partner bought a share in the practice. The cost was the share offered by the practice, of the average gross receipts over the preceding three years. Thus, if the average gross receipts for three years was £8,000 (and few practices exceeded such a high figure), and you were offered a quarter share in the practice, it would cost £2,000: this was paid to the practice, and split between the remaining partners pro-rata. In a partnership of three, if you wished to increase your share from one quarter to one third, by mutual agreement, this would cost one twelfth of £8,000. A retiring partner would be bought out by the remaining partners.

During the first two or three years after the war ended, the lists of practice vacancies, practices required, assistants, and assistants with view to partnership, advertised in the British Medical Journal, were very long indeed. There was a great deal of movement among doctors as they left the forces, completed house appointments, and sought practice vacancies. The British Medical Journal used to be posted on a Friday evening, from London and in many places arrived by first or second post on Saturday. If you lived in a rural area, a little off the beaten track, you were more likely to receive the BMJ on Monday morning.

It used to arrive, tightly rolled, and wrapped its full length in a beige wrapper. To open it, one merely pulled a tear-off strip, so much better than the plastic, transparent envelope used today which allows the contents on the outer cover to be seen by all and sundry.

If you received the BMJ on Saturday, there was time over the weekend to scrutinize the lists, make your choices, enclose copies of your curriculum vitae, and write a letter of application addressed always to a box number. There used to be a postal collection on Sundays at six pm allowing the application to be at the box number by first post on Monday, and reaching the advertiser on Tuesday morning. But if your BMJ did not arrive until Monday morning there was no hope of the advertiser receiving your application before Wednesday morning. Under normal circumstances the advertiser might have waited a week to collect all his replies to his advertisement, but at this time most advertisements attracted over two hundred replies!, and one hundred and fifty or so would arrive at the advertisers surgery on Tuesday morning! Quite clearly he would have made his selection and arranged interviews by Tuesday evening. Any late arrivals would be severely handicapped. Usually the week after the advertisement appeared in the BMJ you would see: 'Box No so and so thanks the two hundred applicants for their replies, and the post is now filled.' Sometimes your letter (apart from the above) was never acknowledged, and your CV never returned. We always thought it was very bad manners and inexcusable, though I did understand the doctors dilemma, surrounded with two hundred letters of application.

Living in Devon, I was at a disadvantage in receiving the BMJ on Monday morning. Some hardy folk travelled to London by train to collect the BMJ on a Saturday to overcome this problem, but I lived too far out, and the expense would have been unjustifiable.

However, despite the problem, and over a couple of weeks, I received replies from a practice in Weston-Super-Mare, Dorchester, and St Ives, in Cambridgeshire, inviting me for interview; all these practices were advertising for an assistant with a view to partnership; the salary was between £850 and £1,000 per annum. I went to Weston-Super-Mare first. It was over seventy miles away, and involved a bus and train journey. The practice was in a salubrious part of Weston-Super-Mare;

it was a sunny day, and the town was clean and bright; post war visitors were in abundance, and demob suits recognizable! Because it lay on the estuary of the River Severn, the sea disappeared from view when the tide was out. I thought this was unattractive compared with the shelving beaches of Dorset and Devon. There were three doctors in the practice, all partners, and no doubt with differing shares. The interview was conducted in the senior partner's house. They were eventually wanting a fourth partner after an assistantship of undetermined length.

The senior partner would be about forty-five years, the others, high, or mid thirties. All were married and I was introduced to their wives. I was so surprised to find the three doctors indigenous, but their wives foreign; one came from France. We had a pleasant lunch in the practice house dining room. Everyone was very lively and the place rocked with laughter as stories unfolded.

I was shown the senior partner's surgery and waiting room. Tools of the trade were in abundance; I noticed a diathermy machine and a frizzling needle hanging from a hook. He saw me looking at it, and he said he dabbled in skins. I was impressed. I was asked if I was married, and he seemed satisfied that I was; I said a baby was nearly full term and this intrigued the foreign wives. Had I taken care to join a Medical Defence Union? Yes I had. A major drawback was the lack of suitable accommodation in the town, but they thought time would solve the problem. There was very little private building for a long time after the war.

I was offered the post, the salary at the current rate, and asked to consider the proposition and let them know soon.

In those days list size was unknown. A firm would have a certain number 'on the panel', but the bulk of their patients would be private until 5 June, 1948 when the NHS was scheduled to commence.

As I returned home it was difficult to know what to think or decide. No doubt many, especially if they possessed a little financial capital, would have jumped at the opportunity. Perhaps I was too discerning. I was concerned about the difference in age between the younger partners and myself. I did not want to be a practice slave. The partners seemed so prosperous, even at this difficult post-war time, that fairly big money would be required to buy a share in the partnership, (if offered). There was a house to buy, build, or rent in the future and I would require a motor car.

My parents would have liked me to accept the post; having been so far off since my student days they would have preferred me to be closer now. However, during the night I concluded that it was an excellent offer for an applicant with capital. To acquire a bank loan with interest at 3.5 per cent was entirely out of my situation; also, there had to be real security. It is so different now.

Rightly or wrongly I made my own decision and rejected the offer. Events proved my decision was probably correct. In a few days I was on the way to Dorchester, a pleasant county capital midst lovely scenery. The practice was close to the main street of the town, at the top of the hill. It was a single-handed practice, the owner was elderly and thin; he did not look well, and I wondered if he was able to manage the practice.

I knew I would have everything to do, but the practice would have been mine in the near future if I could have raised sufficient money to buy him out, should he wish to retire, or even die. The house was dingy. It was not easy to borrow money in those days, and I was unable to afford to be taken on. With regret I rejected the offer.

On to St Ives in Cambridgeshire. It was a long journey for the day, but I managed there and back; the travel across London to another main station used up valuable time.

I found that St Ives was another pleasant market town but I did not like the look of the practice. I wondered why an assistant was required. The doctor said there was good horse-riding in the area and I would enjoy a gallop before breakfast. I was unimpressed. Apart from having to buy a house, and a share in a possible partnership, I did not want to buy a horse, and maintain it. There was nothing about the practice which had any appeal, so I returned home having wasted a day, and the cost of the train fare. If this was the standard of general practice, what could the bad ones be like? No doubt the good offers had already been snapped up.

Next day a telegram arrived to inform me Barbara had been admitted to the Huntly Hospital overnight. I left immediately for Huntly, having planned previously not to arrange any interviews over the next fortnight. When I arrived I was greeted with the news that we had a son and that all was well. We were delighted.

These were the days when mothers spent a full fortnight in a maternity hospital, resting, and learning the skills of breast-feeding and the correct management of infants. Husbands were not allowed to attend the delivery, and could only visit at recognized hours.

After the severe winter of 1947, there was a glorious summer and autumn. When I arrived in Huntly on 25 August 1947 the harvest was in full swing, and the air resounded with noise from small Fordson tractors.

Occasionally the curlew could be heard. It is unusual now for harvest to be so early in that part of Scotland; cutting is rare before the end of September, and has even been later in recent years with the wet summers experienced. It was all hands to get the harvest in, and on this account I cycled to the hospital every day. I would not like to do it now with traffic hurtling past me on the main road, but in 1947 it was peaceful and safe. Barbara was very well, the baby just what we had wished all along, and we spent much time choosing names.

I stayed another few days in Huntly after Barbara returned home with the baby. I was back where I had started; there was no job to consider, and nothing in the pipe-line. The only option was to try again. The BMJ was waiting for me when I reached home, a little weary from so much travel. I applied for several more vacancies addressed to the box numbers in the BMJ as directed. A few days later, I received a telephone call from a doctor in a practice in Alford, Lincolnshire, wishing to interview me. A day was suggested and I said I would be there. When I looked at the map it was a long journey again. To London, to King's Cross, to Peterborough and change, and thus eventually to Alford. There is no doubt the south-west of England is remote from the rest of the country. The motor car and motorways have helped, but even now it is tedious travelling west to east and vice-versa.

Alford was a small market town situated between Louth and the coast. Skegness was about ten miles off, and there was a pleasant sea side resort, Mablethorpe, half a dozen miles away. The countryside was as flat as a pancake; the names of many of the towns and villages ended in letters BY.

There was a small cottage hospital, one or two hotels and an attractive church. The shops would cater for every day requirements. It was a single-handed practice, and had ramifications in the surrounding countryside, and as far as the coast. Most of the patients were elderly. The doctor himself was probably six or seven years older than myself. He was married. He had a pleasant house and a delightful walled-garden. He offered me a job 'on the spot'. I accepted on the spot. He wanted me to start work the following week and I agreed. I was desperate. I sent a telegram to my father informing him I had accepted the post, and made my way back to London. That night at seven thirty pm I was on the train to Aberdeen — Huntly.

My life as a GP was about to begin. It was almost October 1947. It began in Alford, but it did not finish there.

However that is yet another story and another chapter.

6

GP Days

As I travelled through the night to Huntly there was time to ponder the events of the day. Naturally I was pleased and relieved to have found an assistantship in a pleasant rural area, and an opportunity to start work in general practice. I had reached the conclusion that it was going to be difficult to find a suitable post in south-west England due to the popularity of the area, and also, it seemed probable that vacancies there were not advertised in the British Medical Journal, but were filled through consultants recommending certain house-doctors, working in local hospitals, to the GPs in the area whom they knew personally. I thought it was unlikely that this new job would be long-lasting; I was uncertain whether a rural practice would suit me, but time would tell. An important factor was the increased scope now available to find another post later on, because of the greater population in the north. It would be easier, too, to travel the shorter distances to large centres for interviews. I regarded the new job as a stepping-stone; and it would allow further time for Barbara, myself and the baby to adjust to a new life.

There was plenty to do in Huntly, and less than a week in which to do it. We decided to pack our wedding gifts which were stored at Barbara's house, and take them to Alford in a trunk; there would be many items which would be invaluable when we found a corner of our own. The immediate arrangement was for us to stay in the doctor's house.

On the appointed evening we left Huntly by train for Peterborough, travelling overnight: from there it was a change to a branch-line for Skegness, the train stopping at Alford en route. The baby was nearly six weeks old; there was our luggage, and the equipment required for a small baby on an overnight journey.

It was not an easy journey and we reached Peterborough shortly after six am, the baby's feeding time. The rest of the journey was slow and the train stopped at every station. I noticed again the flat terrain, the numerous farms, attractive villages, and the tidy well maintained acres, recently harvested.

We reached Alford about ten am, and were driven to the doctor's house in his car. The doctor and his wife were very kind to us; they had two small children of their own. It was a splendid old house with a large walled garden; fine specimens of apples and pears hung luxuriantly from sturdy mature trees.

During our stay with the doctor and his wife we were treated as members of the family. We occupied a bedroom and used the lounge. It must always be difficult with a baby of such tender weeks in another person's house; babies have to be fed and attended as well, and they are not renowned for patience. Our baby was, however, well behaved, and I cannot recall that he caused the household any particular stress, night or day. We were lucky.

The doctor's wife's parents did not live very far away; once they came over and stayed for a weekend. Her father was a surgeon and drove a sedate, upright, dark saloon car. On one occasion he operated in the local hospital in an emergency. After we had settled in, the doctor gave me a more detailed outline of the practice. It was not very large. He had patients in the town, and there was quite a large rural component. There were patients at Hogsthorpe, and Chapel-St-Leonards; the roads were winding and travel was slow. Three hundred yards up the road was a small cottage hospital which could cater for up to twenty patients. Another firm of two doctors were established in the town and I gathered the opposition was considerable. I thought it was remarkable that four doctors, in their prime, were necessary to attend to the medical requirements of the local population!

The surgery and waiting room were spacious; I noted the usual row of Winchester bottles awaiting their one to three dilution in a separate area off the surgery. There was an examination couch, a writing table with NHI forms, and adequate seating for doctor, patient, and chaperone. A secretary-dispenser appeared for the surgery sessions.

Two purchases were necessary, and quickly; first, a pram for the baby, second, transport for myself.

There were two types of pram on offer all those years ago; for the infant and small baby, there was the large pram with four big wheels, and a roomy compartment for the baby, on a cantilever suspension. A folding hood, and a rainproof cover for the top of the pram kept the baby snug and warm; for an older child there was a smaller, shallower, compartment on four small wheels, and the pram could fold. The modern unsprung, buggy pram used for an older child was not known. They seem popular, but an objection is that the occupant faces the elements, with its back to the mother. We were able to buy a brand new pram in Alford without difficulty; it was well made and served us well.

It was much more difficult to purchase a car. The production of cars in Britain ceased at the onset of war in 1939, and munitions were produced instead; foreign cars were a rare sight, in fact we scorned them, because in those days Britain led the world in car design and car mechanics. Thus in 1947 every car on the road was at least eight years old, probably poorly serviced, and badly repaired, due to scarcity of parts. Most tyres were remoulds and they were scarce too. People held on to their old cars because they could not be replaced; it was 1948 before new cars started to trickle into the garages. There was a great shortage of used models for sale, especially reliable ones.

When I went to the leading garage in Alford there was a choice of two cars, and nothing else. The garage owner was a most pleasant man, and was determined to help. I suggested there might be a bigger choice in a larger town such as Louth or Skegness. He doubted my idea, but said he would ring round his colleagues in the trade.

The two cars he had on offer were a 1938 Morris 8 Saloon with over 60,000 miles on the clock, and a 1939 Flying Standard which used to be a farmer's car. Both cars were showing signs of terminal rust. The Morris was small, and with the carry-cot on the back seat, left no place for luggage except on a folding rack at the rear of the car. It was similar to my father's car, but though three years younger than his, was in a far worse state. The Flying Standard had four doors and was roomy; there was no boot, but there was room for some luggage. Both cars were priced under £100 but that was a large sum in those days; the Morris 8 cost £130 brand new in 1938!

As I feared, the local garage owner had been unable to find other cars for sale elsewhere. The situation was urgent so I bought the Flying Standard, my first car. It was black and had a gleaming chrome radiator. The upholstery was leather; even so I thought I had bought a pig in a poke. Nevertheless, it was my first car, and I was pleased and proud to be the owner. The front seats were very comfortable, and the instrument fascia was well-equipped with an ammeter gauge, an oil pressure gauge, a spring-mechanized clock, speedometer, odometer, and trip. To start the car, apart from turning the ignition key, a button on the fascia required a press. The car had semaphore trafficators between the front and rear doors. These were intended to stick out at a right-angle, and illuminate as well as self-cancel. Ill-disciplined children enjoyed snapping them off necessitating an expensive replacement.

I had already equipped myself with a bell-stethoscope, sphygmomanometer, and a battery-operated, interchangeable, auriscope and ophthalmoscope, and was ready for work. The principal had decided that I should undertake the morning surgery, and also an afternoon surgery at Hogsthorpe, a branch premises consisting of a room rented for the purpose with a small waiting-room area. He would manage the afternoon and evening surgeries at his home.

It did not take long to appreciate that the practice work was light compared with the two assistantships I held in Arbroath in 1943. All new calls were taken by the principal, and I was left with follow-up patients, chronic sick, and the elderly.

He regarded the hospital as his prerogative, and I crossed the threshold on one occasion only when he was unavailable. The bulk of my work was on the Lincolnshire coast north of Skegness to Chapel-St-Leonard, and occasionally to Mablethorpe, a sparsely populated area, and isolated.

However, keen and enthusiastic as ever, I was determined to do my best, though I was disappointed. I could not envisage the situation was likely to change for the better; the practice was unlikely to expand, even in the long term, due to an established opposition. I was the assistant, and not employed to tender advice. I had the impression he feared I might want to take over some of the patients he regarded as his, but nothing could have been further from my mind.

A few days after our arrival the principal said he had been offered an unfurnished flat for our use. The flat was over Lloyd's Bank and I was to contact the manager. Barbara and I went to see the flat and the manager showed us over the premises. The entrance was the side door of the bank used by the bank staff. A flight of wooden stairs led straight into the landing of the flat which embraced a lounge, bedroom, bathroom, and kitchen. There was a small Ideal coke boiler in the kitchen which would heat water, and warm the kitchen. The accommodation was satisfactory for us, and had a view from the lounge window overlooking the market square. It was bare boards everywhere but it had been freshly painted internally, and had not been used as a flat previously. There was no door at the top of the stairs into the flat, ensuring a blast of cold air penetrated the flat every time the side entrance door to the bank was opened. This outer door was also a poor fit and allowed draughts. I pointed out this omission to the manager, and suggested a door was constructed at the top of the stairs into the flat. He would not agree to this reasonable request. However, we needed the flat and agreed the rent which was reasonable. It would take a few days to complete the formalities. We were very pleased to have our own little home, and to enjoy independency.

During my work I detected an ominous tapping noise from under the bonnet of my car, which to me, sounded like a worn 'little end'. I was not off the road, but obviously I soon would be: to save further damage to the engine, I returned to the garage. The garage confirmed the diagnosis of a worn 'little end', and this had to be repaired before the piston broke loose and wrecked the engine. The garage was excellent, and I think they must have worked through the night because the car was returned next day, rebored, with new pistons, and replacement of other worn parts. The cost was minimal. The engine was quiet and smooth and a pleasure to drive after this repair.

At the next opportunity we went to Skegness on a half-day and bought vital furniture for our lounge, bedroom, and kitchen, from a large furnishing house. After the war and for many years later, furniture was described as utility, and that is exactly what it was. The wood was un-named and unseasoned, the workmanship left much to be desired, but the cost was appropriate. Floor covering was a material called condolium.

It was sold in rolls. It had a resemblance to linoleum but it was so thin it could be cut with nail-scissors. It had a high gloss but it could crack easily as it was unrolled for laying. Carpet was not for us, the price outside our financial ability. It was a standard procedure after the war to lay condolium in a square over most of the floor, nail it down, and paint the wood surround with an appropriate wood-stain, and place a rug in front of the hearth. That was what we did. Barbara made curtains, and I was able to lay the condolium and stain the floors at the end of the day's work. When the furniture was delivered from Skegness the flat was very comfortable with a coal fire. Coal was not expensive, coke for the boiler was cheaper.

I contacted a joiner who made a sliding door at the entrance to the flat; it was a great success as we could lock the doors, prevent cold air gaining access, and we were safe from the danger of falling head first down the wooden stairs. When the bank manager saw it he was so impressed that the bank paid for the new door.

No upstairs flat is without objections; the baby's pram lived downstairs, and that of course involved the contents having to be carried up and down stairs whenever the baby went out. Coal and coke had to be carried upstairs. I was always amazed at the plumbing from the coke-boiler; hot water rises, and in so doing creates a circulation through the pipes to a hot storage cistern. This is the reason for the hot cistern being placed at a higher level than the boiler, and the higher the better. In our flat the hot cistern was a foot above floor level, and the in and out pipes from the boiler were horizontal. The result of this extraordinary situation was to produce loud clanking from the pipes as they overheated, instead of circulating the water through the cistern. However, the system worked in an inefficient manner, and it was very necessary that it should, as there were no immersion heaters at that time of our lives. The three of us were very comfortable and happy in the flat and it changed our lives for the better.

We developed a routine quickly. Because the flat was so central it was convenient for Barbara to shop, and as time passed the grocer and butcher were most helpful in producing items of food we had not seen for a long time. I was occupied during the morning with the surgery, making up medicines and counting tablets for patients seen at the surgery, and also preparing repeats to take to Hogsthorpe in the afternoon. After lunch Barbara and baby accompanied me to Hogsthorpe whilst I managed the surgery and did the rounds out there. Pre-war cars had no heating systems, and no screen-washer device; it was therefore very necessary to wear plenty of clothes, and use rugs. We even had a foot-warmer for Barbara which belonged to my mother. We did not feel the cold, and the baby thrived. There was a very kind-hearted old lady living in Chapel-St-Leonard who insisted we had a cup of tea after the rounds there, and this was very welcome.

One half-day we all went to the pleasant town of Louth, and had a look around. As we were driving back I was aware, suddenly, that the front wheels had developed 'wheel-wobble'. This is a frightening sensation, particularly for the driver. There is the impression that the front wheels are loose, the front of the car judders uncontrollably, and the steering wheel shakes and tries to turn against you. The only way to get out of this state is to stop; I did so and the rest of the journey was uneventful. I received such a scare that I went to the garage to be informed the wheel-wobble was due to excessive wear on the 'king-pins'. Modern cars are spared this phenomenon. The treatment involved renewal of the king-pins, and I was soon on the road again.

The weeks passed quickly, but I was unsettled. The area was a backwater and I was wanting to do more; I would have to try again and see if I could improve my position. I knew that I did not want to work in a large industrial town. Many are lured by the bright lights and the amenities of big cities; it was possible to acquire many patients in these areas with the likelihood of a high financial return. Nor did I wish to be so busy that it was a scram to get through a surgery without proper examination of patients. To become a casualty clearing station transferring patients to hospital willy nilly filled me with horror. Surely untrained people could manage to achieve that function.

What then did I want? Perhaps the impossible. I wanted to be a partner in a partnership of no more than three in total, and preferably in a town with a modest population between 20-30,000 inhabitants. If this area was near the coast that would be a bonus. If the town had a hospital with visiting consultants and GP access, that would be Utopia. I was prepared to carry on as at present until I found the goal.

These were the thoughts running through my mind over Christmas, over the dying year, and into the New Year of 1948. Five months away on 5 June the National Health Service was scheduled to start. Judged from the haste of the proposals presented to an unwilling profession (at that time), proposals not whole-heartedly endorsed by the profession's leaders, and proposals confused by the naivety of the Minister of Health, Mr Bevan, the future was going to be difficult for those already established in practice. For the unestablished, confusion and financial hardship lay ahead. The unfortunate public, already confused, were not given adequate information about the proposed changes, and were naturally anxious about the future. It was an extraordinary situation.

My future was slightly eased when the principal mentioned he was experiencing difficulty in paying me my salary, and he advised me to search for another post. Clearly he, too, was very worried about 5 June 1948. I fully understood his predicament and agreed with his suggestion that I look elsewhere. I was prepared to pack up forthwith to ease the burden, but he would not hear of it. His British Medical Journal arrived on the Saturday morning always. Mine arrived on Monday morning even though the BMA had been notified of my change of address to Alford! He agreed to loan me his copy over the weekends and this was a great help in the search for a practice-vacancy.

The pressure was on now to find another post quickly, and it seemed likely that my ambitions would not be realized. I would probably have to accept whatever was on offer to keep the wolf from the door. From the journal the medical manpower situation had not changed; there were still too many doctors chasing too few vacancies. I restarted answering advertisements in the BMJ. Two weeks later the situation was the same, no replies to my applications. One Saturday I noticed an advertisement on the inside back page of the BMJ worded: 'Partner required to replace retiring senior partner in a Partnership of three on NE Coast. Apply Box No ...'. This advertisement was in an unusual part of the BMJ, not included in the list of vacant partnerships. Perhaps it was a late entry. I decided to apply, thinking the practice would be in Newcastle, but I was prepared to consider everything.

Imagine my surprise when a few days later I received a letter from Dr C.R. Taylor stating he had received my letter of application, and I was first in the field. I had better come and see them soon. The name of the town was Bridlington. Having spent my childhood in the south of England, and my student days in Scotland, I had no idea where Bridlington was sited, nor did Barbara. I drove to the railway station, found the large map of Britain on the platform and discovered Bridlington was on the north-east coast between Scarborough and Kingston-upon-Hull. By now we were very interested indeed. I telephoned the doctor in Bridlington and an interview was arranged two days later at two pm. During the two day interval before the interview I discovered more about Bridlington. From the AA Handbook I learned that the population was approaching 30,000. Early closing day was Thursday, and there were several hotels, the Alexandra, the Expanse, the Brentwood and the Southcliffe, and numerous garages for the sale and service of most British car manufacturers; Ripley's Ford Garage, the Buchrose, Trenery and Gambles, Paragon Motors and Holtby and White in Carlisle Road. Another book mentioned that Bridlington possessed a fishing industry, some light industry, and was well-known as a seaside holiday resort for the West Riding. It was sheltered from the North East by Flamborough Head.

I decided to travel by train. I was first in the field and wanted to remain like that. I did not have sufficient confidence in my car to be certain of arriving in time, or even arriving there. I made an early start from Alford and reached the south bank ferry terminus at New Holland. After the ferry crossing to Kingston-upon-Hull there was a bus ride to the railway station. I thought Hull looked dejected, but it had suffered severe war damage which would require time and money to rectify. When I disembarked at Bridlington Railway Station I walked into Quay Road on the east side of the level crossing gates, and headed towards the town centre. I had a request not to mention Dr Taylor's name so I asked a passer-by if he would direct me to Horsforth Avenue; he did not know. I asked another and was informed it might be on the south side, and he walked on. I reached the top of Bridge Street, went into a shop and asked again. I was advised it was somewhere near the Spa Hall. Eventually I found it. I was more than a little astonished at the indifference shown to a polite question, and the unhelpful attitude shown. I assumed that their attitude was due to post-war malaise.

As I walked up Horsforth Avenue, clearly a residential area, I was surprised to see a garage, and coach garage on the east side of the road. I walked on and at the junction of Horsforth Avenue, Belgrave Road, and Roundhay Road stood a large red-bricked two storey house with a red tiled roof and woodwork painted green. The house was on a corner and faced north on to Horsforth Avenue, and east on to Roundhay Road. There was a plate on the gate naming Dr C.R. Taylor, M.D. It was an imposing house with a neat privet hedge surrounding a small front garden; there was a garage opening into Roundhay Road.

There was a quarter of an hour before the interview so I walked along Belgrave Road to South Marine Drive. Although it was a bleak early February day the view across the harbour to Sewerby and Flamborough Cliffs was pleasing. Looking southwards the expanse of clean sand washed daily by the sea was reminiscent of the Brittany coast-line. The quality of the houses impressed me; the good design and solid construction suggested high-grade local builder firms.

I retraced my steps to 63 Horsforth Avenue. As I approached the outer storm doors I noted a brass speaking tube screwed to a door pillar: these were in vogue prior to electric bells and were used by patients at night. The caller spoke into the mouth-piece and the voice was conducted by piping to a bedroom upstairs, enabling a dialogue twixt doctor and caller. I rang the bell. Mrs C.R. Taylor appeared and invited me in; Dr Taylor was waiting in the hall. He was shortish, squat, and had a florid complexion. He wore a black jacket and grey striped trousers, white shirt and stiff white collar. He was most pleasant and jovial as we moved to the lounge.

After some introductory conversation about the weather, my journey, and my present work Mrs Taylor withdrew and Dr Taylor described the history of the practice. He came to Bridlington in 1919, having served in the army in Mesopotamia, and bought 63 Horsforth Avenue. Surgery premises were added to the north wing in 1921. Dr Taylor said he had two partners. He was the senior partner, sixty-three years old, and was anxious to retire. He had intended to retire when he was sixty years, but at that time there was only one other partner, the war was barely over, and it was deemed inappropriate. Dr C.J. Gordon-Taylor was next senior; he came to the practice in 1923 from

Nuneaton and lived in Wellington House, a large Georgian-style house in Wellington Road overlooking the Cenotaph. He conducted surgeries there from integrated premises: he told me Dr Gordon-Taylor was a Roman Catholic, and did some emergency operating in the local hospital. Dr M.R. Linell was the most recent addition to the practice; he arrived in 1946, and had built a bungalow in Fortyfoot for himself, but used Wellington House as his surgery centre. He was in his early thirties.

The practice was mainly private, the NHI component very small indeed. He described it as a high class practice with high grade work expected by the patients. Six medical firms making a total of fifteen doctors attended to the near 30,000 population.

There was a cottage hospital called Lloyd which could care for about sixty-five patients when full. The general practitioners attended their patients within; consultants in surgery, medicine, and ENT, came over from Hull Royal Infirmary on a weekly basis. Another hospital, the Avenue, was for maternity patients, but the north wing, however, was a home for unmarried mothers with babies born in the Avenue maternity wards, awaiting adoption of their infants. Another small hospital in Bempton Lane admitted infectious diseases.

The new partner to replace him would be offered a quarter share based on the average receipts of the partnership over the preceding three years; he would be expected to purchase his house, but he, Dr Taylor, would be prepared to rent it initially for £120 per annum, four quarterly payments of £30.

He suggested we looked at the surgery premises. They comprised a good sized waiting-room, part of the original house, and the surgery, slightly smaller, the extension. Off the surgery was a door leading to a toilet, and a separate wash hand-basin. Another door opened to the outside into a corridor between the surgery and the adjacent house leading to the back gate. The extension, in construction, was identical to the original house, even down to small details such as the finger plates on the doors. Between the surgery and waiting room there was a small area five by seven foot containing a sink, hot and cold water, and a Bunsen burner. There was a working top surface along one side of the wall with sliding cupboards below. Above, there were three rows of shelves. All three rooms were centrally heated, including the toilet which had a mere knuckle of pipe, but sufficient to ease the chill off a small area. Gas fires provided additional heat for the waiting room and surgery. A thick patterned linoleum covered the floors of both rooms. The waiting room furniture was lavish with a leather chaise-longue in the window and a carved light oak table in the centre of the room covered with magazines. Small chairs stood around the room. The surgery furniture comprised a desk, swivel chair, examination couch, weighing scales, a height ruler, a trolley containing dressings and lotions, and table with boxes containing the record cards of private, and panel patients. Patients entered the waiting room via the front door, and left the surgery by the side door. There was a door opposite the clinical lab room leading into the house, saving the doctor the inconvenience of walking through the waiting room to reach the hall. While we were in the clinical room the telephone rang. Mrs C.R. Taylor came through to answer the call and I was most impressed to hear her describe herself as Mrs Dr Cedric Taylor, a charming elegance. Dr Taylor said the cost of the extension in 1919 was £400, and the house cost under £2,000.

Dr Taylor then suggested we moved to Wellington House to meet Drs Gordon-Taylor and Linell. We went in his car, and entered the surgery premises, but did not enter the domestic part of the home.

Dr Gordon-Taylor was nearly six feet tall, well built, and he had a healthy complexion. Born in Peterhead, he had no trace of a Scottish accent, and had received his medical training at Oxford and St Bartholomew's Hospital. He had enjoyed sports in his younger days. He remarked that the practice had always been a three man practice. He said he was sixty-five but was 'pretty fit', but he would be retiring in the not too far away future. Not a verbose man, but courteous and kindly. Clearly he exercised an authoritative attitude. My early impression was that the two doctors respected each other but were not bosom pals.

Dr Linell had little to say. He was married, had a daughter, Lynda, in her early teens, and a father-in-law. He was a sallow man, and not the immaculate figure as demonstrated by the senior partners. My early impression was that he had a large helping on his plate, and not enough money to pay for it. He was pleasant, and hoped I would be joining them. They both wanted to know more about my wife and baby, and I was forthcoming.

As we left the premises, which were similar in design and content, to 63 Horsforth Avenue, I noted a young secretary in the clinical room. I was introduced and she told me she worked in a chemist's shop before employment with the practice. Her name was Miss Wells, and her work was secretarial.

We drove back to 63 Horsforth Avenue and Dr Taylor asked me if I was interested. I replied whole heartedly in the affirmative. I was left alone for a few minutes, presumably whilst he phoned Dr Gordon-Taylor for his opinion. He reappeared and announced they were all in agreement and welcomed me as his successor.

Dr Taylor concluded by inviting my wife, baby, and myself to lunch on the following Sunday. By then he would have some legal instruments drawn up, the practice accounts for me to peruse and I would know what the quarter share was to cost. He would have worked out some dates. He wanted fourteen days to introduce me to many of his patients and show me the ropes. He would empty the house by the end of the fourteenth day and I would take over from then. I thanked him most warmly for his kindness, courtesy, and for giving me such a lengthy and detailed interview. His practice was exactly what I had searched for, and doubted whether I would ever find. He seemed pleased; I had intended he should be.

As I retraced my journey to Alford, euphoria was the predominant reaction. Of course I realized the difficulties. How was I going to pay for the house-purchase? How would we cope with a house that size? What was a quarter share in £.s.d.? What would happen on 5 June? These problems were pushed aside. I had found what I wanted, I was only twenty-nine years old, and it was up to me to make good.

It was past eight pm before I reached Alford Station and home to the flat to break the good news to Barbara. The search was over.

Time passed quickly. The principal was pleased and impressed that I had been fortunate to achieve my wishes. Sunday morning dawned and we set off early in the Flying Standard. Baby Angus was nearly six months old, in a carry-cot on the rear seat. The journey was quiet, the roads flat and the scenery uninspiring as we progressed to New Holland ferry terminus. We were soon in Hull. The city centre was dead quiet, but a policeman shouted at me for creeping forwards when the lights were red/amber for green at the Beverley Road, Springbanks Crossroad. 'There's nowt so strange as folk', thought I. We reached 63 Horsforth Avenue in good time and we were soon seated in the lounge. We were joined by two of Dr Taylor's three daughters. One was married and living in Africa. One was a gymnastic instructress, but I never knew the occupation of the remaining daughter. Dr and Mrs Taylor were excellent hosts and we enjoyed a delicious Sunday lunch.

After lunch Mrs Taylor showed us all over the house. Downstairs were the hall, lounge, dining room, morning room and kitchen, plus the surgery wing. On the first floor there were four bedrooms and a bathroom; on the second floor were two dormer bedrooms (used by maids at one time), and a storage room. There was a toilet off the first flight of stairs, and adjacent, a second bathroom. All the rooms were roughly the same size with high ceilings and large bay sash windows. A cursory glance was sufficient to appreciate that a large amount of curtaining would be necessary for privacy. The house was in a good state of decorative repair despite the war years and building restrictions.

The staircase was superb with thick mahogany supporting pillars downstairs and upstairs too, a mahogany hand-rail, and lathe-turned supporting struts painted white. The hall and lobby floors were made from a hard, shiny composite material, patterned, and akin to marble.

The house was partially centrally-heated with a radiator in the hall, surgery, waiting-room, lab-room, and one north-facing bedroom upstairs, and the landing. I think the lounge and dining room were excluded because of the difficulty in arranging the wide-bore pipes under the composite hall-floor without causing damage. Dr Taylor showed me the gas-fired boiler in an outhouse off the back-yard. He expressed concern that the gas-bill for the last winter quarter had been £14, and throttled down the thermostat by 1°F. Town coal gas was supplied by the Bridlington Gas Company and he praised their efficiency.

The outside kitchen door opened into a medium sized back-yard partially filled with a re-inforced concrete air-raid shelter. Six steps down led to the interior. It was cold and dark, but no doubt it would have withstood a direct hit. Dr Taylor had used the shelter on one or two occasions only. I knew I would have to move it away and I feared the cost, and the difficulty. It looked exactly like an army pill box.

The back-yard led to the rear entrance of the garage via a door. The garage space was the distance between the side of his house and the side of the next house. It had a tarred felt roof covering and could hold two medium sized cars side by side. Large sliding doors opened into Roundhay Road. I thought it provided an excellent arrangement for night calls.

There was a wash-house off the back-yard with a gas-fired copper and a solid wrought iron mangle with wooden rollers. Near the kitchen door there was an outside toilet, and a coal house.

We were both very impressed with the house. It was large, solid, and well-built, dating from 1910. As was the custom at that era, the front and side of the house facing the road were built using high-grade facing bricks, but those at the rear and opposite side were of a lesser quality. We thought it was an excellent family house, with good accommodation in the surgery wing for first-rate medical practice.

Dr and Mrs Taylor had acquired good furniture for the house during their twenty-nine years occupancy; every room was furnished comfortably. Mrs Taylor agreed to leave us the net curtains (only a foot high), and the black-out curtains. We were most grateful for this help and it was several years before we were able to phase them out. Dr Taylor had copies of the practice accounts over the preceding three years ready for my perusal. He said J.C. Beauvais was his accountant, a man with a brilliant brain. I was advised to take the accounts away with me and return them later. He agreed to leave the oak waiting room table for my use, and also the dining-room table. He said he would like to give me fourteen days' introduction to the practice, and to see as many patients as possible before he left. He would vacate the house by the afternoon of 10 March, and I was to take over the house and practice on the morning of 11 March. He was a precise man and I was grateful for this.

It was time to take our leave and return to Alford after an enjoyable and satisfactory day. Dr Taylor suggested that I should return to Bridlington on 24 February and stay at the Southcliffe Hotel for the fortnight before I took over 63 Horsforth Avenue on 11 March. I agreed to this proposal. Barbara and I thought Dr and Mrs Taylor were most kind and helpful to us. He was always ready to discuss any problem and gave direct and detailed replies. We said farewell and set off into the gathering darkness. We crossed the Humber and the enemy fog started to cause difficulty and we lost our way on several occasions. At that time the regulations for car headlamps demanded that the nearside headlamp only, dipped, whilst the off-side, extinguished. The contrast from main beam on both headlamps to the dipped mode was very marked and allowed poor visibility. However we arrived safely back in Alford, well pleased with the day's events. There were two weeks left before I returned to Bridlington. The doctor in Alford was happy to relieve me of my post, and I came off the pay-roll forthwith to save him further embarrassment. I said goodbye to numerous people I had attended over the four and a half months there and handed over.

The immediate action required was to arrange for our furniture to be moved to Bridlington on the morning of 11 March, and to travel to Devon for a long weekend for my parents to see their first grandson. It was unlikely we would have the opportunity to travel to Devon again for many months.

I had a stroke of good luck. Knowing that Dr Taylor was taking his surgery desk with him I bought a desk at a furniture sale room in Alford. The wood was unusual and I think it was a varnished pine; it had four deep drawers on each side of the central recess. The price was exceptionally reasonable and it looked nice. It was in constant use for thirty-four years, and when I left the house for the Health Centre in 1975 it was quickly snapped up by a local practitioner, and is again in daily use at another medical practice in the town.

The final decision taken was that I would return to Bridlington alone by train, leaving Barbara to hold the fort for the two weeks. We could not afford two hotel bills, and the baby might not be popular. I would return to Alford on 10 March as early as the first trains allowed, prepare the flat for the furniture removers next day, and return to the Southcliffe Hotel for the last night, travelling in the Flying Standard with Barbara and baby.

24 February arrived and I set off for Bridlington. Dr Taylor had made a particular request that I kept my business to myself and I must say I found this request difficult to carry out. The Southcliffe Hotel was owned and run by a pleasant man, Mr F. Hartley who was always on the premises, and it was clear that he was puzzled about my fourteen days' sojourn. In the

first place it was surprising the hotel was open in February, out of season when few visitors were around, and when the Spa Hall opposite, from where he derived considerable clientele, was closed. What was I doing there on my own, leaving the hotel at eight thirty am every morning, back for lunch, out all the afternoon and early evening, and back for dinner? Perhaps he was anxious about the account! He fished for information but I made excuses and held my ground. I know he was mystified but he would know one day. Meantime the hotel was very comfortable and I enjoyed my stay there.

On the first morning of the introductory fourteen days I left the hotel just after eight thirty am and walked along Horsforth Avenue to number sixty-three. Dr C.R. Taylor was already in the surgery, pleased to see that I had arrived, and that his retirement plans would go ahead. He did not have receptionist or secretarial help. Appointment systems were not in vogue and were probably unnecessary before the advent of the NHS. He had several open wooden boxes on a table near his desk containing NHI record envelopes, and private male and female cards; these cards measured ten by six inches; name, age, address, marital status were recorded at the top. The appropriate card was produced for each patient as required during the surgery consultation. An entry was made of the diagnosis, any salient features, and medication. On the right side of the card was a column for entry of the fee charged; 3s.6d. was the standard consultation fee, 7s.6d. for a visit. Money did not change hands at the point of contact, but patients were sent an account at the end of every quarter. I was familiar with the NHI envelope, and the continuation card for insertion together with any pathological reports. The small lab-room, adjacent, contained the standard medicines currently in use, and requiring a one to three dilution with aqua tappae. There were tablets of phenobarbitone, ephedrine, thyroid, ferrous sulphate, tabs beneva co, tabs APC, and Codeine immediately visible.

I noted three jars of tabs aspirin, yellow, pink, and standard white in colour. He anticipated my question and said they were all the same strength, grains V, and I would find out that those patients irresponsive to white aspirin improved dramatically with the coloured alternatives. He gave me a wink, and I understood that he, like myself, regarded the practice of medicine as an art as well as a science!

Cod liver oil and malt in two pound jars, and caps vitaminorum helped to bulk up the shelves. There was a test tube rack, test tubes, a wooden holder, litmus paper, benedicts' solution, and glacial acetic acid; cotton wool, gauze, various sizes of cotton bandages, pink and white lint, adhesive zinc oxide plaster, and triangular bandages filled the drawers. There was a dressing-trolley in the surgery well stocked with antiseptic lotions, spirit, green-oiled silk and magnesium sulphate paste. Clearly he was well-equipped and I thought he must be a very sound practitioner. The morning surgery started punctually at nine am, and by nine thirty am it was over. The phone rang about ten times and he rose from the swivel chair to answer it in the lab-room. There was no phone on the desk and he had not found this necessary or desirable, but if he had an additional phone he would place it in the toilet! I enjoyed his pawky humour. He had seen about seven people in the morning surgery and it was soon evident that visits to patients' homes made the bulk of his work. He showed me a Burrough and Wellcome medical diary with well over a hundred patients' names and addresses entered for every month. A cross was placed on the date seen, and carried forward with another cross on the proposed date of the next visit. He said he did about thirty visits a day, and liked to break the back of the work by lunch-time. As he spoke he was making up about ten bottles of medicine, and a linctus; he labelled them, provided instructions, wrapped them expertly, and applied sealing-wax; he placed them then in an aged wicker shopping basket, which he called the egg-basket, for delivery to patients' homes during the daily round. He was a good-natured man and had enjoyed his medical life. There was no coffee break as he considered it an unnecessary luxury and a time-waster.

He picked up the egg-basket and we moved to the garage. Until recently he had two elderly cars, but he had sold them both and bought a new Hillman Saloon painted black, for his retirement. I cursed those two old cars I had never seen as I had to pay a balancing charge for income-tax on both of them at the end of the financial year. However, he left me his professional expenses for the year 1947/8 which were a welcome help.

The Hillman was a smooth quiet car, rather high off the road, but a dream compared with the Flying Standard. We went to

Lloyd Hospital first and parked in Quay Road. As we entered the hospital and reached the lift-cage we noticed Dr Gordon-Taylor, his partner, at the far end of the corridor. Both doctors wore black jackets and grey striped trousers. They bowed low to each other from a distance. I stood rooted to the spot, overcome by such a display of courtesy and mutual respect. How different, thirty-four years later, when I said good morning to a relatively recent addition to Bridlington's practitioners, in the same corridor, to find myself ignored as he brushed past.

Wherever he went, Dr Taylor, or CR, as he was known to many patients and colleagues, introduced me, explained that he was retiring, that I was succeeding him, that they would be in good hands and should support me in the future. We moved rapidly from house to house all over the town. I was in a whirl trying to remember names of streets, names of patients, and realizing that I had a long way to go to know the diagnosis and treatment of everybody seen. He was a welcome figure, and his patients thought the world of him; dogs too, welcomed him — angry alsatians trying to push their noses through letter-boxes on the front door and barking with fury, mellowed as soon as they recognized him.

As he drove, he spoke, and by lunch time that first day I was beginning to understand the set-up, and the style of practice his patients liked and expected. He dropped me near but out of sight of the Southcliffe Hotel, and I was ready for lunch.

The afternoon surgery lasted from two pm to three pm, and this was the busiest of the day. Many patients were nearing retirement age and lived in pleasant roads such as St James Road, Cardigan Road, George Street, Shaftesbury Road, Kingsgate, South Cliff, and Trafalgar Crescent. Many men were connected with Kingston-upon-Hull, and travelled daily there on the eight am business men's train returning after six pm. Some were associated with shipping companies, and ships' fitters at Goole. Others ran their own businesses; accountants, solicitors, the clergy, farmers, a fruit broker, council members and garage proprietors were on the books. The NHI component was a small one, and geographically the premises were unsuitable for them though quite a number made the trek across the town to see him. The other surgery at Wellington House where Dr Gordon-Taylor lived catered more for NHI patients and their families, as it was centrally situated.

After the afternoon surgery we drove to the rural areas; there were patients at Rudston, Bempton, Buckton, Speeton, Reighton and Flamborough. I wondered how the Flying Standard was going to cope with the mileage. Many houses offered us afternoon tea and this was accepted occasionally. It was not always easy to take leave as there were many questions to answer. He did not cater for an evening surgery at 63 Horsforth Avenue but twice a week he managed the evening surgery at Wellington House on Monday and Thursday from six to seven pm. He took a half-day on a Tuesday but was on call that night. There was a Saturday afternoon surgery, and a busy one too; weekend rotas did not exist, each doctor was on call every night, and every day including Sunday. It was not in the patients' interests to do otherwise. Glancing at him I thought his health had stood up to this rather vigorous regime admirably; he was a little flushed and I suspected a raised blood-pressure, but he never mentioned his health.

By the end of the first day of introduction I was aware that a quarter share of the average practice receipts over the preceding three years was to cost £1,975, a great deal of money at that period of time. I had perused and checked the figures and had no doubt they were correctly computed by the illustrious J.C. Beauvais, the practice accountant. Dr Taylor asked if I agreed with the figures and if I was happy with the situation. I agreed. 'OK,' he said, 'I will speak to Mr Turnbull and he will prepare the deed of partnership for our signatures.' Mr Turnbull was the senior partner of a local firm of solicitors Messrs Harland, Turnbull & Co., Mr D. Roberts joined the firm later. At the same time another document was to be drawn stating I was the tenant of 63 Horsforth Avenue, the rental being £30 quarterly.

This large sum of money was foremost in my mind as I approached the Southcliffe Hotel for dinner, and I was not too relaxed to find the kindly Mr F. Hartley in the hotel foyer. He asked if I had been busy, and where I had been. I dodged the question once again, but I knew I was a marked man. I was loth to mislead him as I was certain to meet him again in the weeks and months ahead. (He was a patient of Dr C.R. Taylor but of course I was unaware of this!)

£1,975 was a large sum of money, but I possessed that amount, earned in the RAMC by the sweat of my brow over two and three quarter years, often in unsavoury parts of Africa.

Was I wise to part with it in such a manner in a single blow? If the present system continued there was, of course, no option and I would not have worried. However, although 5 June 1948, the day of the new NHS was scheduled to start, was only three months away, there was uncertainty whether it would commence, so great was the opposition in Parliament, amongst the profession, and its leaders. The purchase and sale of practices was to become illegal as from 5 June 1948; there were veiled threats that doctors not in practice would be directed where to work; those already in practice would be compensated in due course (fifteen years later!), and an annual interest at one and three quarter per cent would be paid on the capital value of their practice as at 5 June 1948. If one delayed the search for a partnership until after the appointed day the possibilities were incalculable. One assumed that many practices would be hard-hit financially and would be unable to afford to take on partners. The search would be even more difficult than it had been previously, but there was always the chance, however slim, that one might find a partnership without having to pay for it, enabling £1,975 to be used for other purposes.

What a dilemma! I cursed Aneuran Bevan for his ineptitude and his offensive words about the medical profession.

However, I agreed that very day to purchase the share; Dr C.R. Taylor had treated me well, and it never occurred to me, seriously, to suggest I was taken on as an assistant and be offered a partnership after 5 June 1948. I would probably have been shown the door. There were plenty of doctors who would have been only too eager to pay up and come to Bridlington.

Moreover Dr C.R. Taylor wanted to retire and collect his asset now, and not in the years to come. He was moving to West Ayton and would require the money. There was no going back. My mind was at ease and the £1,975 was transferred. I was always optimistic, and whatever lay ahead, Bridlington was a pleasant place in which to live, and 63 Horsforth Avenue, a very nice house. Time would tell how the future financial position of the practice would fare after nationalization; it did not augur well at present.

Day followed day in identical pattern as Dr C.R. Taylor spent his last fortnight in the practice and I was introduced to my first. I found it irksome to be continually under public scrutiny and not a little tiring chasing all over the area; I thought that I would not know really where I was going and what I as doing until I was managing on my own. Not that I underestimate in any way the trouble, patience, and hard work of Dr C.R. in introducing me; he certainly did all he could for my enlightenment, and I was well aware that I had his high standard to maintain.

Two days before he was due to vacate the house, two large furniture removal vans arrived at '63', and it took them the best part of two days, travelling the seventeen miles to and from West Ayton, before the house was emptied.

The day before he left I travelled to Hull on the eight am train and before noon I was back in Alford. Barbara had everything organized for the move and all that was left for me was to ease the brittle condolium off the floors, roll it, and tie it.

Confirmation was obtained from our furniture removers that they would empty the flat later in the day and arrive in Bridlington by ten am next morning. We said goodbye to the doctor and his wife at Alford; it was time for us to start our return journey to Bridlington and the Southcliffe Hotel in the Flying Standard car. As we moved through the flat countryside of north Lincolnshire I thought how remarkable it was that I had been offered the post in Alford, because it had been a stepping-stone to a Bridlington practice which possessed criteria I had hoped for but never expected to find. I did not feel annoyed with the doctor in Alford in any way; he had in fact helped me beyond measure. What I could not understand was his need for an assistant, especially so when it was causing him financial anxiety, and with 5 June 1948 just round the corner for further confusion. Soon we were through Kingston-upon-Hull, and along the Beverley Road. At Beverley I took a wrong turn but we continued on through Driffield. After passing Bessingby Hall on our right along a twisty tree-lined road, and before turning right into Bridlington, we noticed a sign-board in a field on our left indicated: 'Site for new Bridlington Hospital'. We were impressed, our luck was holding. It may surprise my readers to learn that the New Bridlington Hospital was built, and opened in 1988, forty years later, not on that notified site either, but on another site a few hundred yards away, west of Bridlington School!

I had retired by then, and apart from choosing my geriatric bed on a preview tour of inspection, I have not had occasion to cross the threshold for medical help.

Mr Hartley was in the foyer as usual when Barbara, baby and myself arrived. If he had been mystified before, he had every reason to be astonished now, as we threaded our way upstairs with a considerable amount of loose paraphernalia, and only for one night too! However, he was genial, and later on in the evening, we were even introduced to his two teenage daughters Brenda, and Leona, now that respectability had been confirmed.

By nine thirty am next morning I had settled the hotel account, informed Mr Hartley that Dr C.R. Taylor had retired, and that I was moving into 63 Horsforth Avenue, now, as his successor. I thanked him for looking after me in his comfortable hotel. It took him a long time to get over the surprise, and he often remarked about my reticence when he came to see me later on. Before ten am I met CR outside the hotel as arranged and he gave me the keys of the house. I wished him a happy retirement (he had bought a large house in West Ayton and intended to undertake market gardening, more as a hobby than for financial gain). He wished us good luck and said he would ask us over to see his garden in due course. He drove off. We drove to '63', parked the car outside the house in Roundhay Road; I thought it looked rather low on the suspension as I glanced backwards.

We let ourselves in by the back door. It is always an anti-climax returning to a house previously furnished and subsequently vacated. Our voices echoed in the lofty rooms and up the staircase. Our footsteps on the bare wooden boards sounded like an infantry regiment on the march. The house seemed huge as we wandered from room to room. The front door bell rang, our furniture had arrived from Alford. It was five past ten am and by ten thirty-five the furniture was in place in the house, the bill settled, and the van on its return journey! I remember it cost £26 to move house, and at the time we thought it was a hefty bill. The baby's pram had arrived with the furniture and it was a relief to transfer him from carry-cot to pram so that he could sleep, and give us time to organize.

The waiting-room and surgery were tackled first as our livelihood depended on the practice, and we expected there might be a few callers during the day. The waiting-room looked bare; certainly the oak-table with its carved legs occupied the centre of the room, and the old, dark-leathered chaise-longue filled the bay window, but there were only three or four chairs, and more would be required, and soon. I was surprised Dr CR had not left me more chairs. There was a gas-fire in the hearth of a tiled fire-side, and a wide mantelpiece; black-out curtains and a low net curtain provided adequate privacy from the road outside, and the house opposite. There was a plain bowl light shade, and strong lino in a green-red pattern wearing well. Yes, it was spartan but would be adequate with a few more chairs for the immediate future; I must see to the matter next day.

The surgery premises came under scrutiny next. The desk of varnished pine I had purchased looked good in position and the swivel chair was satisfactory. There was a chair for the patient I had brought with me. The examination couch in maroon leather in the bay window was in good order: there was a dressing trolley, cupboards concealed by a door, and a kitchen table from Alford for the record boxes at the side of my desk. I thought that by the time I had sorted out the cupboards, and knew the whereabouts of dressings, tablets, and medicines, the room would be more than adequate. The flooring was the same as the waiting-room. There was a gas-fire set in a small tiled surround with the flue opening to the outside wall. Both rooms faced north and would be cold without the central heating. Black out curtains would have to be drawn for a patient on the couch, because I thought peeping Toms would have a good view if care was not taken.

Each bedroom had a large fire-place with a mantelpiece, and were similar in size. Our choice was limited to the room overlooking Belgrave Road to the sea because there was a phone lying on the wooden pine floor-boards; the bedside speaking tube to the front door dangled from the wall and looked like an elephant's trunk.

We had furniture for one bedroom only so we shut the doors of the other three on that floor, and forgot about the attic rooms. The bathroom was the right size with an unboxed bath, wash basin, a large chrome towel rail, and a spacious airing cupboard which pleased Barbara.

The kitchen premises were satisfactory for us. A large maids' parlour opened into a corridor off the hall; it would make an excellent morning/breakfast room, and was likely to become the nerve centre of the house due to its proximity to the side-door from the surgery, the back-door, back-yard, garden and garage.

The room was sheltered from the elements by other houses and it was away from the noises from the road. There was a gas-fire, and a rather unusual gas water-heater with a holding cylinder which transferred the hot water to a hot storage tank in the airing cupboard, and fed the hot towel rail as well. Obviously CR liked gas, but I would have to alter the system to suit my purse later on. The morning-room opened into a small kitchen, noted for an untidy amount of plumbing on one area of the ceiling. The stainless steel sink unit previously installed had been removed, and a white porcelain sink substituted; it stood stark without draining boards and was a horror to behold and something would have to be done about it. A small gas Ascot hot water geyser provided instant hot water for the sink. The elaborate cooker had been removed, and a small electric cooker installed. I noted two heavy duty electric cables lying limply on the floor behind the cooker, their ends wrapped with black insulating tape; I did not like the look of them but there were more pressing problems. Fridges, deep freezers, fitted kitchens, tumble driers and automatic washing machines had not been invented. Groceries were stored in metal cabinets with a drop-down front for pastry work; we had one. The kitchen and morning-room floors were made of red and yellow tiles, unglazed and they could crack: they required a scrub now and again and were probably cut from stone. This was standard kitchen flooring at that time; it was durable, hard, and cold to the feet.

Off the corridor leading to the morning-room was another door opening into a fine pantry with shelves, and a meat cage. Quite clearly we were going to be able to support life, but there was a tremendous task ahead to furnish this house, and it would take time.

During the afternoon Dr and Mrs Gordon-Taylor arrived at the house. I had not met Mrs Gordon-Taylor before. She was short in stature, Irish, and rather pleasant to us. Dr Gordon-Taylor announced that the house would have suited him well. I was surprised at the remark; the stable door was already open, the horse out, and another in; it was too late for such talk if he had wanted to purchase the house. However, he never mentioned it again, and we were left to unpack and prepare for the next day; we had moved on the practice half-day and mercifully we were undisturbed. By late evening I had a list made out for the necessary visits the following day compiled from the Burrough and Wellcome Diary bequeathed me. I had met many of these patients during the previous fortnight; not that I realized it at the time. Also by late evening the gas fire had heated the morning-room, the water was hot, the baby asleep, and we enjoyed supper.

During these early days we were fortunate that Dr CR's milkman continued to call, and also the grocer's traveller. She came to the house every week and took the grocery order which was delivered later in the day. These were the days before supermarkets and large stores (apart from the Co-operative) and small family grocer's shops abounded. Mr F. Maw was our grocer and very good he was too. The butcher would also deliver meat to the house and accept an order by telephone. At that time Mr Rodmell senior was our butcher and had his shop in Richmond/West Street. These facilities were a great help to Barbara, and it was unnecessary for her to shop in the centre of the town except on special occasions when I would make myself available with the car; she had plenty to do without shopping and dealing with the pram in the town.

That first night I checked the telephone at the bedside; there was a switch on the skirting board enabling the instrument to be silenced. To my surprise the switch was in the 'off' position so I switched it 'on'. Next morning before nine am, I was surprised to hear the irate voice of Dr Gordon-Taylor on the phone enquiring why I had failed to answer the phone during the night. He had to 'turn out' for me to an urgent case six miles out in the country. He would drive out with me during the morning to review the situation, and then I must take over. I was upset about this and I could not believe I had slept though the ringing phone at my bedside. It had been an inauspicious start to practice in Bridlington, and those very words were voiced by Dr Gordon-Taylor as we drove to the house in the country.

The 'call' had been to a young lieutenant in the army, serving in a Guards regiment, who lay acutely ill in bed. Apparently with some fellow officers he had been larking; a large table had been tilted to 45°, the officer concerned was pushed rapidly up the table slope by his fellow-officers, the object being a flight across the room, arms out, like an aeroplane! Naturally he fell heavily on his front, but enjoyed the rest of the evening. It was during the night that he showed symptoms and signs of a severe coronary thrombosis. He looked ghastly, his blood pressure barely recordable, his heart sounds imagined rather than heard. Dr Gordon-Taylor said he needed another ¼, (morphine sulphate gr ¼ by injection) and proceeded to administer the dose. So young was the candidate, so ill was he, that it was decided to ask an eminent cardiologist from Leeds to see him and arrangements were made forthwith on the premises. Total bed-rest was imperative, and there was little else the unfortunate patient could do in any case.

It did not take me long to appreciate that weeks of work lay ahead if he survived, and that it was fortunate I had endless energy to attend him and the family. Dr Gordon-Taylor drove me home and he had no further dealing with the patient.

The cardiologist arrived in the mid-afternoon and I was at the patient's house awaiting his arrival. He looked an important figure as he arrived wearing a black trilby and dark overcoat. In addition to a medical case, he carried a portable electrocardiograph; such an instrument had not long been on the market. He was a tall man and did not have much to say to patient, parents, or myself. You could have heard a pin drop as he carefully auscultated the chest and recorded the blood-pressure (he attempted this many times, and I was sure he found it as difficult to obtain a reading as we did earlier on that morning).

The ECG case was opened; the flex was not long enough to reach the ceiling light fixture; wall-points were few and far between in 1948. There was a hold-up as the bed was gently eased beneath a ceiling light, and the flex plugged in.

The cardiologist said the instrument required an 'earth'. I hunted for a cold water pipe and there was of course one in the bathroom some distance off. Extra wire was produced by the household which trailed out of the room to the bathroom and was fastened to the pipe. He wired up the patient with the appropriate leads and switched on. The machine was temperamental and had to be coaxed, but at last the cardiologist expressed his satisfaction at the tracings, and disconnected the instrument.

We assembled over a cup of tea. The expert said that he was a young man to be so ill; certainly he had suffered a massive heart attack, and the prognosis was not good. He must be attended by two private nurses, a night and a day nurse, have absolute rest for a minimum of six weeks, and suitable medication for the pain. At no time was any suggestion made that the patient should be transferred to hospital; it was bad practice and we knew it. I doubt whether he would have survived the trauma of transfer. As he left he gave me a nod and appeared to notice me for the first time. 'He will need good treatment,' he said. He drove off, back to Leeds. I was left to handle the overwrought family and patient.

When I reached home I tackled the bedroom telephone. The switch had been placed upside down, 'on' when up, and 'off' when down, and inadvertently I had carried out the wrong procedure the previous night, and switched the telephone off. To prevent the possibility of future mistakes I contacted the telephone engineers; a fitter arrived, expressed his horror at the DIY switch, and arranged a permanent connection; at the same time he arranged an extension telephone for the morning room and this turned out to be a great improvement. It was a large house, and it was essential to hear the telephone everywhere in it.

It had not been a good day. During the morning surgery (my first in the practice) a patient complained that she had been unaware of Dr CR's retirement, and it had given her a shock; she had sustained a second shock to see such a bare waiting room, and a third shock to see such a young doctor. The shocks had produced an abrasive attitude, but with patience I explained that it was difficult for Dr CR to ensure every patient had been notified of his pending retirement; it was my first surgery since moving in the day before, and more chairs were of course, a high priority. I did not apologize for my age, in fact I was proud of it, but I assured her I would always do my best for her given the chance. The anger subsided, and during the afternoon a wooden chair with a dark green leather seat arrived for the waiting room with her compliments: for thirty-four years I attended her personally before I retired from the practice!

At the bottom of Beck Hill there was a second-hand furniture shop well-stocked with furniture of many types, and here and there, an antique caught the eye. It was owned by Mr Inman, a Bridlingtonian of many years, who was helpful and in no time he had four chairs, all different, but suitable, to augment the number of chairs already in the waiting-room. Over the years I bought many pieces of furniture from Mr Inman. He helped me pile the chairs into the Flying Standard, and after a polish we were well pleased with the purchase.

Those early weeks were busy; quite apart from twenty to thirty visits daily I was learning the practice, the hospitals, and the streets. The surgery attendances increased in number from a handful to a dozen and more, and I was well aware many came for a look at the new doctor and decide whether to stay with the practice. Over and above, the desperately ill lieutenant six miles out required and expected my attention at least twice and sometimes three times during the day. I used to visit him before lunch daily, and I also left my house at nine pm each night for several weeks. The two nurses arrived from an agency; they were middle-aged, staid and required a considerable amount of attention themselves. Two young nurses would have been good for the morale of us all, but no doubt such treasures were otherwise occupied. It was their attitude to the illness I found depressing; they would shake their heads at me and tell me how ill the patient was, and clearly they expected him to succumb. It was the boost to the patient's morale that was lacking, and I had to do it all.

Medically, the patient behaved in the same manner as those severely ill patients with a coronary thrombosis in Arbroath Infirmary. The diagnosis had changed however; the cardiologist wrote that on reflection he thought a traumatic haemorrhage into the pericardium was the most likely diagnosis due to landing heavily on the chest during the aeroplane flight. It was however purely of academic interest in his view, and he had nothing further to suggest in the management of the case. The diagnosis made good sense. I wonder how the thoracic surgeons would handle the situation today! In my opinion, if this diagnosis was correct, it would no doubt take longer to absorb the blood than to absorb an infarct of the heart muscle, but should he recover, the long term prognosis should be excellent.

After ten days we thought we could manage without the night nurse, and she departed; after another week we dispensed with the day nurse. Gradually the patient improved and it became difficult to keep him in bed; the BP rose to 95/60 and stayed there, the heart sounds were clearly audible and of good quality. After two months he was gradually mobilized, and it was gratifying to see such good progress, with no evidence of shortness of breath on light exertion, or any pain.

He made a full recovery and rejoined his regiment, never to experience further cardiac trouble. Forty-one years later, he continues in good health; it was a grateful family with many ramifications over the years to keep me busy.

The Flying Standard had stood the extra mileage of these visits extremely well. However, after two months, as I was crossing the local level-crossing in Quay Road, en route to Lloyd Hospital there was an appalling noise, something dropped and trailed behind me, and then fell into the road. I stopped, walked back, to find the entire exhaust system, front pipe to tail-pipe lying in the road. I kicked it to the gutter and left it there, too hot to handle, and drove to the garage with the embarrassing noise from an unsilenced engine. Mr Trenery owned the Triumph and Standard garage in Hilderthorpe Road; he kept me on the road.

The month of May 1948 was half-way through when, perhaps not unexpectedly, the BMA performed a U turn rather abruptly, and advised its members to join the NHS on 5 June. I had been so busy I had little time to worry about medical politics: events moved rather swiftly as time was running short before the appointed day. Every patient, not already an NHI patient, was required to register with the practitioner of their choice, using a special registration card, available at post offices and doctors' surgeries. It was a large white card at least twelve inches square requiring name, age, marital status, address, and occupation, and to be signed by patient and doctor. Once a week these cards were forwarded to 5 Toll Gavel, Beverley which had been the HQ for the NHI administration for the East Riding of Yorkshire. My personal anxiety was that every unregistered (formerly private patient) was now given the opportunity to register with another practice if he or she so wished, and no questions asked. For a new doctor of two months in the area it was a serious situation, and I could only hope that the other side of the practice at Wellington House would fare better and realize a respectable NHS list. Whatever happened was outside my control; I had spent my savings in order to live and work in Bridlington and I had no regrets about that. It would be imperative for me to keep my head down, work hard, and hope that good results and good example would ultimately bear fruit.

It is necessary at this juncture to state the manner of a practitioner's payment before the NHS, and compare it with the situation after the appointed day, 5 June.

Pre-NHS a practitioner had a National Health Insurance list

comprising males in employment up to retirement age; in addition there were the wives and families of the insured males who were treated as private patients. The NHI list was a comparatively small component of a practitioner's income; it was paid quarterly in arrears; the private patients either paid at the time of service, especially surgery attenders, or were sent an account quarterly, if visited, or preferred an account rather than pay at the point of contact.

As Dr CR retired on 11 March he was entitled to his share of the NHI cheque up to that date, but for accounting purposes he was paid up to 1 April. It was unrealistic for the sum to be split between Dr CR and myself, seventy days attributed to him and twenty for me. I was the April fool!

The private accounts were sent out at the end of the quarter for services rendered during that quarter; the accounts were paid during the following quarter and shared out among the partners on the first day of the next quarter. In other words patients I saw from 1 April to 31 July received their accounts in early August, and they would (I hoped) settle them during the next three months, for share out on 1 October. Similarly the new NHS patients registered on 5 June were not in the pay pipe-line until October (paid quarterly in arrears). The only income I received from the practice from 11 March to 31 July was a quarter share of the NHI cheque on 1 July. At that time the aggregate of NHI patients for both sides of the practice was six hundred, each worth 9s. per annum, i.e. £270 per annum, i.e. £67.10s.0d per quarter, and a quarter share of that sum was £16.15s.8d. Dr Gordon-Taylor remarked that he did not know how I was going to live! Nor did I. He had no suggestions. However I was now in the quarterly pipe-line, and the situation could only improve in future. Not all of Dr CR's former patients joined the NHS 'en bloc'. Some continued as private patients for several years; others joined the NHS and then opted to continue as private patients! This behaviour was illegal, and their NHS registration cards had to be returned to Toll Gavel, Beverley, for removal from the list. It was an offence to charge an NHS patient for any form of service at the onset of the NHS, though minor adjustments for special non-medical aspects such as signatures for certain forms, were allowed over the coming years. Finally the old NHI list was added to the new NHS list to form the NHS list for the future.

The clerk to the old NHI office at 5 Toll Gavel, Beverely was a Mr Swann, a courteous man who carried out his duties with commendable accuracy; he had one helper to manage the secretarial work involved. When the NHS was born, and the public started to register with doctors in their thousands, the large registration forms swamped his office, but it was some time before he was allowed additional staff to cope with the onslaught. The ineptitude, the utter failure to sit down and think out the consequences was incredible to behold. Perhaps it was post-war malaise, but a muddle was created that required many years to correct. We had won the war, but it looked as though we were to lose the peace.

I would not wish to live through such times again.

Two events took place during July which changed my financial life. First, out of the blue, a welcome letter arrived from my father. As a solicitor, he had, no doubt, access to the new regulations governing the NHS; he had perceived the situation of payment in arrears, realized that it would be 1 October before I received a living wage, and he agreed to loan me £500 to be paid back interest free over ten years, the debt to be cancelled in the event of his death. He died in 1955 and I was able to pay back the debt for seven out of the ten years.

This financial help gave me a tremendous boost, and relieved me from seeking a bank loan, no mean feat at that time.

The second event was the start of the post-war summer holiday season in Bridlington. I had no idea how popular Bridlington was as a holiday resort; families, mainly from the West Riding of Yorkshire, arrived in droves on Saturday mornings and stayed for a week in apartments, guest-houses, hotels, holiday camps and private houses throughout the town.

Holiday camps at Flamborough were very popular and were thronged with people. I remember especially Sea Farm Camp, and Thornwick Camp at Flamborough, and Wainds Farm Camp near Flamborough Head and its proximity to the Fog Horn station. If that fog-horn sounded unexpectedly on a dark, damp, misty night if I was on an errand of mercy there, my heart dropped a beat! Charity Farm Camp at Sewerby was another large and popular camp. Nearer to my home was Graingers Camp at Wilsthorpe, subsequently renamed the South Shore Holiday Camp, and then South Shore Holiday Village. Today the Corporation owns a caravan site adjacent to the holiday village.

This influx of people of all ages between 15 July and 15 September produced many patients too; I thought the morbidity was extremely high, and I was frequently shocked at the illnesses, and worse, the undiagnosed illnesses I saw. Many visitors took advantage of another medical opinion whilst away.

The visitors seen on holiday as patients were treated as temporary residents. As expected, the administrators overlooked the obvious fact that people took holidays, and might become ill on holiday, so that initially there was no machinery for their treatment under the NHS! Uproar soon followed, and in a short time, a temporary residents form, Form EC19, appeared which attracted 7s.; it could only be signed once over three months; too bad if the same visitor wanted several bites of the cherry! The generosity was quite overwhelming, our services grossly devalued! Over the years this fee gradually increased, and today is more than adequate.

Wellington House, with its central position, and a chemist shop, J. Whiteside, close by, attracted many visitors, and my house was well situated for the South Shore Camp, beach catastrophes, and numerous guest houses, in Richmond Street, West Street, Pembroke Terrace, Horsforth Avenue, and elsewhere too. The two practices used to collect around 1,000 temporary resident forms during the high season and we were paid on 1 January. We used to say, in jocular fashion, that it paid the half-year income-tax demand. It was very hard work, but it was an essential part of the practice income for nearly thirty years. Although the surgery hours were written on the front gate medical plate, visitors took little notice of surgery hours and whenever I returned home there were usually several to see, patiently waiting my return.

I did not remonstrate, beggars could not be choosers, and it was service with a smile.

Bronchial asthma in children on holiday, especially Flamborough, was a common event during the night. There were few cars, and a visit was the norm. Whether initiated by being away from home, or because a family of five and six persons were cooped in an overheated airless caravan or chalet, parents would tell you it was over a year since their last attack. These children responded well to ephedrine gr ¼ and an aspirin gr V and enjoyed the rest of their holiday; if the attack had been triggered by respiratory infection, that was another matter.

Happily sulphatriad suspension was a recent addition to the limited antibiotic armamentaria, and it worked well, usually within twelve hours. I carried a large stock-bottle of sulphatriad suspension, and poured out sufficient in a cup for several doses. My stock bottle was replenished by a script given to the patient, and another script for the continuation of their therapy. Penicillin was not routinely available, and then it was administered by injection every four hours. There were no inhalers suitable for children. Tabs ephedrine gr ¼ and a sedative were provided as well. The final treatment, or the art of medicine, was to stay on the premises until the agitated patient and parents had settled down, ventilate the premises, have a cup of tea, and engage in light conversation. Often the child fell asleep, the bronchospasm eased, and I made the four mile journey back home, often to find another call to the same camp at Flamborough awaited me! These were grateful patients indeed, and many kept in touch with me over the years. Many a father stuffed a £5 note into my breast pocket as I left, suggesting I had a drink on him.

Severe asthma in a young adult, especially female, could be a nightmare. Steroid therapy was light-years away, but there was a spray called Brovon; many patients had great faith in it, but I cannot say I thought it helped, except psychologically. If on arrival at the house you heard the expiratory wheeze with a final 'twist' to it, trouble lay ahead; often the patient was cyanosed and in a dangerous state. The treatment was to load a minum syringe with 1/1000 adrenaline, take off your watch, drop to your knees, and inject one minum per minute subcutaneously for as long as it took to gain control. I administered a hundred minims over two hours on one occasion in a caravan at Flamborough; an alsatian dog licked my hand during the administration, and I was grateful for its support and trust. Quite abruptly the attack eased and stopped, and the patient enjoyed the rest of the holiday. The hospital was not used for such cases, in the first place the night staff were very busy with surgical emergencies, and second, I would still have been there injecting a minum per minute: it was not reasonable to expect nursing staff to undertake such responsible action. If the asthmatic patient was in a desperate and life-threatening situation, relatives phoned the ambulance, and the patient was transferred to Lloyd Hospital in Bridlington. If oxygen was required, the correct procedure was to place the patient in an oxygen tent. I can remember many dramatic recoveries in oxygen tents before they were considered dangerous and replaced by nasal masks.

Sometimes there was the temptation to give a small injection of morphia to ease the distressed patient; it was totally contra — indicated as it was adding a respiratory depressant to breathing already depressed, but on one or two occasions, with oxygen available, the risk was taken and with good effect. Desperate situations required desperate remedies.

Bronchial asthma was only one of the many acute conditions to treat; surgical emergencies were frequent, especially among the holiday visitors, due largely to the prevalence of peptic ulceration and the inadequate treatment available. At Edinburgh I was taught that peptic ulcer patients must avoid sticks, stones, skins and bones in their diet, and concentrate on milky foods every two hours followed by a dose of magnesium trisilicate. Such a bland diet kept patients' symptoms at bay until their holidays in Bridlington, when, tempted by the odours of fried food, fish and chips, the sight of crabs and lobsters, extra cigarettes, and beer to wash it down, many male visitors suffered a gastric or duodenal perforation. It was easy to diagnose; the scaphoid abdomen, the board-like rigidity on attempted palpation, the pain, the shock, the agonized expression begging the doctor to do something for the pain, and quickly. Treatment was not the simple matter of ordering the ambulance for transfer to a hospital in another town, and 'next case please'. The buck stopped with the practitioner, and the patient arrived at Lloyd Hospital; if the ward was full a bed was erected in the centre of the room, and other patients, less ill, were switched about, until the emergency was settled close to the entrance under closer scrutiny. The admitting practitioner was quickly on the scene, setting up a glucose-saline intravenous drip as senior nurses used their expertise to pass a Ryles stomach tube. The theatre staff, available twenty-four hours a day, seven days a week were warned to be ready and to build up steam for the sterilizers, while the practitioner contacted a surgeon.

The surgeon who came to Lloyd on a regular basis from Hull on Tuesdays was Mr A. Patrick, but it was not always possible for him to leave the Hull Royal Infirmary at short notice, and recourse was made either to Mr Baker from Scarborough or Mr Griffin who came to Scarborough after the war. Both were splendid and gave admirable support to the Bridlington practitioners. They always travelled to Lloyd, and never suggested transferring the patient to Scarborough, thereby saving the patient the agonizing pain and further shock of a seventeen mile ambulance journey. A perforation was a dangerous emergency; we were taught that after six hours the outlook was markedly worse; early operation was essential. Whatever the time, day or night, the anaesthetist, either Dr Linell or myself (for our patients) were waiting for the surgeon to arrive. The patient was in the ante-room, suitable premedicated receiving the intravenous fluid. No time was wasted, and on the surgeon's arrival, the patient was anaesthetized using open ether, or nitrous oxide, oxygen, and ether administered via the Boyles machine. I usually assisted the surgeon. It was amazing the amount of free fluid and particles of food floating about the peritoneal cavity which were removed by the gurgling suction pipe; difficult too, sometimes to locate the perforation, only pin-head in size in many cases; astonishing, also, how quickly the patients condition on the operating table improved when the perforation was closed with sutures, invaginated, and all free fluid removed. If the history was long and the patient's condition was satisfactory, the surgeon might press on, and carry out a gastroenterostomy, or even a partial gastrectomy as the years moved into the late 1950s.

These patients with peptic ulcer perforation did well after surgery, and looked after their stomachs with respect; although many patients who had a gastroenterostomy or partial gastrectomy were relieved of all symptoms for several years, many developed a stomal ulcer, or the 'dumping syndrome', and these operations have fallen from favour now that peptic ulcers heal with the use of the recent histamine H_2-receptor antagonist drugs.

After the operation, whatever the time of night or day, the surgeon would emerge from the shower and dressing-room and have tea and sandwiches with us in the Doctors Room overlooking Quay Road. Many a strange tale was unfolded and we came to know each other well over the years. For night emergencies there was a member of the kitchen staff especially appointed to brew tea and prepare sandwiches for the hungry doctors; she appeared whenever there was an emergency, contacted by a hospital porter, and cycled from her home to the hospital during the night, whatever the hour.

An emergency of this nature wrecked the day, interfered with visits, and sometimes necessitated the cancellation of a surgery. Patients were very understanding and reasonable about such matters.

Night emergencies were more leisurely for everyone concerned and caused less interference with practice work; however, there were occasions when I arrived home after these sessions with time only for a shave before the nine am surgery, and another day.

The arrival of the appointed day, 5 June 1948, initially made little impact on my work and so far as I could tell, the administration and running of the local hospitals continued as before.

There was one hospital secretary, Miss Gardiner, who did sterling work in a small office which subsequently became the telephone exchange room; she dealt with the telephone as well. At night the phone was answered by night sister. Over the years, as the bureaucratic machine moved into an uncontrollable momentum, a vast array of secretaries, porters, cleaners, and domestics evolved; for every appointment there was another appointment to cover their off-duty and so ad infinitum.

Gradually the public realized that everything was free, and inevitably the surgery attendances increased. There was a run on sight-tests and spectacles nationally, causing depleted stocks of lenses and frames by opticians. Whether it was necessary, I know not. Some patients asked for brandy and whisky on a script, arguing that they were drugs, and difficult to refute. Belatedly, instructions were formulated that alcohol, and toilet rolls were not classified as drugs, and if prescribed the doctor would pay the cost.

While I was dealing with the practice, Barbara, too, was busy. The waiting-room was immaculate; the linoleum gleamed, the curtains, cleaned and hanging in folds, the furniture shone with polish; outside the brass speaking-tube glinted in the sun-light, and the front steps looked so clean. Many patients remarked on the cleanliness of the rooms. There was a relay wireless on the mantelpiece with a choice of two BBC radio stations and this proved popular. Some patients bought copies of *Country Life* and the *Dalesman* for the waiting room table. Barbara managed the telephone, answered the front door, and was invaluable with advice in an emergency when I was on the rounds. How she managed to do this, and cope with a small baby midst the interruptions, and provide meals, do the shopping and gradually organize a large house on a shoe-string, yet retain her calm and happy nature, was an inspiration to patients and her husband alike.

There was a situation we did not like; every time the front door was opened to gain entrance to the waiting-room it brought a blast of north sea air into the house. Frequently patients left the front door wide open to aggravate the situation. I was surprised Dr CR had accepted the situation over the years, but later I was informed he had a maid who answered the front door bell and naturally shut the door. On one occasion, to our surprise, we met a patient coming downstairs, having used the upstairs toilet. It upset us to think people could roam the house. Something had to be done as the situation was unacceptable. I considered using the surgery as the waiting-room, with its separate door to the outside, and the waiting-room as the surgery; the waiting-room, then, would have a wash-hand basin and a toilet, no doubt a good arrangement, but I would miss the wash-basin. It would have been possible to fit a wash-basin in the existing waiting-room, but we could not afford the cost. Against the proposal was the entry by patients, using the back gate, to reach the side door of the proposed waiting-room. We thought patients might feel demeaned, so the proposal was rejected, and a partition constructed to shut off the waiting-room door from the hall. This made a tremendous difference to the warmth and comfort of the house, and patients liked the arrangement. It is interesting to note that in the twenty-seven years that this situation existed, only a handful of patients asked to use the toilet; a few children were sick but we were able to accommodate this. Wellington House Surgery had a similar arrangement to mine, a toilet off the surgery.

Over the last ten to fifteen years the public has become 'loo conscious', and adults and children tend to use a toilet whenever one is seen. Many young adults and children seem unable to contain their bladders longer than two hours. In the absence of infection or neurological causes it must be due to faulty training; this is an unfortunate situation requiring better health education. If I had continued with practice at my residence into the 1980s it would have become mandatory to have switched rooms so that patients had ready access to a toilet to accommodate their frequency and ease their weak bladders.

In July 1948 there was an invitation from Dr and Mrs CR to have a strawberry tea at their home in West Ayton. Their house was larger than '63', the garden nearly two acres in size. He had taken up market gardening in a serious way, and rough land had been ploughed using his own rotovator; he had vegetables, fruit, and a hen-battery. The domestic garden, too, was most pleasant with arbours to shelter him from the wind. The strawberries were large by usual standards, and very tasty. He was an affable man, interested in my progress during the previous four months, and anxious to hear about the trials and tribulations of the early weeks of the NHS. He told me that he had heard good reports about Barbara and myself via the bush telephone system, and he wanted me to know this. Practice, he said, could be lonely work and you never knew whether your efforts and good results were appreciated; patients would never tell you because their expectations were high, and your partners would never venture an opinion. He asked if '63' was satisfactory, and I told him we were very pleased with the house apart from the garage roof which leaked badly. Within a week the roof had been refelted and tarred, and never caused further trouble.

Dr CR was always kind and generous to us and we have never forgotten him. We drove home in good spirits. A year later he died in Bournemouth, where he had recently moved, from a heart attack. His retirement was tragically short.

One morning on my rounds I pulled up outside Kidds in Quay Road. When I returned to the car it would not start; it was as dead as a dodo. A man tapped the side window and announced that every time I pressed the starter button there was a gush of water from the exhaust pipe. I expressed astonishment, and had a look while he pressed the starter; he had not been joking. Mr Trenery arrived from the garage, diagnosed a blown main head gasket, and I was towed away, frustrated at the interruption to my work. He promised the return of the car by late afternoon.

In these circumstances I continued my work on foot, and I found it irksome; occasionally he lent me his Triumph Tourer (Bergerac's car!) while he repaired mine. It was exhilarating.

Although four months had passed since my arrival in Bridlington I had little contact with Dr Gordon-Taylor or Dr Linell. I used to call at Wellington House every morning to collect the medicines, now dispensed by Miss Wells, and to see the correspondence from Mr Swann from the Beverley office. Miss Wells was very efficient and knowledgeable. I learned a great amount from her about the practice, and the other two partners as well!

Dr Gordon-Taylor, unrelated to Dr CR Taylor, had served in the navy during the 1914-18 war. He was a general practitioner surgeon, an extinct nomenclature by modern standards. He was a useful man for those times. He could deal with acute appendicitis, perforations, and many other surgical conditions including a Caesarean section. He drew the line at gall-bladder work; however, he undertook prostatic surgery occasionally, but results, even in skilled hands were not good, and mortality rates nationally were high. Other firms in the town sometimes requested his services, but he was sixty-five years old, and many people thought he was too old to be operating, and his work dwindled. Technically he managed well, but naturally he could not command the delicate touch of the full-time surgeon, and he had reached his potential. He liked to operate at nine thirty am after his morning surgery, and he required an assistant (myself) and an anaesthetist (Dr Linell). My surgeries never finished before ten am, usually much later, so I had to drop everything and hasten to the Lloyd Hospital. If you were late it was a very bad show, and you felt you had been playing truant; if the anaesthetist was late it was also a very bad show and I started off the anaesthetic while he paced about to exercise his impatience and cool his irritation. This situation produced an unhappy atmosphere in the theatre and his disapprobation was hard to bear. It was of course difficult for the practice and frustrating to utilize their total manpower at that hour of the day. However we respected our elders and betters whatever their idiosyncrasies, and we did not complain, though there were rumblings of discontent behind the scenes sometimes. He was a man of great integrity, and immaculate etiquette; he was authoritarian, blunt, and did not suffer stupidity easily; he was of course an excellent doctor of his generation. He had a daughter, Sheila, who was a librarian, and a son, Charles, who qualified as a lawyer during my early years.

Dr Linell, several years older than myself, was helpful to us both. However, he had his own problems. His wife had suffered rheumatic fever and had mitral incompetence, he said, and was never too fit; she had a frozen shoulder too, refractory to the available therapy. There was a daughter, Lynda, a young school-girl, and a lively child. His fit father-in-law hovered in the background. He seemed unsettled, and showed a lack of confidence in the future of the practice, which was understandable; he said he had cold feet. Despite the fact he was one of the few people in Bridlington to be able to build a white bungalow on the west side of Fortyfoot, I had the impression he was not going to be a long term partner and was looking for other openings. He liked gardening and seemed to have time to enjoy it. He was not popular with other medical firms in the town but I never understood the reason. On one occasion I witnessed a near brawl with another practitioner outside the Lloyd Hospital in broad daylight. Embarrassed, I made myself scarce.

The long awaited 1 October 1948 arrived, and with it my first proper pay cheque: it was £400. It was my birthday anniversary too, and I remember taking the cheque home and showing it to Barbara. We stared at it with quiet incredulity, never expecting so much. This cheque marked the start of better times, and though we were often very short of money until the Danckwert Pay Award of 1952, which came to the rescue of impoverished doctors, never again did we have to survive for six months at our own expense. There were occasional flashes of irritation that the government of the day devalued the very people trying to make the NHS work, but it was short lived and we threw ourselves with further determination into doing out best for our patients, and leaving the politics to the politicians.

The shock of 1 October 1948 was the practice NHS list — under 2,000 patients. My list was eight hundred, and that of Wellington House 1,100 — 1,900 overall. With a per capita payment of 9s among three doctors, and the remnants of a private practice, this was a depressing reality.

Dr Gordon-Taylor was paid for his surgical appointment by the NHS, and he kept this for himself; at that time he had a 7/16 share of the practice receipts, Dr Linell 5/16 and 4/16 for myself. However the NHS registration cards continued to come to '63', not in big numbers, but in a steady trickle over the months. Optimistic as ever, I could see no reason why I should not prevail provided I was able to stand the pace of twenty-four hours a day, seven days a week. I have previously mentioned there were fifteen practitioners in Bridlington trying to cope with the birth pangs of the NHS, trying to increase their NHS lists, and trying to make a living. Competition was quite intense; if patients were dissatisfied there were no obstacles to prevent them moving to another firm, and doctors were not dainty in refusing them.

I was more interested in obtaining new people to Bridlington rather than accepting disgruntled patients, whose complaints were rarely justified, from other doctors. Geography, in the absence of cars, played a large part in the size of your list, the bulk of patients being in your catchment area. New people to the area were recommended by your patients to register with you. It was a great challenge, and the doctors were kept on their toes.

The Lloyd Hospital and the Avenue Maternity Hospital were the mainstays of my medical work during thirty-four years of practice in Bridlington. Both hospitals performed services of the highest standard with dedicated, motivated, and efficient staff. There were several changes of matrons over the years, retirement age being the usual cause. I have always regretted the demise of matron in the reorganization of nursing status. Whereas a matron used to be a mother-figure, and necessarily, a strict one on occasions, she was non-administrative, and her work centred on the maintenance of high nursing standards; she was a person for nursing or domestic staff to turn to for advice in a domestic or nursing situation. She was there, too, for the benefit of in-patients; her daily round of wards was welcome to patients, and everybody was kept alert. If matron made a visit to the hospital's kitchens, complaints about hospital food were less likely. Sadly, matrons have been replaced by senior nurses, with numericals, who see themselves in an administrative role rather than that of a matron's. To those of mature years, and with good memories, it has been a retrograde step. There has to be a discipline in skilled, life-saving, and high technical hospitals.

Lloyd Hospital was smaller than the Arbroath Infirmary. Bridlington had a larger population by about five thousand, but it had a separate maternity hospital, and the old fever hospital in Bempton Lane was extended and became a geriatric unit. The casualty department was very small indeed, no bigger than an average domestic bathroom, with a very small waiting-room adjacent. Subsequently a new casualty department was built in the 1950s, connected to the old casualty waiting-room by a new corridor. The old casualty became a store-room for the male surgical ward, and the old waiting-room was easily recognizable as a part of the new corridor!

Despite this small area a vast amount of out-patient and casualty work was carried out there. I remember well, a young boy of eight years, a patient of the practice, who was knocked down by a car on a Sunday afternoon at the junction of Marton Road, and Great Barn Street in the early 1950s. He was rushed to this small room, unconscious and with multiple fractures, and lacerations contaminated with road tar. He was resuscitated as best we knew, fractures reduced, and lacerations sutured by a Scarborough surgeon. Finally the surgeon insisted on a laparotomy, fearing a ruptured spleen, and he was transferred to the main theatre upstairs. The spleen was unruptured. He spent several days in an oxygen tent, seemed moribund at times and most unlikely to recover. However he did recover, but was left with damage to the brachial plexus on one side, and although he had full function of his hand, the limb hung limply and never recovered. This young lad became a slater and tiler and I used to watch with amazement as he skimmed over the highest roofs, and scaled ladders with consummate ease. To move the limb, he swung it with his body, and caught it with the hand of the sound side. He was a remarkable young man, and one of a large family.

Lloyd Hospital had a male surgical ward downstairs, above it, a female surgical ward. Balconies were added upstairs and downstairs to these wards and provided a handful of extra beds.

There was a smaller ward, a male medical, facing the Quay Road, and a female medical ward above this. Also downstairs was a small children's ward, and above it, another small female medical ward. The X-ray room was moved twice, first to a room on the right of the front entrance with easier access to the street and front entrance, and second to a building away from the main hospital and adjacent to St Johns Avenue. Entrance was either from St Johns Avenue, or by another new corridor linking it to the new casualty department, and corridor to the main hospital. The operating theatre was upstairs and to the right; it underwent a major modernization in the 1950s, and served the hospital well with a succession of first rate theatre sisters until the hospital closed in 1988.

There was only one entrance/exit from the road when I came in 1948; the opening to the right, facing the hospital, was closed, and green sward graced the area outside the front door. I used to park my car in Quay Road, and it was many years before traffic forced me into St John's Avenue. The view from the doctor's room overlooking Quay Road has changed: there was no roundabout, and all the roads were narrower. A horse-trough existed at the junction of Quay Road and Station Avenue, and many a weary horse, pulling a cart laden with bags of coal, quenched its thirst at this watering point. We were sad when it was moved; it should have remained a relic of past history. Also seen from this window was a blind road, jutting obliquely from Quay Road into the gardens with a line of houses alongside, and subsequently demolished: the Crown Building now occupies this former area of terraced houses.

Mr Adam Patrick, a surgeon from Hull, came to Bridlington every Tuesday morning, and held a clinic, followed by an operating session of three or four cases. He had left by lunch-time, en route for Driffield for an afternoon session. He was a good-looking man with a healthy complexion, and he was upstairs three at a time in Lloyd. He was a slick surgeon, a neat operator, and always composed, whatever the situation. He was a technician, and not so concerned with post-operative care, but that was the custom; there were juniors to carry out post-operative care and routine spade-work.

Although a general surgeon he was renowned for skill in a total hysterectomy, and it was no surprise he had a large private practice in Hull, and Bridlington too, in the earlier days of the NHS. When he had time he would tell us how he saved the lives of prize race-horses, when called upon to do so with various surgical procedures. He was forced to retire, brusquely, and in an uncharismatic manner, characteristic of the times, when he reached his sixty-fifth birthday; he was ably assisted in the operating theatre by Dr Gordon-Taylor up to 1960, aged seventy-seven years. Mr Patrick gave a great service to Lloyd Hospital.

Dr D Muir was the consultant in general medicine, and like

Mr Patrick travelled from Hull on a weekly basis. He had a special interest in heart ailments and over the years he set up a cardiac clinic with Dr Cumming at Kingston General Hospital in Hull. Many of our patients received expert advice and treatment there; their work developed and a coronary care unit was established. Dr Cumming died abruptly in his prime, a sad loss for Hull.

There was Dr Woodrow, a medical consultant from Scarborough who held a clinic in Bridlington until his early death. He was succeeded by Dr Beaton from Scarborough, another medical consultant who worked tirelessly over thirty years in Scarborough and Bridlington.

Mr Debenham, a Scarborough surgeon, operated occasionally on private patients in Lloyd Hospital until the onset of the NHS and his retirement.

Bridlington was particularly fortunate in having a lady obstetrician and gynaecologist resident in the town. Dr Mary Webster, wife of a local practitioner, Dr F.J.D. Webster, came to Bridlington after the war, and for nearly thirty years the female population benefited from her skills in the Avenue and Lloyd Hospitals.

There was yet another medical specialist from Hull who came to Driffield Hospital once a week in the afternoon. His name was Dr Hellewell. He was very willing to do a domiciliary visit to a patient in trouble in Bridlington, provided he had not left Driffield on his return journey. He was an excellent all-rounder, and good on skin disease, and comfortable in patients' houses. He was a humorous and jovial man. I remember warning him on one occasion that the female patient he had come over to see was one of the Victorian era, and unworldly. When we arrived at the house and ascended the staircase, there was a white bust of a man in a corner recess; he bowed low and said, 'William Shakespeare, no doubt.' As we moved into the patient's bedroom we met the patient lying in a brass four-poster bed. 'Ah,' he said, 'you were right, this means she will have to be taken by storm!' He always came to our house for a cup of tea before returning to Hull; he had a glass eye, and drove in all conditions intrepidly.

The Avenue Maternity Hospital was a very busy hospital indeed when I first came to Bridlington. Miss B. Slack was matron for many many years before retirement. In some ways she was like the matron of Arbroath Infirmary, always there whatever the hour or day, and well-informed of all the comings and goings in the hospital. She attended most deliveries, especially if there was a hint of a labour not proceeding according to plan; she was a skilled midwife, very experienced, and excellent at suturing the perineum. She would let you know if a situation was arising requiring the skill of Dr Mary Webster. The two worked well together. Matron Slack invariably assisted her at a Caesarean section, and was theatre sister as well. Such a devoted matron was unlikely to be good at delegation, however, and this was bound to reflect on other senior members of staff who did not always have the opportunity to assume full responsibility. She had a great insight and understood people; everybody knew her but she knew more about them: off-duty (a rare event) she was always pleasant and entertaining. I regarded her as irreplaceable.

These were the days when mothers often spent seven days in bed after delivery, using the bedpan as required. The staff had plenty of hard work to perform. Babies lived in the nurseries night and day, except for feeding when they were brought to their mothers, but mothers fed their babies in the nurseries when they eventually were allowed to totter to their feet. Breast feeding was encouraged, and the majority managed. Those mothers who had to rely on the boat-shaped bottle, were up against an array of powdered and tinned milks of varying constituents. National dried milk was popular and subsidized, but it seemed to produce fat, puffy babies. Other milks were expensive, and mothers, when they returned home were inclined to switch from one type to another, aided and abetted by granny in the corner, and sometimes by the doctor too. The Avenue Hospital was always full; there was a post-war baby boom, and the hospital served a wide area. Even with my modest number of women of child-bearing age I remember five new babies born in a week, the last one lying on an ordinary hospital bed in the main corridor of the hospital. Hospitals never turned a patient away because they were full: how I wish they were like that now.

Apart from our practice there were five others in Bridlington, and all well established; they were staffed by male practitioners. Dr Mary Webster was the sole lady doctor and she had consultant status. Two of the six practices held practitioners related by marriage; one firm was managed by two brothers.

I have listed the practitioners who were established in Bridlington on 11 March 1948, when I started work here, and the addresses of their practice premises. Below, is another list of the practitioners established in Bridlington on 1 May, 1982, as I retired, and their addresses. The endurance test was won by Dr Edgar Watson who worked on for more years after my retirement. Practice D, a single-handed practice managed by Dr P.H.D. Chapman was small numerically; when he retired he was not replaced and his practice list was greedily devoured by the local practitioners.

From 1948-1982 there was considerable movement by doctors in Bridlington. Many retired, having reached their allotted span, and were replaced by younger men; some replacements moved on quickly; two moved to the USA to practice, one doctor sadly committed suicide, another moved for work with the World Health Organization; one or two said they did not fit into the local picture and sought other challenges; one transferred from general practice to community medicine in an area nearby. However, a solid core of the doctors here in 1948 stayed on and retired in the late 1970s and early 1980s, and it was these I knew so well and with whom I had such good relationships. No practitioner died in harness, and no practitioner arrived to put up his plate during these years. There was plenty of stress with work, changing patterns, and with our own parental old age, but it was not allowed to gain control. Bridlington never suffered bad doctors; all were good and had the highest regard for their patients, and were determined to do their best for them; this opinion was confirmed time and time again by visiting consultants.

PRACTITIONERS IN BRIDLINGTON ON 11 MARCH 1948

A	B	C	D	E	F
Gordon-Taylor Linell Cookson	Jarratt Roden	Webster Wilson Swanson	Chapman	Arthur. Johnson + one replace- able assistant	L.A. Watson E. Watson
1) Wellington Hse Wellington Rd 2) 63 Horsforth Avenue	75 Cardigan Road	29 Wellington Road	21 Trinity Road	1 St. Johns Road	34 Victoria Road

PRACTITIONERS IN BRIDLINGTON ON 1 MAY 1982

A	B	C	D	E	F
Lucey Bell McNab	Hart Meldrum	Bayne Mrs. T. Ward Watson Farley	DISBANDED	Robertson Young Hartley Mundy	E. Watson A. Watson McClaren Bowden Gillhespie
Bridlington Health Centre	Bridlington Health Centre	Wellington Road Surgery		Bridlington Health Centre	Victoria Road Surgery

PRACTITIONERS IN BRIDLINGTON ON 1 JUNE 1990

A	B	C	D	E	F
Bell McNab Hillam Elliot	Hart Meldrum Mrs. E.A. Barton	Bayne Mrs. T. Ward R.M. Watson Farley A. Robertson		Andrew Robertson Young Mundy Harris	A. Watson McClaren Bowden Gillhespie Wallam
Bridlington Health Centre	Bridlington Health Centre	35 Wellington Rd. Bridlington		Bridlington Health Centre	18 Victoria Road Bridlington

The Bridlington environment was different in 1948. The West Hill Estate had not been built, and Bessingby Road was a single carriageway, and a narrow one too. There was a dip in the road just before the entrance to the new West Hill Estate, and this was ironed out to improve safety when the road became dual carriageway. The bungalow estate off Bempton Lane had not been built. All the traffic from York to Bridlington on the Sledmere route, passed along Easton Road into Westgate and the High Street, and turned right into Quay Road. There were no traffic lights at this junction despite pleas from many quarters; it became an accident black-spot and I witnessed some horrific scenes there. During the summer season it caused a snarl up of traffic in the High Street, especially at weekends.

A policeman directed traffic at the top of Bridge Street during the season, and another policeman stood in the road outside Batchelors shop at the junction of Queen Street and the Promenade in order to control the traffic, which was two-way, round the narrow right angled turn there. One way streets were years away, and it was permissible to drive and park anywhere in the town. It was often a nightmare during peak season for doctors and ambulances to reach their destination; cars were parked everywhere and anywhere, sometimes even on the corner of a major road junction in the town centre!

Queensgate extension stopped abruptly at the entrance to Nightingale Road and green fields lay beyond. The housing estates to the west of Marton Road, Sewerby Road, and Martongate were green fields, and agricultural land as well. The Northfield housing estate to the west of Scarborough Road is recent, having been constructed during the decade 1970/80. A new road was built linking Easton Road with Scarborough Road and shutting off that portion of Easton Road leading to Westgate. This has stopped traffic from the scenic route from York entering Westgate, causing chaos in the Old Town at weekends, and spared a driver making a right hand turn from the Old Town into a steady flow of two way traffic traversing Quay Road and Scarborough Road at a busy junction, unguarded by traffic lights. The new road also allowed traffic from Driffield to by-pass Bridlington en route for Scarborough.

There is less change to the centre of the town. Carlton's Bon Marché in King Street was demolished, and replaced by Binns, and the Ebor Flats, (the tower block, the Bridlington Carbuncle) overlooking the harbour was built despite the anger of the residents of Bridlington, and the general knowledge that tower blocks aggravate social problems, cause marital unhappiness, and encourage vandalism; and it is clearly unkind that young children should have to live in the sky.

The south side, too, experienced some changes. The Burlington Hotel on South Marine Drive, a building of unusual design with a toothed turret, was demolished and a convalescent home took its place. The Princess Mary Promenade was extended half a mile southward and named Pitts Wall.

It is remarkable that despite the numerous new housing estates, the obvious expansion of Bridlington in a north-westerly direction, and the increase in numbers of retired people living in Bridlington, that the population has changed little over the years, staying around 29,000. The police used to tell us that on a Saturday morning between nine am and noon in peak season, when August Bank Holiday was the first weekend in August, the population was 100,000 at risk, medical risk too! Car accidents and motor cycle accidents were frequent at the entrance to the twisty road to Graingers Camp, Wilsthorpe, from the low Hull Road, and even in the town itself. I remember a bus lying on its side in a garden at the Hilderthorpe, Cardigan, Bessingby Station Roads junction on a Sunday afternoon in the peak season, with many casualties.

Bridlington, like many places at this time, had its share of bad housing. 'Slums', a word widely used to describe them was emotive; the houses were not slums to those who lived in them; they were their homes. Many of their inhabitants were elderly and lived in poverty, but there were young families too, brought up in these old damp houses. One cold water tap, dripping into a cast-iron sink, a black stoved kitchen range, an outside toilet at the end of the back-yard, and the house lighted by coal gas mantles, were the only facilities available. Sometimes the families were large: real family units, everyone caring for and supporting each other. These people were closely-knit, remarkable and praise-worthy folk, without the socio-economic dependency of today, proud people accepting their lot without bitterness. Muggings, attacks on the elderly, and child abuse seemed rare and the doctor was always a welcome figure. I had quite a number of these people to attend in the three months before the advent of the NHS enabled them to be on a doctor's list.

I never felt able to charge them for visits, consultations, or treatment. I had seen too much poverty in Egypt, and around Leith, that to ask for payment seemed obscene. To its credit Bridlington cleared these aged properties quickly in the early post-war years and the occupants were transferred to better accommodation. Most of these aged properties were in the Old Town and had grim names. I remember Paul's Yard, Bell's Yard, and Vickerman's Place. There was some very old property, too, in Prospect Street, reached through a gap between two shops opposite H. Davis Furniture Store.

It was widely known that Bridlington possessed an abortionist based in the Old Town. Termination of pregnancy was illegal in those days, and gynaecologists had to be very sure of their ground in terminating a pregnancy, and in maintaining should the occasion arise, that their action was solely to save the life of the mother. Otherwise it was a criminal offence, and imprisonment, and deletion from the medical register were the likely sequelae.

Termination by an abortionist in an ill-lit area using a knitting needle was fraught with danger, usually infection. Occasionally women terminated by an abortionist came my way; the history and symptoms were vague, nothing was given away and information had to be coaxed from them. They were very loyal to the abortionist, never mentioning a name or an address, and rarely admitting treatment. It was a fact of life that they existed and we had to be on guard with a limited antibiotic armamentarium to combat infection. Many women looked pale and shocked, and many had chronic coughs. Pulmonary tuberculosis was not uncommon, iron deficiency anaemia was very common and the differential diagnosis was rendered complex. The opening dialogue had to be carefully judged. Over and above we were taught never to examine women without a chaperone as your intentions could be jeopardized. Often this advice was ignored, especially if the situation showed emergency implications.

The abortionists' activities ceased with the abortion law of 1960, thus ending a dangerous and criminal practice. The wheel, however, has turned full circle: whereas termination of pregnancy prior to 1960 was a rare event, it became, as a result of the new legislation, a very frequent event indeed.

The wording of the new legislation is such that it seems

possible to make legal any request for termination, thus inviting a termination on demand situation. This demand has upset many gynaecologists, upset many of the nursing and theatre staff for ethical and religious reasons, and added to the work load of the NHS. Some areas have a lower termination rate than others, and no doubt local consultant gynaecological attitudes play a major role in determining this situation. It is ironical that with easy and free access to highly efficient methods of contraception available throughout the UK the high demand for termination of pregnancy still exists. Somewhere along the line from home, to school, to university, to medical propaganda, there must exist a serious failure of communication.

It was now early October 1948. I had just received my first payment of £400 for nearly seven months' work, and it was time to take a holiday. The summer season was over, the visitors had returned home, and many hoteliers, landladies and shop-keepers were on holiday recharging their batteries. At that time, in the early post-war years, it was considered unthinkable to take a holiday in peak season and load your partners with extra work. All hands were required on deck, because the visitor load was a heavy one, and the payment (thought meagre) gave a boost to our small incomes. Everyone pulled their weight, and the Saturday morning visitor head-count over the week became a jovial morale exercise. Records were kept over the year and it was surprising how consistent the numbers were over the corresponding weeks of previous years. This was the first holiday since arriving in March 1948 and we had not experienced a day off. As Barbara had not seen her family for over a year, and funds were low for a hotel holiday, we were only too delighted to travel to Aberdeenshire in the Flying Standard. The procedure, practised over the years was to close up 63 Horsforth Avenue and pin a notice on the front door requesting patients to attend Wellington House surgery. The practice patients were always most understanding about this, and I never heard any complaints about the procedure though I thought it must be inconvenient for them to have to do this. I used to take down the filing cabinets of NHS records and private patients to Wellington House after the last surgery at 63 Horsforth Avenue on the eve of the holiday, to help Drs Gordon-Taylor and Linell maintain continuity of treatment. It was a chore at the end of the day loading up the car boot with cabinets, and then unloading at the other end. It was a worse chore doing the reverse procedure after the holiday! Holidays were regarded as a luxury, not a right, and we were grateful to be able to have them.

I had never driven to the north of Scotland; a road map revealed it was a near 400 mile drive. Motorways were non-existent! Few cities or towns had a by-pass, the River Forth and River Tay Road Bridges had not been built and road surfaces were poor after their neglect during the war years. To negotiate Middlesbrough, Durham, Newcastle, Edinburgh, Dundee and Aberdeen (this was the shortest route during petrol rationing) was clearly going to take time and an early start was imperative if we were to complete the journey in a day and see Mrs Crockatt in Keptie Street, Abroath, as well. Therefore, at four forty-five am the Flying Standard, well down on its suspension, set off on its long journey on a Saturday morning, complete with Barbara and Angus and the driver, and the equipment required for ourselves and a baby of fourteen months. I had collected enough petrol coupons to manage the journey, and return journey. It was dark, the roads quiet, and a little eerie as we traversed the Whitby Moors to Guisborough. The engine never faltered, the off side head lamp repaired by myself with a piece of aluminium, and bolted to the mudguard, quivered, but helped to light the way. However, I was pleased when dawn broke so that I could read the sign-posts and ensure that I was on the correct road out of Middlesbrough to Durham. Our route passed through 'Pity Me' and Chester-le-Street, over the Tyne Bridge, and through the main shopping centre of Newcastle. Then on to Ponteland and into open country once again. It was here that we had our first stop, tea from a vacuum flask, a leg stretch, and a rest. It was nine thirty am. We were doing well. As we motored, the road cleaved the Cheviot Hills; wild-looking sheep with curly horns peered at us from the roadside and care was necessary lest they crossed our path. Otterburn soon was behind us; we noticed large areas of young trees recently planted and other large areas where trees had been felled. Soon Carter Bar was reached, England left behind, and we were gliding along smooth well-engineered roads into the Lowlands. Those Scots, responsible for the environment forty years ago understood the necessity of replacing the gifts of nature they inherited.

Ten years ago, on my journeys to Edinburgh by train on the

old LMS route from Carlisle to Carstairs Junction, I used to admire the gaunt distant hills of the Cheviots, their shadowy shapes at daybreak becoming sharp and majestic as the morning sun rose behind them. To drive through the Lowlands is a sheer delight at any time of the year, but in October with the fall of the leaf from the avenues of trees lining the approach to Jedburgh, and the beautiful colourings of the carpets of leaves formed alongside the main roads, leaves burnt out by the fire of life, is a sight not readily forgotten. This route, the A68, wide and well engineered all those years ago, has required but little alteration to meet the needs of the modern age, and it makes the perfect introduction to Scotland's capital city, landmarked by the characteristic shape of Arthur's Seat, and guarded by the dominance of Edinburgh Castle. It was easy for me to drive through Edinburgh, so well did I know it, as we passed by the Students Union and the McEwen Hall, the book shops of Teviot Place, with a glimpse of the Edinburgh Royal Infirmary as we turned into Forest Road leading to George IV Bridge, down the mound and left into Princes Street. The trams were still there: into George Street, and soon we were on the Queensferry Road with Melville and Daniel Stewart's College on our left, and heading for the River Forth and the ferry, spanned by the artistic, brown-red cantilever rail-bridge.

Before the construction of the Road Bridge across the Forth, two ferries plied back and forth between South and North Queensferry, carrying a cargo of cars. The crossing took nearly thirty minutes. We used to enjoy this part of the journey. First, it was a rest for the driver with the added bonus of lungfuls of Scottish air to clear the head, and second, it gave us a chance to survey from near sea-level, the intricacies and engineering skill of the structure of the rail bridge commenced in 1882. It took eight years to build, and we learned that the painting of the bridge in its red-brown coat was a continuous process, once started never completed.

Later on, the Forth Road Bridge was built and opened by Queen Elizabeth II and the Duke of Edinburgh in 1964; its construction was a fascinating scene. We watched the cable-spinner traverse its seemingly endless journey with wonderment. When the road bridge opened, the ferries disappeared. This event was a great day for Scotland, and now that the Forth Road Bridge is linked to Perth by the M90 it is difficult to remember

213

that previously our route lay from North Queensferry to Inverkeithing and alongside the ship-breakers yards where many a famous naval vessel of World War Two met its grave. HMS *Nelson*, or HMS *Rodney*, a sister ship, was undergoing demolition on one occasion as we drove past. It was then on to Crossgates, Cowdenbeath, Kinross, and Milnathort, towns with their grey stone houses, narrow streets, which always seemed quiet at the times we were there. At the Bridge of Earn we used to stop for refreshment at a cafe near the roadside, close to the Bridge of Earn Hospital. We pressed on, and at a summit of an incline looked down over the fair city of Perth, hazy in the autumn light. We stopped by the side of the River Tay, near the bridge, at Perth, to telephone Mrs Crockatt as we were nearing Arbroath. She always said: 'I'll put the kettle on!', but there was forty miles yet to travel for that cup of tea. Our route now took us along a fast straight road through Glencarse, and Inchture, and by-passed Dundee via its industrial estate. That particular road Perth to Dundee was engineered by the late Mr William Bryce, who subsequently was the county surveyor for the East Riding of Yorkshire. He lived at 94 St James Road in Bridlington, and volunteered this interesting information during a professional visit when the discussion switched from his health to his work in Scotland. The last time I traversed this road it had been converted to dual carriageway for most of its length, and I am sure he would be as proud of it now as he was all those years ago. We were now on the A92, seventeen miles from Arbroath on another smooth, fast, and fairly straight road. As we approached Arbroath, the Infirmary, with its tall chimney on the left was a landmark, and we were quiet as we savoured, with nostalgia, the happy days, the hard and endless work, the meagre salary, friends, and above all, the place where Barbara and I met and found each other. We were delighted to have reached Arbroath by five pm; the Flying Standard had ridden well with the rear wheels separated from the wheel arches by a mere three inches. The engine, with its aluminium cylinder head purred all day, enjoying free rein; baby Angus enjoyed the movement in the carry-cot, occasionally rising to his feet to roll an apple along the rear parcel shelf. We had travelled two hundred and ninety-six miles, and another ninety-six miles lay ahead to complete our journey to Huntly.

'Afternoon-tea' with Mrs Crockatt was always a superb 'high

tea'. She had fresh fried haddock for us, the best there could ever be, and plates of cakes, and bread rolls of every description. There was something very special about her cups of tea which assuaged the dehydration provoked by our journey. She was a skilled conversationalist, seemed to know everybody and everything going on in Arbroath and we were full of fresh knowledge as we bade her farewell. It was six thirty pm, we were refreshed and revitalized, and we have never been able to thank Mrs Crockatt and her son Heb, a potato merchant, adequately for all their kindness, generosity, and support over so many years right up to her death in 1982. Darkness had fallen as we threaded our way back to the main road to Aberdeen. Traffic, mercifully, was light, because a rest, good food, and a hot fire made me feel drowsy. 'Cats eyes' dividing the roads had not been invented, there were few white lines, car lighting was poor, and night driving a hazard. The Flying Standard, in common with many cars of that vintage had a roller-blind which could be drawn over the rear window, controlled by a slide lever above the driver's door, the object being to conceal dazzle from following vehicles. I tended to keep mine down during darkness being more concerned with traffic ahead, and approaching, than traffic astern. However I had a wing mirror which was helpful providing it was not raining. In the modern age, traffic behind has become a real hazard, as drivers bunch together at high speeds, and run into each other from the rear.

We were soon at Montrose and crossing the bridge separating the small harbour from the Montrose Basin, a large inland basin of water on flow tide, but sandy dunes at ebb tide. Latterly I have often thought there was potential for a marina there but it has never been mooted, and is probably impractical. The main shopping street was wide, and spacious, clearly planned by men of vision for the traffic invasion which lay ahead. It was a fine clear night and we made steady progress, descending the twisty hills to reach Stonehaven, a grey little town with pleasant views and a good harbour. We climbed out of Stonehaven and after another seventeen miles we could see the thousands of lights ahead inviting us into the fine granite city of Aberdeen.

After crossing the narrow bridge of Dee (still as narrow forty-one years on, causing traffic delay and requiring a wider bridge and possible fly-over to the A92 South), the city centre was by-passed by the North and South Anderson Drives and joined the

A92 again, linking Aberdeen to Inverness. This was our route, and Huntly was thirty-six miles along it. We soon knew that we were in agricultural country and that there had been cattle and sheep sales in the numerous markets that day. (Saturday was a market day and one of the busiest days of the week in those days.) Heavily laden floats made up most of the on-coming traffic; they were wide vehicles travelling fast and driven by drivers who must have known every inch of the road. We had to get out of the way and concentrate on the verges with the single near-side dipped headlight; the off-side headlight was 'out' by law.

Kintore and Inverurie were the largest towns we passed through with wide main streets, and shopping centres quiet at eight pm. As we sped along the road became quieter as we moved deeper into rural Aberdeenshire. 'Colpy' appeared on a sign-post, and soon we were negotiating the dangerous corners of the Glens of Foudland as we began the gradual descent to Huntly. A small crossroads appeared out of the inky black pointing Gartly to the left, Drumblade to the right. The left turn was for us, and five minutes later we entered the compound of Bothwellseat. I switched off the engine with relief and the weary pistons found respite. We had arrived complete, and in good condition. It was almost nine pm, and we had travelled three hundred and ninety-six miles since leaving Bridlington; such a long time ago it seemed.

We were made most welcome, and for fourteen days we enjoyed rest, fine company, and the best of farm food. The dangers of ingesting animal fat, and high cholesterol and high triglyleride blood levels, were not appreciated at that time, and farm food can produce this situation. However, the farming community appeared fit and strong, taking plenty of rigorous exercise in the very fresh air of north-east Scotland, and their dietary regime did not prevent them from reaching their allotted span, and in many cases, far beyond.

We returned to Drumblade Church for a Sunday service and I remember the well-filled pews, the enthusiastic hymn singing with Scottish accents rising heavenwards in the fine autumn light, and the message from the pulpit, carried home for discussion and analysis later on. Well-educated, sincere, and dignified, were those members of the Presbytery I met and all were deeply respected.

We spent a splendid holiday and the cares of the world seemed far away. Radio reception in the hills was not good in those days and we relied on the daily newspaper (except a Sunday) to keep us informed. However, holidays cannot last for ever, and it was time to take to the road again, and return to the trials and problems facing the new NHS in Bridlington, and especially those of 63 Horsforth Avenue. With the Flying Standard well filled with farm produce we made an early start at six am on a Saturday fourteen days after setting out on holiday. We stopped at 93 Keptie Street, Arbroath, Mrs Crockatt's home, en route. Despite our protests she insisted on giving us a second breakfast with hot freshly baked morning rolls which were delicious; we would not require further food for the remainder of the day. At the last minute she handed me a packet of 'Arbroath Smokies'. Those who have never tasted such a fish dish are recommended to sample this delicacy, hot or cold on their next visit to Scotland.

When we reached the Forth Ferry I left the car for a breath of air, but was well aware of a strong smell of petrol as I returned to it, emanating, so I thought, from an adjacent, aged, truck. Time was precious, summer time ended that night, Angus was a little fractious, darkness expected at five pm, so we pressed on and our next stop was about three miles short of Otterburn. Barbara stayed in the car with Angus, while I had a break. Again I smelled petrol and soon discovered that petrol was leaking from the tank in a steady dribble on to the road; the petrol gauge confirmed that the consumption since the previous fill was heavy. Concerned, I drove rapidly on to Otterburn and stopped at a small garage for advice, to be informed by the attendant that a seam had split in the tank. He attempted to plug it with household soap to no avail, and his advice was to drive to Newcastle as fast as possible and call at the first garage I came across. I required more petrol to get me there and had to part with coupons for two more gallons of (Pool petrol) low octane, the only available petrol then. It was a drab, damp, late Saturday afternoon, Newcastle was busy, and football fans were streaming homewards after the day's matches as we approached the city centre. Eventually we drove on to the forecourt of a garage. Saturday in 1948 was a normal working weekday and two mechanics inspected the tank, announcing that it would have to be removed, dried out, soldered, and replaced, a dangerous undertaking because of a possible explosion, and that it would be impossible to contemplate such work before Monday morning. However, seeing our predicament the mechanics said they would by-pass the leaking tank by standing a ten gallon drum filled with petrol on the floor behind my seat, and connect a tube from it to the petrol pipe feeding the carburettor. It would enable me to get home (one hundred miles away). This procedure was carried out, a modest bill paid and off we went with the car windows wide open, and with the advice not to smoke or switch off the engine as we would never be able to start it again. Angus was now with Barbara on the passenger front seat. I felt sure this procedure was illegal, extremely dangerous, and I drove with the utmost care. Nobody spoke as we approached the Whitby Moors. The engine hammered on relentlessly, the petrol fumes were intolerable, but at ten pm we reached Bridlington and the car came to rest on the garage ramp. We were lucky to be home alive, and with a clear day ahead of us before the onslaught of a Monday morning.

After these long journeys in our early cars Barbara and I always noticed that when we sat or laid down, we felt ourselves surging forwards traversing our route. It took about twelve hours for this phenomena to subside. However in more modern cars, driving faster, and occasionally on even longer distances, we were never troubled. No doubt there is a medical explanation for the sensation experienced, and perhaps the semi-circular canals of the balance mechanism are responsible. Certainly our concentration on the road was intense, our eyes in proptosis, especially in fog, and we were never certain that applying the brakes would stop the car.

On the Sunday morning I telephoned Mr Trenery at his home and explained the situation. To my surprise and relief he was soon on the scene with a mechanic, and once again I watched my car towed ignominiously away. It would not start itself and the Newcastle mechanics had been correct with their advice. Mid-afternoon the car was driven back, the tank repaired, and I had no further trouble in that respect. It was a great relief to be able to drive down to Wellington House, collect the filing cabinets, and gear myself up for the following day. There was no hope of a change of car; in the early post-war period a new car was a rare sight indeed.

The year 1948 drew to a close; it had been an eventful one

for us. Over the Christmas period I remember how amazed and overwhelmed Barbara and I were at the generosity and kindness of so many patients. Bulbs, flowers, fruit, chocolates, cigarettes, and a 'bottle' were gratefully accepted, and Angus received many Match Box models of cars which gave him great pleasure. We had been brought up in the difficult period between the two world wars when money was scarce in Devon, Dorset, and rural Aberdeenshire, and no doubt elsewhere too. We were unaccustomed at Christmas to see decorations apart from a sprig of holly on a Christmas pudding and there were certainly no signs of Christmas during the war in North Africa, the Sudan, and Eritrea.

To see the local hospitals transformed with Christmas trees, and heavily decorated, was a revelation, as were the lights and decorations in many houses.

As the New Year 1949 moved into its stride it became clear that the Horsforth Avenue surgery was on the upswing. More and more registration cards were handed in, and gradually, with every quarterly count of NHS patients conducted at the HQ in Toll Gavel, Beverley, the numbers on the list were increasing. Some registrations were from previous patients of Dr CR Taylor I had never met, who had either misunderstood the need to register on a doctor's list, or who had been lying low waiting for reports about the young new doctor in 63 Horsforth Avenue. Many, however were new arrivals in Bridlington and I was especially pleased about this, and wondered who was advising them! As the list increased, of course, so did the work and the commitment required, but with the valuable help from Barbara who was excellent with the telephone, and who was able to charm callers at the surgery, I worked on determined to maintain the high standard I was taught, and to treat patients as I would hope to be treated myself. At that time the terms of employment were twenty-four hours a day, seven days a week, year in, year out! Dr Gordon-Taylor's ways were set in pre-NHS days and he would not, and could not change. I was able to understand his position; he was sixty-five years old in 1948. Dr Linell seemed to possess a vagueness about his direction and was unable to address himself whole-heartedly to the task of creating a viable practice. Under these circumstances it was little wonder that a heavy load fell to the willing horse, and I found I was having to cope with my own work-load as well as dealing with many patients of the other partners, especially at unsociable hours! The future caused me considerable concern because there was no hint of Dr Gordon-Taylor's retirement, or Dr Linell's change of direction, and I began to wonder for how long I should be able to stand the pace and how long it would be before my first and last coronary thrombosis! Dr Gordon-Taylor was a dominant personality and difficult to approach, but Dr Linell was an amiable man, always helpful in holding the fort in domestic rather than medical situations. We had quite a good relationship though I could not understand his apathy.

Summer 1949 was another good one. My father and mother surprised me by paying us a visit for a week, a long haul for them by train from Exeter to York where I met them in the car. I always thought my father was impressed with Bridlington, and he even inspected a house opposite us to see if it would suit them. However they returned to the blander climate of Devonshire, and never made the journey again, though they often expressed interest in the growth and development of the practice.

During the summer of 1949 Dr Linell's garden was in full bloom, lush with grass, flowers and vegetables. By a twist of fate this idyllic scene was destroyed in less than a week by a plague of caterpillars which confined themselves to his garden only. Everything was reduced to sticks and stalks midst the stench of decaying vegetation. Caterpillars invaded the house, crawled down the flex to the light bulbs, and crawled over the window panes and walls. Caterpillars eyed me from under the glass of the weighing scales. I have never seen such a scene since a flight of locusts destroyed a crop of corn in Eritrea in minutes during the war. This incident was a major disaster for Dr Linell; he felt he had been victimized.

Barbara was expecting her second baby in early August, and we looked forward to this event with happiness.

On a Sunday afternoon about a month after the plague of caterpillars, Dr Linell called at 63 Horsforth Avenue and was escorted to the lounge. He announced that he had cold feet about the practice and the NHS in general, and had decided to resign from the practice at the end of the fiscal year, early April 1950. The poor financial reward was his prime concern; he had decided to emigrate to the US to take up a post in a tuberculosis centre. In retrospect he must have been one of the first of the medical brain drain who emigrated to Canada, Australia and New Zealand between 1949 and 1952 in search of pastures new. Most succeeded and have never returned. The Danckwert Award of 1952 which gave the beleaguered doctors their first financial lift helped in some measure to redress the situation and stemmed the exodus of medical men abroad. Initially I was surprised, though his decision did fit in with my view that he was unsettled and unlikely to change. His decision was irrevocable and I could not persuade him to alter his plans; I could only wish him well.

After he had left the house and I had time for reflection, I thought this was the best possible solution for him, and the future well-being of the practice. The next step, a vital one, was to replace him with a doctor with energy and enthusiasm who would strive to help me build up the practice. I did not see Dr Gordon-Taylor for a day or two; he was non-committal about the news, and my enquiry as to whether he intended to advertise in the BMJ for a successor was a negative one. He said that Mr Patrick, a surgeon from Hull with whom he was on close terms, had told him he could always recommend a house surgeon from Hull Royal Infirmary as required, and he intended to contact him forthwith.

I told him I thought an advertisement would broaden the field of choice, but he refused, dug his heels in, and I was compelled to fall into line with disappointment. There was no immediate urgency, it was the end of July, and Dr Linell did not leave until early April.

6 August, the expected date for the new baby drew near, and the summer season was in full swing, the town and beach packed out with visitors. Barbara was booked into a small maternity home in 148 Cardigan Road. At that time as many babies were born at home or in private nursing homes as in the NHS Avenue Hospital. In 1949 Dr Linell and I had to be very sure that the obstetric situation was satisfactory and unlikely to be complicated for a domiciliary confinement, though a well-equipped midder bag had nearly as much to offer as a maternity hospital, apart from Caesarean sections, rare events and fraught with danger in those far away days. We had nerves of steel, confidence in our abilities, attributes vital for GPs in situations where consultant skill was not readily available or absent altogether.

As events unfolded, Barbara experienced a straightforward uncomplicated confinement and we were delighted to welcome another healthy son whom we named Arthur. Two weeks was the recognized lying in time, and a busy time it was for me because in addition to managing the practice workload I had to keep the home fires burning and look after my well-being as best I could. Angus was in Kent with Barbara's sister and her family, thus freeing us from another anxiety. I remember the journey to Kent there and back in a day, and Dr Linell meeting me at York after midnight. There was a repeat journey too!

It was a relief and a welcome pleasure to visit Barbara and the new baby in the late evenings, to unwind, sit down, and detach oneself from the practice, and discuss future plans.

It was the early years of the NHS and the holiday seasons stand out in my memory. The reason for this was the nature of the work with endless numbers of visitors with acute illness and urgent conditions necessitating urgent treatment. Most visitors from the West Riding stayed for seven days, Saturday to Saturday, and many arrived for an early breakfast in Bridlington on Saturday having travelled by very early train or motor car. Number 63 Horsforth Avenue was situated in an area which had a good quota of boarding houses and hotels around it, and a large holiday camp called Graingers at Wilsthorpe, a mile south from the surgery. This situation ensured plenty of customers. It was not uncommon for the front door bell buzzer close to my ear in the bedroom to activate before seven am. I was able to open the side window of the bedroom, survey the anxious scene below me and engage in a dialogue. Frequently there was an anxious young husband informing me his wife was having a haemorrhage. On numerous occasions the anxious young husband did not know the address of the boarding house. I learned to resist the temptation to demand he should go and find out and let me know, and instead I used to suggest he waited at my garage door whilst I part dressed, and we would drive to the house (if he could locate it). The situation was invariably an inevitable miscarriage, and usually the patient had travelled to Bridlington threatening a miscarriage before leaving home. We used to inject morph gr 1/6, ring the Avenue Maternity Hospital for admission, and contact the local ambulance. It was impracticable to treat these conditions in a busy boarding house in peak season. The landladies did not like it, and the other visitors disapproved. Occasionally an exception had to be made if there was another baby of the same family present, and the husband unable to cope. I did not like it either as my requests to save everything passed fell on deaf ears, and it was conjecture as to whether the miscarriage was complete or not. It was surprising the number of miscarriages presenting in a week. Equally surprising were the visitors who came for a second opinion who were found to have advanced lung cancer, very active peptic ulcers, congestive failure, and left ventricular failure, undiagnosed by their doctors at home. Perforations were very frequent. These latter conditions involved a considerable amount of work and time had to be found to write letters to their doctors about them. The fee for temporary residents, as they were called, was 9s. over a three months period.

The senior partner, Dr Gordon-Taylor, even in 1949 was one of the few remaining general-practitioner surgeons, certainly in this area. He enjoyed surgery so much that he used to assist Mr Patrick, a general surgeon resident in Hull, at his operating sessions once a week in the Lloyd Hospital, Bridlington, when he was well past seventy-five years of age. It was customary, nay, demanded in those days that the patients' GP assisted the surgeon in cottage hospitals. The stress of the interruption of the morning's work routine, which was always heavy, was compensated by assisting the surgeon in the theatre atmosphere. I used to enjoy holding artery-forceps, clipping the bleeding vessels, swabbing as required, and pulling on heavy retractors as the surgeon worked deeply in the abdominal cavity. Often he would chat amiably about his work, and how occasionally he had operated on valuable race-horses, who were first past the post in subsequent races. The blood-vessels, seized by long and short artery-forceps surrounding the incision, had to be tied off using catgut, and this could require a certain skill, elevating them gently for the surgeon to tie the catgut around the nose of the artery-forceps, then depressing the handles so that their nose was directed towards the surgeon whilst he tied the knot. At the correct moment the ratchet of the forceps was released as the catgut received its first tight knot to secure the blood vessel and prevent further bleeding. If you were a fraction too hasty releasing the ratchet the surgeon would find himself merely tying a knot on a piece of catgut for nothing, to his displeasure. If the artery was a large one it would start to spurt blood and the operating field would be soaked in blood, necessitating heavy swabbing and pressure until control was secured again with the artery-forceps. On those occasions when you were holding a heavy retractor with your right hand, and the forceps to be removed was long and strong and tightened to its terminal ratchet, it had to be released using the thumb and index finger of the left hand. This could be tricky and sometimes strength seemed to be lacking; I used to wait until the surgeon said 'Off', and summoned further reserves of strength and dexterity for the manoeuvre which required the delicate approach. Diathermy was available but this was not used by all surgeons. All the time the theatre search-light, inches above you, directed heat and light to your head as well as illuminating the patient's abdominal content.

Cholecystectomy, gastroenterostomy, partial gastrectomy, short-circuiting of the small and large bowel, and occasionally prostatectomy were carried out in the Lloyd Hospital. Post-operative care was in the hands of the GP and it could be time-consuming. There were anxious times, great recoveries, and job satisfaction.

In those days a surgeon was considered an expert technician only, and he did not necessarily follow up his surgical patients in the subsequent days, weeks, or years, though this position has gradually changed and patients would now expect a surgeon to see them post-operatively. Every practice in the town provided the anaesthetist, and assistant for the surgeon so there was a steady flow of different faces and skills every operating session; no wonder there were plenty of rubber boots, rubber aprons, gowns, masks, and head caps in the changing room to garb this influx. After these traumatic intrusions to my work it was off and away in the car to visit new calls, and follow up about a hundred visits a month to the elderly and chronic sick; there was no morning coffee break, in fact I cannot recall morning coffee appearing in the hospital before the mid 1960s, though we were well looked after if there were emergencies at other times. Patients were as demanding then as they are now, and I often set out with thirty calls every morning. I liked to break the back of the work by lunch time, though I rarely succeeded. The practice had a considerable rural component, and the afternoons were required for visits to Flamborough, Carnaby, Rudston, Burton Agnes, Burton Fleming, Ulrome, Skipsea, Speeton, Reighton and Hunmanby. I had patients in Thwing and this was quite a haul. Rural patients did not expect to be seen until the afternoon. My annual mileage was 20,000 miles.

There used to be a wireless training school in Shaftesbury Road, near the sea-front end. It was demolished later and a block of flats took its place. Many students from eighteen years and upwards attended, and they were trained to be wireless operators on ships. There was boarding accommodation attached and students were attracted from many parts of the country. I remember receiving a call there late one evening from the principal, stating that one of the boarders had a very sore throat. I went to the school and was escorted to a bunk bed. Lighting was poor, access not easy, but I found myself looking at the only case of diphtheria I have seen either as a student or in practice. He was acutely ill, and I was most worried for him, and the likely possibility of spread to other students in the school. I was able to transfer him to an infectious diseases hospital in Cottingham where the diagnosis was confirmed. He received anti-toxin and made a complete recovery; it was miraculous there was no spread of this dreaded illness in the wireless school.

Epidemics of children's infectious illnesses could cause a great deal of work, and worry, especially with measles and whooping cough. The high temperature of incubating measles could be present for seven days before the appearance of the rash. Every evening the temperature was higher, 105°F or more sometimes. I was taught to look for Koplik's spots on the buccal mucosa routinely when examining a child with a sore throat, and if seen, (and it was not always easy to see the white grains of salt on an erythematous base) you could with supreme confidence diagnose pending measles. It was a relief to the household and myself when the rash appeared and the diagnosis established. Only ten years ago I remember a medical colleague with two young sons, one of whom I was able to announce would be showing measles in a day or two. Day followed day, and no rash appeared, and the rising temperature and increasing prostration added to the father's anxiety. His nerve nearly cracked, but at last the rash appeared to confirm the diagnosis. He was a young practitioner who had never seen measles and was quite astounded at the severity of the illness before, and during, the invasive stage. I was astounded too, recollecting the many hundreds of children I had seen with measles, but on reflection, he had been trained in the days when measles immunization was routine, thereby practically eliminating an unpleasant illness with dangerous complications, and he had never had the opportunity to see such a case.

Whooping cough, too, could be a dread. The paroxysmal cough could rack a small infant and child to its death. How helpless one was, and how severe the illness used to be. Parents used to chart the number of paroxysms in twenty-four hours and anxiously await a reduction to show the worst was probably over. I remember a small baby, cyanotic with every paroxysm, held in its mother's arms. Medicated steam gently hissed from a steam kettle's nozzle directed at the infant's face, to no avail. I could not leave the house. It was unthinkable to move the baby to an isolation hospital in mid-winter, and what more could a hospital do? For support I asked Dr Gordon-Taylor to come to the house and see the infant. He did so, a formidable figure in black coat and striped trousers. Drawing himself up to his full height he announced that there was one person who could save the baby, and that was the mother. She must nurse it; there was no other treatment. His voice was authoritative, he dominated the room and nobody dared question him. After he departed the effect was electrifying; the mother knew that it was up to her, and help and support for her was rallied from relatives and friends close by.

After some hours I had to leave for further work. That infant survived. Some days later when the danger was past I remarked to the mother how frustrated and ignorant I felt that it had not been possible to help the infant more in such a dreadful illness. She said that my presence in the room had given her the strength and confidence to continue the fight for her baby's life. I was barely thirty years old, and her words left a deep impression on me that I could be valued in such fashion. To this day I sometimes see that infant in our town, now over forty years old, strong and healthy with her family, and I marvel she ever survived that night.

I remember having whooping cough myself when I was five years old, and the paroxysms causing sickness after every meal. It was summertime and I spent most of the six weeks coughing in the garden, and having meals in the garden in the sunshine. The cough lasted many weeks, and I lost weight and strength until one day my father said that the doctor advised that a short walk round the gas works daily would help me. I remember that the cough soon disappeared on this regime, but whether the improvement was due to the coal-tar inhaled, or a natural remission of the disease I will leave for the opinion of those wiser than myself. Again, immunization has worked wonders and although not completely eliminated, whooping cough has become a mild illness causing no anxiety, and can even be difficult to diagnose. In days gone by the whoop could be heard across the street and out of the window, causing mothers and children to scatter to safer areas, and the diagnosis was never in doubt.

Although one attack of whooping cough is said to produce life-long immunity, I had a second dose ten years ago in a mild and modified fashion when there was a small epidemic in Bridlington.

Chickenpox, too, could be a troublesome addition to a workload, especially if there was a measles epidemic simultaneously. Because of its long incubation period an epidemic lingered on over the months, and it took many weeks before a family of three or four children were out of quarantine if the condition was passed on from one sibling to another. Chickenpox used to be quite a severe illness; I used to see children covered with vesicles in all their stages with pyrexia, miserable skin irritation and unwell for four to five days, and it took all of three weeks for the scabs to separate and to be free from infection. We were warned that if the scabs on the face were picked off, the scars were permanent. Adults were affected worse. I had chickenpox as a medical student, and well do I remember the heat and the irritation from the wide coverage of vesicles, especially those in awkward situations such as the outer canthus of the eye and the internal auditory meatus, and the incessant scalp irritation where the scabs were three times the size of those elsewhere. I felt unclean. To my shame I passed it on to my father over the Christmas holiday, and his illness was far worse than mine, and was complicated by a pneumonic patch, happily relieved and contained by M & B 693 (sulphapyridine). The severity with which chickenpox could attack was demonstrated by the case of a middle-aged business man in Bridlington. On the third day after the appearance of the first vesicles he was absolutely covered with the vesicles all over his body, and some were haemorrhagic. He was hyper-pyrexial and in a toxic condition; to add to the problem his extremities were also heavily involved and this is of course unusual in chickenpox. So ill was he, confused, and rambling, and prostrate, that smallpox was seriously considered and I decided to ask the MOH (medical officer of health) to see him and advise. I had not met the MOH previously and he knew I was a newcomer. Perhaps I chose a bad day but when he arrived he was obviously in ill-humour and made it quite clear that he did not regard domiciliary visiting as part of his work. However, he was surprised at what he saw, and said it must be the worst case of chickenpox he had ever seen, but that smallpox was unlikely! He never suggested that he should be transferred to an isolation hospital for skilled nursing, never saw the patient again, nor made further enquiries about him. I was astonished at his unhelpful attitude, and his indifference in leaving so ill a person to the care of his wife and myself. I did not ask for help from the district nurse as I was far from convinced the patient had not been infected with smallpox. The fact that there was no epidemic of chickenpox at the time, his, being the only case in the practice, and the fact that his work was connected with ships at Kingston-upon-Hull that travelled to countries where the disease was endemic, lends support in my view that this man may well have had smallpox. He recovered but it was six weeks before, shakily, he was fit to return to work.

By the time I retired in 1982 chickenpox always seemed a very mild illness; a few scattered spots often passed unnoticed by patient, parent, school-teacher, and often the doctor as well.

Although rubella was often epidemic before the days of immunization I cannot recall any untoward sequelae such as deafness in the offsprings of mothers infected in the early weeks of pregnancy.

Mumps could be unpleasant, especially if all four salivary glands were involved together, producing a bull-neck. Boys at puberty were kept in bed to minimize the onset of orchitis; they did not want a painful swollen testicle, and the possibility of being sterile later on. I thought orchitis was rare. As medical officer to a boys preparatory boarding school for over thirty years I never saw orchitis associated with mumps. In my view adult sufferers were more likely to have this complication. One patient, a girl, from another practice died from mumps encephalitis, but I have never met this complication myself.

The infectious diseases of childhood caused a great deal of work to every practice. If these epidemics coincided with an influenza epidemic, and influenza too was a severe illness fifty years ago, the practice workload became very heavy indeed, and we visited far into the late evening.

Another time-consuming event in the early post-war years, and the early years of the new NHS was the conduct of a post-mortem examination on a patient of the practice, when the doctor did not feel able to issue a death-certificate, being uncertain as to the cause of death. The procedure necessitated the transfer of the deceased to the Bridlington Mortuary, a brick-built structure in Brett Street half-way between St John Street and Brookland Road on the east side of the road. Occasionally when a patient died over-zealous relatives had contacted an undertaker and the body had been quickly removed to the sanctity of a chapel of repose. It was an unpleasant situation when the body had to be removed from there to the harsh coldness of the mortuary for a post-mortem. The coroner for the East Riding of Yorkshire was contacted by telephone and the details of the death unfolded. It was essential to be accurately informed of the deceased's age, address, place of death and how long ago it was since you last saw the deceased alive (any time over twenty-one days meant a post-mortem was mandatory). The coroner always asked why you could not issue the certificate, and what you thought was the most likely cause of death. If the coroner was understanding, realistic, and your account of the death and its likely cause satisfied his criteria, he would consent to the issue of a certificate, and with relief, you did this, completing the space on the reverse side of the certificate that the coroner had been informed.

It is interesting to record at this juncture that there has been no change in the format of a death certificate for over fifty years to my knowledge, and it must surely rank as the sole unchanged survivor of the multitude of forms which have emanated over the years.

If, on the other hand, your account of the death, failed to satisfy the coroner (and there were occasions when you thought his judgement mistaken), he would ask you to carry out a post-mortem, and write a report which was conveyed to him by the police. If he was satisfied after this he would issue a burial or cremation order; (cremation was not so common then).

It was unwise to query the coroner's decision. Usually he was a lawyer (though there was a medically qualified coroner in this area for many years); compliance was advisable. I remember we occasionally met the coroners socially at various functions and we learned to know them well, and they knew us. We had a good rapport. We always tried to make a point of knowing everyone we worked with, so that no-one was faceless.

Sometimes there were medico-legal aspects to the death, unnatural cause of death, and in these cases the coroner would ask for a post-mortem to be conducted by the police-surgeon or a pathologist specialized in such work.

When the coroner instructed the practitioner to perform the post-mortem this caused consternation. It was a major interference with the day's work-programme. In the first place the technique of a post-mortem examination was not high on the agenda for the training of a medical student. I remember purchasing a second hand edition of a text book on the subject from Bryce's bookshop in Teviot Place, Edinburgh, and it accompanied me to the morgue's slabs. There was a female attendant who appeared for every post-mortem who was responsible for cleaning the room, preparing the cadaver, laying out the dissecting instruments, and returning the room to normal after the indescribable mess we used to leave behind us. She was a real character, elderly, motherly, wore a white overall, and there were times when I suspected her knowledge of the matter in hand matched, or even exceeded ours. Her name was Mrs Minnie Trown. She talked steadily whilst we worked away, could narrate a spicy tale about her work there over the many years she had been employed in that capacity, and enlivened what was a gruesome task. She was a patient on my list and begged me never to transfer her to the cold slab on her demise. I acquiesced, and I am relieved to record that she died a natural death at an advanced age, and never occupied a table in the mortuary.

I do not wish to dwell on the details of the post-mortem: suffice it to say that they were carried out conscientiously, to the best of our ability, and with sensitivity. Organs were weighed and closely inspected, and details recorded. When required we removed the brain. It was remarkable that often after what had seemed to be a death from a coronary thrombosis, very little in the way of pathological changes were found macroscopically

230

in the heart and its blood vessels, but this may well have been due to our inexperience. It was paramount that the final suturing was carefully done so that no offence would be caused to the relatives who disliked the necessity for a post-mortem.

I cannot recall ever having received payment for carrying out a post-mortem, though I think there was a fee; a remarkable omission considering the time involved, the importance of the work, and the unpleasant nature of the task. Prior to the NHS it would have been obscene to send the relatives a bill for this service and after the onset of the NHS it was illegal to charge any NHS patient. Over the years, and to our relief, this work was taken out of our hands, and all PMs are now performed by pathologists. A sudden death nowadays always warrants a routine post-mortem, and this attracts a satisfactory fee for the pathologist. A practitioner now merely notifies the police that he has a sudden death to report and is unable to issue a certificate. No questions are asked and that is usually the finale of his involvement. Clearly I was born in the wrong era!

If an inquest is required a pathologist is present to detail and explain the cause of death, though the GP often has to be present as well to give his account of the recent and past medical history of the deceased, and his opinion, too, as to the cause of death. In days gone by we had to battle on in the court-room as best we could. Although the cause of death was usually completely outside our control or knowledge, one could often sense hostility and suspicion from relatives, and occasionally from the coroner himself.

Looking back to those years, so long ago, when a GP seemed to be a jack of all trades, and in whom there was such a high level of expectancy from patients, public, colleagues and consultants, these involvements were an enjoyable challenge.

It was, however, the reduction of the number of hours remaining for patient care that caused stress, and which could almost bring you to your knees if there were a series of similar incidents. Attendance by subpoena at the quarterly sessions in Beverley or the Crown Court in Leeds was exceptionally tedious; there was, often, a mystifying lack of knowledge as to when you were likely to be called to give your evidence as a professional witness: ten am was the usual starting hour and it was crucial to be there on time because occasionally an enlightened barrister for the prosecution, understanding your situation, would be prepared to call you first after he had completed his opening speech. The barrister for the defence would follow suit, and if there were no further questions you were graciously allowed to leave. Failure to be in court on time earned a justifiable rebuke.

This courtesy of an early call to the witness box always pleased me; I used to smile, thank them for their consideration, and was not dainty in my leave-taking. Unfortunately this procedure was not universal; attendances occurred when I would sit on a hard chair in a chilly room with no facilities, and with other witnesses from ten am to twelve thirty pm. Everybody was a stranger to each other, and held their peace from fear of possible collusion, general discomfiture, and the lack of a suitable topic for discussion, until it was announced that the court had adjourned for lunch and would resume at two fifteen pm. The irritation at the delay was assuaged by walking in the fresh air and having a snack in a cafe. I felt sure that the learned barristers would be attracted to the warmth and comfort of the Beverley Arms Hotel for their repast. Certainly my expenses were paid but a retrospective payment did not provide a full purse to pay for the meal at the time. Money was tight.

The court would reassemble at two fifteen pm, and the witnesses returned to the waiting room; at four fifteen pm the day finished and I would drive home frustrated to find that Barbara, with her customary skill with the telephone, had sorted out the new calls for the day, soothed many over-anxious people, and transferred any message with a taint of urgency to the secretary of Wellington House Surgery. Serenity prevailed as I set out on the new calls after five pm knowing that the recipients also knew why I was so late.

The same unhappy procedure could take up most of Day Two as well. With luck I might be called before four fifteen pm to give evidence (and this could be unnerving due to a barrister's skill at disrupting a stream of thought). It was a relief to reach home and read about the verdict in the *Hull Mail* later on in the evening. Well-meaning people said that two days in a chair doing nothing would charge up my battery; I can assure them that the nervous tension generated by being a professional witness, and by being absent from the practice for two days, short-circuited the battery and produced a weak potential.

The nadir of misery was when a subpoena was received which clashed with an annual holiday; hysterical pleading with the client's solicitor sometimes touched a tender chord and the case was delayed for a fortnight or more. Luck was not always my friend, and I remember once, many years ago, leaving my family whilst on holiday on the south coast to attend court, and then retracing my steps to the south again to complete the holiday. The fees for the return journey were paid in full and this helped to flavour the bitter pill.

There were times when I thought it would be sensible to take a holiday without a forwarding address, and be away from it all; sanity, however, always prevailed; I had been schooled to discipline. I am sure the legal profession would think that a doctor who left his practice without trace was not perhaps a conscientious member of his profession. Such bad publicity had to be avoided at all costs.

The year 1950 was getting into stride. Dr Linell had sold his bungalow in Fortyfoot, and, with his wife, daughter, and elderly father-in-law, was winding up his UK connections and preparing for the journey by sea to the US, and a new life. He left Bridlington on a grey morning in early March. Although I kept in touch with him for many years he never returned to the UK to my knowledge, but his wife came over for a holiday over fifteen years ago, called on us, and we spent a pleasant evening hearing how they had fared. It would seem that he had no regrets at emigrating, and had been successful in the various fields he had worked; he had enjoyed good holidays and had managed to see Australia and New Zealand. He died abruptly in his sixties. He was a restless man, capricious, and without a deep root, and no doubt was unable to be happy in a stable, if not monotonous, mode of life.

It was at this time Dr Gordon-Taylor addressed himself to the task of finding a replacement partner by mentioning to Mr Patrick, a surgeon from Hull, that the practice had a vacancy. This dilatory action was just as I feared, and meant that the newly appointed partner would have an inadequate introduction to the practice, and that for several weeks it would be a two-man practice, a daunting prospect for me, already overstretched.

As a result of Mr Patrick's interest two candidates appeared for interview and evaluation. The interviews were on different afternoons at three pm, and were conducted in the drawing room of Wellington House which was Dr Gordon-Taylor's residence as well. I had some pertinent questions to ask because the appointment was of major interest to me, seeing that the new partnership could last for at least thirty years.

The door opened as the first candidate entered the room, and was motioned to a chair. As he sat down it was very clear that he was wearing football stockings, thickly barred in gold and brilliant red. Four hostile eyes surveyed the exhibition in silence. Not that I was shocked, but rather surprised that a candidate should appear for interview in such an ostentatious fashion. Apart from his stockings his appearance was beyond reproach. As the interview progressed (and it did not go well) I felt that he was interviewing us rather than the reverse, and although young myself I gradually formed an opinion that he was a callow youth, and lacked the mature vision which was going to be essential for the survival of the practice! Perhaps I had an inflated physiognomy!; matters came to a head when the candidate asked if there was good hunting, fishing, and shooting in the locality! The interview was terminated rather abruptly, and Dr Gordon-Taylor suggested he saw our secretary, Miss Wells, for his travelling expenses, and that he would be hearing from us in a few days. To receive your travelling expenses was tantamount to being told you had failed in your quest.

After the door had shut behind him Dr Gordon-Taylor turned to me and boomed: 'Did you see his socks?' I had of course. Dr Gordon-Taylor said he would not stand for such stupidity, and obviously he was unsuitable for the post, and expressed his disappointment with Mr Patrick's choice. My opinion was not sought; it did, however, coincide with his, but for different reasons. We hoped for better fortune at the next interview.

As the door opened two days later for the second, and what seemed the final interview, another young man entered the room and was shown the chair. His name was Dr J.D. Lucey; he hailed from Southern Ireland, was ginger-headed, and had trained at Cork University. The interview set off on the right footing as Mrs Dr Gordon-Taylor was from the Emerald Isle too. Dr Lucey told us he had worked in a hospital at Coventry, and subsequently the Hull Royal Infirmary where he had held several appointments under various chiefs. He named Mr Simpson, an ENT surgeon well known for his expectancy of high standards, Mr Patrick, of course, and he also knew Dr Hellewell, the skin specialist, and his prescriptions for skin ailments which he felt sure we would find useful. He possessed the LM from Dublin.

It is interesting to note that there was little discussion about the practice finance, or financial expectation. The figures mentioned were necessarily loose; GPs were inadequately paid, the NHS was groaning with post-natal after-pangs, the future bleak, and we possessed the unpalatable knowledge that the previous partner left because he thought the practice was unviable. There was little to offer.

Hospital-orientated to date he had little experience of the tangled skein of general practice. He was keen and alert, though initially I thought he exhibited some diffidence about the post, and was perhaps wary of the contrasting figures in the interview chairs. Dr Gordon-Taylor always said he was getting on in years but that he was fit for a year or two before retiring; he was sixty-seven years old then. We both considered that he was an eminently acceptable candidate for the post, which was offered to him. After cool reflection he was invited to raise any questions for clarification and to let us know his decision. He returned to Hull. Dr Gordon-Taylor and I were pleased with what had taken place and we awaited his decision with keen anticipation.

How very different is an interview now. There is a high level of expectancy on the part of the candidate who will have been vocationally trained for two years after passing the finals, and will want to know, if taken on initially as an assistant, how long that assistantship will last, how soon will a partnership be offered, and how soon will parity be achieved. Holidays, time off, study leave and rota queries require an answer. Such questioning can be irksome, and one sometimes has to remind a candidate that what is put into a practice is more important than what is taken out of it.

A few days passed and there was no word from Dr Lucey; a week passed and there was still no word. Dr Gordon-Taylor was becoming edgy; he did not like being kept on a string. I tried to calm him by explaining that a house-officer's work was most demanding, and that there was barely time to attend to the calls of nature, let alone phoning a practice thirty miles away, and that he would probably be able to come over on the Sunday when he was perhaps free for a few hours. He accepted the force of this rather unprofessional statement, and the situation was deferred for a day or two. I was beginning to think that, perhaps, Dr Lucey thought the practice on the rocks, and that he would, with his talents, fare better in greener pastures. However, despite the catalogue of gloom and possible doom, I remained as optimistic about the future as ever because in the two years since I joined the practice there was growing evidence that my side of the practice was beginning to pick up. The need was for a similar reaction from the other side of the practice, and I hoped that Dr Lucey would be the man to address himself to the task; if he rejected the offer, it would disappoint me.

However, Dr Lucey remained silent, and Dr Gordon-Taylor eventually phoned Hull to clarify the position, and enquire if he was interested in the offer. I was a little bemused as to why Dr Lucey could not have phoned from night sister's telephone in the Hull Royal Infirmary during a vacant moment.

It transpired, though, that Dr Lucey had not yet made up his mind; it was not an offer on a golden plate, and from my own experiences I was able to understand the reason behind his apparent tardiness.

When he eventually arrived for an afternoon I suggested it would be a good idea if I drove him around, and showed him what bright, breezy, Bridlington had to offer. This was done and we drove all about the catchment area of the practice which was surprisingly varied and scattered, and we had a look at the Lloyd and Avenue Hospitals. I was able to give an account of the problems I faced when I arrived here, my reasons for optimism, and that if he was as keen as I was there was no reason why we should not sew up the town for ourselves! Oh, the naivety of youth! Whether or not this introduction influenced Dr Lucey in any way is unknown to me, but the fact that he accepted the post suggests it may have been a pointer to his affirmation.

Everybody was pleased, including Mr Patrick, and I looked forward to a long and happy partnership. I was not to be disappointed.

It was April 1950 and penicillin by injection had been released for NHS prescriptions. Although used during the war several years elapsed before there were adequate supplies for its general release. When prescribed, the patient received a small rubber-capped bottle containing a pale brown powder requiring a diluent. It was usual to dissolve the powder in two ccs of sterile water, and the injection was given intramuscularly into the upper outer quadrant of the buttock, and it was very painful. If a smaller amount of diluent was used the patient would be fearful of subsequent injections! At that time sterile water in two ccs glass ampoules was a rare sight; there were glass ampoules of coramine (nikethamide) and the mercurial duretic mersalyl, but most other preparations for injection were dispensed as small tablets in a thin glass phial, twenty or more tablets in a phial. In a patient's house the tablet was placed in a teaspoon, very clean water added to the spoon, which was boiled over a spirit lamp until the tablet dissolved. The solution was then drawn up into a glass record syringe, previously sterilized by boiling in the surgery, or the patient's kitchen.

For a penicillin injection in the surgery, sterile water was dispensed in ten ccs rubber-capped bottles which were stored on the practice dispensary shelves; they were used again and again, needles piercing the rubber cap until the bottle was empty, and this could take a month or more. How sterile was the water as the days passed by? Was aqua tappae cleaner?

Oh spare us, modern practitioners, from your criticisms, horror, and withering regard! You, in your ivory towers, with your prepacked throw-away sterile syringes, your medical cases packed with sterile glass ampoules containing water, and the most sophisticated and complex chemical formulae in ampoules, your practice nurse to inject for you, and the numerous preparations of oral penicillin of every flavour and hue, and indeed, even better antibiotics at your command — pause, and reflect on the situation as it used to be, and consider how fortunate you are to have such medication and aid!

We were only too delighted to have penicillin in whatever basic form there was to revolutionize the treatment for our patients' benefit. As for the non-sterile water, I never saw, at any time in my practice life, infection or an abscess at the site of an injection; a reaction to the injection, yes, but never infection. Surely the human body is not so frail as to fall foul to every organism!

The busy days passed by; the new partner settled in. When he arrived he did not have a car, and for the first few weeks his visits were carried out using a solid bicycle belonging to Dr Gordon-Taylor. It was heavy going for him but he carried out his work with good humour and distinction. His surgery consultations were mainly conducted in Wellington House surgery, so he was in closer affinity to Dr Gordon-Taylor than

237

myself: I never knew Dr Gordon-Taylor as well as did Dr Lucey and had little opportunity to do so. Over and above, Dr Gordon-Taylor was not the easiest man for a relationship. However, we all had a high regard and respect for each other, though we did not bow to each other from different ends of the hospital corridors as did my predecessor.

Dr Lucey was not married, and had lodgings in 31 Lambert Road on the north side of the town. The state of bachelorhood however, did not last for long because he found his future wife in Hull where she was nursing in the Hull Royal Infirmary; they were married in 1950.

I write often about motor cars, but so acute was the shortage, that it played a major role in our lives. On the corner of Hilderthorpe Road and Hamilton Road was the Ford Motor Garage owned and managed by Mr Ripley. Mr Ripley was a courteous and charming man who seemed to have a soft spot for young doctors without cars, and sympathized deeply with them when it was brought to his attention that they were wearing out shoe leather rapidly. From out of a top-hat he produced brand new black Ford 8 cars for them for £330; these lucky doctors had been placed at the top of his lengthy queue for new cars.

When Mr Ripley heard that Dr Lucey was riding about town on a Victorian bicycle, it brought tears to his eyes, whether from laughter or grief I know not, but in a very short time Dr Lucey was the proud possessor of yet another black Ford 8 from the top-hat. Good cars they were, too, rather high-sided, but reliable. With Mr Ripley in the background you felt you could not go wrong, and I was well aware myself that what Mr Ripley did not know about cars would go on the back of a postage stamp. He had car sympathy and cared about your car, and would obviously have preferred every local doctor to run a Ford car, bringing kudos to his already flourishing garage.

At nearly the same time, Mr Trenery, who owned the Standard and Triumph Garage at Hilderthorpe Road, and who had given me sterling service was clearly tiring of replacing the main cylinder head gasket of the Flying Standard every 1,000 miles, and towing me to his garage from various corners of the town and beyond; nor was he impressed when I shattered the peace of his garage by driving into it having lost the entire exhaust system from manifold to tail-pipe on the Quay Road

Above: The Flying Standard. New in 1939, it became the author's first car in 1947, and was well-known in Bridlington between 1948 and 1950.
Below: The Standard Vanguard, 1950. The author's second car, the mileometer recorded 130,000 miles at the time the car was traded in.

level crossing. It was time for the Flying Standard to retire. He offered me a brand new Standard Vanguard car; I never ordered it but I could not refuse. It cost £632 including radio, on the road, and it took me three years to pay for it. Fast, powerful, and ugly, it lasted me ten years and went round the clock one and a half times with one re-sleeve. At last it seemed as though we were in business.

It is strange to relate that in our practice the 1950/60 decade was marked by the large numbers of patients who developed acute left ventricular failure, or cardiac asthma as it was widely known, an accurate and graphic description.

Bridlington owned a population with a large elderly component who returned to their homes here after self-evacuation to the rural areas during the war. Whether the onset of an acute attack during the night was brought on from lying flat in bed, or initiated by a cold bedroom (no central heating then) or overactivity during the day, is debatable. What we did not possess was an efficient diuretic for long term use. Also the therapeutics of digitalis were taught differently. Great importance was attached to having a patient fully digitalized in congestive cardiac failure with anasarca, but this was considered of lesser importance in left ventricular failure, possibly because oedema of the extremities was not necessarily present.

The importance of a small dose of digitalis 0.0625 mgms daily for the long term was not appreciated, and even if it was, the available tabs digoxin were 0.25 mgms, requiring division into quarters to provide the small dose.

Whatever the cause, whatever our failings, a patient of sixty years plus could retire to bed in usual health unaware of a pending calamity. A few hours later this patient would waken, short of breath; within minutes a severe asthma attack developed, and minutes later the patient would be cyanosed with a bubbly chest, and moribund. The phone would ring at my bedside; the voice of a frightened relative or neighbour explained the trouble; often I could hear the attack over the telephone in the background. It was 'Come at once'. I did. It was down the stairs, jumping the last half dozen, diving into a long overcoat, wrapping a scarf around the neck, out to the garage, and frequently into the snow. Then a feverish drive with a rising pulse-rate to the house to find the front door open, a lighted bedroom window open, for more air, and the dreadful sound of agonized breathing disturbing the peace of night. Dr Lucey and I had learned to carry oxygen in our cars for the relief of the anoxia. If the cylinder was twenty c.ft., I could balance it on my shoulder, my medical case in my hand and up the stairs; if the cylinder was forty c.ft. (depending on the available stock) I arrived at the top of the stairs in a similar state to the patient. Such was the gross apparition appearing in the patient's bedroom. There was no time for niceties; immediate action was required. The patient was pulled to the sitting position, legs dangling over the side of the bed, and a relative charged to maintain that position. The oxygen cylinder was quickly connected and a BLB mask applied to the patient's face: I opened the medical case hoping I would find what was required. Morphine gr 1/6 combined with atropine gr 1/100 given intravenously to a woman, and morphia gr ¼ with atropine gr 1/100 for a man given intravenously. The effect of this treatment was dramatic; a fast thready pulse could, in twenty minutes, be back to normal, the wheeze and bubbling chest about clear, and the appearance and well being of the patient so improved that a cup of tea was demanded. It was then that we propped the patient high up in bed, with pillows, chair-cushions, and rugs, listened to the heart and chest, took the blood pressure, and decided the future treatment.

If the patient lived alone, transfer to the Lloyd Hospital was arranged when fit to be moved, but patients were kept in their homes if there was good support, good conditions, and good know-how. We never attempted to move a patient to hospital in the fulminating stage; to do so invited certain death. We thought we were far quicker on the scene than the ambulance could be, and in those days ambulances did not carry oxygen.

We used to see dozens of such attacks during a year, and in summer visitors too. Our results were extremely good and we seemed able to resuscitate the most extreme cases, though the underlying weakened myocardium ensured that these patients did not live for many years thereafter.

As I made my way back to the car I sometimes saw the shadowy shape of Dr Lucey in the murky dark, cylinder on shoulder, engaged on a similar task in the same street!

We thought we were years ahead of our time. Back home the parlour light was on, Barbara up, the gas-fire alight, the kettle simmering, and a cup of tea at hand, and so back to bed. Sometimes there were two such episodes in a night. They were hard days and nights, but very happy ones, with never a grumble or word of complaint. I cannot over-estimate the support, care and assistance I received from Barbara on such occasions.

I must, at this stage, pay tribute to Mr Maynard Whiteside who owned a chemist shop in Quay Road. His knowledge and efficiency were outstanding and in addition to the customary work of a chemist, he supplied oxygen, tubes, a gauge, and face masks to GPs on a script. Sometimes during the resuscitation of a patient during the night the gauge on the cylinder showed the supply was running out: a call by phone to his home, (sometimes a neighbour or relative would do this), and he would appear in ten to fifteen minutes with a fresh cylinder, stay, and lend support. The care and compassion, the help and support, in those days was beyond all measure. We shall never forget him.

The house in Horsforth Avenue, the surgery wing is to the right of the house, and left of the tree.
September, 1959 author's 3rd and 4th cars facing the house.

As Dr Lucey and I continued with the daily tasks using, to the best of our ability, the medication and appliances available, the arrival of penicillin to our armamentarium was a revelation indeed, and a striking advance on prontosil red and sulphapyridine, the only antibiotics we knew. The administration of penicillin caused a great deal of work in general practice, first, because the administration necessitated intramuscular injection, and second, in order to maintain the recommended concentration in the body, four-hourly injection was required. It was practical to give an injection morning and evening. If the patient was very ill, the district nurse was asked to provide an injection in the afternoon as well. To add to that work, a syringe and needle were wrapped in gauze, and boiled for at least ten minutes; the steaming bundle was then wrapped in green oiled silk ready for transport to the patient's home in the medical bag. I had a small electric sterilizer in 63 Horsforth Avenue which bubbled merrily, and by the end of the evening surgery, which finished shortly after seven pm, there were three or four sterile syringes in the oiled silk ready for their task. It was rare to be home before nine pm, but the results achieved, which were revolutionary, compensated for the long hours of work. Streptococcal tonsillitis, lobar pneumonia, broncho-pneumonia in children, acute pyelitis, and acute otitis media were common, and acute illnesses in those days and the response was remarkable, even after the initial injection.

Such visiting ensured a close relationship with patients and was instructive for the doctor in that he was able to follow closely, and understand better, the nature of the illness. Is it any wonder that we had many patient friends, and admirers for the rest of our practice lives, and in retirement too!

Why did we not use the local hospital for these acute illnesses? We did when we could, but Lloyd Hospital was not a large one, and one doctor could have filled it in a day. This hospital also undertook major surgery; few patients then were discharged before the tenth post-operative day; thus the hospital was invariably full to overflowing. Why did we not use the district nurses more for these injections? We did within reason, but there were only four or five district nurses and of these, two were district midwives as well. There was a considerable amount of domiciliary midwifery in that decade, which tied them up. District nurses were not attached to practices like today; they

The Lloyd Hospital. Bridlington 1968. Courtesy of Mr. B. Scott.

were zoned, and in Bridlington the Quay Road level crossing divided the town. Depending where the patient lived, north or south of that dividing line, the appropriate district nurse for that area was contacted. We were chivalrous, too. The nurses worked very hard, and we had a high regard for these willing workers, and were loth to ask them to give an injection in the dark evenings which involved a cycle ride. They did not possess cars, and we were zealous for their well-being. To elicit the help of a district nurse the usual procedure was to ring at her home, and to leave a message if she was out; for a district midwife it was usual to contact the appropriate one for the area early on in pregnancy.

Midwives, whether in Leith, Arbroath, Edinburgh, Alford or Bridlington, and any hospital in which I had worked were all well-trained, totally dedicated to their work, skilled, and experienced. With a mother at full term, and with the onset of labour I would notify the midwife, though often she knew before me, and I was notified. She would arrive at the house with her equipment, carried on a bicycle, prepare the patient, organize the room, set up the equipment and did not leave until delivery was complete and the new baby bathed and settled. I was always present at the delivery; it was priority number one, even if sometimes patients were left sitting in the surgery consulting-room chair. They always accepted the situation, returned at another surgery and invariably asked if the new baby had arrived.

The midwife usually conducted the delivery. In my obstetric bag, similar to a large black gladstone bag, were chloroform and mask, ergometrine ampoules, obstetric forceps, catgut, silkworm, local anaesthesia, syringes, and various round-bodied and cutting needles for suturing the perineum. A rubber apron and face mask to shield nose and mouth were additional equipment.

We seemed to have little cause for anxiety as every mother had numerous antenatal checks by the midwife and myself to ensure the situation was safe for confinement at home. Pelvic measurements figured high on the list of antenatal procedures. Many tests and investigations used today were unknown; we had not known too much about the rhesus monkey before the war, and talk of placental insufficiency was years away. Unlike today there was little interference in what was regarded as a normal physiological process. Examinations to determine the state of the cervix and the exact position of the presenting part were carried out rectally; to even consider a vaginal examination showed a disordered mind, quite disgraceful with the danger of infection and the dreaded puerperal fever, so well known. We were all skilled with the foetal stethoscope, midwives even better, and alleged they could hear the foetal heart long before us.

The first stage of labour used to last considerably longer than today, especially in primigravida, but new preparations, prostaglandins, safer uterine muscle stimulants, and apparatus to record the foetal heart, were not available. Eighteen hours in the first stage, even longer if the position was posterior, was not considered abnormal. Happily I never experienced complications with a home confinement, though one mother, seven miles out in the country had a retained placenta. After a lengthy wait, and protected with ergometine, she was transferred to hospital in an ambulance during the night, but on arrival the journey had delivered the placenta for her!

As the years went by home confinements became rare. Increasing knowledge in management, equipment outside a

GP's capacity to possess, fear of litigation, the high level of safety ensured, and reduction of time spent in hospital after delivery, have, to the GP's relief, sounded the death-knoll to home confinements.

My last home confinement was in the early 1970 decade, and against my wishes, but the mother was determined, and dug in her heels. Her two previous confinements had been at home and she insisted her final baby was born at home too. The home was in the country, an additional contraindication. I gave way after prolonged persuasion and explanation had failed, provided she would go to hospital if labour did not proceed normally and she accepted this. With the aid of a willing and compassionate midwife the labour was uneventful, and a grateful family was the reward.

On the departure of my predecessor Dr Cedric Taylor, he left to my care a female patient in her early forties, who had been admitted to Rosegarth, a small private nursing home opposite 63 Horsforth Avenue; this was before the onset of the NHS. She had a respiratory infection, had been ill over a fortnight, and despite a course of suphapyridine, had not progressed. She was dyspnoeic, had an irritable cough, a continued fever, and was propped up in the bed. The owner of the nursing home was an SRN and there were two or three ancillary staff. An X-ray would have been helpful, but in those days, to move an acutely ill pyrexial patient, in cold weather, by ambulance, was regarded askance by patient, relatives, and hospital alike.

An X-ray, therefore, was not carried out. The X-ray department in Lloyd Hospital then was what later became the children's ward. It was entered by a door to the right of the short corridor from the front door to the lift-cage. There was no waiting area for the patient except this short corridor, a draughty area for an ill person. When the room became the children's ward and the X-ray apparatus removed elsewhere, this door was filled in and a new entrance made in the main corridor.

We were taught to make the diagnosis from the physical signs prevailing, and not rely on an X-ray for the diagnosis; understandable then, because X-ray machines were elementary, and in many hospitals, antiquated and neglected during the war years, and later.

246

Thus, from my examination of this very ill woman I was very sure she had a pleural effusion. A white cell count, (carried out by me at home, using a brass microscope belonging to my grandfather), showed a leucocytosis predominantly polymorphs. Empyema was the most likely diagnosis. I was hard pressed with work as at the same time I was driving a round trip of ten miles three times daily to the acutely ill army officer whose illness I described earlier in this chapter, and trying to deal with the difficulties facing a new doctor in a practice, landed at the deep end.

I thought I would have to break convention and transfer this ill woman with empyema to Lloyd Hospital, for rib resection and the insertion of a gas-pipe rubber tube to drain the pleural space. However penicillin was available, not for general release in 1950, but it could be supplied for hospital use, and it could be purchased privately by doctors for those who wished to use it. This patient, before the onset of the NHS, was a private patient, and prepared to do anything to get better.

Penicillin-resistant organisms were rare in the early days of penicillin, and most bacteria overcome by its use, so I decided that this was the treatment for her.

It was therefore with some anxiety that I arrived at this patient's bedside armed with boiled syringes, large and small, a wide-bored chest needle, local anaesthesia, and the precious penicillin, twelve bottles in all. The intention was to carry out a paracentesis, expecting to find fluid, and also pus. The contents of two bottles of penicillin, suitably diluted, were to be injected into the pleural space via the paracentesis needle, already in situ. It was clear that the nursing staff were unused to such heroic measures, and I was regarded with hostile eyes expressing disbelief at my actions. However, I pressed on, and to my relief fluid was aspirated, and I carried out my programme, and asked for the remainder of the penicillin to be given three times daily by the nursing staff intramuscularly.

Next morning when I arrived to assess the situation my reception had improved beyond all measure; I was quickly ushered upstairs, surrounded by smiling faces, to the patient's room. The patient was smiling too, and soon it was my turn to express my delight and pleasure at the amelioration in her appearance, her comfort, the improvement in the physical signs in her chest, and her normal temperature. Penicillin had achieved what I had hoped, yet dared expect, and gave my morale an added boost in those early difficult days in practice. Her improvement never flagged, the course of treatment was extended to last a week, her X-ray became normal, and she was eventually able to return to her work. She died at an advanced age a few years ago. Such patients had an everlasting belief in your ability, sometimes hard to sustain.

Penicillin today is taken for granted, and continues its role as a highly efficient antibiotic; to me, over forty years ago, it was a miracle.

The year 1950 continued to be eventful. A young man, a joiner by trade was out shooting rabbits one Saturday afternoon in the vicinity of Carnaby when his shotgun accidentally 'went off' as he was negotiating a stile. The bullet went through his left forearm about five inches above the wrist joint, shattering two inches of radius and ulna bones, and causing damage to muscles, blood vessels and nerves. He was a strong man and with the help of relatives and friends managed to get back home. I was notified and moved swiftly to the scene, and was startled at the shocked appearance of the patient and the nature of his injury, which, for a joiner, was a serious situation concerning his future employment. I remember giving him morphia gr ¼, and he was transferred to the casualty department of Lloyd Hospital which, at that time was a room ten foot square, and latterly used by the staff of the male ward as cupboard space to store disposable syringes and other items of equipment. Although our orthopaedic colleague in Hull thought we should be able to deal with most situations, leaving him to battle on with the heavy work such as osteotomy and arthrodesis, I really though that here was a situation demanding high expertise so I phoned him and narrated the story of the event.

I was somewhat put out to be told that there was a hospital in Bridlington called Lloyd, and would I please address myself to the task of exploring the wound and doing what was necessary!

It was in situations like this, and they were not infrequent, that I appreciated Dr Lucey's enthusiasm, skill, and manner of speech. Requests made by me to open the theatre were considered outrageous, and no action was forthcoming; the same requests made by Dr Lucey were also considered outrageous but action was taken, especially when accompanied by a pithy command of our language. In this case we were not going to operate in the black hole of Calcutta, but the operating theatre must be opened, steam generated, and the room prepared for major surgery. We seemed to be asking for the keys to remove the crown jewels, but so high was morale, so willing the staff, so determined were we to make the NHS a success, that the theatre-sister appeared from off-duty on a Saturday afternoon, porters were mobilized, and in no time the room was a hive of activity with sterile instruments laid out, and we had all the facilities normally provided for consultant surgeons, at our command. Dr Lucey quickly became involved with the Boyles anaesthetic machine leaving me to wield the knife. He always called me the surgeon on those occasions though often I would have preferred his end of the patient.

However, on this occasion I must confess I felt a 'big shot' as I scrubbed up for twenty minutes, and received the full attention from the theatre staff; I enjoyed diving my hands into the sterile rubber gloves invitingly held out to me, and taking up my position at the table. However the euphoria was tempered by a wave of discomfort as I was not certain what I was going to do. It was really my worry, but on account of the light-hearted atmosphere in the theatre produced by JDL, and his words of wisdom and advice from his side of the screen, I was able to explore the wound, remove shattered fragments of bone lying loose, tie off bleeding vessels, carry out debridement, reconnect severed tendons and join the ends of the severed radial and ulna nerves. I remember the laughter when JDL hoped I had joined up the correct tendons as it would be difficult for the patient to find himself flexing his fingers when he thought he was extending them! I had to bear this ridicule with good humour and dignity. A plaster of Paris cast was applied, and the patient restored to the male ward.

Events though, moved in our favour; there was no infection in the wound, fibrous union of the fractures took place, there was good movement of wrist and fingers, cutaneous sensation returned, and eventually he was able to suspend from a pole using that hand alone. A subsequent visit to an orthopaedic surgeon provided us with the satisfactory opinion that the end result was so good, no further action was desirable. Thirty years later I asked the patient if his injury had interfered with his skill or career as a joiner, and it was pleasing to hear him say that he did not think he had any disability.

As the year 1950 advanced, the partnership Taylor, Cookson and Lucey settled into a regular pattern of work. It was very evident that we had selected a first-rate partner in Dr Lucey, and his ability, geniality, and hard work, soon began to bear fruit. Dr Gordon-Taylor continued to manage a morning surgery, held down a handful of regular patients during a morning, enjoyed an occasional operation, and the additional pleasure of assisting Mr Patrick from Hull on a Tuesday morning. He had his own brand of humour not always appreciated by us, and bemused certain patients, who, requesting a visit at three pm were told: 'You know I gave up night visits some time ago!'

After an exceptionally busy period for us we sometimes thought that his position was so comfortable that he would stay on indefinitely, and that one day in the not too distant future we should require a young partner to share the load, but this was really impractical until he retired. It was with concern that we learned that ten miles south of Bridlington was another doctor in full-time practice, aged ninety-three years, alleged to be in his prime! It was not until later that we learned that a partner, trailing him from a distance, followed his footsteps ensuring that a lapse of knowledge did not merit an alteration of diagnosis or script. Should Dr Taylor elect to stay on until he was ninety-three years, Dr Lucey and I would be ready to hang up our stethoscopes in the attic ourselves, should we live that long, an unlikely prospect. It was a daunting situation which we tried to eliminate from our minds.

It is strange to reflect that fifty years ago, a doctor who had worked hard all his life for a very poor reward, should wish to stay on into advanced old age and require to be gently edged into retirement by his anxious partners, whereas today, at the age of fifty-five years with every modern convenience, ancillary help galore, with seventy per cent of their staff wages paid by the Government, salaries beyond the dreams of avarice, weekends and half-days a routine, a less urgent work-load, and smaller lists, a doctor starts to count the hours left before retirement which cannot come too soon. Whatever is the reason? What has gone wrong?

In our case we thought Dr Gordon-Taylor stayed on because he and his wife could not bear to be parted from our good humour, geniality and sparkling wit! Even in advanced age on social occasions, tears of laughter used to course their wrinkled faces at the strange tales of Irish extraction. We were naive, our attitudes different to those of today, our temperaments ideally suited. It was 'service with a smile'; it was what we were prepared to give, not what we took, that strengthened our morale, produced job-satisfaction, and gave our patients confidence and pride to be associated with the partnership. Of course we had our disappointments. All doctors experience the heavy hand of fate, and the humility of being cut down to size; an unexpected death, death where treatment had failed after hours of toil, death in a young child, death where there may have been an error of judgement. Relatives of patients are very just on these occasions and will forgive a doctor (in my experience) anything, so long as there was no hint of neglect. Happily we were not in that line of business, and never had to excuse or extract ourselves from such degrading charges.

As mentioned earlier, the NHS was precipitated into a delivery, ill-thought through, more concerned with an ideology than with practical details, and showing a lack of regard for those engaged in trying to work the system. Nobody knew the future; those doctors who owned their practices and sunk capital in their purchase, were no longer allowed to sell their share and goodwill; interest at one and three quarter per cent per annum on the estimated value of their share was paid, but it was not until the 1960 decade that full compensation was eventually paid.

The general public thought the NHS was a free for all, and extraordinary demands were made on doctors to prescribe whisky and brandy as cardiac stimulants, toilet rolls, cotton wool and many other questionable border-line medicaments. Initially there was no charge for prescriptions, spectacles, and dental treatment. Gradually lists of preparations which could not be prescribed appeared, and the weekly envelope emanating from executive councils containing standing orders grew bigger each week. The bureaucratic wheel had started to turn, the honeymoon was over.

It seemed to have escaped the planners of the NHS that the public took holidays, or sometimes had to be away from home for many reasons; such people did need medical attention from time to time. There was, however, no arrangement whereby a doctor could be remunerated for such a service. It was illegal to charge any registered patient on a doctor's list, and this applied to visitors as well. It was possible to prescribe medication, but no fee could be claimed. Urgent representations were made to the BMA, and the General Medical Services Committee secured the Temporary Residents Form which was filled in for every visitor and signed by the temporary patient who was not on your own list; one form lasted three months. The form attracted 9 shillings in its early days. Many were the anomalies and the omissions in those early days, and it took time and patience for their correction. I feel sure that if doctors today were treated as we were in the early years of the NHS, there would be a general strike, the NHS would grind to a halt, never to be the same again. To those of us privileged to have been alive to see the NHS through its birth pains, and it took nearly twenty years, the present upset about the Government's White Paper 'Working For Patients' seems a mere ripple on the surface for general practice today. A fraction more work to improve care, maybe, but who dare grumble at that when there are plenty of ancillary helpers, practice nurses, health-visitors, practice-managers, and secretaries in profusion? Some practice reorganization seems to be all that is necessary. It has to be remembered that he who pays the piper calls the tune; no longer is it 'my practice' or 'our practice', but rather 'the practice'. Doctors are employed to work it by the Family Practitioner Committee, and obviously there will have to be certain criteria that must be met. Understandably doctors resent aspersions on their practice standards, but it is easy to slide into the comfortable way of life, forgetting that patient care is the prime concern.

With the shake-up following six years of war, and the new NHS, GPs seemed to fall into two groups. On the one side were a minority fearful of the future, angered at the thought of medicine becoming a political football, displeased at the inevitable bureaucracy, and losing the freedom they thought they had fought for. This group made the brain drain who emigrated mainly to Australia, New Zealand and Canada.

Another large group, and I was a cog, welcomed the ideology but were shocked at the mode of introduction; we lacked the nerve to quit the homeland, having to entice aged and unwilling parents to uproot and accompany us. We stayed, and having decided to stay, supported the principle of the NHS and threw ourselves with energy and determination to make it a success. There was no time for the faint-hearted, even our own partner,

Dr Linell, had disappeared through the brain-drain door, and it was open to all who wished to pass through it.

Despite the poor financial reward, and the confused conditions of service, this challenge never deterred us. Consultants, GPs, ancillary-workers, matrons, nurses, midwives, porters, cleaners, cooks, and ambulance-men seemed to be fired with the desire to make the new NHS the best medical service in the world. There was co-operation, sincerity, appreciation, hard work outside usual hours, and above all, the words care and compassion had a real meaning and it was the patient who came first every time.

Did we succeed? I had thirty more years of work left me in the NHS. Perhaps I shall reach a decision in the final chapter, the twilight of my life.

There was anger too, though it did not reveal itself to patients. The BMA, and the General Medical Services Committee became involved in a dispute with the minister about the remuneration of GPs. The 'Central Pool' from which GPs were paid was funded by multiplying the total population of the UK by 17s. This produced some forty-two million pounds. When, in 1951, the minister said that an extra two million for the Central Pool was all the country could afford at that time, there was uproar, and suggestions that doctors should go on strike. I remember attending some large meetings of doctors in Hull in the late evenings, when angry colleagues, fists clenched, were all in favour of striking, and arguing with others who said it would be a disgrace for the profession to strike.

What about the Hippocratic Oath?!

There was no strike. There was a settlement of the dispute by an adjudicator, Mr Justice Danckwert who was appointed by the Government to soothe the fracas. The Danckwert Award, as it became known, prepared a better basis of payment for GPs in the future, and there was a back-payment to the 5 June 1948 based on the change in the cost of living over those years.

It was not an over-generous award, but the doctors were satisfied and accepted the decision.

One of the recommendations was to reduce the number of patients on a single-handed GP's list; it used to be 4,000 patients, and was reduced to 3,500; for every assistant employed, 2,000 more patients were allowed. A charge of a shilling was made for a prescription, and a small charge made for spectacles. This caused a row in Parliament, as the worthy ideal that everything must be free had been broken.

I was grateful for the Danckwert Award even though the back-payment was very modest due to our small list at the time. I was, however, able to refurbish the waiting room, and there was enough left over to purchase a six inch screen black and white television set. It had a magnifier attached to the front to enlarge the picture to that of a nine inch screen.

We were enthralled to watch the Coronation of Elizabeth II in 1953 in Westminster Abbey, expertly televised all those years ago.

Our family was increasing, and a third son, Dennis, was born at home two days before Christmas 1951. Dr Lucey said I would have to take out another educational insurance policy! Mrs Lucey came to the house with her parents on Christmas Day, cooked a turkey and we had the Christmas dinner together, a kindness we have never forgotten.

We had a private midwife who lived in Whitby. She stayed two weeks and looked after the mother, new baby, his two brothers and myself, with great skill.

To my great surprise and pleasure, Dr Little, who was demobilized on the same day as myself and had been an assistant in a practice south east of London, wrote to say that he was now a partner in a partnership of two other doctors in Whitby, only thirty miles north of Bridlington on the coast.

I remember his two partners, Dr Lyne, the elder, and Dr Rutter, who lived at Robin Hood's Bay near Whitby. For many years, on Sundays, we would alternate visits to each other and enjoy Sunday lunch. His family of three were of similar ages to ours, and we enjoyed the walks, the quaint and picturesque fishing-town, and the Whitby moors all around.

We also enjoyed comparing notes and incidents in our two practices and were intrigued to learn that Dr Gordon-Taylor and Dr Lyne shared much in common! Whitby was often snow-bound and I remember some scarey journeys. It was served by consultants from Scarborough and Middlesbrough.

Dr Little had nerves of steel. He received an urgent message and on arrival found a patient with laryngeal stridor. There was cyanosis, imminent death,and tracheotomy was the only salvation. Using a knife-blade and dressing-forceps he opened into the trachea, and maintained the opening with the blades of the forceps. The patient drew breath and was transferred to the local hospital where the operation was completed with the insertion of a tracheotomy tube. A wonderful achievement indeed, a life-saving feat.

When I first arrived in Bridlington the operation for removal of tonsils and adenoids was almost a routine procedure in five-year old children. The guillotine was the instrument used to remove tonsils, and a snare was used to curette the adenoidal pad of lymphoid tissue. The ear, nose and throat specialists would operate on a dozen or more children at a session in Lloyd Hospital, and it was the same unpleasant procedure I had experienced in Arbroath Infirmary. There was drama, too, because these children had different general practitioners, who had to arrive at the hospital at an estimated time, vacate their cars, and rush up the hospital stairs at the double, grabbing a gown, mask and ethyl chloride for anaesthesia. The surgeon, Mr Simpson, was intolerant of any delay in his flow of work. As one doctor hurtled upstairs, another would hurtle downstairs, anxious to get into the open air after the nerve-racking experience, and to continue his visits. All these children were discharged home the following morning and seemed to show little discomfort, and happily no knowledge of the operation undergone. I always thought the ward nursing staff were splendid in the care of their patients as they came round after the operation.

With the onset of the NHS, this routine removal of tonsils and adenoids quickly fell into disrepute, and after a few years it was difficult to find an ENT surgeon who would undertake the operation. Why was this? Why were thousands of operations a year reduced to a handful in a very short space of time?

Present-day ENT surgeons will say that the operation is unnecessary except in special circumstances. The histology of tonsils and adenoids shows lymphoid tissue; they act as filters against infection, and to remove them in five-year old children who have recently started school where infection is rife, is to remove barriers against infection. Removal of these organs when healthy and unenlarged, and in the absence of nasal obstruction is considered an unwarranted assault.

Yes, indeed, but the fact that tonsils are not chronically infected nowadays, and nasal obstruction reduced, shows that the antibiotic treatment which started to be used in 1950, must take the credit for this altered situation. Its action in controlling the secondary infection associated with colds, sore throat, sinus infection and otitis media have prevented the hypertrophy of the lymphoid tissue which produced the symptoms of obstruction, necessitating the removal of these organs.

Prior to the palatable and pleasantly flavoured oral preparations of penicillin there used to be large numbers of children who had repeated upper respiratory infection every winter, and frequent attacks of tonsillitis. This produced hypertrophy of the tonsils and so enlarged were they that they met in the mid-line of the fauces and gave the impression that they could be plucked out with fingers.

There was always enlargement of the tonsillar lymph gland, often spreading to the chain of glands in the posterior triangle of the neck. Otitis media was a frequent addition to the troubles, and perforated drums, discharging ears, and mastoiditis, all too common and unwelcome. Penicillin has changed this unhappy picture.

If the adenoids hypertrophied the child snored and snorted; the nasal obstruction could interfere with the development of the chest and produce a pigeon chest deformity. The victims breathed through open mouths for adequate air, sucking in cold, unwarmed and unfiltered air to aggravate the respiratory problems, the facies developed abnormally, the voice had a nasal twang, the victim's problems easily identified. Present day ENT surgeons would be amazed at what we saw daily.

Removal of the adenoids in such cases worked wonders, and the child would grow in stature and well-being. Removal of the infected enlarged tonsils, their crypts full of debris and pus reduced the incidence of tonsillitis, and removed the 'chronic foci' of infection alleged to be responsible for nephritis, and bacterial endocarditis. It was the correct and only form of treatment at that time; it seems probable that present-day upper respiratory tract infections are of viral origin, whereas in days past they were bacterial.

Another operation widely employed was the circumcision of male infants, usually carried out in the first few days after birth while the infant was having a feed; anaesthesia was not considered necessary though I was never convinced about this.

The Australian technique using bone forceps to crush, and then grip, the foreskin for two to three minutes was employed.

This usually produced haemostasis, and the skin stitches were unnecessary, though occasionally a ligature was required for the frenal artery. A dressing soaked in tinct Benz Co completed the operation. This operation was usually performed at the request of the babies' parents, and was for aesthetic, and possibly hygienic reasons rather than medical at that tender age. Gradually circumcision in infants fell into disrepute and it was discontinued.

Indications for circumcision still exist at the present time for the treatment of phimosis in young boys, a tightness of the foreskin preventing the retraction of this skin. I have often thought this condition avoidable if daily attempts at retraction were made; I used to show the mother the technique and then she performed the manoeuvre in my presence, and I am sure it was helpful in preventing trouble later on.

Readers may be interested to learn that I examined several thousand young Sudanese soldiers prior to their demobilization in 1946 and every one of them had been circumcised in childhood. I have also seen two men with cancer of the penis and it seems that this dreadful situation is unlikely to occur in circumcised men. In any event it is mercifully rare.

With a better understanding of the value of antibiotics, the British drug houses, and overseas companies as well, turned their attention to the discovery, testing and manufacture of newer, better, and safer chemotherapeutic preparations free from side effects: they had the money and the facilities for research in a field of unlimited potential for the relief of suffering world-wide. May and Baker 760 (sulphathiazole) was a better preparation for staphylococcal infections than M & B 693, or sulphapyridine. Antibiotics, viz, sulphonamides, new penicillins, tetracyclines, cephalosporins were developed with their different effects on various organisms, followed by chloramphenicol, so effective in typhoid fever. The lincamycins came next, the polymyxins, the amino-glycosides, and the chemotherapeutic drugs against tuberculosis followed.

Thus, over a few years, a range of illnesses which could maim or kill people in all age groups, began to disappear from our surgeries and visiting lists. There was much to learn about these new preparations and their correct use, but what an exciting and challenging time it was for the general practitioner. Representatives from all the drug houses descended on our consulting rooms with literature, samples, and advice galore about these new, miraculous, and initially expensive preparations. The results were a wonder to behold. Whereas previously we had been practising 'crisis medicine', we were now engaged in the treatment of the conditions we had been unable to do much good in the past. The time seemed to be approaching when the work-load would change again, perhaps from treatment to prevention. What an exciting prospect!

I have mentioned the chemotherapeutic drugs which were discovered to combat tuberculosis, and my memory goes back to those days without them. Certainly clean milk, the testing of herds and the pasteurization of milk had improved the previous position, and pulmonary tuberculosis was not the killer in its miliary form which devastated families in the nineteenth century. In 1950 children and young adults were not so often infected, but middle-aged and elderly people predominated. We had to be vigilant, never to miss a patient who might be infected. There were several patients in the practice with established pulmonary tuberculosis, treated with artificial pneumothorax to collapse and rest the lung, and a few had thoracoplasty, a more radical surgical procedure to collapse one side of the chest. Many patients seemed to recover, but you never knew when there would be a flare-up. Lassitude, cough, haemoptysis, fever, loss of weight and flesh, and night sweats were cardinal features, and the recovery process had to start all over again.

Streptomycin, isoniazid, PAS and rifampicin, were the new drugs that cured infected patients after twelve to eighteen months with steady treatment as an out-patient. I remember, too, a young, attractive, and active woman on my list was confirmed radiologically as having tuberculosis of a lower dorsal vertebra. She lived in Mayfield Road in Bridlington. She refused admission to hospital which could have lasted months to years; she was adamant. Fresh air, good food, cod liver oil and malt and rest, were all that could be offered. A large plaster bed was moulded to her contours and she lay in the open air during the lovely summer weather, carefully and splendidly attended by her parents. Her general health improved but she developed a psoas abcess, the first and last I was ever to see. She had to be transferred to hospital but not for long. She recovered completely with no spinal deformity. She married, enjoyed good health thereafter but did not bear children. After she was better the new drugs arrived, and I remember the difficulty she had swallowing a PAS sachet, a large preparation, not unlike a miniature straw-hat, taken to complete her treatment.

Gonorrhoea responded to penicillin, and one large injection would cure an acute case; this condition is prevalent to this very day, but the unpleasant sequelae associated with chronicity, viz urethral stricture, bladder trouble, and prostatitis rarely have a chance to develop. We used to initiate the treatment after diagnosis from a urethral smear, and refer the patient to a special clinic in Hull for tests of cure, and follow up, to ensure syphilis did not show its chancre later. The gonococcus was unkind to women, and the salpingitis difficult to eradicate; sterility, and abdominal pains were end-results.

New born-babies fared badly too and could be blinded from gonococcal conjunctivitis at birth. Penicillin has overcome such dreadful tragedy.

Syphilis, caused by the treponema pallidum, responded to penicillin. Those courses of arsenic and bismuth I administered at Arbroath were remembered as a bygone age. Congenital syphilis, aneurysm, osteitis, gummata, and general paralysis of the insane were controlled, but the damage was done; the consolation was the knowledge that new infections would never have the chance to cause such damage in the future.

Syphilis is rare now; in my younger days every person who had a blood test for whatever investigation was automatically screened for this disease using the Wasserman and Kahn tests. There was stigma against syphilis, less so for gonorrhoea, and for this reason the word syphilis was never used in front of a patient. A luetic infection, or a specific infection was the accepted medical terminology. A candidate for an examination, qualifying or higher, who inadvertently used the word syphilis at the bedside would find himself in rough water, and unlikely to satisfy the examiners on that occasion.

During one of my summer visits to my predecessor, Dr Cedric Taylor at his fine home in West Ayton where he grew strawberries as large and luscious as could be found, he announced that he had plans to leave the area and move to Bournemouth on account of his wife's health. Because of this decision he was anxious that I should purchase 63 Horsforth Avenue before he left the area.

This news was disconcerting. I knew that I would have to

buy the house sooner or later and I wanted to do so, but this news came rather earlier than I had expected. The income from the practice at that stage was meagre and there was little margin for further expenditure, but he was always so pleasant and helpful to us in a variety of ways that I felt unable to raise objection. Thus it was that the house was independently valued and a purchase price of £4,000 agreed. At the time the price arranged seemed a frightening figure for Barbara and myself, but it was a solid, well-built house dating from 1910, with a purpose-built surgery wing added in 1921, and considered a high-grade practice premises only a hundred yards from the sea. We could envisage a thirty year period living there, and no doubt it would be a useful asset for the future. At this time there was a tendency for practitioners to have lock-up premises, and live themselves in a smaller house somewhere of their own choice.

Like it or not, the house was the nerve centre of my part of the partnership. No house; no practice, unless I bought a house elsewhere, and rented a lock-up surgery which would be a brash and risky procedure for a recent arrival to the area. There was another established practice close by and I could not afford to take such a chance. Also, I had found that living over the shop provided many advantages for patient care, denied those who elected to live away from the practice office.

I experienced considerable difficulty, as might be expected, in obtaining a mortgage. Money was tight, and the small share I possessed was not good security. Eventually I achieved a satisfactory outcome but it involved two separate insurance policies, and a noose around my neck for twenty-five years. Readers may be astounded to learn that the purchase price of the house was fractionally less than the credit allowance I receive today from a store in Hull where I am an infrequent and stringent customer.

After I had signed the contract Dr Cedric moved to Bournemouth but died a few months later after a short illness. I was very sorry to hear of this; his retirement had been a short one and I was going to miss his encouragement and support. Few doctors could have had a kinder and more helpful predecessor than myself.

The police were most vigilant and 'on the beat' all over the town. I learned that they had a 'rendez-vous' at night behind the hedge of Emmanuel Church fifty yards from my home. My garage doors were of the sliding type and emitted a considerable rumble to disturb the peace of night especially in the early hours. They used to appear as I reversed into Roundhay Road, and sometimes they asked me where I was going. One night a police-officer I had failed to see banged on the roof of my car; if he had been out to get me, he nearly succeeded in producing a cardiac arrest, such was the fright I received!

The traffic lights at the crossroad of Cardigan and Hilderthorpe Roads often stuck at red in the wrong direction, preventing me from crossing; often there was a policeman here. I used to play cat and mouse hoping he would wave me on against the lights but he never did. Eventually I just drove across to see him shaking with laughter. You did not have to travel far to find a policeman at night. Sadly the arrival of the panda car changed the position; it seemed a retrograde step and an invitation to crime.

Bridlington had always relied on Kingston-upon-Hull for provision of the consultancy staff for the Lloyd Hospital. Dr Muir, a physician, and Mr Patrick, a surgeon were Hull-based. With the onset of the NHS it was considered that the Scarborough Hospital would, more conveniently, look after the interests of Bridlington, but there was always considerable local opposition to the proposal. The Scarborough Road could block with snow at the Dottrell Inn and prevent consultants getting through to Bridlington and this was thought to be a potent reason for not utilizing the services of Scarborough, though I must confess this happened very rarely. For many years there was indecision as to the future. Eventually after the upgrading of Scarborough Hospital to a district hospital, both Dr Muir and Mr Patrick, on their retirements, were replaced by consultants from Scarborough, and additional consultants in their own specialities became the responsibility of Scarborough Hospital.

Dr Mary Webster, an obstetrician and gynaecologist, appointed in the early days of the NHS, provided a most efficient consultant service for Bridlington, and the town was indeed lucky her reign lasted over thirty years. She lived in Bridlington. No maternity patient ever had to leave the town for delivery or Caesarean section. Her skills were available to any practitioner who contacted her, whatever the hour. Her work in obstetrics was carried out in the Avenue Hospital, Bridlington, and the hospital in Malton, both busy places in 1948, teaming with activity and coping with the post-war baby bulge. Nobody was ever turned away, the front door did not possess a key, and it opened and shut many times a night with expectant mothers crossing the threshold in early labour.

Sister Fenner, a night sister of great experience and character, could tell when that front door opened from her office upstairs.

Christmas morning 1954, in The Avenue Maternity Hospital. The author is on the right, and Dr Lucey in on the author's right. In the foreground are the author's three sons, left to right Arthur, Angus and Dennis. Matron Slack is fifth on the left. Sister Fenner left foreground.

Dr Mary Webster also ran a gynaecological clinic in Lloyd Hospital, where, with consummate skill, she operated most successfully on the troubles affecting women. When she retired it was forecast gloomily that the maternity service would never be the same again. Retired myself, from my armchair I read of the many mothers transferred to hospitals outside Bridlington in the local press, and in this respect the premonition has certainly proved correct.

Apart from these three specialists there were no consultant

skills available in other specialities for a few years after the start of the NHS. Gradually consultants were appointed to the upgraded Scarborough Hospital by the Leeds Regional Board in most specialities, except for those highly specialized posts found in large district hospitals. It was these specialists who provided the consultant cover for Bridlington.

Prior to the arrival of these new consultants on the local scene, there was, however, a Dr Hellewell, who stood out as a most valuable medical specialist primarily, but who also had a profound knowledge and experience of diseases of the skin. Such combined skills assured him of a welcome place in the affections of the local practitioners. He was Hull-based, and held a medical clinic in the East Riding Hospital, Driffield, every week, an afternoon session. If a local practitioner in Bridlington required his advice and assistance he merely had to phone him at Driffield, and he would drive over after his clinic and meet the practitioner at the patient's house. He seemed to know the streets of Bridlington as well as we did. I would point out, at this juncture, that we always accompanied the consultant on a domiciliary visit. To fail to do this was considered bad manners, and showed a lack of propriety. Times have changed, and unknown faces appear at patients' homes to carry out their speciality, no longer a consultation but an examination, and the GP is informed of their opinion later.

I remember Dr Hellewell as a long-grey-coated figure in his mid fifties and wearing a homburg hat. Despite a glass eye, he drove solo and fearlessly in all weathers, and in darkness too. Always courteous, he had a dry humour; I always suspected he had been a GP in his younger days because he seemed well-versed in a GP's difficulties, and he was a homely figure in a patient's house, putting them at their ease. Unlike many consultants he would sit down, have a cup of tea, and discuss their problem at length. Always he gave valuable and practical advice and we were grateful to him for travelling out of his way home to help us. Sometimes he would come to my house, talk to my children, and step into the kitchen to see what I was going to have for supper!

Barbara invariably had a 'piece' for him.

Younger doctors have told me that it is impractical to accompany a consultant on a domiciliary visit nowadays, and it interferes with their work-load. Quite so, but consider what it did to our work-load! From my own experience, and even just before I retired only eight years ago, I found consultants appreciated my company. I think we knew the consultants as friends, as well as colleagues, because we had numerous social engagements to which they were invited, knew them with their 'hair down' and we would have felt uncomfortable to be thought discourteous if we failed to accompany them on the domiciliary visits. We also learned a great deal from them in their conduct of the examination and their conclusions before reaching a diagnosis.

Before the days of the Icelandic Cod War large numbers of trawlers of comparatively small tonnage plied the North Sea en route to the fishing grounds. During the winter large numbers of these small boats anchored in Bridlington Bay inside the Smethwich Sands to ride out the winter gales which were so frequent and severe. I have counted a hundred vessels and more anchored at one and the same time in the bay, their lights twinkling through the inky night.

It is not surprising therefore that some of their crews fell ill and medical aid was requested via the harbour-master. If the sea was very rough the lifeboat was launched from the south beach and forced its stormy way through perilous seas with waves thundering on the beach, to the craft in distress. If the sea was less rough, an RAF rescue-launch, a fast vessel, set out from the harbour instead. Often the services of a doctor were required at very short notice, and although there were one or two practitioners with naval experience in the town who were prepared to undertake this work, sometimes they were out on an urgent call, or unavailable. The harbour-master would then ring other doctors for their help so that over the years most local doctors had an invitation to share this load. Peacefully sleeping in a warm and comfortable bed, a doctor was woken by the phone, and within thirty minutes or less was on the lifeboat, clutching his stethoscope and medical case, holding on to whatever he could, his life suddenly at risk. Apart from a thick yellow oilskin provided 'on site' the doctor was unsuitably and inadequately clothed for such an ordeal. One doctor, Dr Robertson, had a terrifying experience when the sea was so rough that the trawler's propeller was out of the water, and it was impossible, with safety, to get close enough to the ship for any living soul to embark or disembark. After repeated attempts, the skipper, using a loud-hailer, said he thought the patient was not that bad and he would attempt to return to Hull. The lifeboat returned to its base. Shoes, suits, medical equipment could be permanently damaged. Shakily Dr Robertson narrated his experience to a packed hospital coffee room next morning. Most of the patients seen on these occasions were taken off the ship tied to a stretcher, and transferred to Lloyd Hospital where some were found to require treatment and were ill, others not so. Once, a trawler man walked off the lifeboat on a Sunday afternoon in high season at the harbour top suffering from a dose of clap!

My own experiences were less traumatic. I went out on the RAF sea-rescue launch to a trawler. It was rough enough for me and I did not find it easy transferring to the heaving vessel. My medical case was handed up afterwards. It was a slippery deck and I was conducted down steel steps with a single hand rail to the engine-room to find an Arab sailor lying on the oily floor. It was clear he would have to be transferred ashore, having tripped and fallen down some steps. It was not easy getting him on to the deck and then transferring him to the launch on a stretcher but we reached the Lloyd Hospital safely. I had been able to give morph gr ¼ in the engine-room.

There was a communication problem, and my knowledge of Arabic had begun to fade. Despite X-rays and every investigation he died after a week, the cause obscure. I had seen one or two Sudanese soldiers who died unexpectedly, many days after a scorpion sting. A Sudanese doctor, Dr Zein, did tell me in Khartoum that some Sudanese were able to will themselves to death. 'It was the will of Allah,' he said, but it gave me little comfort.

On another occasion the lifeboat was already out trying to rescue the crew of a ship in distress off Flamborough Head, and we were asked to meet the lifeboat on its return. It was a dark and stormy night, the gale from the north-east. When, after several hours away, the lifeboat's mast-light was visible on its return about a mile out from the harbour entrance, a cluster of people, relatives of the lifeboat crew, Dr Lucey and myself were huddled by the north wall sheltering from the bitter cold.

As the crew and survivors came off the lifeboat it seemed that everyone was safe and unharmed. We were about to leave the scene and return home when we thought we saw an oilskinned mass on the rear deck in the dim light. Somehow his presence had been overlooked. He was dead; he was an older crew member. A post-mortem revealed a fracture of the femur. At the inquest he had been seen at the rescue and it was thought he may have been crushed between the two vessels, and died from shock and exposure. Lifeboat work was risky and dangerous, their crews brave and dedicated, and the elements vicious.

After the cod war we never saw so many ships in the bay again; and the doctors, to their relief, were spared those cold, hazardous trips. But this was not the end of the work. The following morning a report had to be made out, and all details sent to the ship's owners. Usually they had their own medical adviser in Hull and we corresponded with them. I had no secretary; the partnership could not afford a second secretary, and all reports were written in my own hand, often at great inconvenience. There were times when I thought I would never get on top of my work, so many were the interruptions. When the injured man had been discharged from the hospital we used to send an account to the ship's owners for medical services rendered, services which did not come under the terms of the NHS, but I seem to remember that we were not always paid! Underpaid as we were, we preferred to accept the rough with the smooth, and we did not grumble or whinge about it. 'Service with a smile, the patient always first', was our motto, and this resolve strengthened our will to better the NHS!

During the early 1950s, from mid-July to the middle of September, Bridlington was inundated with visitors from the West Riding of Yorkshire. So busy was the town that we looked forward to the Doncaster Races in mid-September when the last horse in the last race came in with snow on its tail. 'That will keep them at home,' an old lady patient used to tell me, and how right she was. These were not day visitors, but visitors who boarded here for a week (two weeks from Scotland!). There have never been so many visitors resident in the town since those days. Family units predominated, and they were here to enjoy themselves on the beach, in the sea, on the motor vessels for trips to Flamborough and Bempton cliffs. There was a converted 'tug' from Hull, the *Yorkshireman*, which came every season for years, and it was a very popular vessel. Also at the harbour was a long rowing-boat, in which an elderly fisherman would row you from South to North harbour walls, and it was packed with people. Those were the days when Bridlington reached its zenith.

Both Dr Lucey and myself soon realized that we were required to visit many young children visitors with very high temperatures after they had been in the area for forty-eight hours, starting on a Monday morning, a busy day in any event. Apart from the temperature and headache there was little to find objectively. With pryexia usually above 102°F, such children felt too unwell to be out of bed. If untreated the condition lasted the entire week, ruining their holiday, and their parents' holiday as well. Every day fresh cases occurred and we saw dozens of such patients through the season. We carried out numerous tests as out-patients, sending normal stools, urine, blood and throat swabs to the laboratory. Never once were pathogens reported. This condition did not occur in local children, nor did it involve adults, and not all the children in a family or guest house were affected; it was worse during a fine hot summer. The only clinical finding, common to all, was the presence of very active bubbly bowel sounds, with a shower of fine crepitations in the background. What was this condition? We were totally puzzled. Enquiries to other doctors suggested that they had not come across this illness. Why not? We spoke to medical specialists, and representatives from the drug houses, and no advice was forthcoming. Sometimes we thought their expressions reflected disbelief in our abilities. At that period of time in the NHS GPs were not held in high regard by their consultant colleagues, and general practice was the place to go for the failures! So unkind, but we managed to change that climate of opinion over the years!

It was suggested that we wrote the cases up and sought publication in the medical journals, but we were busy people practising crisis medicine and we had no time for double-blind crossover trials. If only the birth of the College of General Practice, later to be the Royal College, had been ten years earlier, interest might have been roused, back-up provided, and we might have had advice and help, or even been found to have discovered a new disease to which our names would be linked for evermore!

Right or wrong, and we shall never know, we decided the condition related to the beach, to the sea and the sun, to over-active behaviour, too little sleep, too much excitement, and excessive indulgence by parents to their children, with ice-cream

267

and candy floss; a stress reaction in which the heat centre in the brain lost its stabilizing influence, and the temperature became uncontrollable. But why did the condition take so long to settle down? Why were diaphoretics, anti-pyretics, aspirin, and bed-rest unhelpful?

We called the condition 'beachitis'; for reasons not understood the temperature became normal overnight, and subjective symptoms disappeared, after a single dose of cremosuccidine (a proprietary preparation marketed by MSD containing succinyl-sulphathiazole, kaolin, and a chocolate flavouring agent). Mist kaolin had no effect on the cause of the illness. This treatment was maintained for three days, but the one dose controlled the pryexia, and children rose from their beds and were able to enjoy their holiday as before. Why should a preparation, only of value in bacillary bowel infections, have such a beneficial effect on a condition in which we were never able to demonstrate bacteria?

Certainly the town's sewage was discharged into the sea not far from the harbour mouth, and of course it was overloaded in peak season; witness the seagulls who flocked to the scene and floated there all day. Indeed I had a patient with a B. coli infection of the throat who had bathed in the sea. But this does not explain why the condition became increasingly rare later on (I never saw the trouble again after 1962) though the new sewage outfall a mile out to sea was not completed until 1982. It remains a mystery, but I lived through those days, and the condition caused a great deal of work and spoiled many holidays. MSD benefited by selling hundreds of gallons of cremosuccidine; and ourselves, who were able to sign a temporary resident form for each patient. We used to say that beachitis paid our income-tax demand on 1 January.

An injury often seen in visitors was caused by the fish-hook. Every day a line of amateur fishermen with elaborate and expensive rods and lines enjoyed a day of fishing from the harbour walls, a small collection of worms for bait at their feet. There was no great evidence that their patient hours of waiting were successful. From time to time they would reel in their lines so that the hooks and sinker were visible; then, with a deft ostentatious movement with the rod, attempt to sling the sinker and hooks further out to sea. Unfortunately the innocent passer-by was frequently speared by a fish-hook that had gained considerable velocity. Children in bathing trunks were especially vulnerable, and I have seen fish-hooks in many parts of the body but usually above the waist, in many cases deeply embedded. Ears, lips, cheeks, nostril, and the fingers were frequent sites for the fish hook to lodge.

It was an injury that caused alarm and consternation to the recipient to be wounded in such a manner, and the situation was aggravated by the good intentions of passers-by who would fiddle with the hook, increase the discomfort, and fail to remove it.

I came across the same scene time and time again; the wail of a weeping and frightened child, a group of four or five anxious relatives half-running toward my house, the urgency with which the front door bell rang and my unhappy vision of a small hook firmly embedded in the dorsum of a finger, catgut attached, a piece of slimy bait attached to the hook, and the line, sinker, and framework supported by an anxious parent.

It was not too difficult to remove a fish-hook provided adequate tools were available. The area was first infiltrated with local anaesthesia (novocaine one per cent). It was crucial to have a strong pair of artery forceps to grip the shaft of the hook and with firm pressure push it in the direction in which it entered the skin. Very soon the tip of the hook, followed by the barb appeared from beneath the skin, the exit a short distance away from the point of entry. The end of the hook with barb was sliced off using ordinary pliers and the shaft removed rearwards with smiles of relief all round. The wrong treatment was to try to pull the hook out against the barb; it was too painful to attempt and would cause tissue damage.

No matter how nasty or dirty the hook, sepsis never occurred. Wise men said it was the saline from the sea which prevented the infection.

Most weeks a problem existed with elderly men in severe discomfort with acute retention of urine. I write of the early days of the NHS when a rubber catheter and urine bottle were as essential items of equipment for a GP to carry as a syringe and morphia.

The bladder level was often halfway to the navel before we were informed or reached the patient's home. Sometimes the retention was the first time ever, other times there had been a previous occasion relieved by catheterization, and the patient had re-established a dribbling flow with frequency and discomfort, and yet again, others, especially seen in visitors, had retention with overflow. There were also occasions when acute retention followed indiscretionary behaviour in a public-house, and if the patient was a visitor in a caravan in some distant field at Flamborough at night, you could be assured it was going to take all your skill to relieve him of his discomfort.

Despite these problems we did not seem to be troubled with stress reactions ourselves, and considered the jargon to be associated with fear and inadequacy, undesirable traits in doctors.

In those days an attempt was made to relieve the retention at home in the first place. The rubber catheter was boiled up in a saucepan in their kitchen, the doctor washed his hands carefully, prepared the patient, and proceeded to pass the catheter suitably lubricated with liquid paraffin (KY Jelly was unknown). All went well until the prostatic urethra was reached, and then it was clear a stumbling-block had been reached. Skill was required to pass beyond this area, some doctors attaining a higher rate of success than others in entering the bladder, which was drained to the enormous relief and gratitude of the patient. We were relieved, too, to hear and see water finding its own level. The catheter was removed, and peace reigned. Next morning if the patient was fortunate he had passed or dribbled some urine, continued to do so, and the immediate pressure was off. Sometimes his quality of micturition returned to the standard prior to the attack of acute retention.

If the patient was unfortunate and the doctor found he was up against a brick wall and unable to pass the catheter he was transferred to the Lloyd Hospital casualty department, where, in various cupboards, catheters of all sizes and shapes were available, lying in trays of disinfectants. Gum-elastic catheters were stiffer than their rubber counterparts, and with prostatic curves were easier to pass through the obstruction. We rarely failed with these, but instead of removing the catheter it was retained, and kept in place using zinc oxide plaster strapped to the penile skin. The end was stoppered, and the bladder emptied every four hours. Once this stage had been reached it was evident that prostatectomy was indicated, and the patient was transferred to a hospital where surgery of this nature was performed provided the patient was considered fit for such surgery. What did we do when attempts at catheterization failed whatever we tried? Suprapubic cystostomy was performed. This involved inserting a wide self-retaining catheter through the abdominal wall into the distended bladder via an introducer and draining the bladder into a collecting bottle. Most GPs were competent to perform this surgical procedure, wherever there was a local hospital staffed by GPs. It would have been difficult to have transferred the patient elsewhere in those circumstances; hospital beds everywhere were well-filled; they were practising crisis medicine too. All such patients presenting with acute retention had enlargement of the prostate gland as the causative factor, and no doubt some of the glands would have shown malignant changes.

Those patients who were too old or had additional illnesses, and were not considered suitable subjects for a prostatectomy (the operation had a high mortality rate at that time) spent the rest of their days with a self-retaining de pezzer catheter in their bladders, and walked about connected to a drainage bag. It did not take long for the B. coli organism to infect the bladder producing pus which often blocked the catheter. Bladder irrigation using solutions of silver nitrate, and potassium permanganate were carried out by district nurses, and by GPs too, no doubt introducing more infection; the B. coli was insensitive to the chemotherapy available then. Once a month the de pezzer catheter was pulled out of the bladder with a gush of urine, blood, and pus, and a fresh one inserted. The smell was characteristic and unpleasant, and a patient's bedroom could be unbearable.

Despite these hazards, and the ever present risk of ascending infection to the kidneys, many of these patients reached an advanced age, holding in a de pezzer catheter for ten years and more, and leading active lives.

How did the patients who underwent abdominal prostatectomy fare? It was a hazardous procedure. The bladder was invariably infected before the operation started. As soon as the bladder was opened, the operative field was quickly obscured by blood, and the enucleation of the projecting prostatic mass into the bladder, carried out blind with a sweeping finger. Insertion of a de pezzer catheter completed the operation and the patient was returned to the ward and connected to a collecting bottle standing at the foot of the bed.

271

Shock, haemorrhage, infection, and blockage of the de'pezzer catheter with blood clot, and renal failure, were the enemies the patient had to fight. Was it any wonder the mortality rate was high? Yet, despite these hazards, many patients survived, the urinary flow re-established, the de pezzer catheter was removed, the supra-pubic wound healed, and the patient returned home after many weeks to regain good health without urinary problems. I used to regard these patients with awe and wonder. They were supermen, courageous people, men protected with a robust constitution and their belief in the power of God.

Over the last forty years what a change has taken place! Patients are sent for surgical opinion when the early signs and symptoms of prostate enlargement appear and rarely reach the stage of acute retention. New antibiotics control infection. Modern catheters are manufactured from materials which are less irritant to the urethra and bladder, lessening the likelihood of infection.

Surgical technique has improved beyond all measure, and the retropubic operation, coupled with modern anaesthesia, have allowed prostatectomy to be performed with safety on men aged ninety years. Shock and haemorrhage are prevented, post-operative bladder haemorrhage with clotting controlled using catheters with twin ports for drainage and irrigation, and everything is pre-sterilized and non-touch techniques employed; deep vein thrombosis and pulmonary embolism are hazards of the past.

How fortunate we are to live in this era, and to be spared the trials and suffering I witnessed not so very many years ago.

I had the unfortunate experience of witnessing the deaths of two patients in the consulting room. I had only been in the practice for three or four years, and there was an interval of a few years between the two events. Both patients died from cardiac arrest (though this terminology was not used at that time). Coronary thrombosis was sufficient cause for a death certificate, and I was able to state that the patients died in my presence, evidence accepted without question.

The first death was that of an active man in his early sixties who had taken a long walk on the south beach to Fraisthorpe. He said he had called at the surgery on his way home because he had a pain across the front of the chest while he was walking, but it had passed off now.

I was contemplating whether to send him home by ambulance or order a taxi, so that he could rest, when he slumped forward, dead. Present day attempts at resuscitation, and the use of a defibrillator were not practiced, not orthodox treatment at that time.

The second death was a middle-aged man who had poliomyelitis in childhood, and walked with some difficulty. He was accompanied to the surgery by his wife, and she left to do the shopping with the understanding she would meet him in the waiting room after consultation. He was in his usual health as he entered the consulting room, but he slumped forward, dead, as I was checking his blood pressure.

Both events upset me more than I can describe, and I have never forgotten the difficult task I faced explaining to the shocked relatives what had happened. The fact that their deaths were due to circumstances totally outside my control was my only comfort. Uncomfortable it was, too, contacting the same funeral director on each occasion and watching him remove the victims from the surgery premises, and my embarrassment as I completed the surgery session.

When one considers the number of patients who pass through a surgery premises in a year, a sudden death there is a rare event. I have never met another practitioner who has experienced such an unfortunate incident though I am sure I cannot be alone. I thought I had been very unlucky, and it took me some time to get over the disappointments.

Most practices have their share of the difficult patient, and it is remarkable the amount of time and trouble spent in coping with their demands. I had such a patient. She was in her mid-twenties, was obese, and lived with her parents on one of the council estates in a house as dirty as could be imagined. She had a brother, and there was another sister, marginally less demanding than herself. Despite her rough upbringing and total lack of morality and self-discipline she acquired a superior manner of speech and accent which seemed out of keeping with her station; she was also well-informed about medical benefits, and social security allowances, and possessed a little dangerous knowledge of illness and treatment. She knew every doctor in the town and it became clear as time passed by that she had been in every consulting room in the town and developed a skill in playing off one doctor against another; I have to say she could be very plausible indeed. She never tired of telling me that she was born on Guy Fawkes Day; it was unwise to be flippant, or critical, or slip out an unguarded remark because she would delight in narrating an untrue story about you, carefully embroidered, and shock a packed waiting room. It was embarrassing if you were asked if her story was true by an incoming and refined patient! She could damage your reputation.

She became a victim of the NHS, especially where operative surgery was concerned. It was more in desperation than need that I referred her to a surgeon on account of pendulous breasts, thinking that he would advise her (as I had done and my advice was rejected) to wear a well fitting brassiere and perhaps prescribe one for her. Imagine my surprise when he wrote back advising me he had placed her on his waiting list for a plastic operation, first on one side, followed by the other side, after a short interval, despite the fact his waiting list was lengthy with more urgent cases. I did not think the results of the surgery were a great success. In fact, on one side, with the passage of time, with fibrosis and contracture, the nipple migrated to the axilla. However the patient was very satisfied.

A year or two later she insisted that her pendulous abdomen should be reduced. It was impossible to refuse her request, and once again the same surgeon came to her aid, and removed an apron of fat from the great omentum; this operation reduced her girth.

Removal of her appendix, gall-bladder, and uterus followed, but not before she had borne several children, the last, born in a bucket in the back-garden of a housing estate at West Hill.

I remember my annoyance when I arrived at the scene because every arrangement had been made in advance to avoid such a display of exhibitionism. Mother and baby were unscathed.

Having ruffled and nearly exhausted my patience she began to bother my partners, and I remember a weary time when she attended three surgeries a day and was prepared to carry on indefinitely in that way. Eventually we persuaded her to transfer her affections elsewhere, that she had only a heart, lungs, bowels and pancreas left and because they were all vital organs there was little more we had to offer.

She transferred with ill-grace. We heaved a sigh of relief, and my health improved. It gave us no pleasure to learn later that she embarrassed the doctor who took her on by lying down in the main road (Station Avenue) as his car approached. It was ironic that her pancreas let her down. She developed diabetes mellitus, and at the age of forty-five years she died from a coronary thrombosis.

One surgeon described her as a high-grade mental defective; I doubt whether a psychiatrist would have agreed. I cannot think of any treatment, even with new drugs later on, that could have helped her behaviour. In retrospect perhaps we should all have adopted a firmer attitude and refused her requests, but she was quite capable of lodging a complaint to the powers that be, and we were loth to become involved in further trouble which would have been as futile as timewasting in its findings.

I suspect that many doctors, especially GPs, will have experienced a few disasters in practice, outside their control, which will have left an indelible impression on their memories for the rest of their lives. I remember an event that the passage of time can never erase, and it must be so unusual that I am sure readers would wish to know of it.

The occasion was a Saturday afternoon in the summer in Bridlington over twenty years ago. A business man living in the West Riding of Yorkshire decided to drive over and spend the weekend with a relative. So far as he knew he was in good health at the time. He arrived at his relative's house after an uneventful journey but after thirty minutes he complained of discomfort in the perineum, which, after a further short lapse of time was so painful, and he felt so unwell, that his relative contacted the surgery and asked if I would see him.

I was able to visit him straight away. He had a raised temperature, and the only other abnormal finding was a small area of inflamed skin over the ischiorectal fossa on one side which was exquisitely tender to touch. I remember being puzzled at the rapidity of onset of his symptoms, his toxic appearance, his denial of any previous trouble, and his apparent good health on arrival here, confirmed by his relative, just over an hour ago. He seemed to deteriorate as I watched him. It was evident he had a virulent infection, the site of the infection being in the ischiorectal fossa. I administered a megaunit of penicillin by injection, and arranged his transfer to Lloyd Hospital.

I reached the male surgical ward very shortly after this; by then he was confused and rambling, and to my astonishment the area of inflammation had extended to the upper thigh, buttock and inguinal lymph glands. As I watched I could see bubbles of gas traversing the inflamed areas; it was incredible. This unfortunate man had gas gangrene, and a vicious infection too. Massive doses of penicillin were given and repeated, and anti gas-gangrene serum injected until we had exhausted the hospital's supply, and the chemist's shelf as well. Intravenous fluids by drip followed and I contacted the surgical consultant resident in Scarborough. He expressed his amazement, and said he would drive over straight away and see what could be done. In the meantime Dr Lucey was on the scene and we could only watch the fulminating infection destroying this man; we had injected everything we knew might help, but it was a losing fight in our opinion, unbelievable though it must seem.

The surgeon arrived, expressed horror and amazement. Because the infection was spreading and invading so rapidly he decided the only treatment was a hind-quarter amputation. It seemed to us a heroic expectation of surgery, and in retrospect I would have been content if he had decided to allow the illness to run its dreadful course, though I understood his predicament. Mercifully the patient was unconscious as he mentioned the action he proposed to take.

The theatre-staff mobilized and the operation began. I was assisting, Dr Lucey providing anaesthesia. Every time the surgeon made an incision there was the crackle of gas as it escaped. Sometimes an audible plop was heard as a larger blood vessel was severed, gas escaping from it, and everyone in the theatre was aware of the gentle hiss as foul-smelling gas escaped from the wound. It was a fearsome operation, and I thought the surgeon did well to complete the task; no doubt it was the first, and last time, he would ever be called to undertake a similar procedure. I looked at the result of the surgery and wondered at the future quality of life for this unfortunate man should he recover. However, he was moribund and died half an hour later at nine pm that same afternoon seven hours after leaving the West Riding.

The theatre was shut for a week and stoved. Everyone connected with that afternoon's drama was shocked and distressed beyond all measure. I had an additional worry; I

276

thought one of my fingers had been pricked with the surgeon's needle, but I have lived to tell the tale.

I associated gas-gangrene with the Crimean and Boer Wars, and the 1914-18 World War. That it should occur in Bridlington in the 1960s in a fulminating form, and that with all the potent weapons at our command the patient should die in seven hours, was a devastating experience.

Next day as I drove along the road where the patient had stayed, and saw his car parked as he had left it, I could only shake my head in disbelief. It was a relief to go home to Sunday lunch with my family. I have never forgotten that dreadful afternoon.

In the 1950s the treatment of congestive cardiac failure had shown little advance over the years; the absent medication was an efficient diuretic. It was, therefore, a common situation to have several elderly patients with this condition at any time in the practice, a condition which gradually terminated their lives. The patient lay in bed, propped up high, with gross oedema of feet, legs, buttocks, abdominal wall, and with fluid in the abdominal and pleural cavities; anasarca, it was called. Digitalized these patients were, using tabs Digoxin 0.25 mgm twice daily, but the tab digitalis Pulv. gr 1 was widely used too. Mersalyl injections were given, mercurial diuretics, which helped diuresis initially, but soon lost effect. What was required was an efficient diuretic. The best we could do at that time was to drain the subcutaneous tissues using 'Southeys' tubes. These were fine subcutaneous needles, with multiple holes to the lumen, which were pushed into the subcutaneous tissues and connected with rubber tubes to a drainage bottle. By utilizing numerous needles a large quantity of fluid was removed form the oedematous tissues and did help in some small measure to alleviate the oedema in congestive cardiac failure. The discovery and marketing of the thiazide diuretics, followed later by the loop diuretics, and the potassium sparing spironolactone, et alia, revolutionized the treatment and prognosis of congestive cardiac failure. Salt-free diets were understood, but were of little value on their own. I had an elderly woman with this condition treated at home, and attended by her husband, daughter, and a district nurse. Three months had passed, much work carried out by all concerned, and the situation had become static. Far be it from me to claim that my medication had kept her alive, but after three months her husband said he would like one of the professors of medicine from a teaching hospital in a large university city in the north of England to see her. This was arranged, and I awaited the day with animation.

He arrived shortly after mid-day. I had arranged to meet him outside Lloyd Hospital and he followed me in his car to the patient's house. I soon sensed he did not hold me in high regard. The diagnosis was obvious. Slowly, and methodically, he examined the patient. There was little else to offer, but he produced a salt-free diet from his pocket, and prepared to leave after some encouraging words to the patient. His considerable fee was paid in notes. How undervalued I felt. He had of course travelled a big distance, and lost a day away from his usual routine. As he entered his car he asked me if I would show him a hotel for lunch and I obliged by leading him to a very nice hotel on the North Promenade, the Expanse, overlooking the sea; the dining room tables, visible through the windows, were laid for lunch; it looked inviting. I walked with him to the entrance thinking that a glass of sherry would have gone down well, but no, there was no invitation. The revolving doors turned behind him and I never saw him again. Later on that day I returned to the patient's house to reassess the situation and set in motion one or two of the specialist's suggestions. Her husband asked me if he had driven back straight away, so I said, no, he had his lunch at the Expanse Hotel. He smiled, and dryly remarked that he would have had no difficulty in paying the bill! I smile, too, as I remember those words forty years ago. Perhaps I was unlucky with the high-level consultants from the West Riding. On another occasion, knowing that the consultant smoked, I proffered my cigarette case, and was somewhat offended when he said he only smoked Turkish!

I was startled one surgery session when a fifty year old married woman entered the consulting room and gave a history suggestive of early pregnancy. However I thought the menopause the most likely diagnosis. I requested a pregnancy test on the urine for peace of mind for patient and doctor. The result was positive. It was her first pregnancy and she had not been married for many years. Her pregnancy followed a normal course, consultant advice was neither sought, requested, or required, and delivery was uncomplicated. The male infant was normal in every respect. As I returned home I reflected that

278

when the mother was eighty years, her son would be thirty years, a grand-maternal up-bringing! The father was several years older, but both proved to be model parents. The son thrived, and achieved excellent educational status. Mother always called her son 'my man-child', a designation which suitably impressed me. Only this very year, 1990, from the vantage point of a local shop I watched mother, father, and son parade King Street, Bridlington. Octogenarians indeed were the parents, the son in the full flush of manhood. Nostalgia assailed me as I returned home, and realized that sadly a good memory can produce painful side-effects. Clearly I had not recovered from my bereavement reaction associated with retirement, even after eight years!

Early in the New Year the matron of the Avenue Hospital, Miss Slack, held the annual Avenue Hospital dance. All the local doctors and their wives were invited, together with GPs from Filey, Driffield, and Beeford. There were local people too, closely associated with the hospital. It was a splendid occasion and we all looked forward to the festivities.

Matron Slack was a good organizer. The dance was held in a fair sized ward downstairs, occupied by medical and geriatric patients. At six pm the ward was full, the staff engaged in their work with customary skill and care. By eight thirty pm the transformation was such that it was necessary to check that you had come to the correct venue; the beds with their patients had disappeared, the room was festively decorated, a band occupied a corner of the ward, and the stage was set for an enjoyable evening. Notices directed guests to cloakrooms and toilets.

On entry via the medical door of the hospital, there was a large vessel containing hot 'punch' (more potent than it looked, its constituents, a guarded secret). It was served into glasses from a ladle wielded by Sister Fenner, and sometimes Matron herself. Loud was the laughter, noisy the room, excellent the dance, the ladies' evening dresses making a kaleidoscope of glittering colour. The band played the music of the day, the waltz, slow fox-trot, tango and rumba, and old-time dances too. The Gay Gordons was very popular and we careered about until we were dizzy: heaven forbid, this was before the days of rock and roll, jiving, and ostentatious solo dancing yards away from your partner, and the disco.

As I peer into the past, that dance floor with its happy dancers, hair down, jostling so close together, where everybody knew everybody, epitomized the happy atmosphere in which we carried out our caring work. Co-operation was the password, and refusal of a request for patient benefit never heard.

As the hands of the wall-clock veered on, so the dancing eased and we moved to an adjacent small ward where a buffet was laid on tables groaning under the weight of food which could not fail to satisfy even those with a most fastidious palate. Now and again a telephone rang in the distance, answered by whoever was nearest, who passed on the message to its intended recipient. Now and again a doctor disappeared for a while to attend to a confinement in the main block, only to return and enjoy the rest of the evening. I remember leaving the dance and driving out to an urgent call and giving an intravenous injection into an invisible vein with a skill I did not realize I possessed; to be complimented by the patient remarking how smart I looked in a tuxedo, and she did like the cigar-smoke! 'Come again like that next year!' she said.

As the evening drew to its close, many were invited to Matron's sitting room, again tastefully decorated and adorned with flowers and pot-plants. Lively, interesting, and stimulating were the topics discussed; it was always pleasant to meet other GPs from Filey and Driffield at these dances, and they often provided the only available opportunity.

Two doctors used to revert to herbalistic medicine and enjoyed the taste of chrysanthemum flower-heads year after year, and remarked that they enjoyed the dietary change, and that it did them good.

This annual dance was followed by another dinner-dance given by the matrons and staff of Lloyd and Bempton Lane hospitals. Inevitably it was a much larger occasion with many more nursing staff with their husbands, and male friends attending, and more consultants and local people too. For many years this dance was held at the Alexandra Hotel, a large rectangular building overlooking the north bay, east of Flamborough Road. The downstairs dining room was spacious and lofty with chandeliers suspended from the ceiling; there were two bars leading off from this room. I always thought the building was ideal for this dance on account of its size and position, though the ladies thought it could be chilly in their evening finery. There was a man called Johnny in one of the bars, who could dispense a tray of drinks quicker than anybody I have so far encountered.

After the dinner the tables were moved and the room prepared for the dance which again was a most enjoyable affair. It finished with the hokey-cokey, a hilarious situation. I am sure everybody was sad when the hotel was demolished. On future occasions the three BBB restaurant was used, and Newsome's Cafe once, but the atmosphere was never quite the same. As the years passed, the administration of the hospitals under the NHS became an unwieldy machine, and with so many people employed and attached it became impractical to find adequate accommodation, or the necessary funding for these dances, with the consequence that both were discontinued midst general regret.

The 1950/60 decade was moving inexorably towards its close. Amidst scenes of jubilation, a daughter was born at home in 1955, after a run of three boys; Hazel was her name.

It had been a decade of very hard work with the shoulder to the wheel all the time. Between ourselves, Dr Lucey and I had contrived an arrangement with the post office telephones whereby incoming calls could be intercepted and transferred to another number, enabling us to have a half-day away from the telephone once weekly, and for other special circumstances. For Barbara and I this was the start of fractionally more freedom of movement, and we were now 'off the phone' for a half-day and night for the first time in the twelve years since we arrived. It was a godsend, and we could not believe our good fortune. A 'weekend off' was not permitted by any of the practices, probably because it had never been carried out in the past, and also because the Minister of Health (Mr Aneurin Bevan) in his wisdom had decreed that a doctor was responsible for his patients twenty-four hours a day, seven days a week, fifty-two weeks per year; contravention might be considered a breach of the terms of service with serious consequences. PO Telephones had been known to make mistakes with interception, rendering a patient's telephone useless, and we could not tolerate the risk of that nature for as long a period of time as a weekend. It is not surprising that Nye Bevan had few friends among the medical profession.

Most important was the growth of the practice NHS List of Patients: from a miserly total of 1,900 patients in 1948 the list at the end of 1959 stood at 5,000 patients, an average annual growth of 14.8 per cent over twelve years. It was still a small practice, without a Basic Practice Allowance, or increased per capita payments for elderly patients, and without allowances to help towards the cost of ancillary staff. I have no hesitation in saying, with humility, that the growth was due to the superhuman efforts of Dr Lucey and myself and our only secretary, Miss Wells, in attracting newcomers in the town to our practice, aided by that invisible medium, the bush telegraph system. We can also never forget the assistance given to us by our wives who manned the telephones year in year out with never a word of complaint, and at the same time bearing and rearing a number of babies. They kept us sane, encouraged us, and dismissed our petty irritations inevitably caused by fatigue and pressure of work.

We all worked well together with a high morale. Whenever Dr Lucey saw my car parked in front of the Lloyd Hospital night or day, he would search me out and give his valued assistance; likewise I gave him the same facility. We undertook most procedures, indeed it was vital we did — Colles fractures, Potts fractures, dislocations of shoulders, greenstick fractures, removal of Tarsal cysts, Sebaceous cysts and biopsies, and we had been known to remove teeth when dentists were unavailable.

The casualty staff became familiar with our surgical expertise, and 'Donny' in the casualty department was always pleased to see us, and a most valuable assistant he was too.

Dr Gordon-Taylor was still in the partnership and approaching his seventy-seventh year; certainly he was spared any situation involving stress. Always a strong man with a robust constitution he had not altered in appearance and continued to manage what he thought he was able to do; he had become blander in manner and usually accepted any suggestions we had to make without question. He had good memory, good recall and a good brain. He enjoyed the quality press and had a keen interest in railway timetables and planning a hypothetical journey. 'Bradshaw', a large comprehensive tome on railway timetables was, I believe, his favourite book.

In 1959 he decided to leave Wellington House where he had lived, with the surgery adjacent, for thirty years, and move to a bungalow in George Street. The writing was on the wall for his retirement, the first indication we had perceived.

His two partners viewed this situation with mixed feelings; not that it came as a surprise or shock, but our concern was Wellington House. We did not want the house, but the attached surgery premises were crucial to us. I had my own house and surgery premises, Dr Lucey had built a pleasant family house on the north side of the town. We visualized having to buy the house for the sake of the surgery premises, and then attempt to sell the house separately. It was not an easy house; the kitchen and dining room were in the basement and the entire property was requiring an overhaul. The likely outcome for us was that the property would stick on the market. To find another premises, a lock-up too, in such a central position as Wellington House, would have been difficult.

The present surgery was adequate for our needs, apart from the waiting room, which was too small, and further practice growth might swamp it. If we had to purchase Wellington House, it was going to be difficult to raise capital, and a mortgage was little easier to achieve then than it was in 1948; at that time the economy was stifled and groaning under the weight of excessive taxation.

Happily, and probably via the grape-vine, a purchaser was forthcoming and it was now our turn to rent the surgery premises. We had been spared a major capital outlay, and another mill-stone around the neck, and for this we were indeed grateful.

However, serious trouble lay ahead a few months later. Electricians had been in Wellington House undertaking some alterations for the new owner and as so often happens an electrical fault developed where they had been working. The heat generated from a short-circuit melted the joints of two gas-pipes and in a short time twin gas pokers were doing their damage under the floor of the room above the surgery. There was quite a fire blazing by the time the brigade arrived. It was Saturday afternoon again, and I was oblivious of the event until I called at a grocer's shop in Hilderthorpe Road (now Threshers) on a routine visit. The owner said that Wellington House was on fire! Forgetting that I had come to see her I tore out of the shop, into the car, and along to Wellington House to find that the fire was out, that the brigade had completed its work and had returned to HQ. There was a mess and the typical smell of fire, smoke and char pervaded the surgery. The ceilings were blackened, there was water on the floor and it was clear that the rooms were out of action for a while. Dr Lucey was shifting files of record envelopes from a wet to a dry area.

During the upheaval a patient came up the steps into the room and studied the mess; quite amused she was as she announced that Gordon-Taylor had left in a blaze of glory!

It was not so funny for us. Quite apart from damaged premises we had to endure some warped humour from many quarters that we had set fire to the building ourselves in order to obtain the insurance money. One woman even asked me if I had set fire to the curtains to start it off!

After some discussion we decided to 'jump the gun' and ask the interior decorator to get to work with all speed and decorate the rooms. We contacted Mr Potter and his son, patients of the practice who understood our desperate need to be back in business as soon as possible. Action was swift, and on Monday morning his decorators moved in; it was some days later before the representative of the insurance company appeared, and expressed his irritation that we had commenced decorating, and in some measure destroyed evidence of the fire, and this could nullify our claim for compensation. Our decorator, however, was forthright and was able to describe the fire damage, and the amount of decorative work required: needless to say our claim was met in full.

Mr Potter thought he would be unable to have the rooms ready for us until the beginning of the following week: it was decided therefore that 63 Horsforth Avenue would 'double up'. It became a busy time for my premises. The record envelopes from Wellington House arrived, as did Mrs Wardell, their secretary, who had replaced Miss Wells after her marriage and subsequent arrival of a daughter. Their surgery sessions were fitted in between mine, and for a week the premises were a hive of activity. Inconvenient of course it was for many people but the arrangement saved the day and we did not think there had been any serious break in the continuity of the work. Wellington House surgery looked clean and refreshed after its face-lift, the first time it had been bottomed for as long as records were held. In retrospect we thought the fire had not been such a disaster after all.

Dr Gordon-Taylor eventually retired shortly before the fire in 1960. Wryly we commentated that in March 1948 he thought he would be retiring in two years, and on Dr Lucey's arrival two years later he thought he would be retiring in two years' time! In effect he retired twelve years after I arrived here so by any standards he had enjoyed a long run in general practice, but it was, of course, high time a young doctor filled his shoes.

No doubt, readers, you will have appreciated by now, that both Dr Lucey and I had put immeasurably more into the practice than we had ever taken from it. After lengthy discussion of the pros and cons we decided for a year we would be a two-man practice, and then look for a partner to replace Dr Gordon-Taylor. Without shame, and with minimal embarrassment, the reason for this decision, I have to say, was financial. There may be many people, especially our patients, who would have been astonished to learn that both of us had modest overdrafts and that every penny was a prisoner! How could such a situation possibly have arisen when, for a decade and more, two young men in their prime were working round the clock with skill and dedication, with 'service with a smile' as their slogan, and having increased the practice list by an average of 14.8 per cent annually? Indeed we were anything but extravagant, and the situation was no fault of ours.

The fault lay in the system of payment for GPs. It was based on the number of patients on their list, attracting a per capita payment. What was wrong about that? Nothing, the fault was the low payment per capita which necessitated a doctor holding a list as near the maximum allowable (3,000 in 1960, but 3,500 up to 1950). Thus, the bigger the list, the better the payment, the better your income. It would surely not be unreasonable to assume that with a smaller list and a larger fee per capita, a similar income could be achieved for the small list practitioner as was previously enjoyed by a high list practitioner. More important was the likelihood that a smaller and better paid list would tend to dissuade a doctor from holding a high list, and that a smaller list would enable him to have more time per patient, thus providing a better standard of patient care.

It was a simple exercise in basic logic and elementary mathematics, and as time passed this is exactly what has happened, but why, oh why, did it take from 1948-1965 before implementation?

Dr Lucey and I abided by our decision to be a two-man practice for a year in order to liquidate our overdrafts, put our finances on a better footing, improve our wardrobes, improve our cars, and increase the NHS list by another 14.8 per cent for the year, hoping this would make the practice sufficiently attractive for a new partner to join us. We did not think the work-load would be excessive; in view of Dr Gordon-Taylor's very light work-load before he retired it should make little difference to us.

While we were busily engaged in fulfilling this activity our impression was that the standard of general practice in Bridlington was high and left little to be desired. Indeed, there were no bad doctors. Consultants coming to the local hospitals complimented us on our work and relied on our efficiency to carry out post-operative care on their surgical cases, often heavy work in those days. If there were dissatisfied patients they could transfer to another practice if they so wished, but we all knew each other so well we were loth to do this and stood out against the request unless the circumstances were compelling. Nevertheless patients were your income, and there were other practices who were having as rough a financial ride as ourselves. Many doctors were relieved when a patient who had exhausted them mentally and physically moved on, but recipients soon learned that transfers from other doctors were not always the best.

To strengthen our belief that all was well with the conduct of general practice neither the BMJ, the Lancet, nor the Practitioner Journals, swerved from filling their pages with interesting trials, investigations, advances, and letters. Also in those days the NHS was not receiving daily knocks in the media and on television, starting at first light and repeated over and over again during the day.

We had not realized on our busy piece of coast-line that there was so much that was unsatisfactory about general practice, especially in the industrial cities.

A red book, a thick one, written by another Dr Taylor titled *Good General Practice* appeared and made unsatisfactory reading about the state of general practice in the country as a whole. This doctor had travelled all over the UK, visiting practices of every type, size and composition. Surgery accommodation, furniture, toilets, facilities for children in the waiting room, secretarial help, communication, the doctor's bag, rota systems, list size, prescribing all came under his critical and searching eye. In a nutshell he had little to say what was good about general practice, and indeed there seemed little for him to praise. The book was well written, well researched, and undoubtedly accurate, but it was not a book for the doctor's bedside table to induce sweet dreams.

However, the book was obviously read by many doctors with great concern. Perhaps this was the reason for the Foundation of the College of General Practitioners in 1952. The College produced its criteria for good general practice, faculties sprouted all over the regions. It had a mouth and firm teeth and has striven with outstanding success to further good standards with teaching and vocational training. GPs were invited to become founder members, and Dr Lucey and myself were happy to be included as Members ourselves. The college has continued for twenty-five years to go from strength to strength and has reshaped general practice to make it a speciality in its own right. I hope we no longer hear those demeaning words that general practice is the place for those who failed to make the grade.

If the same author of that red book thirty years ago was able to revisit the scenes of his past travels today, there would be little doubt he would think the age of miracles was not past, and would rapidly commence the task of rewriting the book, and a slim volume at that.

Everywhere he would see modern purpose-built practice premises, or health centres, attractive waiting rooms, an appointment system, secretarial staff in profusion, a practice midwife, a trainee in general practice, an attached health visitor, possibly a practice manager, treatment room, visits by a social worker, and computerization of records. The list is endless.

The passage of time itself can provoke change and induce new thinking, but I would venture to suggest that without the foundation of the College of General Practitioners, the scenery of general practice would never have reached the high standard it now enjoys. The College became the Royal College of General Practitioners in 1967.

I write from a general practitioner's point of view, but what does the patient think? Has this transformation bettered his well-being? Are patients content with the treatment they now receive? I am approaching my final chapter, the Twilight, when there will be time to muse and ponder these questions. At present, the past is still vivid in memory, and this must take precedence before the lamp burns low.

During that year 1960/1 when we worked as a two-man practice it was our holidays that caused most difficulty, because the children of both partners were of school age, and our holidays were tailored to coincide with theirs. Instead of taking a summer holiday in early October when our West Riding visitors had returned home, our holidays were brought forward to the children's holidays in the high season, and this produced a heavy burden for the remaining partner.

Nevertheless we thought it was very important to have a fortnight away at that time, not only to recharge our own batteries, whose voltage was inevitably low due to the demands made on them, but to give our wives a break from the domestic chores, and the telephone, and to show the children there were other places in Britain worthy of a visit.

Holidays then were very different from now; holidays abroad were not for the masses, their cost outside the confines of people's budgets. Dr Lucey purchased a large tent, and with his car weighed down, set off for the Emerald Isle, to white strands, to fish and rest and live under canvas. I was fortunate too; Barbara's home in Aberdeenshire was ever open to us; the peace and quiet, the solitude, and scenery of the coast along the Moray Firth, were the ingredients for the perfect holiday. Also, after my father's death in 1955 from a cerebral haemorrhage, my mother, wisely, left the remote part of Devonshire, six miles inland from Sidmouth, and returned to Swanage where she lived alone in an area she had known since the 1914-18 war, and which had changed but little over the years. Swanage was another splendid place for a summer holiday with a safe beach, a sea temperature often up to 63°F, and my family learned to swim there; it was also a walker's paradise.

Patients were very understanding, different from now. Information was purposely leaked that so and so would be away for a holiday, and if a repeat prescription or a special request was needed it would be wise to come now rather than later, because the remaining partner would be heavily engaged and not *au fait* with their medical history. By the time the partner left for his holiday the Wellington House surgery would merely be 'ticking over', and left in the capable hands of the secretary who was able to contact me at any time, or leave a message if not urgent.

I did not have secretarial help in 63 Horsforth Avenue until 1961. Like Wellington House I tried to reduce my surgery load to a trickle before locking up the house, pinning a notice on the front door advising I was away until ... (and inviting burglars too!), before leaving, eyes glazed with fatigue, either for the long journey north or south; it was eighty miles further to Huntly than Swanage.

A heavy load was placed on Barbara on these occasions as inevitably the incoming telephone calls doubled. However, with her nursing experience and the willing help and encouragement I always received, she used to cope admirably with these demands. The practice was saved the expense of secretarial help we would have found difficult to afford.

For my part it was the burden of writing all practice letters in my own hand that I found irksome, tiring and time-consuming. I experienced little difficulty dealing with the NHS envelopes; they were stacked at the side of my desk, and even though there were open surgeries then, and I had no idea who would be coming, I usually had the envelope on the desk before the patient was ready to sit down. The telephone could be a trial during surgery hours, but if I was delayed in answering Barbara would take the call. This was family medicine!

The patients of both sides of the practice understood and accepted our holiday arrangements, and at no time were there untoward incidents.

However, time and time again many events took place which could make the fortnight very hard-going. To have a surgical emergency barely before your partner's car was a speck in the distance, (and as I have written previously, such emergencies were operated at Lloyd Hospital, and the GP was required to assist the surgeon), could ruin a morning and an afternoon because you were never certain when the surgeon would arrive from Scarborough. It was necessary to keep your eye on the hospital drive to see if his car had arrived, or to ring theatre sister to see is she had any information. It was strange, too, that elderly patients who had held on to life for weeks, sometimes died collectively, the same day the partner disappeared, and as all doctors well know, patient death involves action which is time-consuming. Yes, we had bereavement counselling then; the difference was that the doctor carried it out instead of an ancillary worker, with little or no knowledge of the family situation in that particular instance.

It was a challenging time, but we were happy to see our partner back restored to full vigour; we were not packed up ourselves ready for our fortnight away with the engine ticking over as soon as his car appeared on the horizon. A week or two elapsed for the incoming partner to pick up the threads, and the outgoing partner to unwind, disengage, and prepare for his own holiday.

The year on our own passed quickly and at the end we had achieved our aim, had consolidated our position financially, and increased the NHS count to 5,200. The average list size in the UK at that time would have been around 2,350 patients per doctor, so we were appreciably below that figure for a partnership of three, but to offset that were 1,200 temporary residents, mostly seen between 1 July and 15 September. This TR figure was remarkably constant over the years. We were both tired, physically and mentally, and without hesitation agreed that it was time to find another partner. A carefully worded and accurate advertisement appeared in the British Medical Journal to this end.

Before I describe the details of our eventual selection events were unfolding which were to produce a profound effect on every medical practice in the UK. First was the New Abortion Bill introduced by David Steel, recently knighted, which found its way to the statute book, and second, was the discovery and introduction of the contraceptive pill.

I must confess that every time I signed the 'green form' along the space provided for the first medical practitioner, requesting a termination of pregnancy, when there did not seem to be a specific reason, I wondered that the bill ever became law. Certain clauses seemed so vague that they could be manipulated to suit any occasion. Some obstetricians would sign along the space for the second medical practitioner and agree to undertake the termination provided it was the early months of pregnancy; others would refuse, and you were left with an angry patient, and often, angry parents, considered by many practitioners and consultants as having no role to play in the decision. I cannot see much sense in allowing a pregnancy to continue against the mother's wishes, and I also find it difficult to accept that an unmarried fifteen year old is capable of making a reasoned decision to keep the pregnancy, when oblivious to the problems of unmarried mothers and single parenthood. It was an unhappy situation and could cause practice disagreement. Religious views were factors; all I could do was to interpret the law to the best of my ability, to listen carefully, put forward reasons for and against and reach a decision. It is some years since I retired but my impression from the media, television, and radio is that termination on demand is the order of the day now, and I did not think that was the original intention of the Act.

The arrival of the contraceptive pill was greeted with rapture by patients and the drug houses alike. Caps, diaphragms and sheaths were rejected, though the sheath (now called a condom), has come back to help in the fight against HIV (Homogenous Immuno-deficiency Virus) infection. Initially the Pill had quite a 'high dose' oestrogen component, and although it had been used for several years on the Costa Rica by thousands of women, and considered reliable and safe, it was soon realized here that it had side-effects and could produce dangerous and occasionally fatal consequences. It was very necessary that women taking the pill were regularly examined, weighed, blood-pressure recorded, medical history, and present medication reviewed, and a cervical smear taken at determined intervals. Fears of the pill producing cancer have been discounted, yet I understand carcinoma of the cervix is increasingly common.

It was soon evident that a considerable extra work-load had reached our surgeries. A contraceptive form appeared which required the patient's signature annually, in order to be included on the contraceptive register. This form attracted an annual fee, and was another source of income for the practice, undreamed of previously.

The early euphoria generated by pill-users diminished as time, and experience with its use, revealed that it was not the panacea for the perfect contraceptive. Certainly it seemed to be ninety-nine per cent efficient as a contraceptive for those able to use it, but for those women whose weight increased, whose blood-pressure was elevated to unacceptable levels, for those who had side-effects from its interaction with other medication, and for those who developed prolonged amenorrhoea which might upset their fertility, it was a preparation best rejected. This unfavourable knowledge produced extra work for the general practitioner, which became heavier as newer preparations with elaborate names, varying strengths, and different indications, appeared on the market. More work lay ahead with the innovation of intrauterine contraceptive devices, and referrals to consultants for laparoscopic sterilization. These new techniques came later, unfortunately, as I became older when I would have preferred a lesser work-load. Later pages will reveal my involvement. Nurse Colbeck, a Roman Catholic, and a district nurse, used to pronounce that self-control, not birth control, was required! However, I had to heed patient demand.

Readers will note how meticulous I have been in addressing colleagues by their professional titles, a courtesy expected in those days. It was unusual to address anyone by their Christian name unless related, requested, or exceptionally well known to each other. I had certainly been accustomed to this all my life; at school the surname was always used by staff, and other boys, whom you could regard as your friends. You might have a nick-name but this usually drew attention to some unusual quirk or skill you might possess. If you had one or two brothers at school it was Smith I, Smith II and Smith III. Similarly masters were always addressed as Mr and lady teachers as Mrs or Miss; to be flippant, and call a master by his Christian name in his hearing resulted in an unpleasant visit to the headmaster's study. At Weymouth College we did have one lady teacher who was known as 'the hag' (she never looked one), but of course she was never addressed as such. This form of address applied to my years in Edinburgh too; in the army you were addressed by your rank and surname.

I write of this now because after ten years of close partnership with Dr Lucey with its successes and challenges, its laughter and tears, its support and trust, he is known for the remainder of this tale as 'Des' (short for Desmond).

I return to our task of selecting another partner. Rather to the surprise of Des and I there were many applicants (over forty) for our advertised post. It was interesting that there were few recently qualified applicants; the majority were from doctors already in general practice as assistants, and sometimes partners, who had been attracted by our advertisement relative to the open access of the Lloyd and Avenue Hospitals.

The catchment area was broad; there was one applicant from as far away as Inchture (twix Perth and Dundee), and I remember well a fatigued doctor from Staveley, a highly industrialized area, stamping out a cigarette and gulping the breeze from across the North Sea, with relish.

Wives accompanied their husbands for interview, and we did our best to amuse, entertain, and analyse.

These were the days before vocational training for entry to general practice, and our applicants had completed one, two, or three house-appointments, possibly achieving the DRCOG en route before seeking an assistantship, or assistantship with view to partnership (a misleading term). Those applicants already in general practice were mainly assistants, whose time of employment was running out, and were looking for another post. Assistants were plentiful at that time; many had been mislead and were not, and never were, going to be offered partnership. It was an undesirable situation, but it was cheaper for a principal to have an assistant than an additional partner. It was not entirely a principal's fault; more often than not a practice could not afford two partners; the work was there in plenty, but not the money. Happily the situation was redressed with the years.

Some applicants were unsuitable from the start because of illegible handwriting, a curriculum vitae which was poorly expressed, and it was a surprise that some letters displayed a lack of enthusiasm. Possibly these applicants were writing multiple applications and were weary of not receiving acknowledgement of their application (an experience which was not uncommon).

These failed to reach the interview. All our applicants received acknowledgement and were informed if the post had been filled. One lady doctor applied whom we considered good from her letter of application, but she failed to arrive for the interview. Gradually the field narrowed until there were half a dozen applicants on the short list and all these were interviewed.

Everybody who was interviewed was keen to come, and without exception would have fitted the post admirably, and this of course added to our difficulty; the wheel had turned full circle. We did not realize we had so much on offer that was attractive. I remember an anxious moment when an applicant and his wife arrived at the same time as we were interviewing another applicant; it was not a block-booking but something went wrong with the time machine. As usual our wives (who enjoyed these incidents) were at hand and were able to steer the new arrivals into another room until we were ready to interview them with composure.

We reached a decision which was finalized after a very enjoyable dinner at the Seabirds Hotel at North Landing, Flamborough with the prospective new partner and his wife.

Thus it was that Dr John Bell was appointed and we all looked forward to the future health and wealth of the partnership with keen enthusiasm. A dozen years and more younger than ourselves and already experienced in general practice Des said he regarded him as a colleague, as well as a partner, a fine distinction in the use of the English vocabulary, but with which I concurred.

It soon became clear that the 1960/70 decade was a decade for change. Mr Harold Wilson, the prime minister of the day, talked of the white heat of industrial change, the start of industrial decline as it turned out, but I write of changes that started to permeate the NHS, and the changes in the behaviour of many people which had a direct bearing on my work and involvement with the NHS.

Manners failed early on, rapidly followed by rudeness, bad language, and a *laissez faire* attitude. Sloppy dress, men's hair at shoulder length, side whiskers, and the forgotten razor were soon apparent. Beetlemania accelerated the decline. Expressions such as 'so what', 'if you can't beat em, join em', 'couldn't care less', were the language of the day. People prided themselves on being trendy, and anyone who criticized or failed to conform was regarded as 'square'. Punks, mods, rockers, hells angels, skinheads, flower children, and communal love children appeared to disturb the scenery of the resorts and countryside. Women took to the mini-skirt, and it only suited a few; others strutted about in heavy cloaks or night-dresses. 'Jeans' became popular, and have remained so. I have never understood why.

Sadly these degenerative changes were accepted by many who should have realized the folly, but when these changes were condoned by those responsible for the teaching and education of children and teenagers, was it any surprise that the situation continued to deteriorate, that young people became a problem in their management and that educational standards deteriorated?

Whether these changes were a reaction after the lean post-war decade, or whether it was a swing of the pendulum by the angry young men against accepted standards, codes of behaviour and self-discipline, I must leave to the clearer vision of the historian.

Worse lay ahead. Sexual morality broke down, clearly aided by the use of the contraceptive pill. Sleeping around, infidelity, rape, violence, illegitimacy, drug-addiction, hooliganism, the lager-lout, sexual abuse of children, the break-down of family life, and divorce, dominated the media.

The churches seemed powerless and lacked leadership; the police, overworked, and usually abused, were not entirely blameless, and the judiciary seemed surprisingly out of touch or indifferent.

Of course the medical profession was involved. This catalogue of changes could produce illness and injury: violence and alcoholism caused scenes in hospital accident and emergency departments which were a disgrace to a civilized country. Drug addiction, shared syringes, homosexuality, many different sexual partners, have led to an HIV problem culminating in AIDS (Acquired Immune Deficiency Syndrome). Whereas syphilis was eventually curable, there is no evidence yet that those with HIV infections and AIDS are going to be cured, and the condition shows no signs of containment.

Alcoholism is giving rise to anxiety, and young men are developing cirrhosis of the liver and pancreatitis. Termination of pregnancy has added to the work-load in obstetrics and gynaecology departments. Stress, nervous breakdown, anxiety and suicide have all added to the medical work-load. Vast sums of money are spent year after year to cope with these tragic events; if only that resource was available annually to provide more hip and knee joint replacements, more coronary by-pass surgery, more renal dialysis machines, and a reduction in waiting times for non-urgent surgery.

Happily the NHS has risen to the challenge. Doctors, nurses and ancillary staff have continued to work with dignity, compassion and care, often in the face of adverse criticism from the media, television and radio; criticism so often misinformed and untrue; criticism which must depress the hardiest character and lower the morale of many NHS workers. Despite the problems, the politics and the violence, progress and medical advance continues in all branches, carried out by men and women with vision, determination, and a desire to promote the health of the people of this country, and to cope with those who fall by the wayside.

No! The NHS is not suffering from a degenerative change, and I pray that it never will. Money is poured into the service, but demand is insatiable.

Despite the problems and the increasing work-load, the practice flourished, and the partners did not adapt wayward behaviour.

It was soon evident that Dr John Bell was a practitioner of high quality. He taught us new methods, he had fresh ideas, and he advanced our knowledge; he became a skilled anaesthetist, a valuable asset to a practice at a time when resuscitative measures, airway maintenance, the use of defibrillators, and cardiac monitoring were becoming vital areas of medical knowledge for general practice, and in addition he was a good committee man, representing the Bridlington practitioners over the years with patience, tolerance and wisdom, putting up with the irritations that can be roused by such meetings, and never complaining at the inconvenience caused by being away from his usual practice work.

Steroid therapy came to the practice scene with all the advantages it was known to possess. Soon there was a multitude of preparations from the many drug houses for oral, intra-articular, and intravenous administration, as well as lotions, ointments, creams, drops for eye, ear, and nose, suppositories and sprays as well. These preparations were potent with many contraindications for their use; there was more to learn, more to understand, and special care in their use. The treatment of bronchial asthma was revolutionized; the response to an intravenous injection of hydrocortisone 100m gm in an acute attack, dramatic and life-saving. Certain skin ailments responded rapidly to steroidal lotions, ointments, and creams; inflammatory ocular conditions ceased to give rise to anxiety, and troublesome ear conditions such as otitis externa were quickly relieved.

It was remarkable that as soon as the new steroid preparations became available to treat conditions which I had hitherto seen occasionally, there seemed to be no such shortage of cases in the future. I refer to conditions such as tennis elbow, the carpal tunnel syndrome, and capsulitis of the shoulder joint. Whereas these conditions were intractable and lingered over many months, with physiotherapy the customary remedy, an injection of hydrocortisone succinate into the right spot given in the surgery, usually gave quick easing of the pain, and often cure within ten days. We were fortunate to have an enlightened orthopaedic consultant who showed us how to administer these injections, and he encouraged their use.

In an attempt to keep general practitioners abreast of the rapid changes occurring in medicine, it became necessary for them to attend a specified number of refresher courses each year. These courses were arranged by district hospitals in Yorkshire and Humberside and notified to practitioners by the executive council. Courses were in fact held all over the country and it was perfectly possible to go to London, Edinburgh, or wherever you wished if there was a course to your liking. It was necessary to apply for a course, numbers were sometimes limited, and you received a form of acceptance.

There was no charge, and it was possible to claim for travelling expenses and maintenance, the course being recognized under Section 63, and funded by general taxation. Failure to attend the requisite number of courses per annum involved the forfeiture of the seniority payment, a severe penalty.

Most courses were for a day and a half, usually the whole of Saturday and up to noon on a Sunday. Certain specialized courses in London could last for a week. I remember a refresher midwifery course in York lasting for a week.

I enjoyed these courses, particularly those on paediatrics held in York, and over the years I was to be seen in Harrogate, Hull, Pontefract, York and Scarborough. There was a wide range of subjects to choose, from psychiatry to practice management. Usually the lectures were formal and given by consultants in their various departments. They were well prepared with good delivery, aided with slides, the use of the epidioscope, and sometimes patients were demonstrated as well. I found them valuable, informative and helpful; I enjoyed, as well, the company of other general practitioners from many areas at lunch in the refectories, and hearing their views on current events, and news of their practices.

However, it seemed I held a minority view. Others did not like the weekends broken up in such fashion, or driving a considerable distance two days running in inclement weather. Others wanted more open discussions on a given topic, and I am sorry to say there were those who said they were bored.

Perhaps it was the compulsion that was resented, a sign of

the times. Gradually these courses were reduced, and eventually disappeared altogether. No doubt video tapes seen at home could be as informative, but they were unavailable to us then.

Apart from my work in the practice, escalating each year due to the increase in numbers on the NHS list, to treatment which was becoming more complex and time-consuming, and to the large number of elderly patients over sixty-five years on the list (over twenty-seven per cent), extra-practice events were arising which were important, expensive, and required my attention. Education of my family was the concern. I had always valued my years at school, enjoyed them, and was well aware that my education had stood me in good stead, to the extent that I would have been unhappy if I had not provided a similar opportunity for my children. I had four, and eight years separated the eldest from the youngest, involving a commitment of twelve years expense for each child, inclusive of the parental contribution for university or college after leaving school. If it had not been for the perseverance of the local representative of the Refuge Assurance Society, who convinced me to take out an educational policy for each of my sons, to mature when they were fourteen years old and which covered the fees for five years, I would not have been able to finance the cost without a bank loan (difficult to obtain at that time).

The Refuge representative was a Mr Batty. Invariably he waited his turn in the waiting-room, and set my head reeling with figures of monthly premiums. Many times I had to show him the door, expostulating my inability to pay; he always returned and eventually wore me down so that I signed along the dotted line, anxious to complete the surgery session. However, I have always been grateful to Mr Batty for his persistence, but I never had the chance to thank him adequately because he died abruptly when still in his prime.

It is interesting to record that although the policies were designed to cover the termly fees, these fees had doubled over the ten allotted years of premiums, revealing that inflation had begun to rear its ugly head as far back as 1961!

It was fortunate for my sons that there was a preparatory school at Sewerby called Marton Hall situated in beautiful surroundings half-way between Bridlington and Flamborough. Even more fortunate was the experience, wisdom, and expertise of the headmaster, Mr John Gane, assisted by his wife Georgina.

The school was founded many years ago by his father and had been a family concern ever since. Mr and Mrs Gane possessed an ability to choose teachers, matrons, kitchen staff and gardeners who gave their best, were loyal, and would never consider letting them down. John Gane seemed to understand the physiognomy of boys in the age group of seven to fourteen years. Not over-strict, he expected high standards in their dress, appearance and above all he instilled into them from an early age the importance of manners and sociable behaviour at all times. He kept the boys hard at it and interested all day and every day. Sports played a prominent position in the curriculum, and I was often surprised at the number of. match fixtures arranged with other preparatory schools in the county during a term, the 'away' matches holding a very popular place with the school teams. Everybody admired John Gane. He had ceaseless energy, was stable, fair and charismatic, and highly respected by boys and old boys alike. He seemed to know a boy's capabilities and drew them out to their full potential.

The aim of the school was to prepare boys for the Common Entrance Examination for public schools. He taught Latin himself, and surrounded by a good staff the school was most successful in this respect and boys moved on to public schools far and wide. I had special reason to be grateful to the school. One of my sons made one hundred per cent in arithmetic in the Common Entrance Exam, skilfully taught by Mrs Suggitt, and has maintained his liking for mathematics subsequently, and the two other sons won scholarships to Wellingborough School in Northamptonshire, achievements which were of considerable assistance to me towards the school-fees.

John Gane was older in years than he looked but his appearance never changed and he seemed ageless. Supremely fit himself, he expected parents to enter the hundred yards race on Sports Day; there was no point in hiding behind the trees because he would find you. I remember setting off at a cracking pace in the hundred yards when the gun fired, and for a short time I was in the lead until suddenly both calf muscles seized and I was forced to the ground and out of the race. John Gane completed the race and was the winner.

It was a sad day when John Gane died in retirement some ten years ago. The church at Sewerby where a memorial service was held, was packed to overflowing with Old Martonians from all over the country, a fitting testimony to the affection and respect he inspired. I lost a valued friend, and a man whose ideals and character I admired so much.

There is no doubt that the three phases of education, preparatory school, public school, and university, presented a challenge to recipient and parent as well; with each passing phase a hurdle was overcome, eliciting a sense of relief, only too welcome.

Phase Two was now with us and the boys were at Wellingborough School, 164 miles from Bridlington. Why Wellingborough? Readers will recall that I had been a pupil of Weymouth College on the Channel coast. On the outbreak of World War Two in 1939 Weymouth was considered a vulnerable area due to the proximity of Portland Harbour, an important naval base. There was a torpedo-factory at Portland too. Because the number of boys fell during the first year of hostilities a decision was reached by the Governors to disband the school; thirty-three boys were affiliated with Wellingborough School, and a Weymouth House evolved; three masters, T.S. Nevill, J.W.S. Blake, and F.C. Bowman also moved to Wellingborough: T.S. Nevill became headmaster of Wellingborough in August 1940, and J.W.S. Blake became house master of Weymouth House. It seemed that some Old Weymouthians possessed a loyalty to their old school, and I was not displeased at the thought of Mr Nevill, Mr Blake, and Mr Bowman, who taught me French, history, German and mathematics, teaching my own children. No doubt the values taught at Weymouth College would have permeated Wellingborough over twenty-five years.

However, headmasters come and go, and Mr T.S. Nevill had retired, was ordained, and became chaplain to the Speaker at the House of Commons, before my sons started there, leaving Mr Blake and Mr Bowman who had changed but little over the years.

I held liberal views over their future occupations, though I did suggest that I thought they would be wise to keep to the science subjects, advice which was heeded, and subsequently vindicated. One by one they mastered seven GCE subjects, and moved on to 'A' level studies in physics, chemistry and mathematics.

By now I was under no illusion that any one of them wished

Our family, left to right: Dennis, Angus, Hazel and Arthur.

to consider medicine, and I could not blame them for their decision. Overworked and underpaid, too long hours, their dislike of 'cutting things up' were the reasons put forward. On many occasions certain planned 'outings' were foregone at short notice on account of some medical necessity, and that sort of occurrence was unlikely to endear them to medicine as a career. At their ages one talked boldly of 'going into oil'; another talked of 'electronics', a comparatively new word then, and another was still thinking about his future with no clear decision.

Wellingborough School, however, provided all that was expected of it. Slight rebellion against previous values attempted to penetrate the school in the 1960s, but the staff seemed able to contain this, and so far as I was concerned the only noticeable change during 1960/70 decade was overlong untidy hair, and Beetle-music. Certainly I was spared the horrors of drug taking, rudeness, disobedience or unsocial behaviour, and our family continued manageable and gave us no cause for anxiety. We were proud of them, and fortunate indeed.

For parents there were some enjoyable events; open-days, prize-giving days, Christmas-carol services in the school chapel, and high-powered guests giving instructive addresses. Like Marton Hall, Wellingborough School had spacious and beautiful grounds and playing fields, with chestnut trees in profusion. It was a nice place to be at school and the boys were allowed into the town.

Not so pleasant was the drive from Bridlington to Wellingborough. Traffic on the A1 passed through the town centres of Retford, Newark, and Grantham; there were no by-passes, roads and towns were busy and in those days there was trouble with fog in the evenings. Over nine years I learned to know the road very well indeed, but I had some tough journeys home, sometimes arriving in the early hours. When the three boys were at Wellingborough together for a short time, three school trunks (one on the roof) three boys and driver made the load. The car was a Ford Zephyr six cylinder which ate up the miles, and the petrol too.

The 'A' levels were overcome and phase Two came to a close. I was relieved to be off the A1, especially at night. The boys were students now; one went to Aberdeen University to take a B.Sc. in pure science; another went to Leeds University to study chemical engineering, and another to Nottingham

University to study electric and electronic engineering; it was a relief to be over this hurdle.

It was interesting to have experience of these universities, and three different courses of study. To compare them would be invidious. Some universities possessed more halls of residence than others; flat-sharing between four or five students was more popular with some than others, and in Aberdeen, many students lodged or lived in Aberdeen or close by. Nottingham had an extensive and well-maintained campus; Leeds University was very central. All the universities seemed well-equipped, and had first-class lecturers. The three students obtained degrees of B.Sc. in their chosen faculties, one (Arthur) obtaining First Class Honours in chemical engineering, an outstanding achievement. The dignified graduation ceremonies followed in these three cities, days never to be forgotten by the students or ourselves. My labour and expense for the young men were completed; they had the tools, and what they dug with the spade will be manifest in the final chapter, the Twilight.

But how about our daughter Hazel, the youngest member of the family by four years? She attended the local primary school, sat and passed the Eleven Plus examination. However, to provide her with the same opportunities and values as her brothers, we decided she should be educated at Queen Ethelburga's Girls School in Harrogate. After sitting their entrance exam she was accepted and started her life at the school aged eleven and a half years. We were very sad to see her go, and it was a dismal journey home.

She passed the GCE in eight subjects, and like her brothers took 'A' level science subjects in which she was also successful.

She knew she wanted to be a dietician and we were very pleased she was accepted at Edinburgh College of Domestic Science, at one time the Atholl Crescent School of Domestic Science, mentioned with affection by me in my own student days, oh so many years ago!

Hazel enjoyed her three years in Edinburgh; she shared a flat on the campus with three other girls, made many friends who have maintained contact, and who live fairly close by, in Yorkshire. Time passed quickly for her there; she was successful in the examinations, and on a sunny day in late Autumn 1976 we witnessed her graduation in the McEwan Hall, a dietician at last. Now she had the tools, and what she dug with her spade will also be manifest in the final chapter, the Twilight.

As we drove back through the Borders to Bridlington we knew that phase Three was behind us; we were happy and relieved, and the family was happy. There was, however, not much left in the kitty, a situation not unusual for us. We have never had occasion to regret the expense and the deprivation caused.

Events in the practice had not stood still during these years when I was so heavily involved with education and travelling to and fro. New diuretics were discovered and manufactured by the drug houses. These drugs were capable of exerting their action on the one million nephrons which make the structure of a kidney. There were high, medium, and low potency diuretics, their effect depending on the reduction in sodium reabsorption in the convoluted tubule of the nephron. Some drugs allowed potassium to be excreted from the body and this loss required replacement with potassium preparations. Diuretics were able to rid the body of large volumes of water and resulted in tremendous benefit to the patient in the treatment of cardiac failure. However, care was required in their use in order to avoid the production of other conditions such as gout, and to avoid interaction with other therapy.

Another great advance was the manufacture of histamine H_2-receptor antagonists. These preparations were able to reduce gastric secretion, and were of great value in the treatment of duodenal ulcer, and gastric ulcer. Whereas a duodenal ulcer could take weeks to heal, or never heal, using bed rest, alkali and milk diet, these new preparations allowed a duodenal ulcer to heal in six to eight weeks without a strict dietary regime.

The B_2 adrenergic receptor stimulant preparations were now available, usually administered by inhalation and were of great value in the treatment of asthma, a treatment which could be employed by the patient, and which reduced the urgent need for a doctor to administer hydrocortisone by intravenous injection.

The new drugs used in the treatment of insomnia, depression, and anxiety were widely recognized and prescribed as being helpful in the management of these conditions. Before, during, and after the World War Two there was a very limited range of therapy, the barbiturate group of drugs, bromides, and chloral comprising the drugs usually prescribed. There was another preparation, paraldehyde, with a revolting taste, but usually administered rectally, and essentially for hospital use. Although the barbiturate group of drugs were most efficient and popular for insomnia, unfortunately they produced dangerous side-effects, potentiated by alcohol and many deaths occurred every year from misuse and overdosage. Patients liked these new drugs, and more and more people pressed for a prescription to help them to sleep, young and elderly alike. Very soon the number of patients with depression and anxiety states increased rapidly and sought treatment. Why were there so many people asking for these preparations at a time when the nation's affluence was considered higher than it had ever been, and when the benefits of the welfare state were available to so many, is beyond my capacity to understand.

It was not appreciated at first how addictive most of the new preparations were, and that once started, there were difficulties in their withdrawal. I was frequently surprised that patients under the care of a psychiatrist for depression returned to the surgery with a note asking me to add yet another preparation to the medication, when they were already on one, two, or three preparations prescribed by the psychiatrist, without suggesting that one or two preparations should be withdrawn! It was a persistent fight trying to dissuade patients from starting these drugs, and encouraging their withdrawal by those already taking them. There was, however, no doubt that correctly used and supervised, these new preparations were most valuable and many patients were kept out of hospital who would otherwise have required in-patient treatment. As the years advanced, better preparations with short half-lives were available which were safer and quickly excreted from the body. With a better understanding of their addictive qualities by doctors and patients, the situation became more manageable.

Another group of drugs, the beta adrenergic receptor blocking drugs (the Beta-Blockers) heralded a revolution in the treatment of angina pectoris, essential hypertension, and auricular fibrillation and allied cardiac irregularities. One after the other a newer and slightly different B. Blocker appeared from the drug houses at home and abroad.

The treatment of coronary ischaemia was changing. A better understanding of its cause and relationship to cigarette smoking, lack of exercise, and saturated fats in the diet have led to a better appreciation by the public that a reduction in the incidence of coronary artery disease was possible if they paid attention to their life-style. Public awareness of the treatment of cardiac arrest by the man in the street, and ambulance paramedics has saved lives. Early diagnosis that all was not well with the coronary artery flow, followed by coronary by-pass surgery has reduced the incidence of coronary ischaemia and prolonged lives. However, it is still a major cause of sudden death in the UK, especially Scotland.

The development of the cardiac pace-maker has changed the quality of life for those afflicted with heart-block.

The rapidity of the advances in medicine, and the formidable array of medication available have called for increased knowledge in their correct use by general practitioners. One would have thought that never before were refresher courses so necessary. The drug companies were very helpful with literature, samples, and advice, and many companies would hold a seminar at a local club or a restaurant, and with a film, samples and discussion, followed by a pleasant meal with aperitifs, push the indications and the value of their product. No doubt such meetings helped to fix the name of the preparation in a practitioner's memory, but less emphasis was placed on the nature of the product, its characteristics, and to which group of drugs it belonged.

It was quite easy to find yourself prescribing a product without a full understanding of its therapeutic effects and chemistry, a bad practice which could grow on you, and one to be avoided at all costs.

With these new preparations with new names now available to general practitioners in the late 1960/70 decade, it was little wonder that we were able to do more and more for our patients. Crisis medicine disappeared; once a diagnosis was made, a course of treatment was planned which in many conditions was long-term, and in some cases life-long. Thus more and more demands were made on the surgeries for repeat prescriptions, a situation unlikely to be resolved. In addition, because there was a treatment for most ailments more and more patients attend the surgery. Add to this an increase in the numbers of elderly patients on the NHS, plus annual practice growth, it became clear that more accommodation and additional secretarial help was required.

As a result of the new Charter of 1972, which laid down a

basis of payment less dependent on numbers of patients, but more related to their age group, the elderly attracting higher capitation fees, it was possible to acquire a large income with fewer patients. The size of the NHS list became less important too, because extra-practice allowances covered the cost of seventy per cent of secretarial, practice nurses and managers salaries, hitherto paid in full by the partnership; these were now paid by Humberside Family Practitioner Committee out of general taxation. Fewer patients, more time to spend with them, more money than ever before, we had never experienced such affluence, or such idyllic practice life.

The NHS list now stood at 6,555 and it was decided to hold it at that level for the future. What a contrast to the early days of the NHS when every patient was your bread and butter; if only I was thirty years younger!

To ease the strain on the surgeries it was decided to introduce an appointment system in each of our surgeries: such systems were becoming popular and were recommended by the Royal College of GPs. There was a great deal of discussion about the implementation, and explanation to patients in the use of the new system; clearly there would be an increased load on in-coming telephone messages and additional help might be needed. Appointment diaries would be necessary with pages prepared for entries three months ahead; guide lines were provided by the Royal College of General Practitioners to help our deliberations.

A vital question was the length of time per consultation, five, ten or fifteen minutes. Doctors had different ideas about this; I preferred to work slower, but for longer and remain unstressed; others could empty a waiting room very quickly. The important thing was to be flexible; no patient would ever criticize if you were over-running your time by ten minutes or so, when they had been accustomed to waiting for an hour or more previously. Criticism of you, and the system, could arise when a patient did not receive a consultation on the day he wished, but with flexibility and a willingness to continue until demand was satisfied, these situations were avoided, and it was inexcusable not to avoid them.

Our secretaries became skilled at preparing the appointments and organizing the appropriate record envelopes, but inflexibility by a doctor, determined to finish at a certain time, could stump them.

Surgery demands vary from day to day, and most days are very busy; there can be epidemics, winter weather, national holidays to ensure the next day was a nightmare, and a partner on holiday to upset the average number of patients seen per consulting-room session. It seemed irrational to expect to be able to work the same number of hours every day, to see the same number of patients every day, unless a shift system was introduced and we were not a large enough practice to contemplate such a move.

The introduction of the appointment system was welcomed by patients at both surgeries and no problems were encountered. I was fortunate in having chosen an excellent secretary, Toni Jackson, with good manners, a pleasant personality, a compassion for patients' welfare and a perception of their difficulties, who was well suited to arrange their appointments and cope with demand. Patients quickly appreciated the advantages of this system; other practices followed our example but it took time before they were convinced these systems were workable.

I remained flexible and was prepared to lengthen the sessions to meet the demand. After a month we all agreed we would never revert to the former 'open house', and we wondered why we had not introduced appointments before.

The daily lives of Barbara and I had been greatly improved since the appointment of a secretary at 63 Horsforth Avenue, and over the years I remember Mrs Cawthorne, Mrs Benson, Miss Hoggard, and Miss. Jackson (who stayed, and eighteen years later is still one of the secretaries), with gratitude. Miss Jackson had good legible handwriting, and was efficient with the income tax and PAYE. Taking over the telephone, dealing with the appointment system, and writing letters dictated by me using a magnetic tape recorder, made a tremendous difference to my well-being, though living over the shop was always stressful. Miss Jackson was most popular with the patients, an asset to the practice, and I had every confidence in her ability to deal with any situation when I was unavailable.

There was practice stability during the early 1970s; the three partners were well organized with their work, surgeries and general duties, and since the appointment of a secretary at 63 Horsforth Avenue I was able to take annual holidays without closing the surgery, an obvious advantage to patients, and a relief to me to know there was cover while I was away.

Two changes were introduced relative to Saturday Surgeries; the six to seven pm Saturday evening surgeries were abolished in both premises. Readers may be surprised to learn that the Saturday evening surgeries were the busiest of the week, and work continued long after the entrance door was locked. I was often surprised to see so many young children, drowsy with fatigue, at these surgeries, when there had been surgeries in the morning and afternoon. It has to be remembered that for many people Saturday was a working day, and surgeries and chemists' shops stayed open to accommodate them. With the introduction of the appointment system we tried to dissuade Saturday evening surgeries, and very soon they were redundant. The five-day week was taking effect too, and in no time the afternoon two to three pm surgery became unnecessary; chemists were quick to follow suit and closed at lunch-time on Saturday with the exception of Boots.

I must admit that I found Sunday a difficult day; there was a time when a chemist on rota would open between noon and one pm, and six to seven pm, but the noon to one pm was discontinued over ten years ago. Sunday could be a busy day, and patients seen in the morning with acute infections could not obtain their medication until six pm: often I had to provide samples from my medical case to initiate the therapy, but samples depended on the good nature of the medical representatives from the drug houses, and were not always available: the Lloyd Hospital with its ever open door would provide antibiotics, but it was inconvenient, and used up their supplies. I had always hoped a rota chemist would commence opening at noon to one pm again on Sundays, but it never came to fruition.

Holidays were increasing in number and it became standard to have six weeks holiday annually, and possibly a week's study leave in addition, a welcome contrast to the situation I had known for the previous twenty-five years.

Specificity of patient-care by the practitioner with whom patients were registered became the watchword in our partnership; obviously it was the system most likely to promote good patient care, and continuity of treatment. Occasionally a patient would seek an appointment with another partner; it was important to be flexible and not to eye a patient with disapprobation when this happened, because there was usually a reason for it.

I was having trouble with the road outside my house. As the number of cars on the roads increased, more and more patients came to the surgery in their cars and tried to park wherever there was available space. The situation was aggravated in the summer season by visitors, staying at the numerous guest houses with cars, who parked them around my house making it impossible to find a niche anywhere for my patients.

Councillor Topham came to the surgery one day and expressed his concern at the difficulty he had experienced himself with his car; I asked him if he could help. It was, of course, a difficult situation because my house was at the crossroads of four roads, and the road outside the house was much wider than the others. However, Councillor Topham kept his word, and a plan was drawn up whereby a position of the wide road was converted into a car park for up to ten cars. Unfortunately, but not unexpectedly, this car park became a park for residents who did not possess a garage, as well as for visitors' cars: it did not help my patients and I knew I would have to move elsewhere. I started to look for alternative accommodation, and had some regrets we had not bought Wellington House as it had potential for conversion into a health centre and could have provided car-parking space on both sides of the house; it had drawbacks too.

It was not difficult to obtain a loan through the Family Practitioner Committee and the Practice Finance Corporation for altering or building practice premises, and the repayment terms were generous.

Out of the blue came the answer to our problems. Health centres were fashionable and it was great news for us that in 1973/4 the decision was made to build a health centre in Bridlington, which would be completed in 1975. Wellington House premises were unsatisfactory due to a small waiting room, I was having car park trouble, and we agreed it would be better for the partnership to be under one roof. A suitable site, previously playing fields had been found between the town hall and Station Avenue only 150 yards from Lloyd Hospital; it was close to Quay Road, a main road with access to the town centre and other areas of Bridlington. There were five practices in Bridlington, and three opted to seek accommodation in the

310

health centre.

The structure of this purpose-built health centre was outside our control but the architects were helpful and listened to our suggestions over numerous working lunches; guidelines for health centres had been formulated, and the various rooms had to conform to certain measurements. Unfortunately, the building had a flat roof, like so many modern buildings, and it is well known they have a tendency to leak and are expensive to maintain.

The building was ground floor except for a small area over the main entrance; in retrospect it was regrettable that neither the architects nor ourselves had the vision to appreciate that future long term requirements might necessitate another storey at some time, and to ensure the foundations were adequate.

Briefly the suites of rooms provided, for each practice, either a small consulting room with adjacent examination room, or a larger consulting room without an examination room, for each doctor. These rooms were well equipped with washbasins and a sink, hot and cold water, examination couches with pull-across curtain screening, and angle-poise lighting adjacent to the couches.

A large desk with many drawers, book-shelves, a swivel-chair, a patient's chair, and considerable cupboard space were available.

There was central heating, a window with Venetian blind, telephone, and buzzer switches for the notification of the next patient; weighing scales, and a blood-pressure sphygmomanometer screwed to the wall, completed the equipment. The decor was pastel, the floor covered with flotex carpet.

I found the consulting room claustrophobic; I liked the open spaces, and I was used to a room with a high ceiling. Our three consulting rooms were linked to a large waiting-room by a short corridor. The secretaries were housed in a room with an entrance off the corridor to the waiting room. This room contained the practice records (A4s) housed in steel cabinets with lockable doors, on revolving shelves. There were several telephones. The room was small and from the start was barely adequate to cope with four secretaries at one and the same time; an open front faced the waiting room where patients requests were handled in a face to face confrontation.

Toilets were plentiful for staff and patients.

The waiting room was common to all three practices; pillars subdivided the room, and the chairs were so arranged that patients from one practice did not overlook another. There was also a treatment room with operating table, and facilities for minor surgical procedures; cupboard space was generous. The electrocardiograph lived in this room. Doctors could enter and leave the building without passing through the waiting room, and they could move freely to the other suites if they wished to contact doctors from the other practices. On the opposite side of the building there was accommodation provided for health visitors, baby clinics and family planning, together with a sitting room for the staff. Dentists occupied two rooms on the first floor area of the health centre.

Car-parking was more than adequate for the staff, and there was plenty of space for patients to park around the building.

The practices paid a cost-rent which included heating, lighting, telephone, and cleaning services; we thought it was very reasonable and excellent value for money. There have been some minor changes to the interior structure, involving the loss of the treatment room since I retired, but I write of the building as I knew it. I thought the facilities provided were excellent, and I never had occasion to fault them; it remained to be seen how this new health centre would function.

Excitement mounted as the appointed day in 1975 drew near for the change-over from our surgeries to this grandiose building. Records, files, instruments, typewriters were conveyed to the centre in our cars over a Saturday and Sunday. We received great support from our secretaries and wives who turned out and helped with the arrangement of the records in the cabinets. For a short time flowers hung their pretty heads on the window sills, and one doctor grew tomatoes in his south-westerly window. We were provided with keys to the rear entrance and we were agog for Monday morning. The stage was set.

There was no doubt that the health centre exceeded my expectations from the start and changed my life-style. Older doctors were delighted to drive into a car park to find a space reserved for them, and appreciated the warm, if not overheated building, first thing in the morning; no doubt younger doctors would accept this as a matter of course.

I remembered stoking the large coke boiler in an out-building

312

at 63 Horsforth Avenue before gas took over the task. Last thing at night, and first thing each morning there was a noisy scrape of the shovel on concrete as coke was fed into the boiler's large and hungry mouth, notifying the street I was alive and kicking. I remembered the dismay when the boiler was 'out' in the morning due to lack of draught on a calm windless night, and the pungent fumes if there was a down-draught.

On to the rubbish-tip went the sterilizer and under the heel went the glass record syringes. Cupboards were now stocked with prepacked, sterilized, disposable syringes of various sizes, and with hypodermic needles of differing lengths and bores; packaged sterile gauze swabs and skin cleaners filled the drawers. Specimen screw-capped bottles with a different coloured cap for special tests formed rainbows of colour on the shelves. I stopped asking where it all came from as it did not seem to be my concern any more, but somebody was paying. Basic rate income tax was very high, and a higher band of sixty per cent and over was soon reached. Such luxury could not last and it did not, but it was utopia while it lasted.

Another great advantage was the ease of contact with the district nurses or community nurses as they were now designated, and the health visitor. Both were attached to the practice and were available on the intercom or by personal approach. It was not long before the nurses were available in the treatment room during the main consulting sessions. They gave a grand service in carrying out an electrocardiogram, taking blood samples for the numerous tests on our patients which were sent to the pathology department of Scarborough Hospital, and undertaking dressings.

The laboratory provided a good service; a hospital van collected all specimens from the health centre at noon and conveyed them to the laboratory; often, reports and results were in your in-tray during the early evening of the same day. I valued this service because in earlier days special tests, such as the estimation of prothrombin time (used in the control of warfarin dosage in anticoagulant therapy) were required to reach the laboratory by eleven am. Not all patients were able to be at the surgery by eight thirty am due to lack of transportation or the very nature of their illness. It involved a visit to the patient's house to collect the specimen, which had to be packed in a box, appropriate request form completed, followed by a dash to the

Bridlington bus station off the Promenade to catch the nine am bus to Scarborough (and pay for its cost) before starting the nine am surgery. Those were the days! Sometimes the patience could be a little strained to receive a report back that the specimen arrived too late! It was however always Scarborough's fault, possibly the van sent to meet the specimens at Scarborough bus station was delayed.

Although I was pleased with the health centre and valued its facilities, appreciated the improved conditions for patients, and the opportunity to practice a high standard of medical care, it soon became clear that the faults associated with large offices and bureaucracy were creeping into the buildings. Lights blazed all day in corridors and rooms despite the high light values of summer. Central heating radiators worked flat out irrespective of the time of year and the ambient temperature, and the enemy, 'waste', was all around. Chatter outside the consulting room, telephones ringing, coffee breaks, the sound of doors opening and shutting tended to disrupt the working process. Nevertheless it was still a pleasant place in which to work.

Because it was normal procedure to enter and leave the building by the rear door, away from the hurly burly of the main entrance and the waiting room, it was easy to reach your consulting room and stay there in hermit-mode dealing with your consulting sessions. By the time you had finished, your partners, and colleagues in adjacent suites had perhaps completed theirs and were already 'on the road'. Unless you made a special effort it was easily possible to miss your partners for a day or two!

It would seem that doctors were used to working on their own, preferred it that way, and did not find group practice an easy option, although this was the over-riding purpose of a health centre. Doctors worked according to their whim and in the fashion they preferred.

Patients too, were not slow to sense a remoteness developing between themselves and their doctors in their ivory towers, and this remoteness was aggravated by the decline in home-visiting.

Before the days of the health centre there was a pleasant warm room in Lloyd Hospital on the first floor overlooking Quay road, and the entrance and exit drives of the hospital. The room commanded a good view, and it was called the doctors' room; it contained a respectable medical library and it was also the coffee room. Doctors from all the practices called in during their daily hospital round, enjoyed a cup of coffee, a short rest, and a few stimulating words on any topic from politics to the solution of a medical problem. Often a surgeon, gynaecologist, and an anaesthetist were present, cooling off between cases; the atmosphere was relaxed, sociable and jovial, and it was clearly a useful venue for consultants and doctors, and kept us all in touch. Inevitably a remoteness, due to lack of contact, developed between those working in the health centre who had coffee in their rooms and those outside, who continued to visit the doctor's room; those working in the health centre did not require a second cup of coffee and tended to boycott the doctor's room, an unfortunate sequel.

It did not involve patient care but it caused social aloofness, a major disadvantage of the new health centre, and a situation we had hoped to avoid.

I was unhappy entering the health centre in the small hours. It was spooky. It was occasionally necessary to go there to collect an A4 record, or an emergency preparation. I used to put several lights on; sometimes a door banged, and once I heard people running about on the roof; I was worried lest a person or persons tried to enter as I came out. The health centre was vulnerable, there were items there which were attractive. On one occasion a bullet was fired at point blank range at the glass in the entrance door, but happily it was armour-plated glass which splintered but retained its strength. The break-down of law and order was well under way, and sadly it was becoming unsafe to be alone in certain areas at night. There were young people searching for drugs with 'kicks' who would go to any lengths to obtain them.

Family planning contributed to a large component of practice work. Newer contraceptive pills arrived, and the intrauterine contraceptive device (IUD) was born; every new preparation had side effects and disadvantages and there was more information to absorb.

Although I was nearly sixty years I thought it would be useful to obtain the Family Planning Certificate. It involved a practical course which included instruction in the insertion of an IUD. There were several varieties available, the Gravigard or Copper 7, and the SAF-T-Coil. These courses of instruction were held in Bridlington and Driffield; I went to Driffield on several occasions to attend the late evening clinics there and receive practical instruction. I obtained the certificate and was pleased to have made the effort, tiring though it was after busy days. Apart from instruction in fitting the IUD, I had a better knowledge of the indication, for and against, of the vast array of contraceptive pills available. I used to hold a small IUD clinic every fortnight in the treatment room and with the assistance of a nurse, would fit two or three new patients, and remove or change a couple more; occasionally an IUD could be difficult to remove if the string was not visible or could not be found, and consultant advice was sought in these circumstances.

My mother's bungalow at Swanage.

A difficulty had arisen in Swanage on the south coast. My mother had reached eighty-five years and was living alone. I had been worried for some time that arrangements were necessary to ensure her safety and care. She was unable to go out, and relied on the services of a woman she had known for some years who provided a home-help service, albeit in an inefficient manner. I was concerned that she failed to answer the telephone despite the fact she knew I phoned on a certain day at a fixed time.

It was not easy for Barbara and I; there were no other relations able to offer help due to distance or age. Swanage was three hundred and twenty-five miles away. We used to leave the house at ten forty-five pm on a Friday evening in a motor-caravan, a Commer Van conversion, so we were entirely independent of meals and beds. We drove steadily through the night as far as the Leicester Forest Service Centre on the M1 motorway, and it was not long before we were asleep. Next morning we set off aiming to reach Swanage by three pm when shops would be open to purchase supplies for her.

There was nothing about my mother's health and situation that was different from that of many of my patients in Bridlington, apart from the fact that most of my patients consented to accept care in a home for elderly people, or failing that, received the support of relatives living in the same town. My mother refused to leave her bungalow; she had never seen the inside of a hospital in her life and had been disturbed by a local practitioner who suggested she should be transferred to a geriatric unit in Poole, and who never bothered to see her again! The ideal solution would have been for her to come to our home in Bridlington and give up her bungalow, but the offer was rejected.

I was not prepared to move her against her wishes, and I felt at her age she was entitled to do as she wished so long as she was not a danger to herself or her neighbours; she would have to carry on as best she could, as she wished, with as much support as we could muster, difficult though it was for us so far away. Barbara and I worked hard over the rest of Saturday, and Sunday setting the bungalow in order, dealing with bills and correspondence, stocking up her pantry, and preparing meals which would keep for some time; my mother considered herself independent and would not accept help from an outside source.

On Saturday night in order not to disturb her regime, we drove to a niche off the Studland to Corfe Castle Road and camped in the van again. I had known the area since I was seven years old and I knew where to go; even in winter, tired though we were, it was a delight to look out over the entrance to Poole Harbour in the early morning light.

There was a middle-aged neighbour living opposite my

mother's bungalow who had my telephone number, and who understood and sympathized with the predicament, and who promised to contact me if she thought necessary. Her name was Mrs Leeds, and she used to live in Leeds. Sadly she died from lung cancer several years before my mother died, and her valuable assistance was no longer available to us.

We used to leave Swanage about seven thirty pm on the Sunday night. It was always distressing leaving her alone; I was alarmed at the possibility of fire though everything had been worked out to reduce such risk. Apart from moving her in an undignified manner by force, there seemed no alternative to the present arrangement, and I prayed she would never be found dead, with police and coroner involvement, to add to our discomfiture.

We listened to 'Your 100 Best Tunes' introduced by Alan Keith between Banbury and the M1 and we knew we were on time; his splendid choice of records soothed the jangled nerves as the Commer pushed its way through the night. We were back home to a cold house before two am, and I was back in the health centre at nine am the same morning — Monday was always a busy day, and if I was on rota for the practice on Monday night, readers, perhaps, may appreciate that I was not at my best, though my power of recuperation was remarkably rapid.

For over a year Barbara and I made many similar trips, and time, of course, did not ameliorate the situation in any way. I maintained my attempts to persuade her to return with us to Bridlington, and one day, over the telephone, she consented to come back with us on our next visit. Everything was organized, her room prepared and we set off to Swanage once again. Distressed and embarrassed we returned without her; she had changed her mind in a determined manner.

However, she realized herself as time passed that she had become unfit to continue in that manner, and was beginning to express alarm at her inability to cope: eventually she did come back with us and I remember only too clearly, under cover of night escorting her with walking frame and slow frail steps, as she left her beloved bungalow for what I knew would be the last time. Barbara and I held our breath lest she changed her mind, but she managed to enter the vehicle and with relief I closed the door. Another horizon lay ahead; we should be seeing Swanage many times again before our work was over, and the sale of her home completed. How I wished I had siblings to share the task.

We had moved into the health centre in 1975, and it was formally opened by HRH Princess Margaret in 1976, a great occasion for Bridlington. After we moved there the surgery premises at 63 Horsforth Avenue fell into disuse; peace reigned, the telephones slept, and the front door remained shut. Barbara and I surveyed the scene, our voices echoing in the eerie quiet. We moved from room to room. The children had flown, the nests were cold. Only my mother dozing in her chair, and ourselves, were left to live in that large house; it seemed incredible that for the twenty-seven years we had lived there, the house, which had been a hive of industry, every room occupied, happy with the sound of children's laughter, the surgery wing coping with a through-put of over 7,000 attendances annually, had at long last earned its rest. We remembered with nostalgia the dinner parties we gave for every doctor and his wife, a dentist and his wife, and special friends known to all, who sat down to food and drink to menus prepared and cooked by Barbara. We remembered the sight of their cars parked as far as the eye could see, and the noise, immeasurable in decibels, of happy people enjoying themselves. We certainly did our best to promote good relations and professional contact.

It was time to leave the house for a small house in the same area and five minutes from the sea. Happily 63 Horsforth Avenue was sold with ease to a neighbour with a guest-house, who joined the two properties into one large establishment.

Thus in September 1976 we left 63 Horsforth Avenue with its happy memories, and with my mother we moved into 6 Trafalgar Crescent which we had altered for her comfort, and our retirement, not so many years ahead.

In the health centre a routine developed with almost clockwork precision, and there was a proficiency in management and administration which was a pleasure to witness. Our partnership of three doctors linked with another practice of two doctors solely for duty rota purposes. With five doctors it became possible for a doctor to enjoy only one night per week on duty, and a weekend on duty from a Saturday morning to a Monday morning every fifth week, though adjustments were necessary for holidays which were thirty-five weeks for five doctors.

During the years 1976-1981 the pattern of work continued

to change with the new developments in medicine. We had grown accustomed to the change over to SI units, and from the imperial to the metric system; the change over required some discipline and concentration when for so many years we had been accustomed to the apothecaries' weights and measures. The scanner had arrived in the hospitals, tomography had narrowed diagnosis to fine limits, and there seemed few conditions beyond the scope of accurate diagnosis. The endoscope was developed, a most useful tool, for the diagnosis of gastric and duodenal disorders.

More and more tests were employed. The treatment and dosage of thyroid conditions depended on thyroid function tests; the treatment of diabetes was controlled by estimating the serum glucose. Patients who were medicated with anti-convulsive drugs, and patients on long-term digitalis, had the levels of these drugs estimated in the serum and were ensured of not acquiring too high or too low blood concentrations, thus avoiding troublesome sequelae. Anticoagulant therapy was controlled by the estimation of the prothrombin time. Gout was diagnosed by the level of serum uric acid, and polymyalgia rheumatica diagnosed and controlled from estimations of the plasma viscosity. All these tests involved collection of venous blood specimens, passage to the correct container, form filling, and transport to the laboratory. We had nurses able to take samples. I did many myself as it was important not to lose skill when confronted with a difficult and invisible vein.

New drugs were so potent that constant vigilance was required for evidence of interaction with other drugs; most drugs had side-effects. The non steroidal anti-inflammatory group of drugs was well known to cause gastric haemorrhage, yet there was no reduction in their use. Many drugs caused skin rashes and rendered the skin sensitive to sunlight. It was easy to treat a condition and produce another! Iatrogenic medicine was the terminology used when this occurred.

A blood count and haemoglobin estimation were practically routine procedures for every patient seen.

There was a great increase in the numbers of sexually active women coming to the consulting sessions with unpleasant vaginal discharges caused by candidiasis and trichomonas infections. Was it the pill causing these troubles? Was it the life-style, or tight jeans, or simply bad hygiene? Despite the fact that there were good preparations which cured these conditions there were many recurrences. Time was spent in taking swabs for accurate diagnosis, and more swabs to ensure the conditions were eliminated.

Cancer of the cervix was steadily on the increase, and considerable time was spent in taking cervical smears for early diagnosis. Many patients had reduplication of cervical smear tests by gynaecologists when referred for other causes, and the family planning clinics became involved as well. Many tests were inconclusive and required repetition. It all took time.

Every condition had a diagnosis, every diagnosis commanded a treatment, and there seemed little we were unable to manage.

I enjoyed some chiropody in the consulting room, and was surprised how easily patient discomfort was overcome by treating corns, removing callosities, and providing proper shoes for flat feet and sagging transverse arches. It was indeed a challenging time with never a dull moment. Enthusiasm was nurtured by age; there was so much to do and insufficient time for its completion.

It was autumn 1980 and my mother was ninety years old. Never happy away from her bungalow I had to resist attacks to return her there on numerous occasions. Barbara had attended to her needs with extreme care and kindness, patience and good humour, but she was beginning to tire. We were unable to take proper holidays due to her determination to stay where she was, and it was not easy to find caring people prepared to live in the house whilst we went away. It was over six years since we had enjoyed real relaxation, and a proper holiday.

I was aware that I was tiring and I understood why sixty-five years was the retirement age. Apart from fatigue my lower back was troubling me and I was finding it painful to get in and out of the car. The height and position of the examination couches aggravated the situation and the symptoms.

I was slower too; I noticed that at the end of the day I was invariably the last out of the health centre, a curious situation since I was sixty-two years and the oldest there by some years. Occasionally I had queer colicky lower abdominal pains, felt faint, and had to lie down for five minutes. I wondered whatever was wrong with me, but did not wish to find out.

I found the rota system trying, especially at weekends when one doctor was looking after the interests of five doctors and nearly 10,000 heads from a Saturday morning to Monday morning. I thought it a bizarre situation to be working as hard when I was near retirement, as I had been in my younger days. The spirit was willing, the flesh had become weak. I had worked hard at school, as a student, in the army, and in the practice, under initially most adverse conditions, for many years. I was burned out, and I knew it. It was time for me to pull my horns in!

In January 1981 my mother died quite suddenly. She had experienced a small haematemesis on two occasions but lost consciousness while I was talking to her one evening. I had no doubt that she had a cerebrovascular accident as well as internal bleeding. She was transferred to the East Riding Hospital in Driffield, her first visit to a hospital ever, but she never regained consciousness and died twelve hours later.

Twenty-four hour retirement was a relatively new and rather extraordinary procedure permissible under NHS regulations. I need not enter into details because present-day doctors will be familiar with them. Basically you resigned from the partnership to enable you to draw your lump sum and receive your superannuation, to be re-employed by the partnership within twenty-four hours. You retained your NHS list, but you were only allowed to draw a much-reduced income from the practice, and if you exceeded the amount, there was a 'rebate', and it was mandatory to refund it. The conception was remarkable, presumably designed to ease a practitioner into full retirement, yet ensure the practice would be able to employ an additional doctor without financial reduction in their incomes.

I decided to take up this remarkable scheme, and my partners agreed to re-employ me. It was decided to advertise for another partner, preferably young, who would take over my NHS list eventually when I retired in toto. After many interviews and much deliberation over highly qualified vocationally trained applicants, Dr Hamish McNab was appointed.

Thus it was that I commenced twenty-four hour retirement and Dr H. McNab joined the partnership. I hoped he would be as happy in it as I had been. That summer Barbara and I set off for the French Riviera in the Commer Caravan, and spent time in the warm sea at Le Lavindeau as well.

I felt better and fitter on my return.

Twenty-four hour retirement involved spending a considerable number of hours consulting, the number of hours laid down in regulations in the little red book, the doctors bible. I also undertook the examinations for the Department of Health and Social Security for attendance and mobility allowances, while Dr McNab gradually found his feet in the practice with the patients on my list.

It was a strange coincidence that at that time there was a big increase in the number of attendance allowance requests, and at one time I had over thirty application forms on my desk for examinations in and around Bridlington, Filey, Hunmanby, and even Scarborough. It was not an exciting occupation, the appropriate form containing contradictory questions, and I never knew the result of my efforts which was demoralizing. The travel and form filling involved a great deal of work.

After three months I thought it was time to retire completely. Many of my former colleagues had already retired and I missed them in the hospital and elsewhere; they seemed to be enjoying a life of bliss. It was time to follow suit. Three months notice was required and I left with regret at the commencement of the fiscal year. The one situation I did not miss was rising in the middle of the night on Friday nights, to drive to the police station to collect specimens of blood for the blood alcohol estimations on those unfortunate drivers of cars who had been stopped by the police. It was usually around two am, and relatives of the accused turned up in the main entrance; they were always abusive, and on one occasion I was greeted with 'here comes the creep', as I pushed my way into the unhospitable police station. It did not strike me as funny!

The partnership arranged a splendid farewell dinner at a fashionable restaurant in the Old Town, a memorable and emotional occasion. I spoke at some length of the history of the practice, and in ringing terms of their heritage, and the future prosperity and well-being of the practice, followed by a toast.

Diane, one of our treasured and chatty secretaries casually mentioned the toast should have been in champagne. I remarked that I would attend to the observation because she had never tasted champagne. I did so and we all enjoyed a glass of champagne, a fitting termination to my thirty-four years in the practice, and the end of a memorable evening.

I received many many retirement cards which gave me great pleasure. One in particular stands out as showing me on a magic carpet floating over sun-drenched beaches accompanied by two beautiful and scantily dressed girls with the caption:- 'And this is only the beginning'!

The lamp of memory is burning low. Now it has flickered; alas, it is out. Does it matter? No! the tale is written and just in time. Whatever light remains can only be for the present, and possibly a short peer into the future too.

$$7$$

The Twilight

When I retired in 1982 I had no intention of undertaking any further activity in medicine. I had been qualified for forty years and spent thirty-four years as a general practitioner in Bridlington; during that time I had put all my energy and effort, and most of my time in pursuit of the career I had chosen. Readers may remember as I set out for Edinburgh in 1937, and barely nineteen years old, that I was filled with excitement, hope and expectation. I was setting forth to do something in my life that I really wanted to do, and I was grateful to my parents for enabling me, though with difficulty, to study medicine and to fulfil my wish. Readers know now how I fared, but have I enjoyed those forty-seven years?

Yes, indeed I have, and I write of my enjoyment in the practice of medicine, irrespective of my private life, which has also been a supremely happy one.

It is surely a natural instinct to want to help others less fortunate than yourself. People do this in a variety of ways: the nursing profession and the ministry can help; some help financially, others help in a more physical manner, and there are those who help by lending their support to various causes and beliefs. Doctors, of course, can help those who are ill, and throughout my medical life it has given me profound pleasure and happiness to have been able to do this. It has also been remarkable, over the years, to have witnessed and taken part in the great changes brought about by an increasing knowledge of disease, and to have efficient treatments available to cure these diseases; this has been a great challenge.

Most sick people have great faith in their doctors and this

can indeed be a humbling experience when there is nothing more that can be done for them apart from compassion and care. On the other hand to be able to restore a patient in diabetic coma to full consciousness, to be able to relieve an elderly person from fear, distress, and pending death in an attack of cardiac asthma, to help a middle-aged man through a major coronary ischaemic attack back to health over several weeks can give a satisfaction, and a sense of kudos to yourself as well as the everlasting gratitude of the patient.

Readers may wonder that having enjoyed my medical life to such an extent that I was able to drop it in a day; one day a partner with full responsibilities and a full time-table, the next day unemployed. I formed a planned determination not to fret, not to be silly and continue to work when I was unable physically to do so. Of course I was sad to retire and end my hopes and aspirations, sad to realize that I was not immortal, that my life was inexorably approaching its final chapter. I had enjoyed the friendship of my partners, and enjoyed hearing their views for the future benefit of the partnership. I enjoyed the cheerful and willing help of the youthful secretaries, the laughter, the atmosphere, the bustle, the camaraderie, and the occasional snippet of scandal.

Doctors have to come to terms with the possibility that no matter how much value they think they are contributing to a practice, there is such a situation as over-staying their time. Younger partners may feel that deep-rooted ideas about the direction their elders think a practice should take are not shared by them; they may even think their older partners are out of date, but are too polite to say so. Older doctors may disagree with new policies; the generation gap has always been wide, but they should not stand in the way of younger partners who may think they are being restrained by older doctors. Perhaps I had a slight feeling of guilt; in desperation I remember telling Dr Gordon-Taylor when he was well past seventy years that it was time he 'pulled his horns in' and reduced his share. Eventually he did reduce his share but stayed on in the practice wearing loose harness for a further six years! Obviously he did not regard the remark as a retirement hint!

I never intended to be told when to go; I would see myself out of the door when the time was ripe. Of course I did not want to retire; I had enjoyed my life and work too much to wish to drop out. There was so much to lose.

The Commer Motor Caravan that took us all over Europe.

The medical profession and the church are closely related; just as it is unusual and undesirable for a vicar to return to his flock, or even worship in his former church after he has retired, so I knew that as the health centre door closed behind me, I would only be returning as a patient requiring help.

I did not think it desirable to look in and have a chat with the staff, disturb their work, or become involved; not kind to be breathing down the neck of the replacement partner; so easy to criticize, advise, or patronize, that it was best to disengage entirely. Of course it hurt all the more but retirement does cause pain.

Barbara and I have been lucky to have enjoyed good health for many years so that visits to the old haunt are few and far between (annually for an influenza vaccine which we administer to each other); it still hurts to return and I have to brace myself to cross the threshold. Familiar faces are still there; I see the door to my old consulting-room; the staff are very kind; after eight years they still tell me they miss me, that things have never been the same, that I am as youthful as ever, they have never

At Lake Thun, Interlaken, Switzerland, May 1985.

seen me so well, and that I am graceful in retirement! I disbelieve them, inwardly I am flattered, and once again the door closes behind me; there is no place for me now. It is a grief reaction for which there is no bereavement counselling likely to help. Does one ever overcome it?

For the retired general practitioner there are few opportunities for further medical work. To ease the shock and prolong their working life I have known some hardy practitioners undertake a series of locum employment; others have managed to retain their position as examiners for invalidity and mobility allowance applicants, and some sit on medical boards and act as medical referees. These positions, however, are more often associated with a practice rather than an outside appointment.

Those who managed to continue in some capacity or other found that their pension was reduced in the past when they exceeded the earnings allowance, but this anomaly was corrected in the budget of 1989. They also discovered that their earnings, as entered in their tax return, naturally attracted tax, but in a following year an estimated sum was demanded by the

Inspector of Taxes even though their earnings had ceased, and there was nothing to enter on the tax return. To make matters worse the demand for this tax necessitated payment in full by 1 January. This situation involved a letter to the inspector of taxes explaining the matter before the demand for tax was cancelled, and this was an unwelcome hassle during the adjustment to living on a reduced income.

Because I was sorry to retire I find it strange to meet former colleagues in streets or supermarkets, with many years to go before retirement becomes an issue, complaining of stress, their workload, and their longing to retire at their earliest. Perhaps it is bravado; perhaps they will not feel that way when they choose to retire. If it is a genuine distaste for their work, it is sad, and perhaps they entered the wrong profession. It cannot be due to the conditions of service, because never before has there been so much ancillary help, secretarial help, computerization, purpose-built health centres, long holidays, time off, and a high financial reward. Every dream seems to have been realized. Certainly the Government is there, and he who pays the piper calls the tune!

I appreciate that the nature of the work is changing all the time; is it becoming dull and boring? Whereas I had to practice crisis medicine for many years, when every patient was acutely ill and required urgent treatment, the work has gradually changed. With new knowledge, new medication, I realized that I was more occupied in dealing with less urgent conditions, but conditions which were requiring long-term treatment and maintenance therapy for the rest of a patient's life. Gradually I was learning to find and diagnose conditions early, and emphasis was on prevention.

The former conditions of osteomyelitis, diphtheria, scarlet fever, tuberculosis, rheumatic fever, measles, mumps, whooping cough, lobar pneumonia, poliomyelitis and nephritis have virtually been wiped off the face of Britain, but it had been my generation who were involved with these illnesses and our hard work under adverse conditions no doubt helped in their elimination. Perhaps this is the reason we become so attached to our work, were satisfied that we were doing good, and doing our best, and seeing the results of our efforts; under such circumstances boredom was an irrelevance.

Yes indeed, I think the realization that present day practice rarely utilizes the skills, training and knowledge a doctor possesses, may be depressing, and that it may well be boring to be holding well women, well men, well baby, diabetic, anti-smoking, and BP clinics which I would have thought were within the capabilities of well-trained nurses and health visitors. Practitioners may, in some measure be to blame for referring simple surgical procedures to accident and emergency departments of larger hospitals when they could deal with such situations perfectly well themselves. Surely it is more interesting and valuable to remove a sebaceous cyst from the scalp, remove a big toe-nail, deal with a simple fracture, become skilled at suturing and expert at cardio-pulmonary resuscitation than to be recording a series of blood pressures in an overheated consulting room, and undervaluing yourself.

I have noticed over the years that visiting elderly patients and keeping a medical eye on them was falling out of fashion. I heard a doctor on the radio this very week stating that visiting the elderly was valueless, and that most of them would be on the golf-course! Some, maybe, might be enjoying this activity but the majority would not be in such a fortunate position, and would be coping with their disabilities at home, or in homes for the aged.

I was taught to visit elderly patients on a long-term basis, who were unable to attend the surgery. There were plenty of them and more to come in the future. So many elderly are on potent medication with cumulative effects, others exhibit the symptoms of interaction of drugs, others have gastric bleeding caused by drugs, and I have been surprised how rapidly a macrocytic hyperchromic anaemia can occur requiring urgent treatment, and how insidiously myxoedema can reduce the quality of life. More than ever before blood requires checking and someone has to decide when; surely this is the work of the general practitioner who has knowledge of his practice patients?

I should have felt uncomfortable if I had not undertaken this work and I found it interesting and rewarding; it certainly kept boredom at bay. Screening the elderly, possibly by a health visitor, on a seventy-fifth birthday may well pick up a modest list of minor defects requiring treatment, but I would only regard it as complementary to a doctor looking for side-effects of drugs and following up illnesses outside the scope of a health visitors training.

330

When Mr Bevan, Minister of Health in 1948, was defending the introduction of the NHS he announced that disease would now be rapidly conquered and suffering removed from the lives of the British people. Many doctors regarded it as a fanatical and irresponsible statement flavoured with ignorance. Nevertheless forty-two years later, if he had been alive today, he might with some justification have said his remark had been vindicated. I have already listed a formidable number of some of the illnesses of the past which are rarely seen now, and the burden of their treatment has vanished. However doctors are still as busy as ever; their previous work has been replaced with the treatment of long-term medical illnesses using the advances in medicine of today. The treatment of the elderly, treatment of conditions caused by wear and tear, the surgical treatment of conditions made possible by high-technology have transformed the quality of life for countless numbers of people. Heart-transplantation, liver and kidney transplantation, coronary artery by-pass surgery, hip and knee replacement are now available for those in need of such treatment. What lies ahead? Will cancer be preventable or curable? Will the life-span increase from three score years and ten to a century and more?

Such advance as we have seen unfortunately costs money, and the cost of the NHS already is astronomical. Pundits have remarked that the entire wealth of the UK could be spent on the NHS and within a year there would be clamour for more resources. Can the country afford the NHS any longer? Other countries, larger and wealthier than the UK, have not followed our example, yet they seem to be able to provide a medical service which is highly efficient and have shorter waiting lists than ours. Indeed one does not hear grumbles from these countries, nor the daily whinge of the short-comings of their service as we do here. I think there may have to be additional measures of funding over and above what is provided by the tax-payer.

I do not think the media has been kind to the NHS; sometimes I think there must be representatives of the unions, the press and television huddled together outside every large hospital waiting for an incident to occur whereby they can criticize, or try to pin blame on some unfortunate doctor, nurse, hospital administrator, or even the government. Unfortunately there always seems to be someone who is prepared to face the camera, usually make unfortunate and ill-considered remarks, and aggravate the situation out of all proportion. This is bad for the morale of those working within, and confuses the public who, not unexpectedly, support the NHS.

In my student days there were long waiting lists for the repair of herniae, and for the treatment of varicose veins. Forty-seven years later there are still long waiting lists for the treatment of these conditions. Why is this? It is evident that at present these conditions cannot be prevented, but they can be treated successfully and easily. Is it because they are not a threat to life that the sufferers are relegated to the end of the surgical queues? Certainly such operations do not hit the headlines.

Forty-seven years ago a patient was treated for over a fortnight lying flat on his back, and without a pillow, after a hernia operation: ten years ago in Bridlington in a small, basic, and non-high-tec hospital, hernia operations were often carried out as day-cases, or at most for an overnight stay on the day of operation, thus relieving the necessity for in-patient admission, and utilizing a bed. These patients do not require high-tec operating theatres or complex and sophisticated surgical instruments; they need surgeons prepared to repair their herniae, and basic theatre facilities. The general practice team takes care of the post-operative requirements.

I can understand that repairing a hernia is mundane, but someone has to do it. If surgeons are too busy with major surgery, surely there are general practitioners with a surgical bent developed perhaps from house-officer days, who could be trained over a period of time under the direct supervision of a surgeon, possess a recognizable certificate, and carry out these operations? I am not, of course, suggesting that a strangulated hernia requiring the resection of a portion of non-viable bowel should have surgery by anyone other than an experienced surgeon.

It is probable that a long waiting time for straight-forward cold surgery is a reason for dissatisfaction about the performance of the NHS. It seems to be failing those people on the queue.

It cannot surely be beyond the ingenuity of the medical profession to correct this lapse: in other respects, especially the treatment of emergencies and high technological skills the NHS must be second to none.

Excitement, hope, and expectation were my dreams in 1937

en route to Edinburgh; all three have been fulfilled in full measure. I have no regrets. With the help of Barbara I witnessed the birth of the NHS, nurtured it through fragile infancy, watched it grow to a towering giant, and worked hard in it through thick and thin during all its phases; I enjoyed what I set out to do, and hope, in some measure, I helped my patients and enhanced the practice.

Would I do it again next time around?

Yes, I would hope to train as a doctor, would hope to receive a student loan to ameliorate the stringency I had to endure. When qualified, and with surgical qualifications I would leave for an under-developed country and give to its inmates what I tried to give to my patients in Bridlington. But who would come with me?

Do patients like the NHS? After forty-two years since inception, the majority of the population are unaware there could be any alternative. Certainly there is anathema at any scheme which involves payment at the point of contact, and anger should a charge for a certain item be introduced. The fact that it is a 'free service' weighs heavily in its favour by patients.

It is remarkable that the public will pay vast sums for the well-being of their dogs, cats, rabbits, and tortoise, yet resent any payment for their own health care by the NHS, though huge sums are spent on permissible medication over the counter of a chemist's shop; remarkable too, that the millionaire with the ability to pay, uses the NHS, tends to be criticized if he does not use it, but is criticized for paying the same community charge as others, for similar local authority services!

For the freedom of payment at the point of contact, the public has become tolerant, and will put up with delay in receiving an appointment, occasional discourtesy from receptionists, failure to visit when requested, and unhelpful attitudes by doctors too; a waiting time of several years for non-urgent operations of common conditions produces rumbles of discontent.

Would the public accept this if there was payment? Probably not. I must beware, I touch lightly on medical politics, and in a story of this nature I should not wish to dwell. Yes, the public support the NHS; it is here to stay, and most people have occasion to be extremely grateful for it. As I have said before the emergency service is probably the best in the world.

No doubt further resources are required over the years, but

the public and the medical profession must be realistic that this small country does not possess a bottomless purse, and that other means of funding may be an additional necessity. I would venture to suggest that some form of insurance for those above a certain level of income will be necessary, or the tax payer will be unable to foot the bill.

In earlier pages I mentioned that Des and myself had put a vast amount of hard medical work into the NHS especially during its first twenty years, with a good morale, and oblivious to the poor financial reward. I queried if we would succeed and I suggested that in the twilight I would be able to review the thirty-four years and form an opinion.

Yes, I think we did succeed. The very fact we increased the practice NHS list from 1,800-6,500 in fourteen years, at a time when the other practices in Bridlington were attempting the same activity, and with a static population numeracy, must point to a success story.

We tried to break down the barriers between the consultants and the GPs, and put an end to the remark — 'he's only a GP'. We developed excellent relations with our consultant colleagues, a mutual trust and respect, and we went out of our way to assist them in their work.

Reciprocity was the reward, and this was maintained up to our retirement day.

We like to think our patients trusted us, respected us, and were grateful to us; we, in our turn tried to do our best for them with good humour, kindness, and medical skill. We were happy in our work, and our patients were happy with us. The fact that over the years the NHS grew into a monstrous political machine, unfortunately to its detriment, was no fault of ours. We worked hard at the treatment of our patients under the terms of the NHS, and we did our best, and nobody can do more than that.

The light of the present day is flickering as it burns, and I must hasten to finish.

What happened to those places of learning of my youth? The red-bricked school at Swanage (Oldfeld by name) with its windmill to generate electricity, still stands. It is now Harrow House, a language school and sports centre. Swanage bay retains its beauty and has changed little over the sixty-five years I have known it, apart from some concrete flats and houses in the area where the demolished Grosvenor Hotel once stood and towards

Peveril Point. The knowledge that it is now known as the Costa del Swanage will inform my readers of the nature of those buildings! My mother's bungalow in Rabling Road has new window units, and is squashed by a house of two flats which has been built on the adjacent empty site. We walk past and remember the happy days when the children were small and we ran down to the beach. We remember, too, our nightmare journeys of fifteen years ago to attend my mother as best we could in her old age, and her steadfast determination to stay at home.

Weymouth received my first visit in 1988 since leaving the College in 1937, fifty-three years ago. From the Radipole Road aspect I found it little changed; it is now a youth training centre under the auspices of the Dorset County Council Education Department; the extensive playing fields behind were filled with houses. I was surprised to see the junior school and College House, opposite the school, where Rev. E.V. Tanner (the school priest) was house-master, were empty and windows boarded. The school chapel, the scene of many memorable occasions, looked the same on first sight, though the memorial windows and oak-panelled war memorial had been transferred to St Aldhelm's Church, Radipole. The eagle lectern and choir stalls had made their journey to the school chapel at Wellingborough.

Lodmoor, a barren dyke-filled waste-land, the scene of the annual steeple-chase had improved, and sported a large car park, a housing development on the periphery, and there were plans for recreational activities. The Stainforth memorial trophy had been moved from the school to the Greenhill Gardens, mounted on a tall pillar. The town had changed but little, the Victorian promenade clock was still ticking away time, and the sea and Purbeck cliffs were as inviting as ever.

How has Edinburgh fared? The former LMS Railway Station at the West End of Princes Street has closed, and the route from the south is King's Cross to the Waverley Station, the eastern route. The fine trams have disappeared and I think the commuters' problems might be improved if they returned. The city now has a new by-pass road linking the A68 to the A1, and the A68 to the Forth Road Bridge, and motorway to Glasgow. Edinburgh Royal Infirmary is screened, from the meadows, which remain unchanged, by trees which have grown considerably. The University Medical School, Surgeons Hall,

Our present day Renault at Bothwellseat.

the book shops in Teviot Place, the Students Union and the McEwan Hall remain untouched by time, though new additional university buildings have mushroomed, and a students health centre has been built close to the older buildings. Princes Street is as serene as ever, the Walter Scott Memorial, unique as ever, bearing testimony to its great author. The castle still dominates the city, and the Princes Street Gardens remain the haven of peace from busy streets.

I was disappointed at the degeneration of Nicholson Street and the Haymarket; they seem neglected and dilapidated; perhaps these areas are being run down and plans exist to upgrade them. I hope so. Edinburgh remains the gracious capital of Scotland, but, as teachers write in their end of term reports, 'should do better'.

I hasten north to Arbroath; a wide road bridge spans the river Tay to Dundee for those travelling through Fifeshire. The approach to Arbroath is unchanged, the Infirmary perched on rising ground overlooking pleasant gardens and the sea. I have been inside once a few years ago; it teemed with staff; they were surprised I knew so much, the ward names, the former doctors.

They were more surprised when I said I had been house-surgeon in 1943 and 1947, and frank disbelief that I had been the only resident doctor in 1943 with everything to do. The town centre is now walk-about, and a new road linked the main coast road to Montrose with the approach road from Dundee. The harbour was busy and attractive.

I thought Arbroath looked good and was flourishing. I relived the walk along the north cliff to the Deil's Heid. Queen's Drive is a fine promenade and I have often wondered why bulldozers have not been to the beach and excavated the large rocks and stones, or even used explosives to flatten out the foreshore and encourage the deposition of sand; this would give Arbroath the potential to become a first class holiday seaside resort.

Before leaving Arbroath Barbara and I went to Keptie Street and looked up at Mrs Crockatt's flat's window and remembered her great kindness and friendship to us both during and long after World War Two. She died in 1982 and we have missed her very much. On to her son, and daughter-in-law's home, Denley, in Arbirlot Road for a brief visit; he has retired and his knee joints are worn from much hard work. It makes us feel old; we have been around for a long time.

We speed on to Aberdeen; from the approach the granite city looks strong, formidable, beautiful on a sparkling day. How I wish they would demolish the few tower blocks because they do not suit this city, and should never have been built! Aberdeen, its economy enriched by the discovery of North Sea oil fields, has become one of the wealthiest cities in the UK and would seem to enjoy every facility, luxury and indulgence. Union Street has lost its green trams and traffic is heavy; I would venture to suggest that, like Edinburgh, their return would benefit the community. There is new development along George Street, some of the large stores in Union Street moving to this area.

We cover the thirty-six miles to Bothwellseat. The main road is wider and fast and straightened out, but the narrow approach road to the farm is not as quiet as of yore. Heavy transport occasionally thunders at speed along it, and the slipstream makes walking hazardous. The farm is quiet with little activity apart from the grazing of cattle and many sheep. Brothers-in-law and a sister-in-law have passed on; there are few replacements and we await the new generation to mature and carry on the tradition. The well-built granite house wears well, and we love

The granite farmhouse, at Bothwellseat, Aberdeenshire, September 1988.

to travel there, to see the sun rise over the Ordes-Nacht, to hear the curlew, and the wind roaring in the trees in the autumn, and to reflect on those busy days in the post-war period when the air was filled with the sound of small Fordson tractors working away at harvest time, reaping the crops. Farming was at its zenith then.

What was the fate of Alford, the little market town in Lincolnshire where I was assistant to Dr Nicoll in 1947/8? I was there to see for myself in 1989, my first visit since I left. The railway had closed, victim of Dr Beeching's axe. The centre of the town with its fine old church had changed little, and I had no difficulty in finding Lloyds Bank and its side-door leading to the little flat where we lived for six months with baby Angus.

I experienced difficulty in finding Dr Nicoll's house, the Chauntry. Enquiries failed, and nobody knew of him except an elderly lady who said she thought she knew the name and that he might have moved to Lincoln.

I came across Merton House Surgery and then I realized where I was; this new building was attached to a nice house which I recognized as the Chauntry, and it was part built in that lovely old garden. The remainder of the garden was the

338

practice car park! Yes — there were the old brick walls where hung those luscious pears.

Merton House Surgery was small; I moved inside to find that five doctors formed the medical staff; I asked the secretary if I could speak to a doctor socially for two minutes, that I would wait, and I explained who I was.

The request was refused, he was too busy; there were only two people in the waiting room! I smiled wryly, knowing the population had not increased, and thought how unsociable and entrenched doctors and secretaries could be. I moved to the small cottage hospital and rang the bell; an elderly nurse said the hospital was due for closure and a petition had been sent to the health authority to keep it open. Foolishly I asked if surgery was still carried out in the theatre upstairs and I received a queer look that I might not be quite normal.

I was not dainty in my departure, and I shall not return to Alford.

Is that house in Devonshire, two miles from Ottery-St-Mary, on the West Hill, where my parents lived through those World War Two days, and from where so many of my journeys started in the early light of dawn, still standing?

It is thirty-five years since I last saw it, though my eldest son was there two years ago and pronounced it little changed.

Barbara and I have planned to travel there this autumn to see for ourselves; I want to peer through the high hedge and survey the two thirds of an acre of rough field which I turned into a lawn using a twelve inch hand mower all those years ago, when the strength of youth coursed my veins. I want to shut my eyes and hear the ever-monotonous cawing of the rooks squatting on the tall pine-trees at the bottom of the garden, and to savour the solitude and peace of that beautiful county.

What has happened to Lloyd Hospital after it was vacated in 1988, closed, and superseded by the new Bridlington and District Hospital at a cost of £15 million? Sadly a purchaser has never been found, and the building now 122 years old is suffering from neglect. Every window is boarded, the woodwork darkened by the ravages of the climate. The entrance drive is used as a parking area for cars willy nilly, and sadly litter is blown into the entrance. I drive past with tunnel vision and in silence; it was a splendid hospital and served the population of Bridlington, and the many ill holiday makers from the West Riding with skill, care and compassion over a generation and more.

What has become of those persons I knew so well? Dr Seymour Halkett, who dragged me in toxicity to my finals, specialized in anaesthetics and moves in retirement twix Aberdeenshire and North Yorkshire.

Dr J.D. Little moved from the partnership in Whitby to become á partner in another practice in Darlington where he spent the remainder of his practice life. In retirement now, he and his wife Esme live in the secluded village of Walworth six miles from the centre of Darlington. His cello, golf clubs and walking boots ensure his retirement is never dull.

Dr Lucey (Des), his coronary arteries by-passed, thrives in recent retirement; he is a fisherman, his Irish humour and stories as breath-taking as ever, and guaranteed to raise a laugh on the darkest day.

Dr J.R. Bell works on; he has seen many changes, and worked hard to introduce many himself, especially in the area of computerization. He has seen the practice extend from three partners, to four partners and a trainee, seen the introduction of a practice manager, a practice nurse, and additional secretaries. No doubt further changes lie ahead as there is a growing tendency to leave multi-group practices in a health centre, and to provide practice premises for your own group, a trend which does not surprise me as way back in 1975 I was not convinced that doctors were comfortable in multi-group practice in health centres.

Dr Gordon-Taylor died aged ninety years; I used to visit him every Christmas Eve, a bottle in my hand, and we talked of the past. He was pleased to see me and said he was glad to be 'out of it'. How could I believe him?

And what news of Louise Petrie? I have never seen or heard of her again since I last saw her in Cairo in 1946.

The light is steady again but the oil is low. I hasten on.

Finally our family and ourselves. Our four children gleaned great advantage from their education and have occupations which we muse with wonderment and pride.

Angus, our eldest son, with his bent on mathematics, started as a Blue Button on the floor of the London Stock Exchange, to become, after a series of examinations, a Member of the Stock Exchange. He is now a regional director of the York branch of the National Investment Group, a useful man for any household to know.

Arthur, our second son, wearing a hard hat, worked at the Stanlow Shell Refinery at Ellesmere Port. After two years he left Shell temporarily and became an inspector of taxes after three years of further study. Armed with dual qualifications he was re-employed by Shell and is now taxation consultant for the Company. He lives in the Hague, travels world wide, involved with finance and taxation involving millions of pounds.

Dennis, our third son started with Marconi in Chelmsford. He left, and was employed by University College London, and was sent out to New South Wales in Australia to be involved with the electronics of a massive telescope at Coonabarabran. From there he joined Reuter; he has risen to the position of global strategic planner of Trading Room Systems and also travels widely in Europe and the USA. Chicago and New York and Geneva are his main cities of call, though Australia and Japan have required his presence on several occasions.

And how about our dear daughter Hazel? Her qualification as a dietician took her first to Aberdeen Royal Infirmary. From there she was employed by Scarborough Hospital to found the Dietetics Department, and had contact with Malton and Whitby Hospitals as well.

She married, the stork was busy, and like us she has three sons and a daughter; this has enforced her loss to dietetics, but the other day I heard her say she was hoping to find a part-time post in dietetics as her family grows up.

We are happy for our family and do not have to worry over their prospects; all are married and we have eight grandchildren, six boys and two girls; the eldest is ten and the youngest two weeks.

I left for Edinburgh, alone, full of expectation, but I never expected three daughters-in-law, a son-in-law and eight grandchildren.

Barbara and I are very fortunate; our health is good and we never have to consider our ages. We have been able to travel to the USA, and visit Washington and Houston. At that time Arthur, our son, working with Shell was resident in Houston for eighteen months, and we experienced a memorable holiday there. We spent a day exploring NASA (National Aeronautics and Space Administration Lyndon Johnson Space Centre) and learned with profound interest, about the medical aspects of the astronauts' space flight to the moon and back, the calorific value of their food packs, the medication, and their exercises, which revealed the detail and precision undertaken to ensure the safety and well-being of the astronauts on their remarkable voyages.

Amazed, too, we were at the sheer size of the Medical Centre in Houston; helicopters take off from pads around and attached to the hospitals. There are separate hospitals for every speciality, and separate cancer hospitals for men and women. The centre covers an area comparable to a town the size of Scarborough.

I was very surprised to see a young woman in Houston pushing a pram, and to be informed she had a Caesarean section three days previously. I was also surprised to see most children, especially girls, wearing braces on their teeth.

A memorable evening was a visit to a rodeo, to witness the skill of the Texans with horse and cattle. On another occasion we attended a base-ball match, a massive family gathering, with bands, gymnastics, and competitive games between young people of both sexes. The behaviour was excellent, and the entire atmosphere very different from the scenes we are accustomed to in the UK.

We also travelled to Alexandria in Louisiana, by coach from Houston, where I have another cousin, and from there, to Baton Rouge, through typical Texan terrain.

A week or two after retirement started, we set out in the Commer Caravan for Italy for a month. It was a sensible action because it is a dread returning to work, and this time I did not experience that sensation; it broke me into retirement.

We stayed at camp sites. Florence, Rome, Venice, and Pisa came under our gaze. We shall never forget that month of relaxation, pleasure, and the sheer beauty of Italy. We were exceptionally lucky to meet a Pole, with an English wife from Pontefract, on a camp site on the outskirts of Rome; they were Catholics and although we were not of their faith, they provided us with passes for an audience with Pope John Paul.

It was a wonderful experience; the great square was thronged with seated people of every nationality, the hot sun blazed on our heads, and Pope John Paul, only twenty yards away, spoke with ease in six languages for ten minutes in each language. We returned via the Italian Riviera to Genoa, to Aosta, to Switzerland, France and back to Bridlington.

Since retirement we have also managed a trip to the Aegean

Dr and Mrs Cookson with their eighth and youngest grandchild. 1990.

Sea and Turkey, have experienced the charm of the Canary Islands and Madeira, and traversed the Norwegian Coast from Bergen to the North Cape. We were late starters but we could not travel far for domestic and financial reasons when we were younger.

Life is never dull; there is different work and plenty of it. There is the quality press to absorb, and I read the medical journals; there is television, the dog, the garden, the grandchildren, our caravan for summer travels in the UK, and I have written this book in my own hand. I have learned new skills with wood, metal, and paint, and my house possesses many clocks, accurate to the minute.

Yes, retirement is bliss, and long may it last. We shall not live long without each other. I do not grieve for my work now that the memory is lost, knowing the record is there.

The lamp has flickered again, and now it is out. I have finished my task in the nick of time.

Tikka, our Shih Tzu, on his 13th birthday, he has kept us to daily walks.